Connectionist Models of Behaviour and Cognition II

PROGRESS IN NEURAL PROCESSING*

Series Advisor

Alan Murray *(University of Edinburgh)*

Vol. 6: Neural Modeling of Brain and Cognitive Disorders
Eds. James A. Reggia, Eytan Ruppin & Rita Sloan Berndt

Vol. 7: Decision Technologies for Financial Engineering
Eds. Andreas S. Weigend, Yaser Abu-Mostafa & A.-Paul N. Refenes

Vol. 8: Neural Networks: Best Practice in Europe
Eds. Bert Kappen & Stan Gielen

Vol. 9: RAM-Based Neural Networks
Ed. James Austin

Vol. 10: Neuromorphic Systems: Engineering Silicon from Neurobiology
Eds. Leslie S. Smith & Alister Hamilton

Vol. 11: Radial Basis Function Neural Networks with Sequential Learning
Eds. N. Sundararajan, P. Saratchandran & Y.-W. Lu

Vol. 12: Disorder Versus Order in Brain Function: Essays in Theoretical Neurobiology
Eds. P. Århem, C. Blomberg & H. Liljenström

Vol. 13: Business Applications of Neural Networks: The State-of-the-Art of Real-World Applications
Eds. Paulo J. G. Lisboa, Bill Edisbury & Alfredo Vellido

Vol. 14: Connectionist Models of Cognition and Perception
Eds. John A. Bullinaria & Will Lowe

Vol. 15: Connectionist Models of Cognition and Perception II
Eds. Howard Bowman & Christophe Labiouse

Vol. 16: Modeling Language, Cognition and Action
Eds. Angelo Cangelosi, Guido Bugmann & Roman Borisyuk

Vol. 17: From Associations to Rules: Connectionist Models of Behavior and Cognition
Eds. Robert M. French & Elizabeth Thomas

Vol. 18: Connectionist Models of Behaviour and Cognition II
Eds. Julien Mayor, Nicolas Ruh & Kim Plunkett

*For the complete list of titles in this series, please write to the Publisher.

Progress in Neural Processing • 18

Proceedings of the Eleventh Neural Computation and Psychology Workshop

Connectionist Models of Behaviour and Cognition II

University of Oxford, UK 16 – 18 July 2008

NCPW11

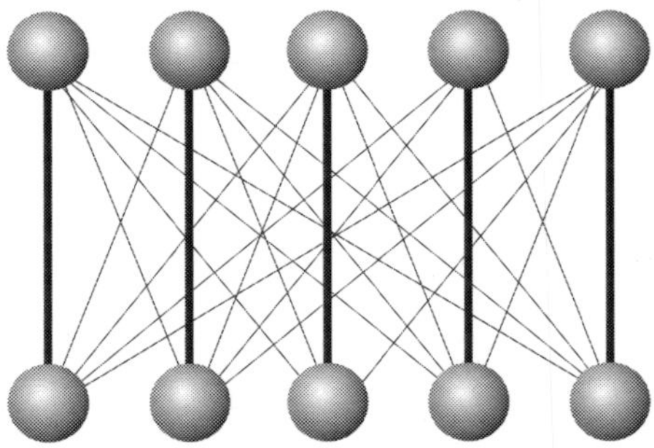

OXFORD 2008

Editors

Julien Mayor
University of Oxford, UK

Nicolas Ruh
Oxford Brookes University, UK

Kim Plunkett
University of Oxford, UK

World Scientific

NEW JERSEY • LONDON • SINGAPORE • BEIJING • SHANGHAI • HONG KONG • TAIPEI • CHENNAI

Published by

World Scientific Publishing Co. Pte. Ltd.
5 Toh Tuck Link, Singapore 596224
USA office: 27 Warren Street, Suite 401-402, Hackensack, NJ 07601
UK office: 57 Shelton Street, Covent Garden, London WC2H 9HE

British Library Cataloguing-in-Publication Data
A catalogue record for this book is available from the British Library.

Progress in Neural Processing — Vol. 18
CONNECTIONIST MODELS OF BEHAVIOUR AND COGNITION II
Proceedings of the 11th Neural Computation and Psychology Workshop

ISBN-13 978-981-283-422-5
ISBN-10 981-283-422-2

Printed in Singapore.

PREFACE

After the very successful Tenth Neural Computation and Psychology Workshop held Dijon, the Eleventh Neural Computation and Psychology Workshop, NCPW11 took place at the University of Oxford from July 16-18, 2008.

This well-established and lively series of workshops aims at bringing together researchers from different disciplines such as artificial intelligence, cognitive science, computer science, neurobiology, philosophy and psychology to discuss their work on models of cognitive processes, with previous themes encompassing categorisation, language, memory, development, action, to name but a few.

In this issue, we have collected 30+ original contributions from presenters coming from four continents. This diversity is not geographical only, as articles target different aspects of cognition; from amnesia to concept formation, from spatial cognition to language acquisition, this collection of papers emphasises the scientific contribution of neuro-computational models in order to bring new ideas to a wide range of subjects of studies in psychology.

We would like here to take the opportunity to thank all attendees, for making this conference a success, with special thanks to our invited speaker, Prof. David Plaut. We are also grateful to the Oxford Foundation for Theoretical Neuroscience and Artificial Intelligence for its financial support. The organisers would also like to acknowledge the contribution of the ESRC through their research support: Nicolas Ruh's research is supported by the grant RES-061-23-0129 awarded to Gert Westermann whereas Julien Mayor's research is supported by the grant RES-062-23-0194 awarded to Kim Plunkett.

We already look forward to the next edition and wish the readers all the best in their journey through the different contributions to neural computations in psychology.

The organising committee,

Oxford, December 4th, 2008

Julien Mayor
Nicolas Ruh
Kim Plunkett

CONTENTS

Embedded Cognition

UNDERSTANDING COMMUNICATIVE INTENTIONS USING SIMULATED ROLE-REVERSAL

M. KLEIN*

Center for Language and Speech Technology, Radboud University Nijmegen, Nijmgen, 6500 HD, Netherlands
**E-mail: M.Q.Klein@let.ru.nl*

Understanding the communicative intention of a speaker is the ultimate goal of language comprehension. Yet, there is very little computational work on this topic. In this chapter a general cognitive plausible model of how an addressee can understand communicative intentions is presented in mathematical detail. The key mechanism of the model is simulated role-reversal of the addressee with the speaker, i.e., the addressee puts himself in the state of the speaker and — using his own experience about plausible intentions — computes the most likely intention in the given context. To show the model's computational effectiveness, it was implemented in a multi-agent system. In this system agents learn about which states of the world are desirable using a neural network trained with reinforcement learning. The power of simulated role-reversal in understanding communicative intention was demonstrated by depriving the utterances of speakers of all content. Employing the outlined model, the agents nevertheless accomplished a remarkable understanding of intentions using context information alone.

Keywords: Understanding Intentions; Communicative Intentions; Non-Verbal Communication; Multi-Agent-Systems.

1. Introduction

When a baby cries, the information content transmitted in the acoustic signal is very low[a]. Nevertheless, a mother can usually understand what the baby desires. She can do so because she understands (i) the context of the cry (last meal, state of diapers, etc.), as well as of (ii) the normal desires of a baby (to be fed, to be dry, etc). While utterances with such a low information content are exceptional, it is generally the case for almost every utterance that the literally transmitted information is not sufficient to understand the communicative goal of a speaker, but *context* and *likely*

[a]i.e., although the individuals cries might be quite different, these differences do not systematically related to a difference in content (at least not in the early stages of development).

desires are required as additional key parameters. To understand the communicative goal of a speaker is not a minor side issue, but it is the overall purpose of every act of inter-human communication. At the very fundament of human communication lies the understanding that a speaker (or, as in the example above, a crying baby) has a certain intention and wants you to understand this intention.[1] And to understand this intention, the context (including the current state and history of the speaker, as far as it is known the the addressee), as well as our estimation of likely desires of the speaker are essential sources of information. Only an approach integrating these can be considered a good model of human communication. In fact, our good understanding of each other, despite the fact that our utterances are so imprecise and sparse in terms of content can only be explained within the framework of such an integrated approach. Embedding cognitive processes involved in communication and language in a more general framework of processes concerned with the understanding of intentions is considered essential,[2,3] but so far very little computational work uses such an approach.

To understand intentions in the way described above requires a number of cognitive abilities. First of all, a person must have the ability to attribute a desire to another person, even if this desire is different from desire the attributing person has himself. This ability has been coined *Theory of Mind.*[4] This term is generally considered to include the second precondition of the model outlined above: the ability to regard actions as caused by those attributed inner states. Given that these two conditions are fulfilled, we can ask the question of *how* it is possible for a person to compute the underlying desire of an action.

The contemporary philosophical literature distinguishes two contrasting approaches to solve this problem: *theory-theory* and *simulation theory.*[5–7] While theory-theory would describes this computations as a detached theoretical process, simulation theory postulates that we simulate the mental state of the observed person in our own cognitive system. In other words, we put ourselves in the shoes of the other person. This means, for example, that we could estimate an emotional state of a person by simulating the situation or context of that particular person.

One of the main computational advantages of simulation theory over theory theory is that the machinery used for understanding an action is more or less the same as the machinery used for selecting your own action. The model I will present in this chapter draws heavily on this advantage. All the components an agent uses to understand an intention are the same as those the agent uses for the selection of his own goal-directed actions. What I will present is a first simple computational approach to model the understanding of communicative intentions taking into account the context *and* likely desires. To demonstrate how effective these two parameters can be used in understanding a communicative intention, I will use communication signals that are utterly empty in terms of content (comparable to the cries of a baby), with the only information transmitted being that an act of communication has been made. A multi-agent system is used in which agents receives a reward if they are in a certain class of states of the environment. Using reinforcement learning,[8] the agents learn which states of the environment are desirable. Agents can perform a set of non-verbal actions to get into these desired states. In certain cases a desired state cannot be produced by an action of the agent itself, but by the action of another agent. In these cases, an agent is allowed to produce a communication signal without any content. The desired state that the signaling agents is trying to accomplish is considered the communicative intentions. The agent decides which action (among non-verbal and the one verbal) to perform by means of a Markov decision process using a value function and a pre-programmed forward model as it was described in previous work.[9] Using their own experience - their knowledge about which states of the environment are desirable, as well as their full awareness of the current state of the speaker, the addressees computes the plausible intentions of the speaking agents by a form of role-reversal. After putting themselves into the state of the speaker, the addressed agents use their forward model to test which of the plausible intention of the speaking agent they can actually bring about (assuming that the speaker wants them to bring about a certain state). Of those role-reversed states that the addressee is able to bring about, it is the one with the highest value that is considered the communicative intention of the speaker.

2. Method

Value Function

In the simulation work presented in this chapter, a value function $V()$ maps complete states of the simulated environment to a value (equation 1).

$$V^{\pi}(s_t) = E_{\pi}\{\sum_{k=0}^{\infty} \gamma^k r_{t+k+1}\} \qquad (1)$$

The value is an estimations of how good it is for an agent to be in this particular state (i.e. how much he desires the state). Values are positive or negative real numbers. $V^{\pi}(s_t)$ is the estimation of the value of state s_t at (discrete) time step t under a *policy* π.[10] Here, π is a mapping from states s and actions a to the probability $\pi(s, a)$ of performing action a when in state s. $V^{\pi}(s_t)$ is defined in terms of the expected sum of discounted rewards r. The expected value is taken with respect to the Markov chain $\{s_{t+1}, s_{t+2}, ...\}$ where the probability of transition from state s_{t+k} to s_{t+k+1} is given by π. Future rewards are *discounted* by the discount factor γ. The higher the value of γ, the more importance is given to later rewards, i.e. the less they are discounted (see Ref. 10 for a more detailed explanation of the formula and the theory that goes with it).

The value function is implemented as a single-layer feed-forward neural network. To train this network we used *TD(0) reinforcement learning.*[8] In TD-learning, the so-called TD-error gives the distance from the correct prediction and the direction of the deviation. Thus, it can be used to change the weights of a neural network. The TD-error δ is computed by subtracting the current state value of state s_t $V(s_t)$ from the sum of the reward r_{t+1} and the value of the next state $V(s_{t+1})$ times the discount factor (equation 2). Given δ, the value of the state $V(s_t)$ is changed to $V(s_t) + \alpha\delta$, where α is the rate of change (equation 3).

$$\delta = r_{t+1} + \gamma V(s_{t+1}) - V(s_t) \tag{2}$$

$$V(s_t) \leftarrow V(s_t) + \alpha\delta \tag{3}$$

Action Selection

The value function allows to determine the *most desired state* of every agent in every state: the desired state is the state with the highest value. However, not every state can be reached from every other state. In fact, apart from the context state s_t only those few states are accessible which can be produced from s_t through a single action in a single time step. Therefore, the value function only needs to compute the value of those states which can be reached from the current state. To compute which states are accessible, or, in other words, to select a (verbal or non-verbal) action the *consequence* of actions needs to be estimated. This is accomplished with another device - a so-called *forward* model.[11] Within motor control, forward models are used to predict sensory consequences from efference copies of issued motor commands.[12] In the model described in this paper, we use forward models for the selection actions in the following way: the outcome of all possible actions in the present context is predicted with the forward model and then the action which produces the most desired effect is chosen. F predicts a subsequent state s^*_{t+1} based on a current state s_t (context) and a possible non-verbal or verbal action (utterance) u^*_t.

$$s^*_{t+1} = F(s_t, u^*_t) \tag{4}$$

Given the forward model F, utterances and actions are selected by means of a function $\arg\max_u$ which selects the verbal or non-verbal action that produces the most desirable state (equation 5).

$$u_t = \arg\max_u [c(s_t, u^*_t) + V(F(s_t, u^*_t))] \tag{5}$$

This function returns that one from all possible a^*_t's which, given the context s_t, is mapped by the forward model F into a state s for which the value function V returns the highest value. Since $\pi(s, u)$ can be determined on the basis of the function described in equation 5, we will, for the rest of this article, no longer talk about π, but only about the forward model and the value function.

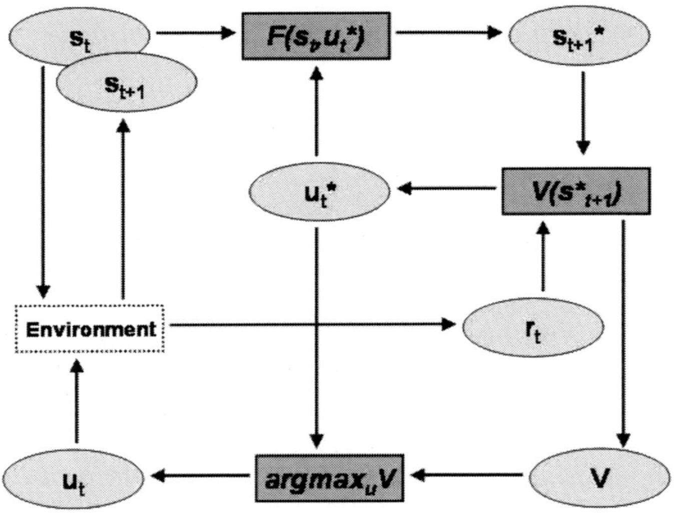

Fig. 1. The figure shows the architecture of action selection. In the current state s_t, the forward model $F()$ is used to predict the outcome of possible non-verbal or verbal actions. The value function $V()$ then estimates how desirable such an outcome is. The selected action is the one which leads to the most desirable outcome. After action selection, the environment determines the reward r and the next state s_{t+1}.

To be able to choose a *verbal* action, an agent needs to be able to compute the outcome of such a verbal action. In the simulations described in this chapter this is done in the following manner: Given the current state the speaker computes the outcome of all possible actions of a possible addressee with the pre-programmed value function and estimated the value of those outcomes with his trained value function. If any of the actions of a possible addressee leads to a state with a higher value than those states he can bring about himself he will choose to signal this addressee. This, of course, assumes (i) that the addressee will understand what the speaker want from him - which is only the case in later stages of training and (ii) that the addressee will actually cooperate. To keep things simple and we avoided all issues related to cooperation and made it a general policy of the addressee to cooperate.

Understanding Intentions

Here we state the mathematical and computational core of the theory presented in this paper. It is based in the following assumption:

(i) The addressee assumes (correctly in our simulations) that, if he is spoken to, the speaker desires that the addressee performs an action and that this action is the one that is the optimal action for the speaker in the current circumstances.

(ii) The value function of the addressee can serve as an approximation of the value function of the speaker, i.e. speaker and addressee desire similar things in similar situations.

Therefore, to understand the communication intention of a speaker, an addressee needs to (i) understand the current state of the speaker, including, of course, the speaker's environment. This is, of course, a highly idealized assumption. In the simulation presented in this chapter, agents, however, have full access to the complete state of the game. The state, however, needs to be role-reversed, i.e. the addressee needs to *put himself in the shoes* of the speaker. On the basis of this role-reversed current state, the addressee can find the action that is optimal for the speaker using his own value function to serve as an approximation of the value function of the speaker

$$a = argmax_{V_{sp}} a(F(s_c, a_{ad})) \tag{6}$$

The role-reversed value function is denoted by V_{sp}. I use the term *desire* and *intention* in the following manner. States of the world which the agents know to be beneficial for themselves are desired states, while states of the world which they are actually trying to reach by some action or utterance are called intended states. In our theoretical framework an agent has many desires. However, only some of these desires actually become intentions. The desired state that triggered the verbal action is regarded as the communicative intention of the verbal action. If the addressee chooses an action that brings about this intended state he has correctly understood this intention.

The Acquisition Environment

We test our hypotheses about language acquisition and communication in a simulation of a multi-agent game. The goal in this game is to obtain food through verbal and non-verbal actions. In this simulation, *food* grows in certain intervals on *trees* (how this time interval is calculated is explained in the appendix). There are three trees $T_1 ... T_3$, growing three types of food. Every tree T_i can hold maximally 5 pieces of food. Time is supposed to advance in discrete jumps, from $t = 1$ to $t = 2$, $t = 2$ to $t = 3$ etc. Each two successive times t_i and t_{i+1} are separated by an action a_{t_i} of one of the agents, so that the state $s_{t_{i+1}}$ at t_{i+1} is the result that action a_{t_i} produces in the state s_{t_i}.

Within a certain time interval (d_o) invariably one piece of food gets *digested*, i.e. it disappears. Once the total amount of food in the game is below the threshold n_o, 3 pieces of food grow simultaneously on one of the three trees. Because of this design, the agents cannot afford to rest once they have gained a sufficient amount of food items. Agents never starve to death, but for every time step during which they do not have any food they get a very negative reward.

Agents can perform one of the following 12 actions:

- harvest a tree, i.e. collect all its food (3 possibilities)
- give one piece of food to another agent (2 other agents $\times$ 3 food types = 6 possibilities)
- send a communication signal to one of the other agents (2 other agents = 2 possibilities)
- *no action* (1 possibility)

At each transition between two successive times, only one agent can perform an action. This agent can perform either one non-verbal or one verbal action. Generally, the agents take turns. However, when an agent asks another agent for a type of food, the normal order of play is suspended for one time step and while the addressee gives (or fails to give) the desired object to the speaker. An agent can only address one of the other agents, never both of them.

The goal of the agents in the game is to have at least one piece of each food type at all times. Therefore, the reward function was designed in the following way: Each agent gets a reward at every time step. If an agent has at least one item of every food type, he gets a reward of +3, otherwise he gets −1 for every food type which is missing in his store at that time.

3. Results

We performed a number of simulations during which the neural network based value function of the agents were trained and the percentage of correct understood communicative intentions were measured. Figure 2 shows a Hinton diagram of the weights of trained value function (at the end of the simulation). In that simulation a high γ-value was chosen and, as a result, the agents have learned that it is good to have more than one item of every type, although a direct reward is only given for the first item of each type. The diagram also shows that the agents all have a good understanding of

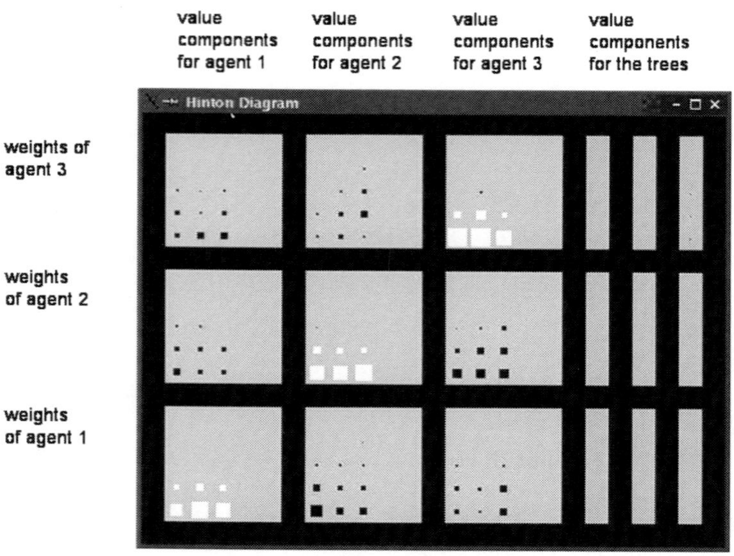

Fig. 2. This figure shows the weights of the value functions of the three agents for a γ - value of 0.9. The size of the squares represents the strength of the weights; the color represents the polarity (white is positive, black is negative).

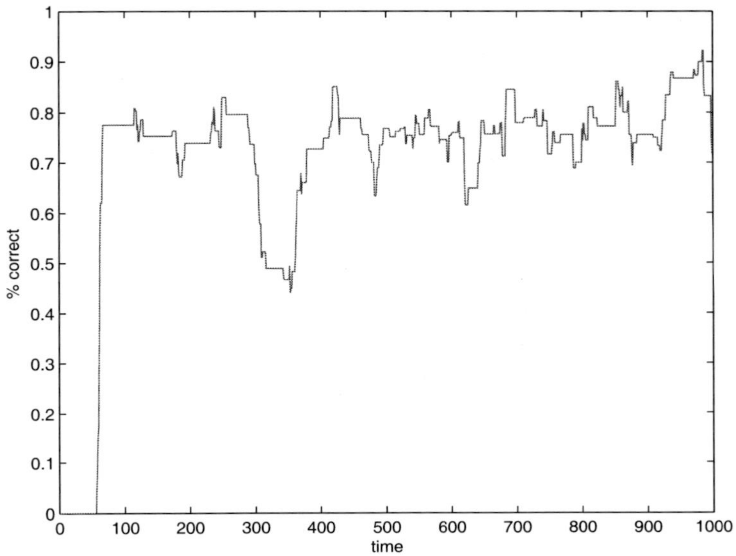

Fig. 3. The figure shows the average percentage of correctly understood communicative intentions over 15 runs.

which states of the game are desirable. Note, however, that there are subtle differences between the weights of each agents — even when the states are role-reversed the computed value will not be exactly the same.

This is also the reason why the number of correctly understood communicative intentions does not go up to 100%, but reaches a plateaux of about 80% after an initial fast increase of performance in the beginning (see Figure 3. This slight difference in value function is probably due to the fact that the weights are initialized randomly and for exploratory purposes during action selection a random number is added to the value of every action outcome. Nevertheless, given that no verbal information is given to the agents, the number of correctly understood utterances after a short training interval is remarkably high.

To illustrate the exact way the system works, two example *conversations* are shown here (see Figure 4 for the exact situations in which the two interactions took place). The first one is an incorrect case from early training (time step 2066 of 20000), i.e. the addressee does not understand the communicative intention of the speaker, due to his incompletely trained value function.

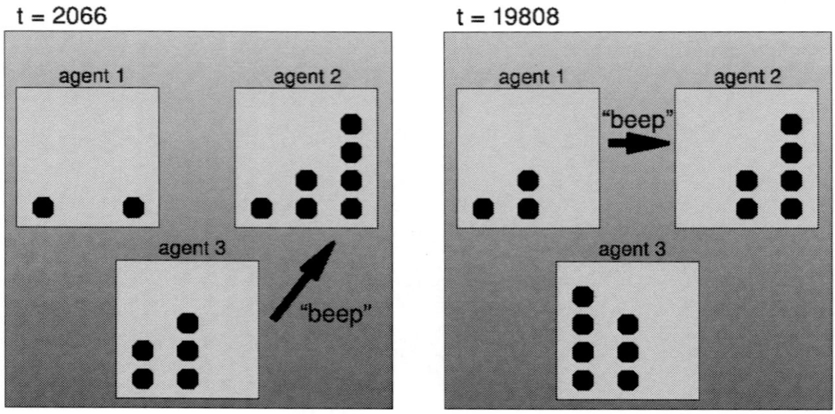

Fig. 4. This figure shows the situations of the two example interactions.

(i) Agent 3 needs food type 3. He correctly addresses agent 2 who is the only agent who has this type of food.

(ii) Agent 2 has items of all three food types. For each of the three food types he computes the consequent state should he give agent 3 an item of this type. Then, using role-reversal, he computes what value the three consequent states would have for agent 3. Due to his insufficient training he computes 0.2649376 for food type 1, 0.25863677 for food type 2, and 0.2633224 for food type 3. As a result, he gives agent 3 and item of food type 1 — clearly the wrong interpretation of the speaker's intention.

The second example is a correct case from the later stages of training (time step 19808 of 20000) when the addressee correctly understands the intention of the speaker.

(i) Agent 1 needs food type 3. He beeps agent 2, since agent 3 does not have food type 3.

(ii) Agent 2 has food type 2 and 3. He applies his value function (role reversed) to the outcome of the possible actions of giving agent 2 food type 2 (value: 1.2755736) or food type 3 (value 1.28508). Consequently, agent 2 gives food type 3 to agent 1 — the correct interpretation of the speaker's intention.

4. Discussion

This chapter introduced a general cognitive plausible theory of intention understanding in mathematical detail. Its effectiveness was demonstrated in a number of simulations using multi-agent systems. The estimation of intentions was performed with a value function implemented as a neural network and trained with reinforcement learning. To demonstrate the power of the approach we used utterances without content, so the only information an addressee did receive was that an utterance has been made. Nevertheless the amount of correctly recognized communicative intentions was around 80% after training.

One of the reasons for the recognition rate to be that high is the current implementation uses two major simplifications of the simulated world in comparison to real communication situations. The first one is that the state of the speaker and its context is fully accessibility to the addressee. The second one is that there is a close similarity between the value function of all agents. The similarity is accomplished by the fact that they are given exactly the same rewards and they also use the same γ parameter (i.e., they have the same attitude towards the relation between short term and long term goals). And while it can be generally assumed that all humans have somewhat similar goals just by the fact that they are the same species, difference in goals are given by genes and environment.

Simulations that do not use these simplifications are bound to be interesting and would be a possible extension of this work. However, when the value function of the agents start to differ due to differences in experience and hard-wired parameters, agents need to rely stronger on the verbal content of an utterance to determine the communicative intention. Therefore, a model needs to be developed that can use information given literally in an utterance (as in previous work[9]) together with the context and information obtained through role-reversal.

References

1. H. P. Grice, *Philosophical Review*, 377 (1957).
2. M. Tomasello, *Constructing a Language - A Usage-Based Theory of Language Acquisition* (Harvard University Press, 2003).
3. S. C. Levinson, On the human interaction engine, in *Roots of Human Society*, eds. N. J. Enfield and S. C. Levinson (Berg, 2006).
4. D. G. Premack and G. Woodruff, *Behavioral and Brain Sciences*, 1, 515-526 (1978).
5. A. Goldman, *Behavioral and Brain Sciences*, 16: 15-28 (1993).

6. J. Decety and P. L. Jackson, *Behavioral and Cognitive Neuroscience Reviews*, 3, 71-100 (2004).
7. S. D. Preston and F. B. M. de Wall, *Behavioral and Brain Sciences*, 25, 1-72 (2002).
8. R. S. Sutton, *Machine Learning* **3**, 9 (1988).
9. M. Klein, H. Kamp, G. Palm and K. Doya, *Neural Networks* (2008), submitted.
10. R. S. Sutton and A. G. Barto, *Reinforcement Learning - An Introduction* (MIT Press, 1998).
11. M. Jordan and D. E. Rumelhart, *Cognitive Science* **16**, 307 (1992).
12. M. Kawato, *Current Opinion in Neurobiology*, 718 (1999).

AFFORDANCES AND COMPATIBILITY EFFECTS: A NEURAL-NETWORK COMPUTATIONAL MODEL

D. CALIGIORE[*§+], A. M. BORGHI[§*], D. PARISI[*§] and G. BALDASSARRE[*]

[*]*Consiglio Nazionale delle Ricerche, Istituto di Scienze e Tecnologie della Cognizione, Via San Martino della Battaglia 44, I-00185 Roma, Italy {daniele.caligiore, domenico.parisi, gianluca.baldassarre}@istc.cnr.it*

[+]*Università Campus Bio-Medico, Via Alvaro del Portillo 21, I-00128 Roma, Italy*

[§]*Università di Bologna, Dipartimento di Psicologia, Viale Berti Pichat 5, I-40127 Bologna, Italy annamaria.borghi@unibo.it*

Behavioural and brain imaging evidence has shown that seeing objects automatically evokes "affordances", for example it tends to activate internal representations related to the execution of precision or power grips. In line with this evidence, Tucker and Ellis [1] found a compatibility effect between object size (small and large) and the kind of grip (precision and power) used to respond whether seen objects were artefacts or natural objects. This work presents a neural-network model that suggests an interpretation of these experiments in agreement with a recent theory on the general functions of prefrontal cortex. Prefrontal cortex is seen as a source of top-down bias in the competition for behavioural expression of multiple neural pathways carrying different information. The model successfully reproduces the experimental results on compatibility effects and shows how, although such a bias allows organisms to perform actions which differ from those suggested by objects' affordances, these still exert their influence on behaviour as reflected by longer reaction times.

1. Introduction

According to the traditional view of cognition, perception precedes action and is not influenced by it. Sensory stimuli determine how the world is represented in organisms' nervous systems whereas processes underlying actions play only a role on how they intervene on the environment to modify it. This passive view of knowledge is challenged by recent behavioural [2], physiological [3] and brain imaging [4] evidence showing that organisms' internal representations of the world depend on the actions with which they respond to sensory stimuli.

In this perspective, the notion of affordance [5] has been given new relevance. An affordance is a quality of an object which is directly accessible to an organism and suggests its possible interactions, uses and actions. Many works provide evidence in favour of an automatic activation of affordances during the observation of objects [6][7].

One way of studying how internal representations of objects and concepts rely upon motor information is to devise experimental tasks in which participants are shown objects and are asked to produce actions which are either in agreement (congruent trials) or in contrast (incongruent trials) with the actions typically associated with those objects (e.g., to grasp an object with the appropriate grip). As objects automatically elicit the activation of their related affordances, if participants find it more difficult (e.g. as revealed by longer reaction times) to act in incongruent trials than in congruent ones, one can infer that objects are at least in part represented in terms of potential actions.

Tucker and Ellis [1] performed an experiment with this compatibility paradigm. Participants were asked to classify large and small objects into artefacts or natural categories by mimicking either a precision or a power grip while acting on a customised joystick. Importantly, object size was not relevant to the categorisation task. The authors found a compatibility effect between object size (large and small) and motor response (power and precision grip), namely shorter reaction times (RTs) in congruent trials than in incongruent ones. These results show that object knowledge relies not only on objects perceptual features but also on the actions that can be performed on them.

This work presents a bio-mimetic neural-network model which allows interpreting the results of the aforementioned experiments on the basis of the integration of three general principles of brain functioning. The first regards the broad organization of brain cortex underlying visual processing into the “dorsal and ventral streams” [25]. The ventral stream is a neural pathway which carries information, among other things, about the identity of objects (“what”). The dorsal stream is a neural pathway which carries spatial information, for example about the shape and location of objects (“where/how”). This pathway implements the “affordances” of objects which can be learned during the first months of life, but also in the rest of life, on the basis of spontaneous environment explorations. The second principle concerns the general theory on the functions of prefrontal cortex (PFC) recently proposed by Miller and Cohen [8]. This theory views PFC as an important source of top-down biasing where different neural pathways carrying different types of information compete for expression in behaviour [8][24]. Finally, the third principle is about the use of neural networks based on the dynamic field approach [21] which allow accounting for reaction times on the basis of biologically plausible mechanisms.

In agreement with the computational neuroscience approach [9], the model is not only requested to reproduce behaviours observed in experiments but it is also constrained, at the level of the model overall architecture and functioning, by the known anatomy and physiology of brain structures underlying the behaviours investigated [10].

2. The model

2.1. *Simulated robotic set-up*

The model controls a simulated 3D artificial organism endowed with a visual system, a human-like 3-Segments/4-DOF arm, and a 21-Segments/19-DOF hand (Fig. 1a). The visual system is formed by a simulated "eye" (a 630×630 pixel RGB camera with a 120° pan angle and a 120° tilt angle) mounted 25cm above the arm's "shoulder" and leaning forward 10cm. The organism can see four different objects: two natural objects (orange and plum) and two artefacts (glass and nail) (Fig. 1b). For simplicity, the image that is sent to the system is caused only by the objects and not the hand: this amounts to assuming that the hand is ignored on the basis of a suitable non-explicitly-simulated attention mechanism (Fig. 1c; cf. [36]). The simulated arm and hand have the same parameters of the iCub robot (http://www.robotcub.org). The model controls only 2-DOF of the hand: one for the thumb, whose DOF are controlled together proportionally to commands, and one for the four same-sized fingers, controlled as a whole "virtual finger" [11] again proportionally to commands. Reaching is not simulated as not relevant for the experiment (DOF of the arm are kept still).

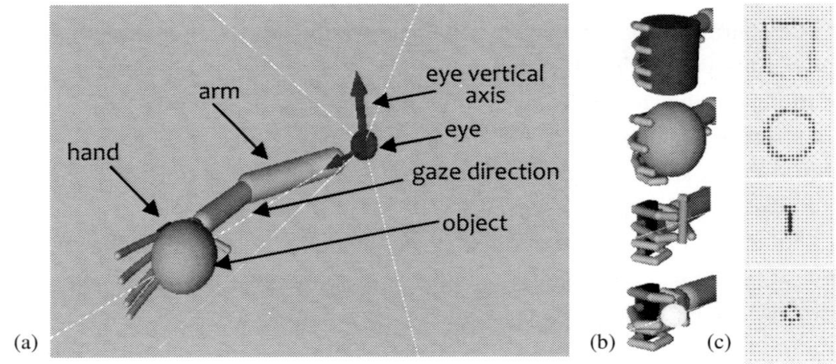

Fig. 1. (a) The simulated arm, hand, and eye interacting with a simulated object (orange). (b) Hand grips for four objects: glass, orange, nail, and plum. (c) The corresponding activation of PC neurons.

The activation of the output map of the model (premotor cortex) encodes (see Sect. 2.2) the desired hand's posture used to continuously feed the hand muscle models with "equilibrium points" [12]. Here, similarly to what is done in [13], single muscle models are simulated as simple Proportional Derivative controllers (PD) [14]. The equation of a PD muscle controller is as follows:

$$\mathbf{T} = \mathbf{K_P}\tilde{\mathbf{q}} - \mathbf{K_D}\dot{\mathbf{q}} \tag{1}$$

where $\mathbf{T}$ is the vector of muscles' torques applied to the joints, $\mathbf{K_p}$ is a diagonal matrix with elements equal to 300, $\tilde{\mathbf{q}}$ the difference vector between the desired joints' angular position and the current joints' angular position, $\mathbf{K_D}$ is a diagonal matrix with elements equal to 10, and $\dot{\mathbf{q}}$ is the vector of current joints' angular speed. The PDs' action is integrated by a gravity compensation mechanism here implemented by simply ignoring the effects of gravity on the arm and hand.

2.2. *Architecture and functioning of neural network model*

The model is formed by nine 2D maps of 21×21 neurons each (Fig. 2). Visual cortex (V1) receives the visual pre-processed signal supplied by a simulated camera. Its neurons have an activation ranging in [0, 1] and encode the information about shape and colour of the foveated object obtained through three edge-detection Sobel filters [15]. Each filter is sensible to a particular component of the object's colour (red, green or blue: this simulates the functioning of the three kinds of cones in the human retina). The model assumes that the eye always foveates the target, in line with the current neuroscientific literature suggesting that primates tend to foveate the target objects with which they interact and that their brain exploits gaze centred reference frames as much as possible for sensorimotor coordination (see [16] for a review).

The neurons of parietal cortex (PC) encode the information about the object shape but not colour. To this purpose the neurons are activated with the average activation of the topologically correspondent RGB neurons of V1. This assumption is in accordance with recent neurophysiological data showing that the information about the object's shape plays a crucial role during learning and use of affordances related to objects [17][18].

The neurons of premotor cortex (PMC) encode the output of the system in terms of desired hand fingers' angles: these angles, mapped onto the 2 dimensions of the map, are "read out" as a weighted average of the neurons' position in the map with weights corresponding to the neurons' activation ("population code hypothesis", [19]). The PMC supports the selection of postures [20] on the basis of a dynamic competition between its leaky neurons having lateral short-range excitatory connections and lateral long-range inhibitory connections [21]. When input signals from PC and PFC activate neurons of PMC, they tend to accumulate activation and form clusters (due to lateral excitatory connections) and, at the same time, to suppress other clusters (via lateral inhibitory connections). This dynamic process continues until a cluster succeeds in suppressing all other clusters, overcomes a threshold (set to 0.75), and so triggers the hand movement based on the reading out of the map:

$$s[j,t] = \overbrace{\sum_{i=1}^{N} w_{(PMC\to PMC)\,ji}\, a_{PMC}[i,t]}^{Inner} + \overbrace{\sum_{i=1}^{N} w_{(PPC\to PMC)\,ji}\, a_{PPC}[i,t]}^{Dorsal\ stream} + \overbrace{\sum_{i=1}^{N} w_{(PFC\to PMC)\,ji}\, a_{PFC}[i,t]}^{Ventral\ stream}$$

$$u[j,t+\Delta t] = \left(1-\frac{\Delta t}{\tau}\right) u[j,t] + \frac{\Delta t}{\tau} s[j,t] \qquad a[j,t] = \mathrm{f}[u[j,t]] \tag{2}$$

where $s[j, t]$, $u[j, t]$ and $a[j, t]$ are respectively the total signal, the activation potential, and the activation of neuron j at t time, Δt (set to 0.01s) is the integration time step (100 steps = 1s), τ (set to 0.3s) is the relaxation time, f is an activation function equal to $[\tanh[.]]^{+}$.

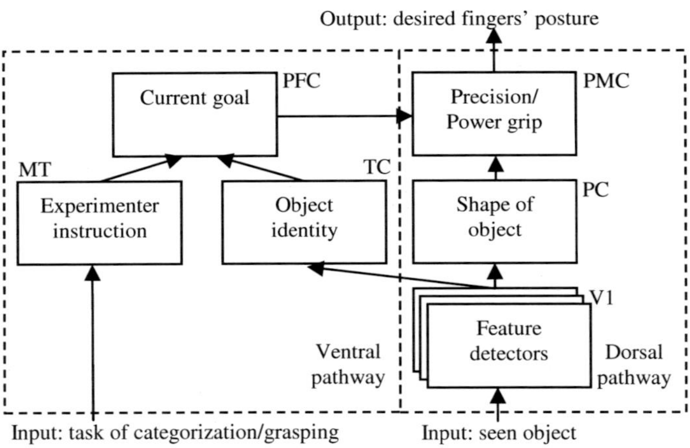

Fig. 2. Schema of the neural network model. V1 includes three RGB neural maps. Downstream V1, the model divides into two main neural pathways: the dorsal stream, implementing suitable sensorimotor transformations needed to perform action on the basis of perception, and the ventral stream, allowing a flexible control of behaviour due to the biasing effects of prefrontal cortex.

The *Inner* component of the formula accounts for signals received from lateral PMC connections with hardwired connection weights $w_{(PMC\to PMC)}$. These weights, excitatory for connections between neighbouring neurons and inhibitory for connections between distant neurons, are set to fixed values on the basis of a Gaussian function and an inhibition term as follows:

$$w_{ji} = \exp\left[-\frac{\left(d[j,i]\right)^2}{2\sigma^2} \right] - I \tag{3}$$

where w_{ij} is the weight between two neurons i and j of the map, $d[j, i]$ is the distance between the two neurons in the map "neural space" (where the measure unit is equal to 1 for two maximally-close neighbouring neurons), σ (set to 0.6) is the width of the Gaussian, and I (set to 0.9) is the inhibition term.

The *Dorsal stream* component accounts for the signals received from PC neurons modulated by the connection weights $w_{(PC \rightarrow PMC)}$; finally, the component *Ventral stream* accounts for the signals received from PFC neurons modulated by the connection weights $w_{(PFC \rightarrow PMC)}$. The reaction time is the time required by at least one neuron of the winner cluster of PMC to reach the threshold [21].

The neurons of temporal cortex (TC) encode objects' identity. In accordance with visual physiology findings [22], from lower (V1) to higher levels (TC) of the visual hierarchy receptive field size and stimulus selectivity of neurons increase, whereas visual topography is progressively lost. In the model, TC is a Kohonen self-organising map (SOM) which activates as follows [23]:

$$a_j = \exp\left[-\frac{\left\| \mathbf{w}_{(V1 \rightarrow IT)j} - \mathbf{a}_{V1} \right\|^2}{2\sigma^2} \right] \tag{4}$$

where a_j is the activation of the TC neuron j, σ is the size of the clusters of active neurons equal to 0.55, $\mathbf{w}_{(V1 \rightarrow TC)j}$ is the vector of connection weights from V1 to TC neuron j, and $\mathbf{a}_{V1}$ is the activation of V1 neurons. After learning, TC responds to different objects with different neuron clusters (see Sect. 2.3).

The neurons of medial temporal cortex (MT) encode the category of actions to be performed on objects, namely either those required by a grasping task, as performed by participants in everyday life, or those required by the psychological experiment specified by language. To this purpose, neurons of MT are activated with two random patterns with 20 neurons set equal to one and the rest equal to zero. The neurons of prefrontal cortex (PFC) encode information about the current goal of action depending on both the task (MT) and object identity (TC). To this purpose, PFC neurons are activated according to the Kohonen activation function of Eq. (4). The use of a Kohonen network for both TC and PFC is based on studies which suggest that these cortical areas are involved in high-level visual processing and categorization [24][26][35].

2.3. *Learning phases*

The organism undergoes two learning phases, one representing experience gathered in "normal life", during which it learns to suitably grasp objects, and one representing the psychological experiment, during which the organism learns to trigger a power or precision grip on the basis of the objects' category.

Before learning, the connection weights of the model are set to values uniformly drawn in [0, 1]. Learning during life involves learning of the affordance-based behaviour within the dorsal stream [27] and learning of objects' identity in TC [28]. To this purpose, the four objects are repeatedly presented to the system in repeated trials during which MT is always activated with the pattern corresponding to the grasping task. Note that during this "life learning" the PFC and MT are activated, notwithstanding this would not be required to execute actions via the dorsal pathway, to avoid biasing the results when the ecological and experimental conditions are compared. In each trial the hand is open and the object is located in close to the hand palm, V1 performs Sobel-based colour-dependent edge detection of the object image, and PC performs colour-independent edge detection (that is it encodes object's shape) by averaging the activation of RGB neurons of V1 with same topography.

The PC-PMC connection weights are developed using a Hebb covariance learning rule while the organism performs randomly-selected power/precision grip grasping actions in correspondence to the perceived object. This "motor babbling" [29][30] is a general learning process [37] for which the production of rather unstructured behaviours allow the formation of basic associations between sensory representations and motor representations [31]. Here, motor babbling is composed of these phases: (a) either a large (orange and glass both with a 7cm diameter) or small object (plum with a 2cm diameter or nail with a 8mm diameter) is set close to the system's hand palm; (b) the hand moves its fingers around the object with constant torques (this is done by issuing suitable desired angles to the PD muscle models; objects are kept fixed in space to avoid that they slip away from fingers during closure); (c) when the fingers have been closed on the object (see Fig. 1b), the Hebb covariance learning rule reported below [32] is used to update the all-to-all connection weights between PC and PMC neurons so as to form associations between the object's perceived shape (PC) and the corresponding hand posture (PMC):

$$\Delta w_{ji} = \eta\left(a_j - \bar{a}_j\right)\left(a_i - \bar{a}_i\right)\left(w_{max} - \left|w_{ji}\right|\right) \tag{5}$$

where η is a learning rate (set to 10), w_{max} (set to 0.2) keeps the connection weights within a small range, a_j is the activation of the PMC neuron j, a_i is the activation of the PC neuron i, $\bar{a}_j$ and $\bar{a}_i$ are moving decaying averages of the neurons' activations calculated as $\bar{a}[t+\Delta t]=(1-\xi)\bar{a}[t]+\xi a$ (ξ is set to 0.8). This rule strengthens the connections between each couple of neurons which have both an activation above or both an activation below their own average activation, and weakens their connections in other cases. Within the ventral pathway, during motor babbling the V1-TC connection weights develop the capacity to categorise objects on the basis of a Kohonen learning rule [23][33]:

$$\Delta w_{ji} = \mu\Lambda\left[j, j^*\right]\left(a_i - w_{ji}\right) \qquad \Lambda(j, j^*) = \exp\left[-\frac{d^2\left[j, j^*\right]}{2\sigma^2}\right] \tag{6}$$

where μ is a learning rate (set to 1), a_i is the activation of V1 neuron i, j is the index of an TC neuron, j^* is the index of the TC neuron with maximum activation ("winning neuron"), $\Lambda[j, j^*]$ is a proximity Gaussian function which determines the size of the cluster of neurons whose weights are updated, $d[j, j^*]$ is the Euclidean distance between j and j^* on the TC map, σ is the width of Gaussian function. During the model tests, the value of σ is set to a larger value for larger objects, in particular it is set within [0.5, 0.9] in proportion to the activation of V1 neurons for the various objects. This assumption is motivated by the following considerations. The Kohonen neural network is an approximation of the dynamic-field neural network of Eq. (2) and is used here because it is computationally faster and because it offers a well-understood learning algorithm. Contrary to the dynamic-field neural network, however, the Kononen neural network has the implausible feature for which it forms clusters of active neurons having a *constant* number of units and overall activation level. As the total activation of clusters may have important effects on RTs, and this was important for the goals of the paper, this limit of the Kononen network is overcome with the assumption on the variable σ. Note that a similar assumption is done also for PFC (see below). Having a larger number of active neurons in correspondence to larger objects seems a better approximation of what might happen in real brains (e.g., in this way information on objects size is encoded in terms of overall activation of neurons, cf. Hu and Goodale, 2000).

During the psychological experiment learning involves acquiring suitable "goal representations" in PFC, that is representations of which action to select (stored in the PFC-PMC connections) in correspondence to which combination of task and object identity currently tackled by the organism (stored in the (MT, TC)-PFC connections). To this purpose, the four objects are repeatedly presented to the system in multiple trials during which (a) MT is always activated with the pattern corresponding to the categorisation task, and (b) the hand has performed the grip requested by the psychological experiment. The connection weights between (MT, TC)-PFC are updated using the modified

Kohonen algorithm of Eq. (6). Similarly to TC, also within PFC the use of the modified Kohonen algorithm allows obtaining larger clusters of activated neurons for larger objects. In this way the model assumes that the ventral stream stores information about the object size in terms of number of activated neurons (cf. [34]). During the objects presentation, accompanied by the hand closure requested by the categorisation task of the simulated psychological experiment, also the connection weights between PFC and PMC are updated, in this case on the basis of the Hebb covariance rule of Eq. (5). This allows the system to associate the particular combination of task (MT) and object identity (TC) with the suitable action required to correctly categorise the observed object (PMC).

3. Results

The model reproduces the experimental results of [1] (Fig. 3). An ANOVA on response times was performed with two factors: congruency (congruent vs. incongruent) and object size (large vs. small). Participants were ten different simulated organisms trained and tested with ten different random-number generator seeds. In agreement with the experiments run with real subjects, both factors were statistically significant: RTs were faster in congruent than in incongruent trials ($p<0.01$) and for large than for small objects ($p<0.01$).

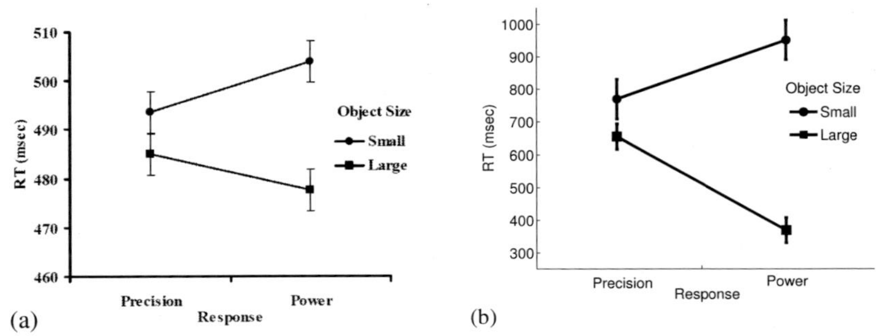

Fig. 3. Reaction times (y-axis) versus kind of grip (x-axis). (a) Real experiment [1] (copyright of Taylor & Francis, Visual Cognition, http://www.informaworld.com). (b) Simulated experiment.

The analysis of the system during "life" (i.e. while performing a grasping task) shows that the dorsal pathway tends to trigger an action on the basis of the affordances elicited by it (a power grip for a large object, a precision grip for a small object). In particular, after the learning phase, when organisms see an object the neurons of V1 become active by encoding shape and colour, and thus the neurons of PC become active by encoding the shape. The activation of PC causes a neuron cluster in PMC to gain activation until it reaches the action-triggering threshold. This leads to the execution of either a power or precision grip through the muscle-models and the simulated hand. In parallel, when the task requires grasping objects the ventral pathway evokes the same congruent action in PMC as the dorsal pathways (see Fig. 4a). In particular, TC activates four different clusters of neurons, one for each different object, PFC does the same, and each PFC cluster evokes the action congruent with the object.

In the case of the categorisation task, TC activates four different clusters of neurons, one for each different object, as during "life". On the contrary, PFC activates four different clusters with respect to what happens during "life", as now the MT activation pattern indicates to the system that it needs to respond to each object with an action which depends on its category (artefact vs. natural) and not on its size (small versus large). As a consequence, in incongruent trials the ventral pathway evokes an action different with respect to the dorsal pathway (e.g. a precision grip to categorise as artefact an orange) via a suitable bias issued by the PFC to the PMC, thus causing a conflict within the latter (Fig. 5b). As the PFC-PMC signal is stronger than the PC-PMC signal, the bias from PFC wins the competition (e.g. by triggering a precision grip) but the RTs is longer with respect to the congruent cases. In fact, when PFC and PC signal clusters mismatch they lead to a slower charge of the PMC leaky neurons, and hence reaching of the threshold requires more time than when they match.

(a)

(b)

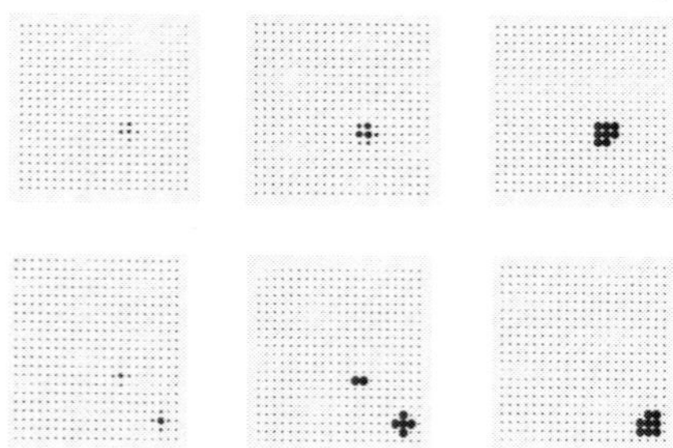

Fig. 4. (a) Activation of PMC in a congruent trial. (b) Activation of PMC in an incongruent trial.

The results also show faster RTs for the larger objects, as in real experiments. The reason is that large objects activate more neurons of V1 than small ones, and these activate a larger number of neurons in PC, and, in turn, in PMC. The signal arriving to PMC via the ventral pathway is also greater for large objects than for small ones due to the use of the modified Kohonen learning rule. Both phenomena tend to produce a faster "charge" of the leaky neurons of the PMC and hence faster RTs (see Eq. (1)). In incongruent trials, the two signals from PFC and PC to PMC do not overlap but are both large: a competition between two large activation patterns again leads to faster RTs in PMC than when there is a competition between two small patterns. However, these RTs are slower than RTs of congruent trials.

4. Conclusion

The proposed model successfully reproduces the experimental results of [1], in particular faster reaction times in congruent conditions vs. incongruent ones, and with large objects vs. small objects. The architecture of the model *integrates* three important principles, namely the interplay between ventral and dorsal visual pathways, the top-down biasing effect of prefrontal cortex on selection of actions, and the dynamic-field competitive processes, which make it quite general and suitable to tackle other empirical experiments in future work.

Acknowledgments

This research was supported by the EU FP7 Project ROSSI, contract no. 216125-STREP.

References

1. M. Tucker and R. Ellis, *Vis Cogn* **8**, 769 (2001).
2. L. W. Barsalou, *Annu Rev Psychol* **59**, 617 (2008).
3. G. Rizzolatti, R. Camarda, L. Fogassi, M. Gentilucci, G. Luppino, M. Matelli, *Exp Brain Res* **71**, 491 (1988).
4. Berthoz, *Philos T R Soc B* **352**, 1437 (1997).
5. J. Gibson, *The ecological approach to visual perception* (1979).
6. M. Borghi, C. Bonfiglioli, L. Lugli, P. Ricciardelli, S. Rubichi and R. Nicoletti, *Neurosci Lett* **411**, 17 (2007).
7. U. Castiello, *Trends Cogn Sci* **3**, 264 (1999).
8. E. K. Miller and J. D. Cohen, *Annu Rev Neurosci* **24**, 167 (2001).
9. P. S. Churchland and T. J. Sejnowski, *The Computational Brain* (1993).
10. J. Grèzes, M. Tucker, J. Armony, R. Ellis and R. E. Passingham, *Eur J Neurosci* **17**, 2735 (2003).
11. M. A. Arbib, Grounding the mirror system hypothesis for the evolution of thelanguage-ready brain, in *Simulating the Evolution of Language*, eds. A. Cangelosi and D. Parisi, 229 (2002).
12. G. Feldman, *J Mot Behav* **18**, 17 (1986).
13. N. E. Berthier, M. T. Rosenstein and A. G. Barto, *Psychol Rev* **112**, 329 (2005).
14. D. Bullock and S. Grossberg, Vite and Flete: neural modules for trajectory formation and postural control, in *Volitional Action*, ed. W. Hershberger (1989).

15. I. Sobel and G. Feldman, A 3x3 isotropic gradient operator for image processing, *Presentation for Stanford Artificial Project* (1968).
16. R. Shadmehr and S. P. Wise, *The Computational Neurobiology of Reaching and Pointing* (2005).
17. Murata, V. Gallese, G. Luppino, M. Kaseda and H. Sakata, *J Neurophysiol* **83**, 2580 (2000).
18. R. T. Oliver, E. J. Geiger, B. C. Lewandowski and S. Thompson-Schill, *J Vision* **5**, 610 (2005).
19. A. Pouget, P. Dayan and R. Zemel, *Nat Rev Neurosci* **1**, 125 (2000).
20. M. L. Platt, *Nature* **400**, 233 (1999).
21. W. Erlhagen and G. Schooner, *Psychol Rev* **109**, 545 (2002).
22. Tanaka, *Annu Rev Neurosci*, **19**, 109 (1996).
23. T. Kohonen, *Self-Organizing Maps* (1997).
24. E. K. Miller, D. J. Freedman and J. D. Wallis, *Philos T R Soc B*, **357**, 1123 (2002).
25. D. Milner and M. A. Goodale, *Neuropsychologia* **46**, 774 (2008).
26. D. J. Freedman, M. Riesenhuber, T. Poggio and E. K. Miller, *J Neurosci*, **23**, 12, 5235 (2003).
27. P. Cisek, *Philos T R Soc B* **362**, 1585 (2007).
28. H. R. Rodman, *Cereb Cortex* **4**, 484 (1994).
29. D. Caligiore, D. Parisi and G. Baldassarre, Toward an integrated biomimetic model of reaching, in *Proceedings of 6th IEEE International Conference on Development and Learning*, eds. Y. Demiris, B. Scassellati and D. Mareschal (2007).
30. C. von Hofsten, *Dev Psychol*, **18** (1982).
31. Piaget. *The origins of intelligence in children* (1952).
32. T. J. Sejnowski, *J Math Biol* **4**, 303 (1977).
33. H. Ritter, T. Martinetz and K. Schulten, *Neural Computation and Self-Organizing Maps - An Introduction* (1992).
34. Y. Hu and M. A. Goodale, *J Cognitive Neurosci* **12**, 856 (2000).
35. K. Shima, M. Isoda, H. Mushiake and J. Tanji, *Nature* **445**, 315 (2007).
36. D. Ognibene, C. Balkenius and G. Baldassarre, Integrating epistemic action (active vision) and pragmatic action (reaching): a neural architecture for camera-arm robots, in *Proceedings of the Tenth International Conference on the Simulation of Adaptive Behavior (SAB2008)*, eds. M. Asada, J.C.T. Hallam, J.-A. Meyer and J. Tani (2008).
37. D. Caligiore, T. Ferrauto, D. Parisi, N. Accornero, M. Capozza and G. Baldassarre, Using motor babbling and Hebb rules for modeling the development of reaching with obstacles and grasping, in *International Conference on Cognitive Systems*, eds. R. Dillmann, C. Maloney, G. Sandini, T. Asfour, G. Cheng, G. Metta, A. Ude (2008).

MIRRORING MAPS AND ACTIONS REPRESENTATION THROUGH EMBODIED INTERACTIONS

ALEX PITTI[†]

ERATO Asada project, JST, University of Tokyo
Tokyo, Japan

HASSAN ALIREZAI and YASUO KUNIYOSHI

ERATO Asada project, JST, University of Tokyo
Tokyo, Japan

In this paper, we present a neural architecture aimed to reproduce the qualitative properties of the mirror neurons system which encodes neural representations of actions either performed or observed. Several biological researches have emphasized some of its important aspects, for instance, the tight coupling between perception and action, the crucial role of timing (temporal information for encoding and detection), or its particular neural connectivity. We attempt to model these in a network of spiking neurons to learn the accurate temporal relationships between sensorimotor maps for action representation. After the learning, the neural connectivity efficiently induces functional capabilities in the whole network exhibiting statistics similar with observed evidences in the mirror neurons system and comparable to those of small-world networks (e.g., scale-free dynamics and hierarchical organization).

1. Introduction

The discovery by Rizzolatti and his team of particular neurons triggering to specific actions, whenever performed by the subject himself or observed from someone else executing it [1], brings out the tight coupling that exists between perception and action. This neural population –, coined by the term "mirror neurons system" (MNS) and found in the premotor cortex,– is important since it sheds light not only on how our actions are represented within the brain but also how we understand those performed by others; action understanding is hypothesized to be the first stage for infants to develop higher cognitive skills such as social interaction and imitation [14, 15]. Recent observations of human and monkey MNS have permitted to dress an overall good picture of its characteristics and functionalities [1, 2, 14, 17-19]. For instance, it fires robustly with exact timing to executed and observed actions, even when the action

[†]Work supported by grant from ERATO Asada project, JST.

sequence's end is occluded. Nevertheless, despite the advances done, few is known about its underlying neural mechanisms and computational principles. As these neurons represent a very small portion within a larger population of broadly congruent neurons (10 to 30 percent neurons only present effective visuo-motor congruency), some researchers ever questioned about their real significance and importance [17, 18]: How such system might support any important functionality relying on so few neurons? We propose to investigate this question and present our hypothesis on how the MNS *could be* organized to represent actions, fulfilling its qualitative and quantitative properties; computational models proposed recently never addressed this issue (cf. [14]).

To rely on so few neurons, the MNS must be critically organized as in complex systems (e.g., [6, 16, 20]). Efficient neural connectivity might permit to have specific neurons to support the network's functional integration for cross-modal associations. We introduce in the first part our motives to develop such kind of neural network that can exhibit the same functionality as the MNS. Next, we show that its characteristics make it a small-world network which are networks with exceptional structure (e.g., fault tolerance, short path length). Using this network, we reproduce then the Rizzolatti's experiment exhibiting the mirror neurons features to trigger either during action execution and during action observation (e.g., for grasping). We show that the network generates similar characteristics with the MNS revealing sensorimotor coupling and multi-modal integration (e.g., the re-enaction of one modality from experiencing the other) relying on critical neurons.

2. Motivation

The particular organization of the MNS presents some similarity with those of complex systems which may permit to understand (and model) its functioning. For instance, mirror neurons fire to either performed or observed action but with *accurate* timing (e.g., firing only at the time-to-contact during grasping). We believe that this temporal characteristic is important since it requires efficient information propagation and therefore efficient neural connectivity to respond robustly. However, the neurons firing at exact timing represent a minority within the MNS: Gallese and Rizzolatti discovered that the MNS has an atypical distribution [1] following roughly two classes labeled "strictly congruent neurons" and "broadly congruent neurons" with respectively 1/3 and 2/3 ratio suggesting that actions are represented by few neurons ([17, 18] report a 1/10 - 9/10 partition). Since timing is crucial, these neurons must be efficiently connected within the MNS in order to trigger contingently. Therefore, these critical neurons must somehow generalize the spatio-temporal structure of one action sequence into its action primitives ([14]). Reversely, their damages can cause the degradation of the network performance and its functional integration (e.g., one hypothesis of the cause for autism [10]). In addition, new evidences demonstrating that actions are represented both spatially and temporally at different description levels [2] support once more the hierarchical nature of the MNS organization. Altogether, these considerations suggest us that, in order to exhibit pragmatic representations implicit from which appear the tight links between perception and action, the MNS should follow a complex systems architecture exhibiting *(i)* robust and redundant information processing relying critically on time, *(ii)* asymmetric density distribution of the neurons connectivity, and *(iii)* hierarchical and distributed representations.

Those properties, summarized in table 1), are an hallmark of scale-free and small-world networks (SWN) [6, 7, 16, 20]. These are types of graph with characteristic nodes connectivity distribution that follow a power-law distribution and present efficient information propagation and synchronization at different time scales (i.e., scale-free dynamics [7, 16]). A majority of units possesses short path lengths connections with their neighbors, forming a semi-closed cluster, whereas a minority possesses long path lengths linking those clusters to distant ones. These special neurons represent hub connectors that link the "small-worlds" to each other. Information exchange is particularly fast because of the hierarchical organization that combine centralization and distribution making the network robust to fault tolerance [20]. The suppression of an important number of provincial units might weakly affect the network performance whereas the suppression of the most connected ones might drastically affect it, making them critical.

Table 1. Qualitative and quantitative comparisons between the properties of the mirror neuron systems and of small-world networks.

Mirror neurons system	*Small-world networks*
Tight coupling between perception and action: critical timing [1]	*Critical timing* SWN relies on few but critical units integrating globally the local processes.
MNS distribution [1]: 60% "coarse" neurons 30% "accurate" neurons Autism: no global integration of modal processes [11]	*"Hub Connectors"* Connectivity distribution of the units in a SWN follow a *power-law* curve. SWN relies on few but critical units integrating globally the local processes.
Neural representation at different description levels [2]	*Scale-free dynamics* Information is represented in hierarchies at multiple time scales.

3. Experiments

3.1. *The neural network model*

We attempt to model the particular entanglement between perception and action characteristic to the MNS for action representation (e.g., grasping a cup). To this aim, we define two networks to receive respectively the visual information from the camera and the somatosensory input from a haptic device (the force feedback of our fingertips), see Fig. 1. Each neuron of the visual map is associated to one pixel value. As the camera resolution is reduced to 60x90 pixels, 5400 neurons constitute the visual map. The somatosensory map has for itself 1000 neurons, each ones associated to a spatial location of the haptic device [5, 9]. The neurons, all excitatory, are defined by the formal model proposed by Izhikevich [11, 12] to which we add 2000 inhibitory neurons in a separated hidden layer to stabilize the overall system. The initial neural network is to a standard random graph so that the node connectivity has a uniform distribution: each neuron, either excitatory or inhibitory, has 100 synaptic connections equally weighted to other ones randomly selected over the whole network. Therefore, the neural pairs within the same map support the intra-map information processing (specialization) whereas the distant neural pairs support the inter-map information processing (integration). Before learning, these neural associations don't correspond to any particular sensorimotor patterns; the mechanism of spike timing-dependent plasticity (STDP) [4] regulates then the learning by updating the synaptic weights.

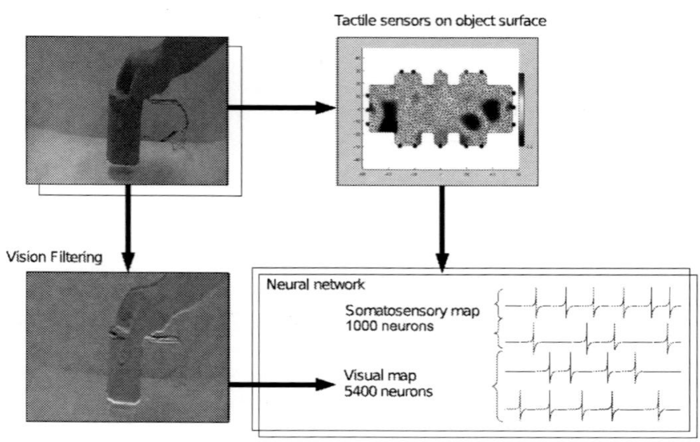

Figure 1. Schematic of the experiment. The network receives the co-occurent visuo-tactile inputs during grasping from the camera (bottom-right corner) and from the pressure sensitive device (in the upper-left corner).

3.2. *The learning procedure*

The first stage consists of repeated grasp of the tactile device. During execution, the neurons of each map learn the invariant contingent relations between their siblings within the same map (intra-map specialization) and of the other map (inter-map integration). During time, they assemble themselves to form robust spatio-temporal clusters between the vision map and the somatosensory map. The result is such that, after the learning period, if we reproduce again the grasping sequence, the network anticipates this time the exact time-to-contact: the specific somatosensory pattern is activated *before* the effective contact within dozens of milliseconds in advance (see Fig. 2).

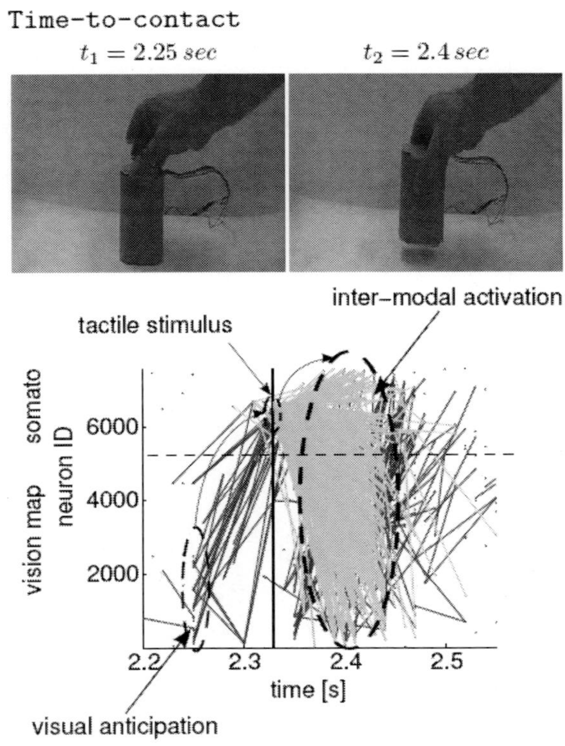

Figure 2. Neural dynamics of the visuo-tactile maps during physical interactions; the dots represent the neurons spikes. In dark gray (resp. in light gray) the synaptic activation from the neurons of the vision map (resp. the somato map). The retina anticipates the perceptual stimulus in the somatosensory map *before* the time-to-contact. At the time-to-contact, the somatosensory map generates in return a global activation.

This phenomenon, described by Berthoz as "anticipated touch" [14], shows how the neurons of the visual map literally *simulate* the activity of the tactile modality with precise timing. The tactile and the vision modalities get intertwined reproducing the mirroring effect of the F5 area's neurons. It follows that, when we effectively touch the device at the time-to-contact (receiving tactile stimuli), it is then the tactile map that generates a global activation in the whole network. The two modalities are such functionally integrated that one perceptual stimulus can activate (or simulate) the modality missing. Such case occurs for example when we grasp an object with closed eyes and mentally reconstruct its shape from our touches (tactile → vision). Or, when observing someone else grasping, we mentally reconstruct the respective tactile information (vision → tactile).

3.3. *Functional comparison with the MNS*

To fulfill the comparison with the MNS, we test the network's response in the conditions of action observation i.e., we provide to the network only the visual stimuli (see Fig. 3).

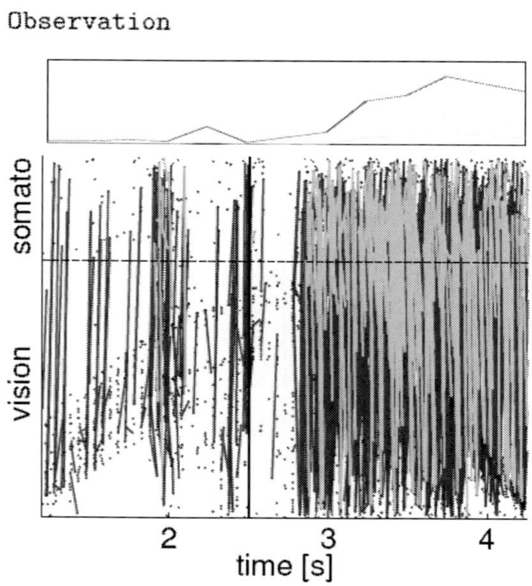

Figure 3. Neural activity during observing a grasping sequence (no tactile information received). At the time-to-contact and during handling, the visual map, without tactile information, re-activates nevertheless the somatosensory activity as during enaction.

Without tactile stimuli, the network nevertheless re-activates the same neural pathways as during enaction (see Fig. 3) and reconstructs the missing modality from only the visual information: the tactile information is perceived from the visual information (dark gray links) and fires back (light gray links). Their dynamics thus reverberate each other in a coherent fashion through a resonant-like process at precise timing. It assesses the tight coupling between the two modalities and suggests that the network is efficiently organized.

4. Analyzing the dynamics of the neural network

We analyze the network statistics with respect to the neurons connectivity. Fig. 4a) presents the distribution of the neural groups size relative to their time span. Fig. 4b) displays the neurons density distribution relative to the number of synaptic connections. In Fig. 4c), we analyze the network tolerance when confronted to an attack (pruning neurons). The first one displays the wide distribution of the clusters temporal range whereas the second shows the power-law distribution of the units connectivity. These two graphs explain how actions are represented inside the network as spatio-temporal clusters at multiple time scales and at different hierarchical levels.

As we introduced it in section 2, these properties are those of small-world networks [7] and match the MNS quantitative data separating the neurons into two classes asymmetrically distributed, those broadly congruent, the majority, and those strictly congruent, the minority. This functional architecture is hypothesized to imply efficient interregional communication, enhanced signal propagation speed, computational power, and synchronizability [3, 6, 7]. For instance, the network performance –, computed as the firing rate in the somato map normalized between a lower and a higher limit interval,– decrease linearly when we suppress neurons selected in an aleatory order (Fig. 4-c, continuous line) whereas the performance falls drastically if we prune the most connected neurons first (Fig. 4-c, dashed line): the suppression of 37.5% of neurons randomly selected or of the 7% most connected ones achieve the same performance score.

The power laws curve means that neurons in a small-world network are not completely independent from each other, and a few ones dictate the action. In our experiment, it means that the neural network has evolved into an efficient system shaped by the synchronized and coordinated visuo-somatosensory stimuli. The network produces different description levels of the action across multiple time scales assembled dynamically into short and long range clusters. These clusters are organized around neurons highly connected (Fig. 4b) which articulate the scale-free temporal binding between the short-range time scale of

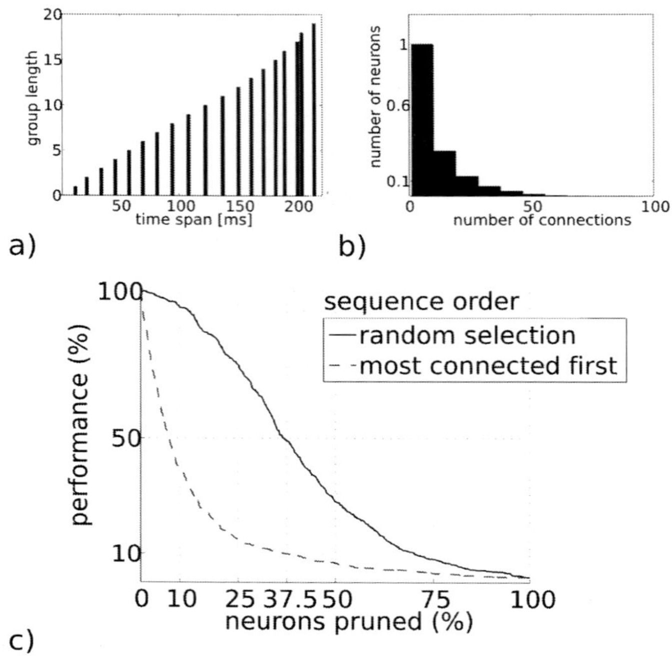

Figure 4. Clusters statistics. Density distribution of the neurons connectivity ordered by their time span (a) [resp. the longest path of cluster defined and their time span]. The density of the neurons connectivity in (b) follows the characteristic power law curve typical of small-world networks. The network produces scale-free dynamics. In c), we compare the network performance (firing rate of the somato map) depending if we prune the neurons in a random sequential order (continuous line) or the most connected neurons first (dashed line).

the neurons (millisecond order) to the long-range time scale of the "body" (hundred milliseconds to seconds order).

Precisely, some of the neurons are found critical within the network due to their large number of connections. Thus, not all of them have the same importance. These particular neurons direct the neural dynamics and sustain the network functional capabilities. It is remarkable that the network functional integrity relies on a relatively small population of neurons compared to its dimension: lesser than 5 percents of the neurons in the network possess more than ten synaptic connections which represent approximately 300 neurons. We circled these critical neurons in figure 5 and in thin black lines, some clusters connecting some of them during grasping. As it can be seen from the graph, they follow the trends of the visuo-somatosensory patterns (the continuous and dashed lines). They represent therefore the primitives on which the dynamics of

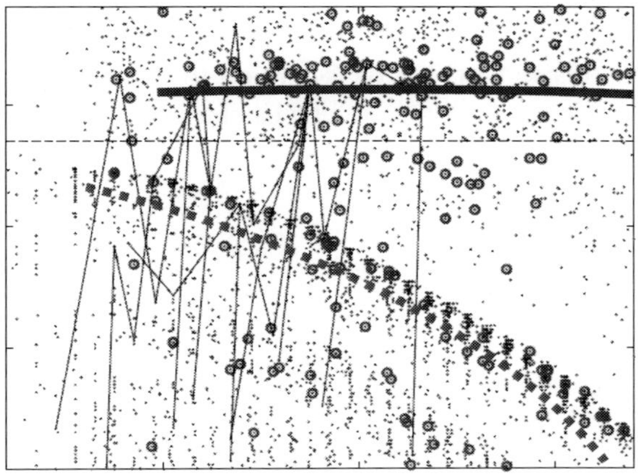

Figure 5. Critical neurons. We circled the neurons with more than ten synaptic connections during the period of tearing [taken from Fig. 4]. They are critical for the functional integrity of the network on which the clusters rely on. We plot also some clusters passing by some of these neurons. The plain and dashed lines plot their trends, the action primitives.

the network are articulated and show how actions can be represented as scale-free dynamics.

5. Discussion

In this paper, we proposed the hypothesis that the mirror neurons system is organized critically as a complex network to represent actions. Our proposal is supported by recent findings suggesting that action representation in the MNS are modeled at different description levels with scale-free dynamics [1, 2, 17] relying on very few neurons [18, 19]. The neural organization of our model has a topological connectivity similar to scale-free networks [3, 6, 7] which permits the cross-modal integration between the visual and haptic information. Although the network is highly robust against pruning, global integration is nevertheless sensitive to the suppression of particular neurons only, highly integrated. One hypothesis suggested for autism [10]. We expect that such neural mechanism might provide some principles to understand how cross-modal integration occurs for action representation and action understanding during infant development [9, 15].

Acknowledgement

We would like to thank the JST ERATO project for the support to this research and the anonymous reviewer for his helpful comments.

References

1. Rizzolatti, G., Craighero, L., "The Mirror-Neuron System", Annu. Rev. Neurosci., 27:169-92, 2004.
2. Lestou, V., Pollick, F., Kourtzi, Z., "Neural substrates for action understanding at different description levels in the human brain", Journal of Cognitive Neuroscience 20(2), 324-341, 2008.
3. Bassett, D., Bullmore, E., "Small-world brain networks", The Neuroscientist 12(6), 512-523, 2006.
4. Abbott, L.F. and Nelson, S.B., "Synaptic plasticity: taming the beast", Nature neuroscience, (3), pp. 1178-1182, 2000.
5. Pitti, A. Alirezaei, H. and Kuniyoshi, Y., "Cross-modal and Scale-free Action Representations through Enaction", Neural Networks (in press).
6. Watts, D., Strogatz, S., Collective dynamics of 'small-world' networks. Nature 393, 440-442, 1998.
7. Buzsaki, G., Rhythms of the Brain. Oxford University Press, 2006.
8. Alirezaei, H., Nagakubo, A., Kuniyoshi, Y., A highly stretchable tactile sensor skin for smooth surfaced humanoids. IEEE-RAS 7th Intl. Conf. on Humanoid Robots, 512-523, 2007b.
9. Rochat, P., Five levels of self-awareness as they unfold early in life. Consciousness and Cognition 12, 717-731, 2003.
10. Just, M.A., Cherkassky, V.L., Keller, T.A., Kana, R.K. and Minshew, N.J., "Functional and anatomical cortical underconnectivity in autism: evidence from an FMRI study of an executive function task and corpus callosum morphometry", Cerebral Cortex, 17:4, p. 951-961, 2007.
11. Izhikevich, E., Gally, A.J. and Edelman, G.M., "Spike-timing Dynamics of Neuronal Groups", Cerebral Cortex, 14, p. 933-944, 2004.
12. Izhikevich, E., "Polychronization: Computation With Spikes", Neural Computation, 18, p. 245-282, 2006.
13. Berthoz, A., The Brain's Sense of Movement, Harvard University Press, 2000.
14. Oztop, E., Kawato, M. and Arbib, M., "Mirror neurons and imitation: A computationally guided review", Neural Network, 2126, pp. 1-18, 2006.
15. Zukow-Goldring, "Assisted imitation: affordances, effectivities, and the mirror system in early language development", from Action to Language via the Mirror Neuron System, M.A. Arbib, 2005.
16. Barabási, A.-L. and Albert, R., "Emergence of scaling in random network", Science, 286:509-512, 1999.

17. Chong, T. Cunnington, R. Williams, M. Kanwisher, N. and Mattingley, J. "fMRI Adaptation Reveals Mirror Neurons in Human Inferior Parietal Cortex" Current Biology 18, 1576-1580, 2008.
18. Dinstein, I., "Human Cortex: Reflections of Mirror Neurons", Current Biology 18, R956-R959, 2008.
19. Dinstein, I., Gardner, J. Jazayeri, M. Heeger, D., "Executed and Observed Movements Have Different Distributed Representations in Human aIPS", The Journal of Neuroscience, 28(44):11231-11239, 2008.
20. Albert, R. Jeong, H. and Barabási, A.-L., "Error and attack tolerance of complex networks", Nature 206, 2000; p. 378-382. Erratum: Nature 409; p. 542, 2001.

MODELING VISUAL AFFORDANCES: THE SELECTIVE ATTENTION FOR ACTION MODEL (SAAM)

CHRISTOPH BÖHME* and DIETMAR HEINKE

School of Psychology, University of Birmingham
Birmingham B15 2TT, United Kingdom
**E-mail: cxb632@bham.ac.uk*

Classically, visual attention is assumed to be influenced by visual properties of objects, e.g. as assessed in visual search tasks. However, recent experimental evidence suggests that visual attention is also guided by action-related properties of objects ("affordances"),[1,2] e.g. the handle of a cup *affords* grasping the cup; therefore attention is drawn towards the handle. In a first step towards modelling this interaction between attention and action, we implemented the Selective Attention for Action model (SAAM). The design of SAAM is based on the Selective Attention for Identification model (SAIM).[3] For instance, we also followed a soft-constraint satisfaction approach in a connectionist framework. However, SAAM's selection process is guided by locations within objects suitable for grasping them whereas SAIM selects objects based on their visual properties. In order to implement SAAM's selection mechanism two sets of constraints were implemented. The first set of constraints took into account the anatomy of the hand, e.g. maximal possible distances between fingers. The second set of constraints (geometrical constraints) considered suitable contact points on objects by using simple edge detectors. We demonstrate here that SAAM can successfully mimic human behaviour by comparing simulated contact points with experimental data.

Keywords: Affordances; Visual Attention; Modelling; Action; Grasping.

1. Introduction

Actions need to be tightly guided by vision in our daily interactions with our environment. To maintain such a direct guidance, J. J. Gibson postulated that the visual system automatically extract "affordances" of objects.[2] According to Gibson, affordance refers to parts or properties of visual objects that are directly linked to actions or motor performances. For instance, a handle of a cup *affords* directly a reaching and grasping action. Recently, experimental studies have produced empirical evidence in support for this theory. Neuroimaging studies showed that objects activate the premotor cortex even when no action has to be performed with the object.[4,5] Behavioural studies indicated response interferences from affordances despite the fact that they were response-irrelevant.[6,7] For instance, a recent study in Ref. 8 demonstrated that pictures of hand postures (precision or power grip) can influence subsequent categorisation of objects. In this study, participants had to categorise objects into either artefact or natural object. Additionally, and unknown to the participants, the objects could be manipulated with either a precision or a power grasp. The study showed that categorisation was faster when the hand postures were congruent with the grasp compared to hand postures being incongruent with the grasp. Hence, the participants' behaviour was influenced by action-related properties of objects irrelevant to the experimental task. This experiment together with earlier, similar studies can be interpreted as evidence for an automatic detection of affordances.

Interestingly, recent experimental evidence suggests that not only actions are triggered by affordances, but also that selective attention is guided towards action-relevant locations. Using event-related potentials (ERP) Handy *et al.* showed that spatial attention is more often directed towards the location of tools than non-tools.[9] Pellegrino *et al.* present similar evidence from two patients with visual extinction.[10] In general visual extinction is considered to be an attentional deficit in which patients, when confronted with several objects, fail to report objects on the left side of their body space. In contrast, when faced with only one object, patients can respond to the object irrespective of its location. This study demonstrated that this attentional deficit can be alleviated when the handle of a cup points to the left. Pellegrino *et al.* interpreted their results as evidence for automatically encoded affordance (without the patients' awareness) drawing the patients' attention into their "bad" visual field.

This paper aims to lay the foundations for a computational model of such affordance-based guidance of attention. We designed a connectionist model which determines contact points for a stable grasp of an object (see Fig. 1(a) for an illustration). The model extracts these contact points directly from the input image. Hence, such a model could be construed as an implementation of an automatic detection of object affordances for grasping. To realise the attentional guidance through affordances, we integrated the selection mechanisms employed in the Selective Attention for Identification Model (SAIM).[3] Since this new model performs selection for action rather than identification, we termed the new model Selective Attention for Action Model (SAAM). There are only few computational models of affordance.[11,12] However, Fagg's *et al.* model does not process multiple-object scenes. On the other hand Cisek's model considers attentional processing with respect to pointing actions. However, in order to model crucial aspects of affordance-oriented processing, it is necessary to consider behaviours that require true physical interactions with objects, since this characteristic leads to an entirely different processing objective compared to classical perceptual processing, e.g. object recognition, where the physical environment is passively analysed. In this paper we will present first simulation results as well as an experimental verification of the model.

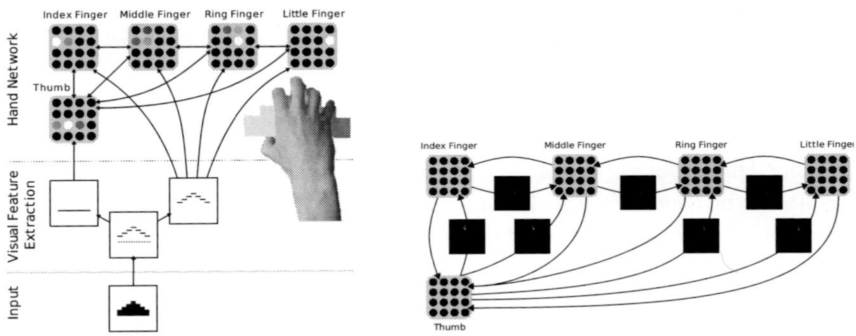

(a) Overall structure.

(b) Excitatory connections between fingers.

Fig. 1. The Selective Attention for Action Model.

2. The Selective Attention for Action Model (SAAM)

Figure 1(a) gives an overview of SAAM. The input consists of black&white images. The output of the model is generated in five "finger maps" of a "hand network". The finger maps encode the finger positions which are required for producing a stable grasp of the object in the input image. At the heart of SAAM's operation is the assumption that stable grasps are generated by taking into account two types of constraints, the geometrical constraints imposed from the object shape and the anatomical constraints given by the hand. In order to ensure that the hand network satisfies these constraints we followed an approach suggested in Ref. 13. In this soft-constraint satisfaction approach, constraints define activity patterns in the finger maps that are permissible and others that are not. Then we defined an energy function for which the minimal values are generated by just these permissible activity values. To find these minima, a gradient descent procedure is applied resulting in a differential equation system. The differential equation system defines the topology of a biologically plausible network. The mathematical details of this energy minimisation approach are given in the next section. Here, we focus on a qualitative description of the two types of constraints and their implementation.

The geometrical constraints are extracted from the shape of the object in the visual feature extraction stage. To begin with, obviously, only edges constitute suitable contact points for grasps. Furthermore, edges have to be perpendicular to the direction of the forces exerted by the fingers. Hence, only edges with a horizontal orientation make up good contact points, since we consider only a horizontal hand orientation in this first version of the model (see Fig. 1(a)). We implemented horizontal edge detectors using Sobel filters.[14] Finally, to exert a stable grasp, thumb and fingers need to be located at opposing sides of an object. This requirement was realized by separating the output of the Sobel filters according to the direction of the gradient change at the edge. In fact, the algebraic sign of the response differs at the bottom of a 2D-shape compared to the top of a 2D-shape. Now, if one assumes the background colour to be white and the object colour to be black, the signs of the Sobel-filter responses indicate appropriate locations for the fingers and the thumb (see Fig. 1(a) for an illustration). The results of the separation feed into the corresponding finger maps providing the hand network with the geometrical constraints. Note that, of course, the assumptions about the object- and background-colours represent a strong simplification. On the other hand, this mechanism can be interpreted as mimicking the result of stereo vision. In such a resulting "depth image" real edges suitable for thumb or fingers could be easily identified.

The anatomical constraints implemented in the hand network take into account that the human hand cannot form every arbitrary finger configuration to perform grasps. For instance, the maximum grasp width is limited by the size of the hand and the arrangement of the fingers on the hand makes it impossible to place the index, middle, ring, and little finger in another order than this one. After applying the energy minimisation approach, these anatomical constraints are implemented by excitatory connections between the finger layers in the hand network (see Fig. 1(a) and 1(b)). Figure 1(b) also illustrates the weight matrices of the connections. Each weight matrix defines how every single neuron of one finger map projects onto another finger map. The direction of the projection is given by the arrows between the finger maps. For instance, neurons in the thumb map feed their activation along a narrow stretch into the index finger map, in fact, encoding possible grip sizes. Each neuron in the target map sums up all activation fed through the weight matrices. Note that all connections between the maps are bi-directional whereby the feedback path uses the transposed weight matrices of the feedforward path. This is a direct result of the energy minimisation approach and ensures an overall consistency of the activity pattern in the hand network, since, for instance, the restriction in grip size between thumb and index finger applies in both directions. Finally, since a finger can be positioned at only one location, a winner-takes-all mechanism was implemented in all finger maps.

2.1. *Mathematical Details*

2.1.1. *Visual Feature Extraction*

The filter kernel K in the visual feature extraction process is a simple Sobel-filter.[14] In the response of the Sobel-filter the top edges of the object are marked with positive activation while the bottom edges are marked with negative activation. This characteristic of the filter is used to feed the correct input with the geometrical constraint applied into the finger maps and the thumb map. The finger maps receive the filter response with all negative activation set to zero. The thumb map, however, receives the negated filter response with all negative activation set to zero:

$$I_{ij}^{(\mathrm{f})} = \begin{cases} R_{ij} & \text{if } R_{ij} \geq 0, \\ 0 & \text{else.} \end{cases} \qquad I_{ij}^{(\mathrm{t})} = \begin{cases} -R_{ij} & \text{if } -R_{ij} \geq 0, \\ 0 & \text{else.} \end{cases}$$

with $R_{ij} = I_{ij} * K$ whereby I_{ij} is the input image.

2.1.2. *Hand Network*

We used an energy function approach to satisfy the anatomical and geometrical constraints of grasping. In Ref. 13 an approach is suggested where minima in the energy function are introduced as a network state in which the constraints are satisfied. In the following derivation of the energy function, parts of the whole function are introduced, and each part relates to a particular constraint. At the end, the sum of all parts leads to the complete energy function, satisfying all constraints.

The units $y_{ij}^{(f)}$ of the hand network make up five fields. Each of these fields encodes the position of a finger. $y_{ij}^{(1)}$ encodes the thumb, $y_{ij}^{(2)}$ encodes the index finger, and so on to $y_{ij}^{(5)}$ for the little finger. For the anatomical constraint of possible finger positions the energy function is based on the

Hopfield associative memory approach:[15]

$$E(y_i) = -\sum_{\substack{ij \\ i \neq j}} T_{ij} \cdot y_i \cdot y_j.$$

The minimum of the function is determined by the matrix T_{ij}. For T_{ij}s greater than zero, the corresponding y_is should either stay zero or become active in order to minimize the energy function. In the associative memory approach, T_{ij} is determined by a learning rule. Here, we chose the T_{ij} so that the hand network fulfils the anatomical constraints. These constraints are satisfied when units in the finger maps that encode finger positions of anatomically feasible postures are active at the same time. Hence, the T_{ij} for these units should be greater than zero, and for all other units, T_{ij} should be less than or equal to zero. This lead to the following equation:

$$E_{\mathrm{a}}(y_{ij}^{(g)}) = -\sum_{f=1}^{5} \sum_{\substack{g=1 \\ g \neq f}}^{5} \sum_{ij} \sum_{\substack{s=-L \\ s \neq 0}}^{L} \sum_{\substack{r=-L \\ r \neq 0}}^{L} T_{sr}^{(f \mapsto g)} \cdot y_{ij}^{(g)} \cdot y_{i+s,j+r}^{(f)}.$$

In this equation $T_{ij}^{(f \mapsto g)}$ denotes the weight matrix from finger f to finger g.

A further constraint is the fact that each finger map should encode only one position. The implementation of this constraint is based on the energy function proposed in Ref. 16:

$$E_{\mathrm{WTA}}(y_i) = a \cdot (\sum_i y_i - 1)^2 - \sum_i y_i \cdot I_i.$$

This energy function defines a winner-takes-all (WTA) behaviour, where I_i is the input and y_i is the output of each unit. This energy function is minimal when all y_i are zero except one, and when the corresponding input I_i has the maximal value of all inputs. Applied to the hand network where each finger map requires a WTA-behaviour, the first part of the equation turns into:

$$E_{\mathrm{WTA}}^{\mathrm{a}}(y_{ij}^{(f)}) = \sum_{f=1}^{5} (\sum_{ij} y_{ij}^{(f)} - 1)^2.$$

The input part of the original WTA-equation was modified to take the geometrical constraints into account:

$$E_{\mathrm{f}}(y_{ij}^{(f)}) = -\sum_{f=2}^{5} \sum_{ij} w_f \cdot y_{ij}^{(f)} \cdot I_{ij}^{(\mathrm{f})}, \qquad E_{\mathrm{t}}(y_{ij}^{(1)}) = -\sum_{ij} w_1 \cdot y_{ij}^{(1)} \cdot I_{ij}^{(\mathrm{t})}.$$

These terms drive the finger maps towards choosing positions at the input object which are maximally convenient for a stable grasp. The w_f factors were introduced to compensate the effects of the different number of excitatory connections in each layer.

The Complete Model To consider all constraints, all energy functions need to be added, leading to the following complete energy function:

$$E(y_{ij}^{(f)}) = a_1 \cdot E_{\mathrm{WTA}}^{\mathrm{a}}(y_{ij}^{(f)}) + a_2 \cdot E_{\mathrm{t/f}}(y_{ij}^{(f)}) + a_3 \cdot E_{\mathrm{a}}(y_{ij}^{(f)}).$$

The parameters a_i weight the different constraints against each other. These parameters need to be chosen in a way that SAAM successfully selects contact points at objects in both conditions, single-object images and multiple-object images. The second condition is particularly important to demonstrate that SAAM can mimic affordance-based guidance of attention. Moreover, and importantly, SAAM has to mimic human-style contact points. Hereby, not only the parameters a_i are relevant, but also the weight matrices of the anatomical constraints strongly influence SAAM's behaviour.

Gradient Descent The energy function defines minima at certain values of y_i. To find these values, a gradient descent procedure can be used:

$$\tau \dot{x}_i = -\frac{\partial E(y_i)}{\partial y_i}.$$

The factor τ is antiproportional to the speed of descent.

In the Hopfield approach, x_i and y_i are linked together by the sigmoid function:

$$y_i = \frac{1}{1 + e^{-m \cdot (x_i - s)}},$$

and the energy function includes a leaky integrator, so that the descent turns into

$$\tau \dot{x}_i = -x_i - \frac{\partial E(y_i)}{\partial y_i}.$$

Using these two assertions, the gradient descent is performed in a dynamic, neural-like network, where y_i can be related to the output activity of neurons, x_i the internal activity, and $\partial E(y_i)/\partial y_i$ gives the input to the neurons.

Applied to the energy function of SAAM, it leads to a dynamic unit (neuron) which forms the hand network:

$$\tau \dot{x}_{ij}^{(f)} = -x_{ij}^{(f)} - \frac{\partial E_{\text{total}}(y_{ij}^{(f)})}{\partial y_{ij}^{(f)}}.$$

To execute the gradient descent on a computer, a temporarily discrete version of the descent procedure was implemented.

3. Verification of the Model

This study tested whether SAAM can generate expedient grasps in general and whether these grasps mimic human grasps. To accomplish this, simulations with single objects in the visual field were conducted. The results of the simulations were compared with experimental data on grasping these objects. In the following two sections we will at first present the experiment and its results and then compare its outcomes with the results from our simulations with SAAM.

3.1. *Experiment*

We conducted an experiment in which humans grasped objects. Interestingly, there are only very few published studies on this question. Most notably D. P. Carey *et al.* examined grasps of a stroke patient.[17] However, no studies with healthy participants can be found in the literature.

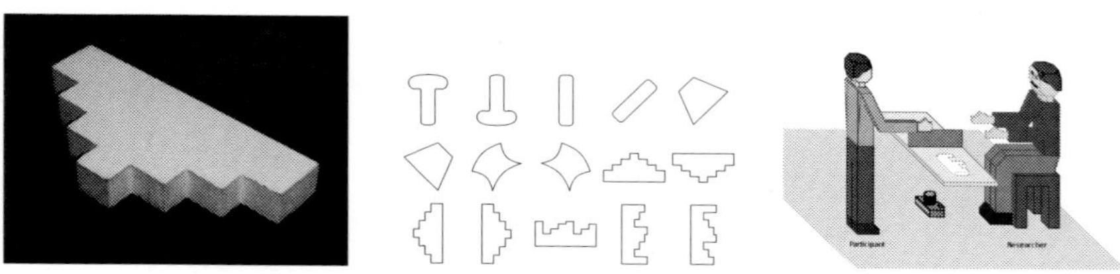

(a) Object used in the study. (b) Conditions of the experiment. (c) Placing of experimenter and participant.

Fig. 2. Material and procedure of the grasping experiment.

Participants We tested 18 school students visiting the psychology department on an open day. The mean age was 17.8 years. All participants but two were right-handed. The left-handed participants were excluded from further analysis because the objects had not always been mirrored correctly during the experiment.

Material For the experiment we designed six two-dimensional object shapes. The objects were made of 2.2 cm thick wood and were painted white. Their size was between 11.5×4 and 17.5×10 centimetres (see Fig. 2(a) for an example). By presenting the objects in different orientations we created fifteen conditions (see Fig. 2(b)). Note that the shapes are highly unfamiliar, non-usable. Hence, the influence of high-level object knowledge is limited in the experiment. We chose this set-up in order to be compatible with the simulations in which SAAM possesses no high-level knowledge either.

Procedure Figure 2(c) illustrates the experimental set-up. During the experiment participants and experimenter were situated on opposite sides of a glass table facing each other. The glass table was divided in two halves by a 15 cm high barrier. Participants were asked to position themselves so that their right hand was directly in front of the right half of the glass table. In each trial the experimenter placed one of the objects with both hands in the right half of the glass table. The participants were then asked to grasp the object, lift it and place it into the left half without releasing the grip. The experimenter took a picture with a camera from below the glass table (see Figure 3(a) for an example). After taking the photo, the participants were asked to return the object to the experimenter. The last step was introduced to ensure that the participants would not release their grasp before the photo was taken. As soon as the object was handed back to the experimenter, a new trial started by placing the next object in the right half of the glass table. Each participant took part in two blocks with fifteen trails each. The order of the trials was randomised.

Results To analyse the pictures taken in the experiment, we developed a software for marking the positions of the fingers in relation to the objects. In Figure 3(b) the resulting finger positions are shown for the first condition. Even though the grasps show some variability, in general, participants grasped the object in two ways: they either placed their thumb at the left side of the object and the fingers on the right side or they placed the thumb at the bottom of the object and the fingers on the top edges. These two sets of different grasping positions are indicated with two markers in Figure 3(b) (circle and square). Such sets different of grasping positions were observed in all conditions.

To determine a "typical" grip from the experimental data, averaging across these very different set of grasping positions would not make sense. Therefore, we calculated the mean finger positions for each set of grasping positions separately. The resulting mean positions for the first condition are shown in Figure 3(c). Sets of grasping positions containing only one or two samples were discarded as outliers. For the comparison with the simulation results we only considered the set of grasping positions for each object chosen in the majority of trials.

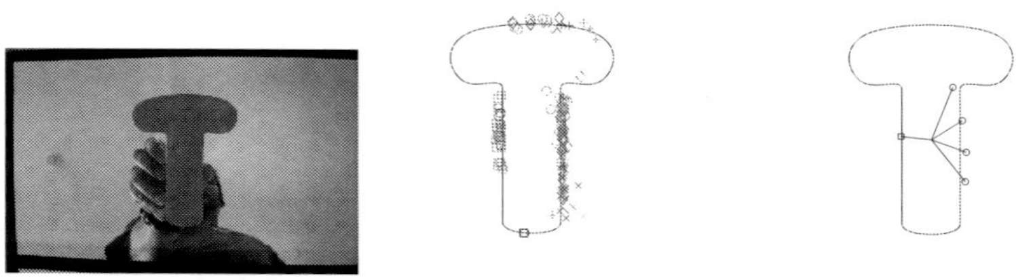

(a) Photo taken during the experiment. (b) Extracted finger positions. (c) Mean finger positions.

Fig. 3. Mean finger positions: Finger positions (b) are extracted from photos (a). For each finger its mean position is calculated (c). The thumb position is highlighted by a square box.

3.2. *Simulations*

We conducted simulations with SAAM using the same objects as in the experiment. Figure 4 shows two examples of the simulation results. These illustrations also include the mean finger positions from the experimental results for a comparison with the simulation data. The ellipses around the mean finger positions illustrate the variations in the data. The comparison shows that most finger positions lie within the ellipses. Hence the theoretical assumptions behind SAAM that geometrical and anatomical constraints are sufficient to mimic human behaviour have been confirmed. Note that not all experimental conditions could be simulated with SAAM, since the model is currently only able to create horizontal grasps.

We also tested simulations with two objects in the visual field to test SAAM's ability to simulate attentional processes. The simulations were successful in the sense that contact points for only one object were selected and the second object was ignored (see Conclusion for further discussions).

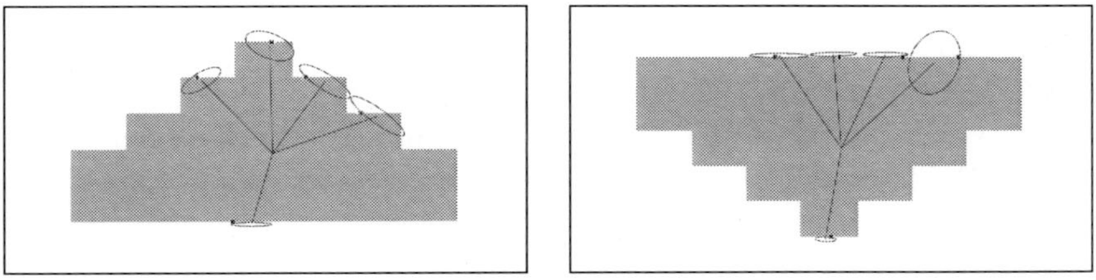

(a) Simulation 1 (b) Simulation 2

Fig. 4. Comparison of experimental results and simulated grasps. The ellipses indicate the variation in the experimental data. The black dots mark the finger positions as generated by the simulations.

4. Conclusion and Outlook

Recent experimental evidence indicates that visual attention is not only guided by visual properties of visual stimuli but also by affordances of visual objects. This paper sets out to develop a model of such affordance-based guidance of selective attention. As a case in point we chose to model grasping of objects and termed the model the Selective Attention for Action Model (SAAM). To detect the parts of an object which afford a stable grasp, SAAM performs a soft-constraint satisfaction approach by means of a Hopfield-style energy minimisation. The constraints were derived from the geometrical properties of the input object and the anatomical properties of the human hand. In a comparison between simulation results and experimental data from human participants we could show that these constraints are sufficient to simulate human grasps. We also tested whether SAAM cannot only extract object affordances but also implements the guidance of attention through affordances by using two-object images. Indeed, SAAM was able to select one of two objects based on their affordance. The interesting aspect here is that SAAM's performance is an emergent property from the interplay between the anatomical constraints. Especially, the competitive mechanism implemented in the finger maps is crucial for SAAM's attentional behaviour. This mechanism already proved important in SAIM[3] for simulating attentional effects of human object recognition. However, it should be noted that SAAM does not select whole objects as SAIM does. But, since SAAM and SAIM use similar mechanisms, it is conceivable that they can be combined to form one model. In such a model SAIM's selection mechanism of whole objects can be guided by the SAAM's selection of contact points. Hence, this new model could integrate both mechanisms, selection by visual-properties and by action-related properties, forming a more complete model of selective attention.

Despite the successes reported here, this work is still in its early stages. First, we will need to verify the priorities of object selection predicted by SAAM. We also plan to include grasps with a rotated hand to simulate a broader range of experimental data. Finally, there is a large amount of experimental data on the interaction between action knowledge and attention (see Ref. 18 for a summary). Therefore, we aim to integrate action knowledge into SAAM, e.g. grasping a knife for cutting or stabbing. With these extensions SAAM will sufficiently contribute to the understanding of how humans determine object affordances and how these lead to a guidance of attention.

References

1. J. J. Gibson, *The senses considered as perceptual systems* (Houghton-Mifflin, Boston, 1966).
2. J. J. Gibson, *The ecological approach to visual perception* (Houghton-Mifflin, Boston, 1979).
3. D. Heinke and G. W. Humphreys, *Psychological Review* **110**, 29 (2003).
4. S. T. Grafton, L. Fadiga, M. A. Arbib and G. Rizzolatti, *NeuroImage* **6**, 231 (1997).
5. J. Grèzes and J. Decety, *Neuropsychologia* **40**, 212 (2002).
6. M. Tucker and R. Ellis, *Journal of Experimental Psychology* **24**, 830 (1998).
7. J. C. Phillips and R. Ward, *Visual Cognition* **9**, 540 (2002).
8. A. M. Borghi, C. Bonfiglioli, L. Lugli, P. Ricciardelli, S. Rubichi and R. Nicoletti, *Neuroscience Letters* **411**, 17 (2007).
9. T. C. Handy, S. T. Grafton, N. M. Shroff, S. Ketay and M. S. Gazzaniga, *Nature Neuroscience* **6**, 421 (2003).
10. G. di Pellegrino, R. Rafal and S. P. Tipper, *Current Biology* **15**, 1469 (2005).
11. A. H. Fagg and M. A. Arbib, *Neural Networks* **11**, 1277 (1998).
12. P. Cisek, *Philosophical Transactions of the Royal Society* **362**, 1585 (2007).
13. J. J. Hopfield and D. W. Tank, *Biological Cybernetics* **52**, 141 (1985).
14. R. C. Gonzalez and R. E. Woods, *Digital Image Processing* (Addison-Wesley, 1993).
15. J. J. Hopfield, Neural networks and physical systems with emergent collective computational abilities, in *Proc. of the Nat. Academy of Sciences*, (8)1982.
16. E. Mjolsness and C. Garrett, *Neural Networks* **3**, 651 (1990).
17. D. P. Carey, M. Harvey and A. D. Milner, *Neuropsychologia* **34**, 329 (1996).
18. G. W. Humphreys and M. J. Riddoch, *Psychology of learning and motivation* **42**, 225 (2003).

Memory

STDP AND AUTO-ASSOCIATIVE NETWORK FUNCTION

DANIEL BUSH, ANDREW PHILIPPIDES, MICHAEL O'SHEA and PHIL HUSBANDS

Centre for Computational Neuroscience and Robotics, University of Sussex, UK

Auto-associative networks have proven extremely useful when modelling the hypothesised function of the hippocampus in both episodic and spatial memory. To date, the majority of these models have made use of rate coded neural implementations and Hebbian plasticity rules mediated by correlations between these firing rates. However, recent neurobiological evidence suggests that synaptic plasticity in the hippocampus, and many other cortical regions, depends explicitly on the temporal relationship between afferent action potentials and efferent spiking – a formulation known as spike-timing dependent plasticity (STDP). Few attempts have been made to reconcile the STDP rule with previous models of rate coded plasticity or auto-associative network function. Further complications arise from the fact that there are many computational interpretations of the empirical data regarding STDP which can each precipitate distinct network dynamics. This paper examines an STDP implementation that has been identified by previous research as able to replicate rate coded Hebbian plasticity within a spiking, recurrent neural network. We consequently demonstrate that the STDP rule and spiking neural dynamics can be reconciled with auto-associative network function, allowing the successes of previous hippocampal models to be replicated while providing them with a firmer basis in modern neurobiology.

1. Introduction

The idea that activity-dependent changes in the strength of connections between neurons might underlie the phenomena of learning, memory and the development of neural circuits dates back to the late nineteenth century. This theory was more precisely delineated by Donald Hebb, who hypothesised that "...when an axon of cell A is near enough to excite cell B and repeatedly or persistently takes part in firing it, some growth process or metabolic change takes place in one or both cells such that A's efficiency, as one of the cells firing B, is increased" [1]. Hebbian learning rules, which have come to include any formulation that is driven by positive correlations between pre- and post-synaptic activity, have been at the centre of computational models of synaptic plasticity ever since.

Hebb's postulate has received subsequent support from a wealth of neurobiological investigation in which tetanic stimulation protocols have been used to induce the long-term potentiation or depression of synapses [2, 3].

Elsewhere, computational studies have successfully applied Hebbian learning rules to a wide variety of learning and memory models [6]. Issues of positive feedback are often encountered, however, as the potentiation of a synapse increases the correlation between pre- and post- synaptic firing rates. This inherent instability reduces the functional performance of the learning rule and drives synaptic weights and neural firing rates to saturation. Fortunately, these problems can be avoided by introducing some form of competition into the Hebbian framework, and several methods (each with a distinct influence on emergent dynamics) have been commonly implemented [5].

Three general mechanisms for generating competition in Hebbian learning rules exist – those that adjust the propensity for further synaptic plasticity (i.e. metaplasticity); those that limit the resources available to synaptic inputs; and those that adjust the intrinsic excitability of neurons. The best known example of metaplasticity is the BCM rule, which was inspired by studies of synaptic plasticity in the visual cortex [4]. The BCM rule posits that there is some post-synaptic firing rate threshold above which potentiation is induced and below which depression is induced. The position of this threshold is determined by the history of activity at a synapse, so that potentiation becomes more difficult after prolonged periods of high neural activity, and vice versa. This formulation has been very successful in replicating known features of the visual cortex such as ocular dominance and orientation selectivity, and characterises many of the properties of rate coded plasticity observed in vivo.

More recently, neurobiological investigation has established that not only the rate but also the precise temporal order of pre- and post- synaptic firing plays a critical role in directing changes in synaptic strength [7]. In its most common form, the observed spike-timing dependent plasticity (STDP) rule dictates that synapses at which afferent action potentials shortly precede post-synaptic spike generation are potentiated and vice versa. This formulation, like Hebb's original postulate, places an emphasis on causal activity relationships, and the temporal coding which it allows can vastly increase the computational power of neural networks. It also implicitly generates competition between synaptic inputs for the control of post-synaptic spike timing, thus allowing the homeostatic control of neural activity [8]. However, it is not yet clear how the STDP rule might be reconciled with previous rate coded observations of synaptic plasticity and models of Hebbian learning. It seems certain that these two induction protocols activate the same molecular mechanisms, and a phenomenological plasticity model which can replicate both sets of data should allow rate and temporally coded data to be processed by a single learning rule.

Although STDP and BCM-type synaptic plasticity have been observed in the visual cortex, the vast majority of empirical studies have focussed on a different brain region – the hippocampus. Along with surrounding parts of the medial temporal lobe, the hippocampus is strongly implicated in declarative memory function, although some debate exists as to whether it primarily mediate episodic or spatial learning [14, 15]. Observations of neural structure and activity patterns, as well as the ease with which synaptic plasticity can be induced, have led many researchers to postulate that the function of the hippocampus is mediated, at least in part, by auto-associative dynamics [6]. Auto-associative networks comprise of a recurrent neural architecture which implements some form of Hebbian learning rule. These models have had great success in replicating many of the functions ascribed to the hippocampus, both by those who propose that it primarily processes episodic memory, and those who suggest that its main function is to mediate spatial learning.

Auto-associative networks are attractive because they represent a unified description of encoding, storage and recall processes. However, these models can easily be criticised on the grounds of biological realism [16]. Rate-coded plasticity formulations have been almost exclusively employed, or weight matrices pre-wired, and methods used to introduce competition between synapses are often unrealistic of the hippocampus. Neural activity in typical auto-associative network models also bears little resemblance to that observed in vivo, with neurons either silent or firing close to saturation and in a very regular manner. Furthermore, learning and recall processes are often separated arbitrarily in order to avoid issues of interference [18].

The aim of this research is to establish whether the STDP rule can be reconciled with previous rate-coded plasticity formulations in a recurrent neural network and therefore demonstrate some of the properties that are critical for auto-associative network function. Several previous studies have indicated that STDP can produce the selective potentiation of higher rate neurons and be reconciled with the BCM model under certain conditions, but the majority of these results apply to feed-forward architectures, or are purely analytical and rely on a number of biologically unrealistic assumptions [9, 10, 12, 17, 18]. In this paper, this form of the STDP model is assessed for the ability to stably store and recall discrete, rate coded patterns of afferent activity using auto-associative dynamics in a spiking neural network. It is demonstrated that synaptic weights are rapidly re-arranged to reflect activity correlations, and pattern completion can be achieved by selectively and significantly elevating the mean firing rate in neurons which form part of a previously learned pattern during recall.

These findings provide support for the analytical reconciliation of STDP and BCM rules proposed previously [9] and, to the best of our knowledge, represents the first demonstration of a temporally asymmetric STDP rule successfully replicating rate-coded auto-associative network function [13]. However, the model faces one significant functional issue, as the level of recurrent excitation generated by synapses during recall is insufficient to precipitate firing rates which approach those in externally stimulated neurons. This dichotomy is at odds with observations of neural activity in the hippocampus and previous auto-associative modeling studies, and induces the depression of synapses during the recall process. The next stage in this research is to identify a biologically plausible method of addressing this issue, and several possible approaches are discussed.

2. Methods

The artificial neural network (ANN) consists of 125 neurons, of which 80% are excitatory and 20% are inhibitory. The network is fully recurrently connected except for self-connections. Each simulated neuron has a randomly chosen axonal delay in the range [1ms : 20ms]. The neurons operate according to the Izhikevich (2004) spiking model, which dynamically calculates the membrane potential (v) and a membrane recovery variable (u) based on the values of four dimensionless constants (a, b, c and d) and a dimensionless current input (I) according to Eq. 1. This model can exhibit firing patterns of all known types of cortical neurons by variation of the magnitude of applied current and the parameters a – d [11]. The values used for regular spiking in a standard excitatory neuron are [a=0.02, b=0.2, c=-65, d=6]. Inhibitory neurons are assigned values of [a=0.1, b=0.2, c=-65, d=2], which generate a fast spiking (FS) mode that is believed to be more realistic of their neural dynamics [11].

$$v' = 0.04v^2 + 5v + 140 - u + I$$
$$u' = a(bv - u) \tag{1}$$
$$\text{if } v \geq +30\text{mV then } \begin{cases} v \leftarrow c \\ u \leftarrow u + d \end{cases}$$

Mathematically, with s = t_{post} - t_{pre} being the time difference between pre- and post- synaptic spiking, the change in the weight of a synapse (Δw) generated by STDP can be calculated using Eq. 2. The parameters A_+ and A_- effectively correspond to the maximum possible change in the weight of a synapse per spike pair, while τ_+ and τ_- denote the time constants of decay of these potentiation and depression increments respectively [see 18 for a detailed review]. During simulations, only excitatory-excitatory synapses are plastic, while inhibitory synapses are assigned a constant negative value of w_{inh}=-5. Synaptic weights between excitatory and inhibitory neurons are also assigned a value of zero, so that the inhibitory firing rate is constant and driven by external input only. Throughout these simulations, a hard limit of w_{max} is placed on the achievable strength of synapses. The value of w_{max} is varied in these simulations, but consistently kept below the single level of current required to generate a post-synaptic action potential (I=16.5 for RS neurons).

(2) $$\Delta w = F(s) = \begin{cases} P_+ = A_+ \exp(-s/\tau_+) & \text{for s} > 0 \\ P_- = A_- \exp(-s/\tau_-) & \text{for s} < 0 \end{cases}$$

The STDP model examined in this research, which is inspired by the results of previous modeling studies, has parameter values of [A_+=0.24, A_-=-0.12, τ_+=20ms, τ_-=50ms]. This STDP parameter set has been identified as able to produce the most important feature of rate-coded Hebbian learning for auto-associative network operation – the selective potentiation of synapses adjoining neurons which are firing at a higher than background rate [18]. The evolution of synaptic weights under the STDP rule is also affected by the choice of which pre- and post- synaptic spike pairs are allowed to influence plasticity processes. Several common implementations will be tested here, each of which is also described in detail in previous research [10, 18]. Each of these places some temporal restriction on spike pairings, such that consequent neural activity will affect the relative magnitude of potentiation and depression processes.

The nature of external input to the network during tests of auto-associative function is inspired by previous models of the hippocampus and biological data from this brain region [6]. Five binary and orthogonal input patterns of density σ=0.1 are selected at random and applied to the network in a random order for a period of five seconds each (i.e. 10 'foreground' neurons from the total of 100 excitatory neurons fire at an equal elevated rate while the remaining neurons fire at a background rate), interspersed with a two seconds period of background activity only. This process is repeated twenty times to constitute the learning period of a single trial. Foreground neurons are externally stimulated to have a mean firing rate of ~20Hz, while background neurons are externally stimulated to have a mean firing rate of ~0.5Hz - these values being realistic of the hippocampus [6, 18].

During recall, a single partial cue is created for each of the original input patterns by randomly selecting 50% of the foreground neurons in that pattern. These partial cues are presented to the network in a random order for five seconds each, interspersed with two seconds of background activity only, this process being repeated five times to constitute the recall period of a single trial. The performance of each incarnation of the STDP rule can therefore be assessed on the basis of how it re-arranges the synaptic weight matrix to reflect externally applied rate correlations during the learning period, and on its ability to perform pattern completion during the recall period. For this latter criteria to be successfully achieved, the mean firing rate in neurons which form part of a learned pattern but are not being externally stimulated (while other neurons which form part of that pattern are) should be significantly higher than that in the background neurons.

3. Results

Previous research has indicated that setting STDP parameters such that depression dominates overall but potentiation dominates at shorter ISIs allows the learning rule to be reconciled with the BCM model, provided that some temporal restrictions are placed on spike pair interactions. Typical emergent synaptic dynamics in a recurrent network are illustrated in Figure 1 [see 18 or further discussion]. This form of the STDP rule therefore provides two of the primary features that are required for efficient auto-associative network function – the selective potentiation of synapses that connect neurons firing at an elevated rate, and the hetero-synaptic depression of those which connect neurons firing at a background rate.

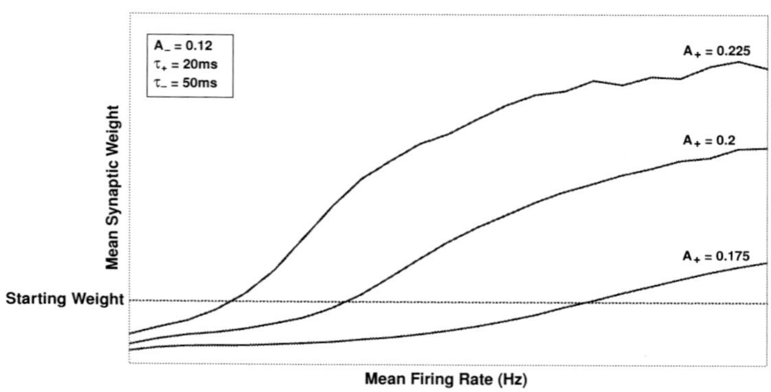

Figure 1. Sample 'BCM' curves generated by the STDP rule in simulations with the lax nearest neighbour spike pairing scheme and w_{max}=5. Mean synaptic weights were sampled from random network incarnations after 200s of simulated time over a range of equal pre- and post- synaptic firing rates [see 18 for further discussion of these results].

This process of selective potentiation is also illustrated by the relative mean synaptic weight values obtained at the end of the learning period in auto-associative network tests (see Figure 2). The mean weight of connections between foreground neurons is significantly higher than that of all other synapses in the network in each of these simulations. It is interesting to note that the mean weight of 'redundant' synapses (those that connect neurons which are active in different patterns) is consistently higher than that of the 'background' synapses (those that connect neurons which are not active in any pattern). Because the synaptic inputs to these redundant neurons (which form part of a learned pattern that is not currently being stimulated) become higher than those to the background neurons (which do not form part of any learned pattern), mean firing rates are also generally higher in these neurons. This consequently manifests a slight increase in the mean synaptic weight of redundant synapses, as compared to background synapses. Figure 2 also illustrates how inhibitory input enhances the selective potentiation process by both increasing the relative mean weight of foreground synapses and significantly reducing the mean weight of redundant synapses, in accordance with previous research [18].

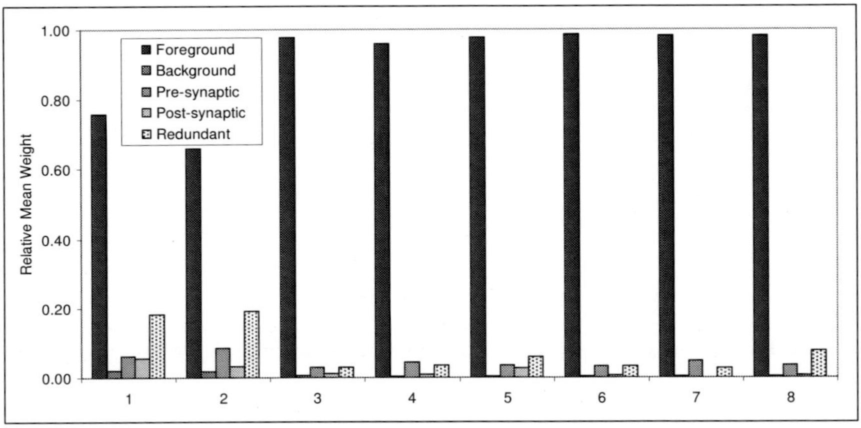

Figure 2. Relative mean weight (i.e. w/w_{max}) of foreground, background, pre-synaptic, post-synaptic and redundant connections at the end of the learning period in auto-associative simulations with (1) Output-restricted (OR) spike pairing, no inhibitory input and $w_{max}=5$; (2) Lax nearest neighbour (LNN) spike pairing, no inhibitory input and $w_{max}=5$; (3) OR spike pairing, 40Hz inhibitory input and $w_{max}=5$; (4) LNN spike pairing, 40Hz inhibitory input and $w_{max}=5$; (5) Strict nearest neighbour (SNN) spike pairing, 40Hz inhibitory input and $w_{max}=5$; (6) OR spike pairing, 40Hz inhibitory input and $w_{max}=10$; (7) LNN spike pairing, 40Hz inhibitory input and $w_{max}=10$; and (8) SNN spike pairing, 40Hz inhibitory input and $w_{max}=10$.

It is interesting to note that the mean weight of pre-synaptic connections to the foreground neurons can, in some cases, approach or exceed the mean weight of redundant synapses. This result suggests that high post- (as oppose to pre-) synaptic firing rates tend to induce potentiation, in accordance with the BCM rule and typical rate-coded Hebbian learning models. Similarly, biological data indicates that synapses with high pre- and low post- synaptic firing rates are generally depressed, and this result is also replicated in these simulations (as illustrated by Figure 2). Furthermore, the mean weight of foreground synapses exceeds a value of $w_{max}/2$ (and often approaches the value of w_{max}), which indicates that strong bi-directional connections are developing between foreground neurons. The development of strong bi-directional connections is essential for efficient recall from any partial cue in auto-associative networks, and previous research into the STDP rule has suggested that this feature might not be generated by an asymmetric learning rule [8].

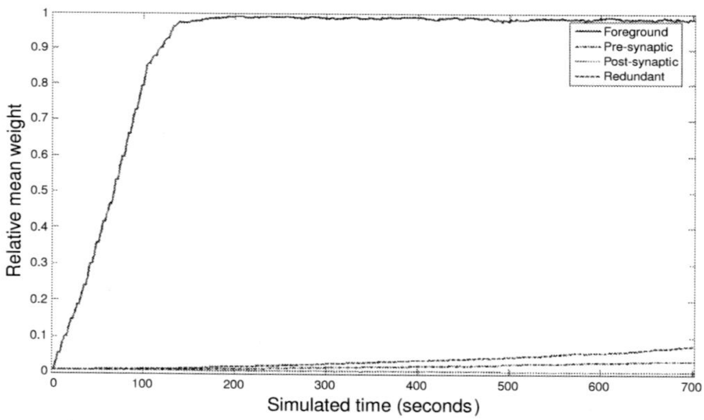

Figure 3. Dynamic changes in the mean weight of foreground, pre-synaptic, post-synaptic and redundant connections in a typical auto-associative simulation. The data illustrated here is obtained from simulation (8) in figure 1 – i.e. SNN spike pairing with 40Hz inhibitory input and w_{max}=10.

An inspection of synaptic weight dynamics during the learning period of a typical simulation (illustrated in Figure 3) demonstrates that the potentiation of foreground synapses is also a much more rapid process than changes in the strength of other connections in the network. This result can be accounted for by the greater frequency of more proximate spike pairings that are generated by high pre- and post- synaptic firing rates. It is interesting to note that, while the mean weight of foreground synapses reaches an equilibrium (imposed by the maximum weight limit) after only a few exposures of each pattern, the strength of pre-synaptic and redundant connections (which are significantly lower) increase throughout the learning period. Over a more protracted period of operation, these weights may approach the strength of foreground synapses and thus interfere with the long-term efficiency of auto-associative network function. This issue might be addressed by the inclusion of some slower mechanism for stabilising weight distributions, such as synaptic scaling, or by direct modulation of the BCM threshold itself. Further testing is required to fully elucidate this issue.

Because the process of selective potentiation generates foreground synapses that have a significantly higher mean weight than other connections in the network, the mean firing rate in 'recall' neurons (those that are not being externally stimulated, while other neurons that form part of the same learned pattern are) is significantly higher than that in background and redundant neurons in each of these simulations. As illustrated by Figure 4, however, typical recall firing rates are also significantly lower than those in externally cued neurons, which is at odds with both biological observations of hippocampal activity and previous computational modelling.

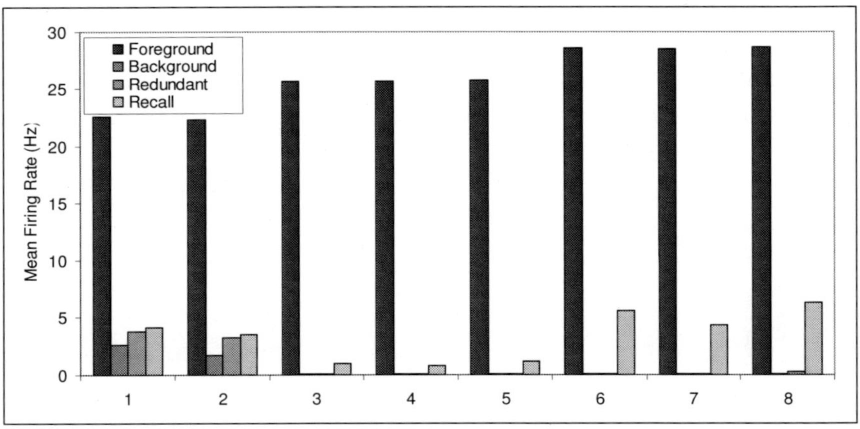

Figure 4. The mean firing rate in foreground (i.e. those that are externally stimulated), background (those that do not form part of any learned pattern), redundant (those that form part of a learned pattern which is not being stimulated) and recall (those that form part of a learned pattern which is being stimulated) neurons during the recall period of auto-associative tests. Results are illustrated for the same simulations as in Figure 2.

In this network, the recall firing rate is solely precipitated by recurrent synaptic currents, which are in turn determined by several parameters: the rate and strength of inhibitory input, the mean weight of foreground synapses, the firing rate in cued foreground neurons and the number of neurons which are being cued. Increasing the value of w_{max} indirectly increases the absolute mean weight of foreground synapses, and therefore the recall firing rate that is incurred, but, in the spirit of biological realism, synapses must not be allowed to approach a strength whereby they can solely provoke post-synaptic firing. It is also important to note that, due to the dominance of potentiation at low ISIs which is dictated by this form of the STDP rule, runaway saturation of neural firing rates and synaptic weights is possible, and the value of w_{max} must therefore be limited to avoid excessive recurrent excitation destabilising network operation. Similarly, an absence of inhibitory input might allow an increase in excitatory firing rates, but will also have an impact on synaptic dynamics (as illustrated by Figure 2), and inhibitory input is a prominent (and functionally important) feature of the hippocampus.

Conversely, the number of neurons in the network, and the number being cued during recall (which is proportional to the size, in number of neurons, of the discrete activity patterns being stored) deviates significantly from that which is theorised to exist in vivo. Increasing the value of σ (and, therefore, the number of neurons being cued during recall) has little effect on synaptic dynamics, but does significantly increase both recall and redundant firing rates. Consequently, because the mean weight of foreground synapses is much greater than that of redundant synapses in these simulations, the functional performance of the model (as assessed by the ratio of recall to redundant firing rates) is also improved, as illustrated by Figure 5.

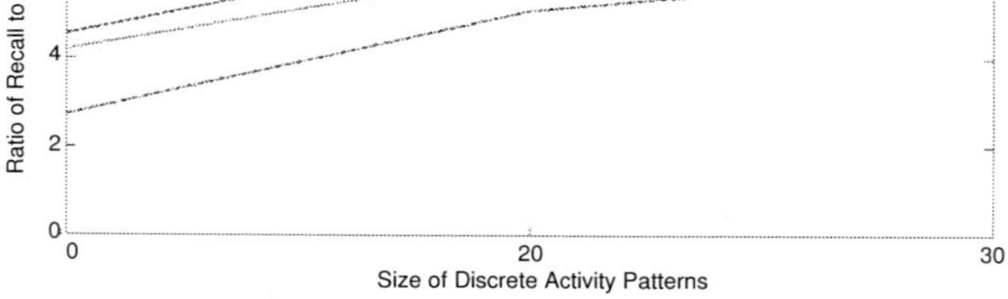

Figure 5. The change in the ratio of mean firing rates in recall and redundant neurons during the recall period as the value of σ is increased, which corresponds to an increase in the size of activity patterns and the number of cued neurons during recall. Results are illustrated for three different spike pairing schemes with 25Hz inhibitory input and w_{max}=5.

One critical difference between the auto-associative network model presented here and the majority of those examined previously is that synaptic plasticity continues during recall in these simulations. Consequently, the dichotomy between firing rates in externally 'cued' and recurrently 'recalled' neurons incurs significant weight change during this period. As Figure 6 illustrates, the strength of synapses which connect cued neurons change very little, while the strength of synapses connecting cued and recall or recall and recall neurons decrease significantly. It is also important to note that the dynamic decrease in the strength of connections between externally and recurrently stimulated neurons during the recall period provokes a concurrent dynamic decrease in the magnitude of recall firing rates. Interestingly, although recall firing rates are higher in simulations with higher maximum weight limits, the increased frequency of spike pairings precipitates a greater degree of relative depression during the limited time period examined here. Whatever the functional implications of this decrease in synaptic weights, it seems likely that the discrepancy between foreground and recall firing rates must be eliminated to prevent some degree of relative depression during recall.

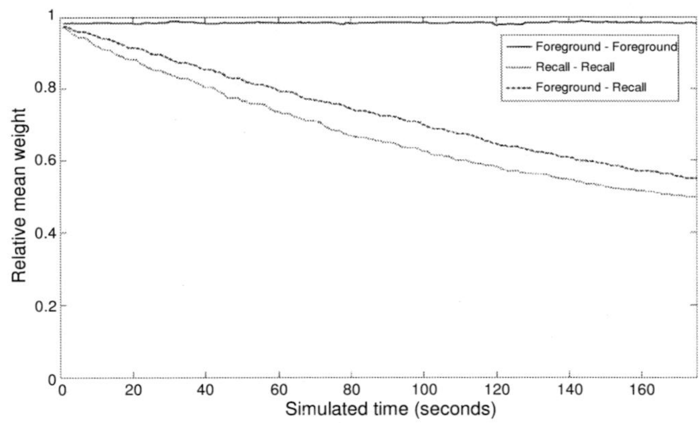

Figure 6. Dynamic changes in the mean weight of foreground synapses during recall for a typical simulation. The data presented here was generated with LNN spike pairing, 40Hz inhibitory input and w_{max}=10.

4. Conclusions

To our knowledge, this research provides the first computational modelling evidence that temporally asymmetric STDP can replicate many of the properties observed in biological studies of rate-coded synaptic plasticity and generated by traditional Hebbian learning rules, and can thus be integrated with basic auto-associative network function. As the STDP rule presented here is also ideally suited to processing temporally coded data, these results raise the possibility that both spike-timing and rate coded data might be encoded, stored and recalled within a single auto-associative network framework. Developing such a model is the next step in this research.

In order to achieve this aim, one significant issue regarding the operation of this model must be addressed, but fortunately, this seems to relate to the structure and dynamics of the network itself, rather than the synaptic plasticity formulation employed therein. Recall firing rates generated by recurrent excitation in these simulations are significantly lower than those in cued neurons generated by external stimulation, and this precipitates a further decrease in foreground synaptic weights and firing rates during recall. This result is at odds with both neurobiological data and previous modelling studies, although it may have some useful functional implications for associative network function (i.e. gradually 'forgetting' the variant sections of repeatedly encountered activity patterns). It also seems likely that this problem may be addressed by simply increasing the size of the network and patterns stored within it.

Elsewhere, it is possible that the dynamic modulation of synaptic strengths and synaptic plasticity, in line with models of Acetylcholine modulation and theta phase coding, may also allow recall to proceed more efficiently [19, 20]. Boosting recurrent excitation during recall will provide higher firing rates, while suppressed plasticity during this period avoids the dynamic depression of foreground synapses and the possibility of positive feedback processes arising. This approach might also address the gradual increase of pre-synaptic weights during the learning period – a feature which could represent a significant issue for the long-term efficiency of this auto-associative network model. However, it seems likely that more straightforward methods of synaptic scaling or BCM modulation will also be capable of eliminating this issue.

References

1. D. O. Hebb, Wiley, New York (1949)
2. T. V. Bliss and T. Lomo, Journal of Physiology 232, 331 (1973)
3. G. S. Lynch, T. Dunwiddie, V. Gribkoff, Nature, 266, 737 (1977)
4. E. L. Bienenstock, L. N. Cooper, P. W. Munro, J. Neurosci., 2, 32 (1982)
5. K. D. Miller and D. J. C. Mackay, Neural Computation, 6, 100 (1994)
6. E. T. Rolls, Hippocampus, 6, 601 (1996)
7. G. Q. Bi, M. M. Poo, J. Neurosci., 18, 10464 (1998)
8. S. Song, K. D. Miller, L. F. Abbott, Nat. Neurosci., 3, 919 (2000)

9. E. M. Izhikevich, N. S. Desai, Neural Computation, 15, 1511 (2003)
10. A. N. Burkitt, H. Meffin and D. B. Grayden. Neural Computation, 16, 885 (2004)
11. E. M. Izhikevich, IEEE Trans. Neural Networks, 15, 1063 (2004)
12. G. Mongillo, E. Curti, S. Romani, D. J. Amit. European J. Neurosci., 21, 3143 (2005)
13. T. Samura, M. Hattori, Int. J. Neural Systems, 15, 13 (2005)
14. P. Andersen, R. Morris, D. Amaral, T. Bliss, J. O'Keefe, OUP, Oxford (2007)
15. R. Morris, OUP, Oxford (2007)
16. Y. Roudi, P. E. Latham PLoS Comput Biol, 3, 1679 (2007)
17. D. I. Standage, S. Jalil, T. P. Trappenberg, Biol. Cybernetics, 96, 615 (2007)
18. D. R. Bush, DPhil Thesis, University of Sussex (2008)
19. D. Bush, A. Philippides, P. Husbands and M. O'Shea, Proceedings of the 10th International Conference on Simulation of Adaptive Behaviour, Springer-Verlag (2008)
20. M. E. Hasselmo, Current Opinion in Neurobiology, 16, 710-715 (2006)

THE HIPPOCAMPAL SYSTEM AS THE MANAGER OF NEOCORTICAL DECLARATIVE MEMORY RESOURCES

L. ANDREW COWARD

Department of Computer Science, Australian National University, ACT 0200, Australia

A model is described in which the hippocampal system receives inputs from cortical columns throughout the neocortex, uses these inputs to determine the most appropriate columns for declarative information recording in response to the current sensory experience, and generates outputs that drive that recording in the selected columns. Evidence in support of the model is described, including physiological connectivity, neuron structures and algorithms, and psychological deficits resulting from damage. Preliminary results from an electronic implementation of the model using leaky integrator neuron models learning via the LTP mechanism are described.

1. Introduction

Physical damage to the hippocampal system results in a striking combination of memory deficits [1], including loss of ability to acquire any new declarative memories (anterograde amnesia), loss of episodic memories for a period of years prior to damage (retrograde amnesia) [2], but preservation of semantic memories including those acquired during the period with lost episodic memories [3]. General intelligence, speech capabilities and skills are retained. New simple skills can be learned, but not skills requiring new declarative memory.

The recommendation architecture model for the mammal brain has been proposed [4] on the basis of theoretical constraints on the architecture of any system which learns to perform a complex combination of behaviours with limited resources. This model has several major subsystems. One subsystem (*clustering*) is made up of modules that define and detect different groups of similar circumstances within sensory experience. Another subsystem (*competition*) interprets the detection of any one group of circumstances (indicated by an output from the corresponding module) as a recommendation in favour of a range of different behaviours, each with a specific weight. The competition subsystem determines and implements the behaviour most strongly recommended across all currently detected similarity circumstances. Modules learn their groups in the course of sensory experience, in such a way that the overlap between the similarity circumstances of different modules is minimized.

Module outputs can recommend many different behaviours, hence any changes to a group in the learning process must minimize undesirable side effects on behaviours already dependent on that group. Such minimization of side effects means that a group can expand by addition of circumstances similar to those already detected by the group, but with some limited exceptions existing circumstances cannot be changed [4]. Groups of similarity circumstances cannot in general be evolved to correspond with cognitively unambiguous circumstances like features or categories. The presence of such features or categories is detected on the basis of predominant recommendation weights across the population of currently detected groups.

On the basis of an extensive range of psychological and physiological evidence, Coward [4, 5] has argued that the neocortex can be identified with the clustering subsystem, and the receptive fields of cortical columns correspond with groups of similar circumstances. Subcortical structures including the thalamus and basal ganglia form the competition subsystem that associates groups of similar circumstances and different types of behaviours.

A primary driving force on learning is the requirement that, to ensure a high integrity behaviour, at least a minimum range of recommendations must be generated in response to every sensory input state. At least a minimum number of columns must therefore detect their circumstances in each sensory input state. If necessary, some columns must expand their receptive fields in order to reach the minimum. These expansions are the declarative memory of the input state.

To reduce the risk of undesirable side effects, receptive field expansions must occur in such a way that the total change is minimized. A set of columns must be identified which achieves the minimum total activity with the least total change. In the proposed model, the hippocampal system identifies the appropriate set of columns in response to each sensory input state.

The model is a hierarchy of descriptions relating neuron level phenomena to psychological memory phenomena. Pyramidal neuron receptive fields are described using leaky integrator neuron models. Cortical columns are described using three layers of pyramidal neurons (and some associated interneurons). The interactions between cortex and hippocampus are described in terms of column outputs flowing along known anatomical connection pathways. Finally, memory deficits are described in terms of damage to specific more detailed capabilities.

2. Pyramidal neuron model

The leaky integrator model for the pyramidal neuron has been widely used for dynamic modelling of cortical activity [e.g. 6]. The neuron model used for the cortico-hippocampal model and illustrated in figure 1 is a generalized version of this neuron model which incorporates the concept of staged integration [7].

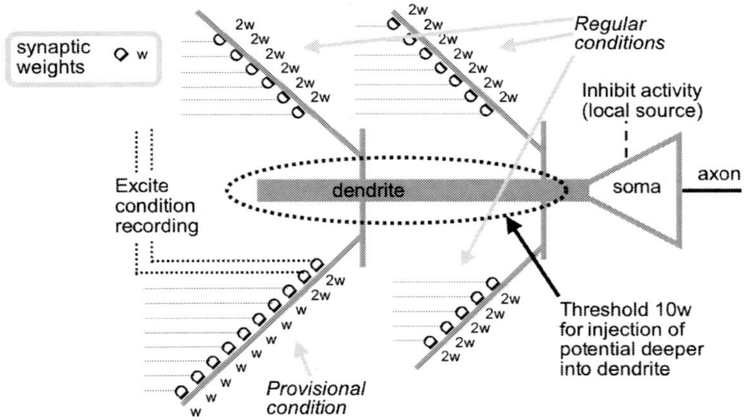

Figure 1. Leaky integrator model for pyramidal neuron with staged integration across its dendritic tree. The LTP mechanism is used to change provisional conditions into regular conditions.

The dendritic tree is divided into branches, each branch having a number of synaptic inputs. Action potential spikes directed to a synapse inject potential into the branch proportional to the synaptic strength. This potential rises and decays over a timescale of about 25 milliseconds. If the total branch potential derived from all recent synaptic inputs exceeds a threshold, the branch injects a potential into the dendrite. Injected potentials rise and decay, and the neuron generates an action potential only if the total dendritic potential at some point in time exceeds another threshold.

The set of synapses on a branch form an information condition within sensory inputs. The neuron receptive field is defined by a group of similar conditions. The neuron generates an output if a large number of these conditions is present within a relatively short period of time.

Receptive field expansions occur by addition of conditions to the group. Conditions are added using branches configured with "provisional" conditions, made up of synapses from neurons detecting simpler sensory receptive fields, with total synaptic strengths too small to result in the branch threshold ever being exceeded. Hence input sensory receptive fields alone cannot trigger condition detection. However, the branch has additional inputs labelled "excite condition recording" in figure 1. If these inputs are also receiving spikes, the branch threshold may be exceeded. If the resultant branch potential injection is followed shortly afterwards by a neuron output, the long term potentiation (LTP) mechanism [8] increases the synaptic weights of recently active synapses on the branch. This increase can result in synaptic weights sufficient to lead to future total potential injections exceeding the branch threshold, independent of the excite condition recording inputs. Hence effectively a new condition has been recorded on the dendrite, slightly expanding the neuron receptive field. This learning algorithm requires excite condition recording inputs. Cortical columns generate the information needed to indicate when such inputs are appropriate.

3. Cortical column model

Cortical columns (figure 2) form areas of columns that detect receptive fields at one level of complexity in terms of sensory inputs. An area must detect at least a minimum number of receptive fields in every sensory input state. A succession of areas detects receptive fields of gradually increasing sensory complexity and pass detections to the next area. An example is the succession of visual areas V1, V2, V4, TEO and TE making up the ventral stream [9].

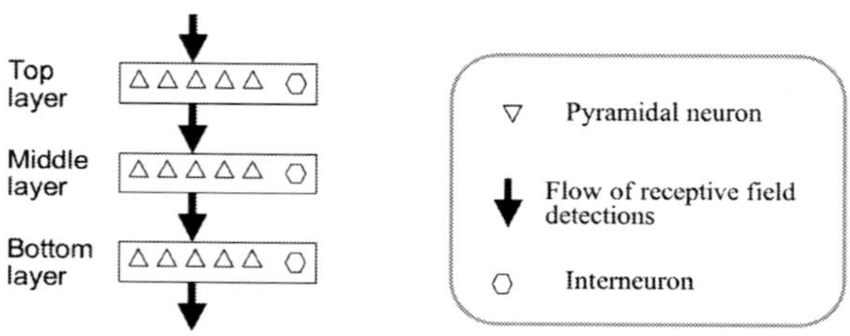

Figure 2. Neocortical column model.

There are three layers in a column. Conditions defining receptive fields of top layer pyramidals are combinations of receptive field detections by the columns that provide input to the area. Conditions in middle layer pyramidals are combinations of top layer receptive field detections, and conditions in the bottom layer are combinations of middle layer detections. Detections by bottom layer neurons are the outputs from the column passed to the next area. Receptive field complexities gradually increase between top and bottom layers. Pyramidals in the top layer detect their receptive fields in a relatively wide range of input states, those in the middle layer in a somewhat more narrow range, and those in the bottom layer that generates column outputs in a yet more narrow range [4].

If the total number of columns generating outputs in the area is less than a required minimum, some columns must expand their receptive fields. Columns with no current output but strong activity in their middle layer are good candidates for such expansion, because their middle layer activity indicates that the required expansion will be fairly small. A competition is required between the middle layer activity of all the columns in the area to determine the most appropriate columns for such expansion. Pyramidal neurons in the selected columns must then receive inputs that excite condition recording.

One additional factor is relevant to the selection of appropriate columns. If all of a set columns have often expanded their receptive fields in the past in response to the same sensory input states, and if many in the set are selected for expansion, the others in the set may well be good candidates even if their internal activity is lower. The competition should therefore take account both of current internal activity and past simultaneous information recording.

Interneurons limit overall activity within columns and within areas. For example, interneurons in the top layer could receive inputs from pyramidals in columns throughout the area, and inhibit pyramidals in their own column layer, and interneurons in the middle layer could receive inputs from their own column and layer, and inhibit the same pyramidals. This inhibition is general to the pyramidal neuron and not specific to individual branches.

4. Cortico-hippocampal system model

The major anatomical structures and connectivity paths of the cortico-hippocampal system in the human brain are illustrated in figure 3. The model interprets these structures and connectivity paths as managing selection of appropriate cortical columns to record information.

Columns in the perirhinal cortex (PRC) and parahippocampal cortex (PHC) have receptive fields corresponding with groups of cortical columns in sensory areas that have expanded their receptive fields at similar times in the past. Entorhinal cortex (EC) columns have receptive fields that correspond with larger groups of columns in many different sensory and polymodal areas that have recorded information in the past at similar times. Information on the current activity of these extensive groups is provided to pyramidals in CA1 and CA3, and to granule cells in the dentate gyrus (DG), by connectivity from the EC.

DG granule cells have receptive fields corresponding with extensive but relatively randomly selected groups of neocortical columns. The receptive fields of pyramidal neurons in CA3 correspond with extensive groups of neocortical columns that have tended to record information at similar times in the past. The receptive fields of CA1 pyramidal neurons correspond with extensive groups of neocortical columns that have recorded information at similar times in the past. There are general similarities between the receptive fields of individual granule cells, CA3 pyramidals and individual CA1 pyramidals in that their receptive fields are all combinations of the same EC outputs. However, in CA1 the fields are sharply focussed in terms of simultaneous past information recording, in CA3 they are less sharply focussed, while the receptive fields of granule cells are relatively unfocussed.

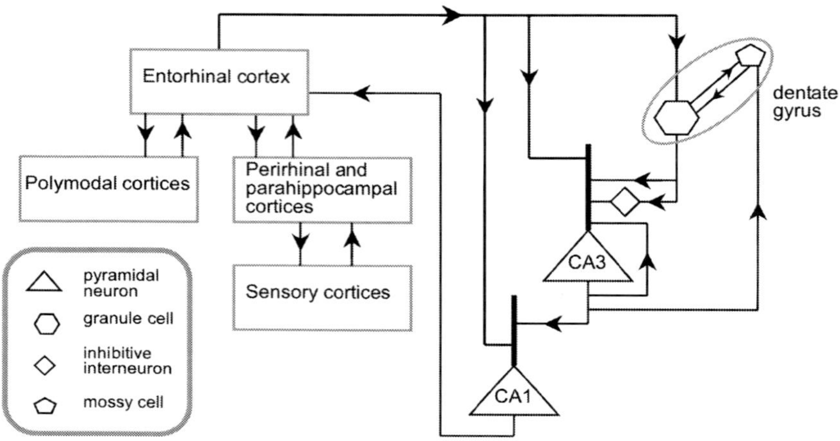

Figure 3. Major connectivity paths of the cortico-hippocampal system. For cortical connectivity see [10]. For EC to hippocampus proper see [11]. For internal hippocampal connectivity see [12].

All hippocampal system receptive fields need to be learned, just as sensory receptive fields are learned. Signals to drive expansions of receptive fields are therefore required, but the conditions recorded are groups of neocortical columns that expand their receptive fields at the same time. In the model, granule cell outputs drive expansions in CA3 pyramidals, CA3 pyramidal outputs drive expansions in CA1 pyramidals, CA1 pyramidals drive expansions in the EC, EC outputs drive expansions in the PRC, PHC and some polymodal cortices, and PRC and PHC outputs drive expansions in the sensory and other polymodal cortices.

4.1. *Flow of inputs to the hippocampal system*

Middle layer activity of a column indicates the degree of appropriateness of the column for receptive field expansion. Middle layer outputs from the sensory cortices target PRC and PHC columns. Middle layer outputs from these PRC and PHC columns indicate the degree of internal activity in the groups of sensory columns forming their receptive fields. PRC and PHC middle layer outputs target EC columns which produce top and middle layer outputs indicating the degree of internal activity of the large groups of sensory columns forming their receptive fields. Pyramidals in CA1 and CA3, and granule cells in the DG, receive inputs from the top and middle layers of EC columns.

4.2. *Competition within the DG and CA3*

Within the hippocampus proper there are two excitatory feedback loops, one in CA3 and the other in the DG, with strong links between them (figure 3). In CA3, pyramidals target large numbers of other pyramidals. In the DG, granule cells target mossy cells and mossy cells target granule cells. Between the two feedback loops, CA3 pyramidals excite DG mossy cells, and granule cells both excite and (via interneurons) inhibit CA3 pyramidals. The excitatory connections are the signals exciting CA3 pyramidal receptive field expansions, and the inhibitory connections reduce general CA3 pyramidal activity. As granule cell activity increases, inhibition predominates over excitation.

Strong input from the EC indicates that the current input state is familiar and little receptive fields expansion is required. Such a strong input will result in strong granule cell activity, leading to strong CA3 interneuron activity which cuts off CA3 pyramidal activity. Lack of CA3 pyramidal activity will mean little CA1 activity which will mean little neocortical receptive field expansions.

A smaller degree of EC output means that initially the indirect inhibition of CA3 pyramidals by granule cells will be low. Granule cells also provide outputs exciting condition recording by CA3 pyramidals, targetting pyramidals that receive inputs from EC columns similar to those that provide inputs to the granule cell. There will be initial CA3 pyramidal activity from detection of receptive fields as currently defined within EC inputs. Granule cell outputs targetting CA3 pyramidals directly will increase this initial CA3 activity by expanding receptive fields. As CA3 activity increases, the activity of mossy cells (targetted by CA3 pyramidals) increases, and this increases the activity of granule cells. The increase in granule cell activity increases the activity of CA3 interneurons, limiting the increases in CA3 pyramidal activity.

The activity of CA3 pyramidals will therefore be inversely proportional to the degree of activity in the EC, which is itself inversely proportional to the novelty of the current sensory input state. The most active CA3 pyramidals will be those with receptive fields corresponding with large groups of neocortical columns that currently have strong internal activity. Because new such groups are recorded when the CA3 pyramidals are producing outputs, and such outputs ultimately drive condition recording in those new groups, the CA3 pyramidal receptive fields will evolve to correspond with groups of columns that tended to record information at the same time. The competition thus produces outputs from CA3 pyramidals favouring groups that are currently active internally and that have tended to record information at the same time in the past.

4.3. *Flow of outputs from the DG-CA3 competitive system*

CA3 pyramidals target CA1 pyramidals, both to generally excite those pyramidals and to encourage receptive field expansions. The CA1 pyramidals targetted by a CA3 pyramidal are those receiving inputs from the EC similar to the CA3 pyramidal inputs. Hence CA1 pyramidals will develop receptive fields that are generally similar to those developed by CA3 pyramidals, but more sharply focussed on groups of columns that record information at the same time.

The outputs of a CA1 pyramidal target pyramidals in the columns of the EC from which it derives its inputs. These CA1 outputs both generally excite pyramidals in those columns and drive pyramidal receptive field expansions throughout the columns. The overall effect is that the EC columns most targetted by currently active CA1 pyramidals will produce bottom layer outputs, expanding their receptive fields if necessary. Interneuron activity within those columns limits overall column activity.

Similarly, EC column bottom layer outputs target the PRC and PHC columns from which they derive their inputs, and the PRC and PHC columns target the sensory cortex columns from which they derive their inputs.

The overall effect is that neocortical columns are selected to expand their receptive fields on the basis of a combination of current internal activity and past simultaneous expansions at the same time as other columns with strong current internal activity. The outputs of the selection process both drive current expansions in neocortical sensory receptive fields and evolve pyramidal neuron receptive fields in the hippocampal cortices and hippocampus proper to reflect those current expansions.

5. Accounting for psychological phenomena

The loss of ability to create new declarative memories of any type can be understood as the result of the loss of CA1 outputs driving receptive field expansions. Damage limited to CA1 results in anterograde amnesia. However, damage to the hippocampal system does not affect the receptive fields of existing neocortical columns, only their ability to change. Those receptive fields and their recommendation strengths will be unaffected. Hence hippocampal damage will not affect skills, general intelligence, speech etc.

A loss of episodic memories is also observed following hippocampal damage, but not of semantic memories derived from the same time period as the lost episodic memories. [13] has argued that the information mechanisms supporting episodic and semantic memory are qualitatively different. Episodic memories are constructed by indirect activation of neocortical columns on the basis of past simultaneous information recording. For example, during the experience of a novel event (e.g. watching a report of the first Bali bombing on television), there will be receptive field expansions in a wide range of columns. Later, hearing appropriate words (e.g. "Bali bombing") could activate a primary population of columns including a proportion of the columns active during the original event. If this population is evolved by activating a secondary population made up of columns that most often expanded their receptive fields at the same time as columns in the primary population, and then activating a tertiary population on the same basis and so on, the end point will be an active column population approximating the population active during the original experience. Such a final population would have recommendation strengths in favour of speech behaviours describing that original experience etc. Semantic memories, on the other hand, are based on frequent past simultaneous activity of different groups of columns, generally without receptive field expansions (e.g. groups of visual columns directly activated in response to seeing dogs, and groups of auditory columns directly activated in response to hearing the word "dog").

The hippocampal system role in managing the selection of columns that will expand their receptive fields means that the information required to manage episodic memory retrieval is readily available. The required indirect activation on the basis of past simultaneous condition recording can be driven by PRC, PHC or EC columns, targetting somas or dendrites of pyramidals in appropriate columns, but not provisional condition branches.

The information to drive indirect activation on the basis of frequent past simultaneous activity (generally without receptive field expansion) is qualitatively different. Collection of such information by the hippocampal system would corrupt the receptive field expansion information required for its primary role. This collection must therefore occur in a different neocortical area, which will be unaffected by hippocampal damage.

6. Computer implementation of the proposed model

A simple version of the cortico-hippocampal model has been implemented, including models for neocortical columns and CA1. The flow of time is broken up into 0.33 millisecond timeslots, and the states of all the neurons making up the model are recalculated in each timeslot, using new system inputs and the states of all the neurons in the previous timeslot.

One neocortical area with ten columns is modelled. Each column has three layers (figure 2). Each layer has 50 pyramidal neurons and the top two layers each have 10 inhibitory interneurons. Pyramidal neurons are modelled as two stage leaky integrators. Interneurons are modelled as single stage leaky integrators. Pyramidal neurons in the top layer have 20 branches, each with 25 inputs from randomly selected sensory inputs. Pyramidals in the middle and bottom layers have 10 branches with inputs from 15 randomly selected pyramidal neurons in the preceding layer. Interneurons target pyramidal neurons in the same column and layer. Each top layer interneuron has randomly selected inputs from pyramidals in the top layer of every column except its own, these interneurons therefore limit the overall activity of the area. Each middle layer interneuron has randomly selected inputs from pyramidals in the middle layer of its own column, these interneurons limit the overall activity of their column.

Learning occurred by the LTP algorithm. When a neuron produced an output, the weights of any recently active synapses were increased by about 10%, provided their branch had injected potential into the dendrite. However, unless there were five such increases within a 200 millisecond period, increases were reversed. Permanent learning therefore only occurred if a provisional condition contributed several times to the production of an action potential by its neuron. Total increases for one synapse were limited to doubling its original strength.

CA1 had 10 pyramidal neurons and 10 interneurons. Each CA1 pyramidal had inputs from a randomly selected set of middle layer pyramidals in a randomly selected set of columns, and targetted branches of pyramidals in all layers of the columns from which it received inputs. CA1 pyramidal receptive fields are therefore learned to a very limited degree, and are comparable with granule cell receptive fields in the full model. Overall CA1 activity is limited by interneurons receiving randomly selected inputs from CA1 pyramidals.

Inputs to the cortex emulate inputs that would be received from sensory systems. There are 200 sensory input streams, and the input state in one time slot is a 200 element vector indicating the presence or absence of a spike in each input stream. Spikes occur at different average rates in each input stream. Each input stream has a spike generation probability, and the presence of a spike is determined randomly on the basis of this probability in each time slot.

There are different categories of input experiences. These categories could be interpreted as different categories of visual object. A category is defined by a set of spike generation probabilities for the set of 200 input streams. For each category the 200 spike generation probabilities are created by random selection.

Category instance presentations last for 200 milliseconds, and are generated for each of the 600 time slots by using the appropriate spike generation probabilities. Hence every category instance presentation is different, there is simply a tendency for some input streams to have higher average rates and others to have lower rates for all instances of the same category.

Column #		1	2	3	4	5	6	7	8	9	10
Category											
1		450	300	100	91	0	73	0	0	268	350
2		0	50	139	329	50	0	112	905	152	0
3		0	0	200	0	100	306	250	0	0	0
1		0	288	268	0	149	50	0	120	50	50
2		26	0	36	50	0	50	0	1291	122	0
3		0	0	50	0	50	1001	0	50	0	0
1		112	579	0	0	0	157	123	100	150	0
2		0	0	117	0	0	51	0	1141	0	50
3		41	0	0	0	0	1236	100	50	0	0
1		0	206	50	0	50	200	0	576	0	0
2		0	0	0	0	0	50	0	2753	0	0
3		0	0	0	0	0	1453	37	268	0	0
1		50	131	643	0	0	523	0	150	114	0
2		0	0	0	0	0	135	0	2277	50	0
3		0	0	0	0	50	2156	0	217	0	0
1	▪	0	50	14	0	0	947	0	1112	0	0
2	▪	0	0	0	0	0	56	0	3094	90	0
3	▪	0	0	0	0	0	2925	0	200	0	0

Figure 4. Results of a run of the computer model. The total number of action potentials generated by the pyramidal neurons in the bottom layer of each column during the presentations of 200 millisecond instances of three different categories are shown. The first five and the last groups of three category instances from a total of 10 (i.e. 30 instance presentations) are shown.

The objective of the computer model is to demonstrate that the model columns can self organize to generate outputs that discriminate between different categories, and that the hippocampal activity improves the effectiveness of the discrimination achieved.

Results of one simulation are shown in figure 4. In this simulation, ten columns were presented with ten sets of different instances of three object categories. The total action potentials generated by the fifty bottom layer pyramidal neurons in response to the first five and the tenth sets of instances are shown. The array of columns rapidly settled into a mode in which category one instances produced activity in columns 6 and 8, category two instances only in column 6 and category 3 instances only in column 8. This pattern of response can support an adequate discrimination between the categories from a behavioural point of view [14].

Discrimination effectiveness varied between runs, but without CA1 signals the effectiveness was less: column activity tending to be more uniform across columns for all categories. The simulation thus demonstrates the feasibility of the model to support column definition. Implementation of a full CA3-DG system should improve the effectiveness and consistency of the model.

7. Conclusions

The proposed model for the cortico-hippocampal system provides a novel but plausible role for the hippocampal system in managing the recording of declarative information in the neocortex. This model makes it possible to understand the operations of the neocortex on multiple levels of detail from physiological to psychological, is consistent with known anatomy and physiology, and provides a straightforward account for the memory deficits that result from physical damage to the hippocampal system. Computer modelling confirms the general feasibility of the model.

References

1. W. B. Scoville and B. Milner, J. Neur. Neurosurg. Psychiat 20, 11-21 (1957).
2. J. H. Sagar, N. J. Cohen, S. Corkin and J. H. Growden, Ann. New York Acad. Sci. 444, 533-535 (1985).
3. E. A. Kensinger, M. T. Ullman and S. Corkin, Hippocam. 11, 347-360 (2001).
4. L. A. Coward, J. Cogn. Sys. Res. 2(2), 111-156 (2001).
5. L. A. Coward, A System Architecture Approach to the Brain: from Neurons to Consciousness. New York: Nova (2005).
6. M. Diesmann, M-O. Gewaltig and A. Aertsen, Nature 402, 529-533 (1999).
7. M. Hausser and B. Mel, Curr. Opin. Neurobiol. 13, 372-383 (2003).
8. G-g Bi and M-m Poo, J. Neurosci. 18, 10464-10472 (1998).
9. M. Mishkin, L. G. Ungerleider and K. A. Macko, Trends. Neurosci. 6, 414-417 (1983).
10. W. A. Suzuki, Semin. Neurosci. 8, 3-12 (1996).
11. R. Insausti and D. G. Amaral, In G. Paxinos and J. K. Mai editors. The Human Nervous System 871-914 (2004).
12. J. E. Lisman, Neuron 22, 233-242 (1999).
13. L. A. Coward, Modelling Language, Cognition and Action, A. Cangelosi, G. Bugmann and R. Botisyuk editors, 311-320 (2005).
14. L. A. Coward, T. D. Gedeon and U. Ratanayake, Lect. Notes Comp. Sci. 3316, 458-464 (2004).

THE ROLE OF STRUCTURAL PLASTICITY AND SYNAPTIC CONSOLIDATION FOR MEMORY AND AMNESIA IN A MODEL OF CORTICO-HIPPOCAMPAL INTERPLAY

A. KNOBLAUCH

Honda Research Institute Europe
Carl-Legien-Strasse 30, D-63073 Offenbach/Main, Germany
E-mail: andreas.knoblauch@honda-ri.de
www.honda-ri.de

This simulation study explores how structural processes and synaptic consolidation during hippocampal memory replay can improve the performance of neocortical neural networks by emulating high effective connectivity in networks that have only low anatomical connectivity. We model ongoing structural plasticity such that, in each time step, a certain fraction of the unconsolidated synapses are eliminated and replaced by new synapses generated at random locations. Simultaneous replay of novel memories consolidates some of the cortical synapses according to Hebbian learning. By this procedure sparsely connected networks can become functionally equivalent to densely connected networks, thereby storing a large amount of information with a tiny number of synapses. In particular, it is possible to store up to $\mathfrak{C}^S \leq \log_2 n$ bits of information per synapse in simple networks of n neurons. This is much more than the well-known bound $\mathfrak{C} \leq 0.72$ bits per synapse for static networks. It turns out that sufficiently fast learning requires a significant number of silent unconsolidated synapses. Thus, with lifetime and stored memories, the number of unconsolidated synapses and thus the ability to learn will decrease gradually. This leads to the discussion of various memory-related effects such as catastrophic forgetting and Ribot gradients in retrograde amnesia.

Keywords: Synaptic plasticity; Associative memory; Willshaw model; Catastrophic forgetting; Ribot gradients.

1. Introduction

Traditionally, learning and memory are attributed to synaptic plasticity, typically by modification of synaptic strength or weight according to variants of the Hebb rule.[1–4] Similarly, artificial neural networks rely almost exclusively on synaptic plasticity in fully connected neural networks.[5] In contrast, connectivity of real neural networks is low even on a local scale. For example, pyramidal cells make synapses to only 10 percent of the neighboring cells within a cubic millimeter of cortical tissue.[6,7] Moreover, plasticity in the brain includes also structural processes on larger time scales such as elimination and generation of synapses, growth and retraction of spines, and remodeling of dendritic and axonal branches.[8–11] There is increasing evidence that structural plasticity occurs not only during development but is also a regular feature of the adult brain.[12,13]

Here we explore functional implications of structural plasticity[14,15] and synaptic consolidation[16] induced by hippocampal replay[17–19] for storing memories in neural networks of the cerebral cortex. To this end we develop a simple model of structural plasticity and synaptic consolidation and apply it to simple associative networks of the Willshaw-type employing binary synapses.[20–22] It is well known that such network models, in their basic form, can store at most 0.69 bits per synapse, and even more sophisticated models employing real-valued synapses cannot store more than 0.72 bits per synapse.[23–29]

However, our work suggests that, by employing structural plasticity, the storage capacity of these networks could increase to values up to $\log_2 n$ bits per synapse for networks of n neurons.[30–33] This becomes possible because in our model structural plasticity and synaptic consolidation induced by Hebbian learning work together in order to eliminate and replace "useless" synapses by new synapses at possibly more "useful" locations. By this selection procedure a sparsely connected neural network can "place" the rare synapses at the most effective locations and thereby becomes equivalent to a static network with much higher anatomical connectivity. It turns out that sufficiently fast learning consistent with memory transfer from the hippocampus to cortex[18,19,34–37] requires a significant number of silent or unconsolidated synapses which can be re-"placed" by structural plasticity. Thus, with lifetime and stored memories, the number of unconsolidated synapses and, consequently, also the ability to learn will decrease gradually. This leads us finally to the discussion of various memory-related effects such as catastrophic forgetting[38,39] and Ribot gradients in retrograde amnesia.[17–19,34]

2. A simple model of structural plasticity, synaptic consolidation, and cortico-hippocampal interplay

In the following we propose two simple models of structural plasticity that abstract from biological details described in the introduction. For this we apply the concept of a *potential synapse*[15] defined as a cortical location where a presynaptic axon and postsynaptic dendrite are close enough such that a connection could potentially be formed by spine growth and synaptogenesis. We consider the synaptic connections from a neuron population u of size m to another population v of size n that can be described by a synaptic (weight) matrix W of size $m \times n$. We further assume that there are Pmn real synapses and $P_{\text{pot}}mn$ potential synapses. Here P is the *anatomical connectivity* and P_{pot} the *potential connectivity*, where

$0 < P < P_{\mathrm{pot}}$. Further we assume that each real synapse is either silent (weight 0) or consolidated (weight 1).

For our first model variant (see Fig. 1) we assume that there is at most one potential synapse ij that may connect neuron u_i to neuron v_j. Thus, the network can be described by states $W_{ij} \in \{\nu, \pi, 0, 1\}$. Here state $W_{ij} = \nu$ means that synapse ij does not exist and cannot be realized, $W_{ij} = \pi$ means that ij is a potential synapse not yet realized, $W_{ij} = 0$ means that ij is already realized but still silent, and $W_{ij} = 1$ means that ij is realized and consolidated. States are updated in discrete time steps. Let $p_g := \mathrm{pr}[W_{ij}(t+1) = 0 | W_{ij}(t) = \nu]$ be the *generation probability* that synapse ij changes from a potential synapse at time t to a real silent synapse at time $t+1$. Similarly, the *elimination probability* is $p_e := \mathrm{pr}[W_{ij}(t+1) = \nu | W_{ij}(t) = 0]$, the *consolidation probability* is $p_c := \mathrm{pr}[W_{ij}(t+1) = 1 | W_{ij}(t) = 0]$, and the *deconsolidation probability* is $p_d := \mathrm{pr}[W_{ij}(t+1) = 0 | W_{ij}(t) = 1]$. In order to keep the total number Pmn of real synapses constant, we have to balance generation and elimination of synapses, for example by choosing $p_g = p_e P_0 / (P_{\mathrm{pot}} - P)$, where $P_0 mn$ is the number of real silent synapses.

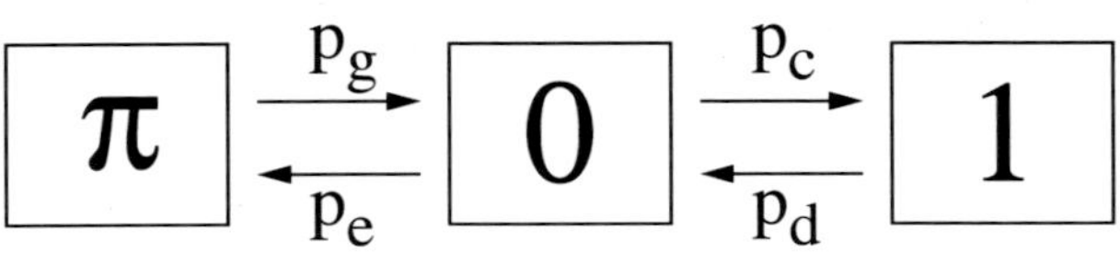

Fig. 1. State diagram illustrating our model of structural plasticity. A synapse can be either potential but not yet realized (state π), realized but still silent (state 0), or realized and consolidated (state 1). Transitions between the states occur with probabilities p_g, p_e, p_c, and p_d as explained in the text.

During the process of *synaptic consolidation* we assume that each synapse receives a binary *consolidation signal* $C_{ij} \in \{0, 1\}$. For a synapse ij we generally assume $p_c = 1$ if $C_{ij} = 1$ and $p_c = 0$ otherwise. Thus, C_{ij} can be interpreted as the "desired" weight matrix for storing a new set of memories in the synaptic connections between neuron populations u and v. Very similar to Hebbian-type learning, the consolidation signal C_{ij} could be provided by coincident presynaptic and postsynaptic neuron activity. The degree to which the actual synaptic connections resemble the "desired" connections can be assessed by the *effective connectivity* $P_{\mathrm{eff}} := (\sum_{i,j} C_{ij} W_{ij}) / \sum_{i,j} C_{ij}$ denoting the fraction of "desired" synapses that are actually realized and consolidated. Here the first sum assumes weight zero for states $W_{ij} \in \{\nu, \pi\}$.

To achieve significant *memory consolidation*, C_{ij} must be provided over longer time intervals matching the time scales of structural plasticity. This may be no problem in the case where the new memories correspond to frequently recurring stimuli. However, *episodic memories* typically have only a single training event and thus require a hippocampus-like memory buffer and repetition system that is able to store and replay new memories for some limited time.[34,36] In fact, experiments support the idea that such episodic memories are first buffered by one-shot learning in the hippocampus, and later replayed to become permanently consolidated in the neocortex.[17–19,34–37]

Figure 2 shows a highly simplified model of *cortico-hippocampal interplay* where u and v are interpreted as two cortical neuron populations, and the hippocampus is modeled by an additional neuron population HC. The basic idea is that incoming novel activity patterns are temporarily stored in the connections between neocortex and HC associating each memory u^μ (and v^μ) with an arbitrary index pattern HC^μ. This must happen by one-shot learning such that structural plasticity will be of little use here. However, HC can replay all buffered memories and thereby provide the consolidation signal C_{ij} necessary for final storage of memories in the high capacity cortico-cortical connections from u to v. For this we can assume that the hippocampal indices HC^μ are organized into a sequence, for example, in the local HC connections such that ordered replay is possible.[40] We can further assume small deconsolidation probability for synaptic connections within neocortex, for example $p_d = 0$, but a much larger deconsolidation probability for connections from, to, and within HC. By this choice, memory lifetime is limited in HC, but virtually unlimited in cortex.

We have also investigated a second model variant of structural plasticity assuming that a newly generated synapse is placed randomly at one of the potential locations. In contrast to the first model, this variant allows multiple realizations of synapses connecting neuron i to neuron j.[41] In fact, if a consolidation signal corresponding to a given set of memories is replayed for too long a time, this will have the effect that all remaining unconsolidated synapses will clutter the few potential locations ij with $C_{ij} = 1$. We have the idea that the first model variant is better suited for spine plasticity where realization of potential synapses is strongly limited by axonal and dendritic geometry (and thus avoids the described cluttering), while the second model variant may be better suited for axonal and dendritic remodeling on a large time scale. In any case, our simulations show that both model variants lead qualitatively to very similar results.[31]

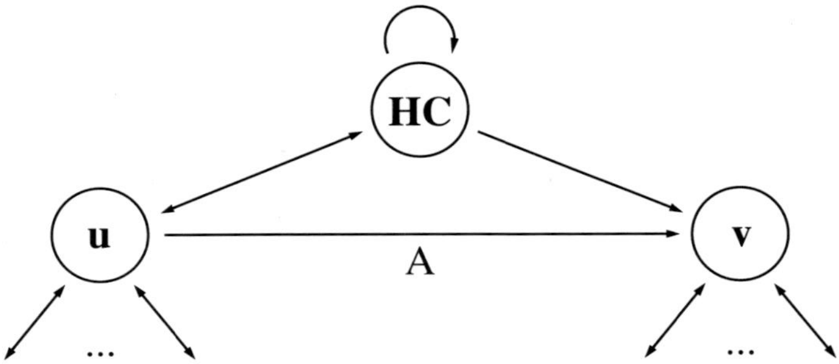

Fig. 2. Model of cortico-hippocampal interplay for memory consolidation. Storing memories means establishing associations between neural activity patterns in cortical areas u and v. These associations are first buffered in the connections from and to the hippocampus (HC) capable of one-shot learning. During the process of consolidation HC can reactivate memories in cortex. By ongoing structural plasticity and synaptic consolidation memories get finally stored in the cortico-cortical connection from u to v. See text for more details.

3. On the function and benefits of structural plasticity for memory storage

We hypothesize that an important function of structural plasticity is to compensate for sparse anatomical connectivity. According to our model, neural networks endowed with structural plasticity are able to increase effective connectivity P_{eff} from the level of anatomical connectivity P towards the level of potential connectivity P_{pot}. Thus, such networks may finally become equivalent to static networks with high anatomical connectivity $P \approx P_{\text{pot}}$ which would be much more expensive to maintain for the brain in terms of space and energy requirements.[42–44]

Figure 3 illustrates simulations of our first model variant showing that this idea actually works if the number of "required" synapses, $P_{\text{pot}} \sum_{i,j} C_{ij}$, does not exceed the number of available synapses, Pmn, or, equivalently, if the *consolidation load* $p_{1C} := (mn)^{-1} \sum_{i,j} C_{ij}$ does not exceed the bound $p_{1C} \leq P/P_{\text{pot}}$. The simulations also show that emulating high effective connectivity comes at the price of long replay periods if p_{1C} is close to P/P_{pot}. Thus, in order to achieve sufficiently fast consolidation the number of synapses required to be consolidated should be sufficiently smaller (for example factor $1/2$) than the number of available synapses. For more details see[31] where I have given a quantitative analysis of consolidation time required to achieve a desired effective connectivity.

What then are the concrete benefits of structural plasticity and increasing effective connectivity? To answer this question let us consider neural associative networks commonly used as cortical models for storing memories. In our scenario the task is to store a set of M memory associations $u^\mu \to v^\mu$ ($\mu = 1, \ldots, M$),

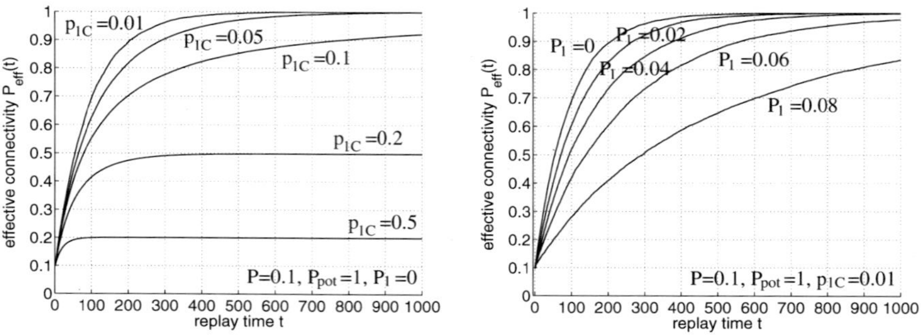

Fig. 3. Results from simulations of the model of structural plasticity for population sizes $m = n = 1000$, anatomical connectivity $P = 0.1$, and full potential connectivity $P_{\text{pot}} = 1$. The plots show effective connectivity $P_{\text{eff}}(t)$ over replay steps t for different consolidation loads p_{1C} (left panel) and different numbers $P_1 mn$ of initially consolidated synapses (right panel). During each replay time step a fraction $p_e = 0.1$ of the silent synapses was replaced.

where u^μ are address vectors corresponding to activity patterns in the neuron population u having k out of m active units, and, similarly, v^μ are content vectors having l out of n active units. A particularly simple network model is the so-called Willshaw network.[20,21,33,45] In the fully connected static Willshaw network the memories are stored in a binary $m \times n$ weight matrix W by Hebbian learning where $W_{ij} = \min(1, \sum_{\mu=1}^{M} u_i^\mu v_j^\mu)$. This means, a synapse ij has weight 1 iff there is at least one μ with coincident pre- and postsynaptic activity, $u_i^\mu = 1$ and $v_j^\mu = 1$. It turns out that this simple model can store a quite large number of memories, $M \sim mn/\log^2 n$, and that it is possible to store about $\mathfrak{C} \leq 0.7$ bits per binary synapse which is quite close to the information theoretical optimum.[20–22,33] Some theory (e.g., see[22] for a concise description) shows that the storage capacity $\mathfrak{C} \approx \text{ld} p_{1W} \ln(1 - p_{1W})$ (in bits per synapse) writes as a function of the memory load $p_{1W} := (mn)^{-1} \sum_{ij} W_{ij} = 1 - (1 - kl/(mn))^M$. Here for static networks maximal $\mathfrak{C}$ is achieved for $p_{1W} = 0.5$, while $\mathfrak{C} \to 0$ for low memory load $p_{1W} \to 0$ or large memory load $p_{1W} \to 1$.

However, now consider the Willshaw network endowed with structural plasticity and a consolidation signal identical to the weight matrix of the static network, $C = W$ and $p_{1C} = p_{1W}$. Further we assume, without loss of generality, that the anatomical connectivity is low and equal to the memory load, $P = p_{1W} \ll 1$, and that the potential connectivity is maximal, $P_{\text{eff}} = 1$. Because the condition $p_{1C} \leq P/P_{\text{eff}}$ is fulfilled the network can emulate full connectivity, $P_{\text{eff}} \to 1$, for sufficiently long a consolidation time. This means that the sparsely connected Willshaw network with structural plasticity becomes functionally equivalent to the fully connected static Willshaw network. Thus, it is possible to store the same number of pattern associations as in the fully connected network, but employing only a small number of synapses. Thus, the storage capacity per synapse is much larger for the network with structural plasticity, $\mathfrak{C}^S = \mathfrak{C}/p_1$. It is easy to see that $\mathfrak{C}^S \to \infty$ for $p_{1W} \to 0$. Thus, in large networks with $n \to \infty$, a single synapse can store an arbitrarily large amount of information. A closer analysis reveals that indeed $\mathfrak{C}^S \sim \log n \to \infty$ (see[30,31,33]). In contrast, it is well known that any static network model of distributed storage cannot exceed the bound $\mathfrak{C} \leq 0.72$ bits per synapse, even if endowed with real-valued synaptic weights.[23–29,46]

Thus, structural plasticity allows us to store large amounts of information with a tiny number of synapses. The intuition is that structural plasticity with hippocampus-like replay and consolidation can "place" the rare synapses at the most useful locations. By this procedure a sparsely connected network can become functionally equivalent to a fully connected network with pruning of irrelevant (i.e., weak or silent) synapses. For that reason, such "zipped" networks can achieve a much higher storage capacity per synapse than static networks.

4. Structural plasticity and catastrophic forgetting

Artificial neural networks are well known for suffering from catastrophic forgetting (CF) also known as the stability-plasticity dilemma.[38] CF means that optimizing synaptic weights for storing a set of new memories will deteriorate or even destroy previous memories. On the other hand, freezing synaptic weights prevents the ability to learn new memories.

In contrast, the learning methods described here for associative networks do not suffer so seriously from CF because the learning contribution for a new memory is independent of other memories. From a functional perspective, associative networks are closely related to look-up tables, where adding a new memory does not affect previous memories.[22] However, associative networks store memories in a distributed way and therefore still may suffer from a weak form of CF, the so-called *Hopfield catastrophe*:[39] This means that a static neural network can store many memories without any problems until the capacity limit is reached. Then storing a single or few further memories can destroy all previously learned memories. This effect is a problem for technical applications but also for modeling memory processes since CF does not normally occur in our brains.

We argue that sparsely connected networks employing structural plasticity do not suffer from CF. Figure 4 (left panel) shows a simulation where we store a larger number of memories exceeding the capacity of the network. Memories are ordered within blocks and each memory block is replayed and consolidated for some time one after the other. The simulations show that approaching the capacity limit implies that storing new memories becomes more and more difficult, while older memories remain intact even if the capacity limit is exceeded. Thus, in contrast to static networks, there is no CF. The reason is essentially that with storing more and more memories the remaining silent synapses (necessary for storing new memories) become rare and, eventually, are used up right before CF can occur.

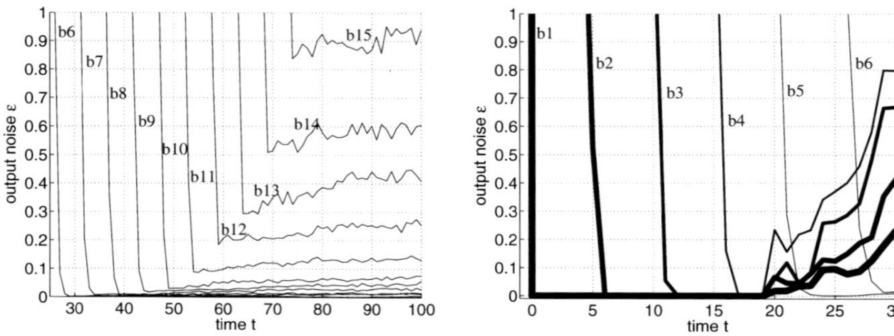

Fig. 4. Results from simulating the model of structural plasticity and cortico-hippocampal interplay for memory consolidation in neocortex. We stored 25 memory blocks (b1,b2,...) each consisting of 4 memories. Each block was replayed by HC for 5 time steps (e.g., block 10 between $t = 45$ and $t = 50$). During each replay step all silent synapses were replaced. The plots show normalized output noise ϵ for each memory block in population v with inactivated HC. Left panel: When storing more and more memories approaching the capacity limit of the network there is a gradual increase of output noise only for new memory blocks while old memories maintain high retrieval quality. Thus, there is no catastrophic forgetting. Right panel: Similar simulation as before, but at time $t = 20$ the cortical network was lesioned by deactivating half of the neurons in population u. This leads to Ribot-like gradients in output noise, i.e., retrieval impairment is more severe for recent memories than remote memories.

5. Retrograde amnesia and Ribot gradients

The same mechanism that prevents CF may be responsible for another salient effect of memory: Patients with lesions of the hippocampus or neighboring neocortex often suffer from graded retrograde amnesia.[34,47–49] This means that lesions impair recent memories more severely than remote memories. These so-called Ribot gradients can also be seen in our model (Fig. 4, right panel). When consolidating more and more memories the number of consolidated synapses (P_1) increases and, correspondingly, the number of unconsolidated silent synapses decreases. Thus, assuming constant replay time per memory block, the effective connectivity that can be achieved for recent memories is smaller than for remote memories (see also Fig. 3, right panel). And this is actually the reason why in our simulations, after lesions, remote memories are better preserved than recent memories.

In previous theoretical models Ribot gradients have typically been generated by gradients in consolidation time,[17,19] where the Mth memory obtains a $1/M$ share of consolidation time, for example assuming a random walk over the attractor-landscape in Hopfield-type networks with M attractors. Then Ribot gradients occur because early memories can accumulate a much larger total consolidation time (and thus resulting memory trace strength) than recent memories. However, these models implicitly assume that memories are maintained in and consolidated by the hippocampus forever. This contradicts evidence that new memories are buffered by the hippocampus for a limited time only and that replay of novel memories is controlled by the hippocampus.[36,37]

6. Discussion

In this paper we have proposed a simple model of structural plasticity and its relation to synaptic consolidation and cortico-hippocampal interplay. We abstracted from many biological details such as different time scales and geometrical constraints of spine plasticity and remodeling of axons and dendrites. The essence of our model is that structural plasticity can eliminate "useless" synapses (those with low synaptic weights) and regenerate new synapses blindly at potentially more "useful" locations. If a synapse turns out to be actually "useful" it gets consolidated and escapes the process of elimination and regeneration. Since structural plasticity is slow this requires replay of the memories to be consolidated, presumably controlled by the hippocampus.[18,34,35,37]

In contrast to previous approaches[14,15] we apply these ideas to well known associative network models as often used for modeling cortex and memory.[20,21,50,51] By introducing the concept of effective connectivity we have shown that sparsely connected networks with structural plasticity are functionally equivalent to more densely connected static networks. Thus, under some conditions, networks endowed with structural plasticity can store the same large amount of information as fully connected networks, but require only a relatively small number of functional synapses. A closer theoretical analysis reveals that the bits of information stored per synapse can reach the theoretic bound $\log_2 n$ where n is the network size.[30,31,33] Further analyses indicate that these results apply also to biologically more realistic networks based on synapses with gradual weights.[52] In contrast, static neural networks can store at most 0.72 bits per synapse even if endowed with real-valued synapses.[23–29,46] Thus, we propose that the main function of structural plasticity is to emulate higher effective connectivity in networks with sparse anatomical connectivity in order to minimize space and energy requirements.[42–44]

Besides these functional considerations, our model avoids common problems of static neural networks and can reproduce memory effects found in psychological and neurophysiological experiments. For example, networks endowed with structural plasticity inherently avoid catastrophic forgetting of repeatedly presented memories.[38] Instead, they gradually reduce the capability to acquire new memories, but leave previously stored memories intact. The reason for this behavior is that the number of consolidated synapses will increase with the number of stored memories, and, correspondingly, the number of remaining unconsolidated synapses diminishes. Since silent unconsolidated synapses are necessary for learning new information this process prevents exceeding the storage capacity of the network and thus catastrophic forgetting.

The same mechanism leads to gradients in effective connectivity and thus memory trace strength. Recent memories achieve a lower effective connectivity than remote memories. By this our model can reproduce Ribot gradients as found in patients suffering from retrograde amnesia after cortical lesions.[34,47–49] In previous models[17–19] Ribot gradients have been reproduced by a gradient in total consolidation time. These approaches assume ongoing replay and consolidation of any memory such that the Mth memory gets a time share of only $1/M$. In contrast, our model can reproduce Ribot gradients even for constant replay time per memory. This seems more consistent with common ideas and physiological evidence that new memories get consolidated only for a limited time by hippocampal replay.[18,34–37]

Acknowledgments

The author is grateful to Edgar Körner and Marc-Oliver Gewaltig for providing the opportunity to do this work at the Honda Research Institute. He is also grateful to them and to Ursula Körner, Friedrich Sommer, and Günther Palm for many fruitful discussions and comments.

References

1. D. Hebb, *The organization of behavior. A neuropsychological theory.* (Wiley, New York, 1949).
2. T. Bliss and G. Collingridge, *Nature* **361**, 31 (1993).
3. O. Paulsen and T. Sejnowski, *Current Opinion in Neurobiology* **10**, 172 (2000).
4. S. Song, K. Miller and L. Abbott, *Nature Neuroscience* **3(9)**, 919 (2000).
5. J. Hertz, A. Krogh and R. Palmer, *Introduction to the theory of neural computation.* (Addison-Wesley, Redwood City, 1991).
6. V. Braitenberg and A. Schüz, *Anatomy of the cortex. Statistics and geometry.* (Springer-Verlag, Berlin, 1991).
7. B. Hellwig, *Biological Cybernetics* **82**, 111 (2000).
8. F. Engert and T. Bonhoeffer, *Nature* **399**, 66 (1999).
9. S. Witte, H. Stier and H. Cline, *Journal of Neurobiology* **31**, 219 (1996).

10. C. Woolley, Structural plasticity of dendrites., in *Dendrites.*, eds. G. Stuart, N. Spruston and M. Häusser (Oxford University Press, Oxford, UK, 1999) pp. 339–364.
11. R. Lamprecht and J. LeDoux, *Nature Reviews Neuroscience* **5**, 45 (2004).
12. A. Holtmaat, L. Wilbrecht, G. Knott, E. Welker and K. Svoboda, *Nature* **441**, 979 (2006).
13. V. DePaola, A. Holtmaat, G. Knott, S. Song, L. Wilbrecht, P. Caroni and K. Svoboda, *Neuron* **49**, 861 (2006).
14. P. Poirazi and B. Mel, *Neuron* **29**, 779 (2001).
15. A. Stepanyants, P. Hof and D. Chklovskii, *Neuron* **34**, 275 (2002).
16. S. Fusi, P. Drew and L. Abbott, *Neuron* **45**, 599 (2005).
17. R. Alvarez and L. Squire, *Proceedings of the National Academy of Sciences (USA)* **91**, 7041 (1994).
18. J. McClelland, B. McNaughton and R. O'Reilly, *Psychological Review* **102(3)**, 419 (1995).
19. M. Meeter and J. Murre, *Cognitive Neuropsychology* **22(5)**, 559 (2005).
20. D. Willshaw, O. Buneman and H. Longuet-Higgins, *Nature* **222**, 960 (1969).
21. G. Palm, *Biological Cybernetics* **36**, 19 (1980).
22. A. Knoblauch, *Information Processing Letters* **95**, 537 (2005).
23. M. Tsodyks and M. Feigel'man, *Europhysics Letters* **6**, 101 (1988).
24. G. Palm, On the asymptotic information storage capacity of neural networks., in *Neural Computers*, eds. R. Eckmiller and C. von der Malsburg (Springer Verlag, Berlin, Heidelberg, New York, 1988) pp. 271–280.
25. G. Palm, *Concepts in Neuroscience* **2**, 97 (1991).
26. J.-P. Nadal, *J.Phys. A: Math. Gen.* **24**, 1093 (1991).
27. P. Dayan and D. Willshaw, *Biological Cybernetics* **65**, 253 (1991).
28. G. Palm and F. Sommer, Associative data storage and retrieval in neural nets., in *Models of Neural Networks III*, eds. E. Domany, J. van Hemmen and K. Schulten (Springer-Verlag, New York, 1996) pp. 79–118.
29. A. Knoblauch, *Neural associative networks with optimal Bayesian learning.*, Internal Report HRI-EU 08-xy, Honda Research Institute Europe GmbH (D-63073 Offenbach/Main, Germany, in preparation).
30. A. Knoblauch, *On compressing the memory structures of binary neural associative networks*, Internal Report HRI-EU 06-02, Honda Research Institute Europe GmbH (D-63073 Offenbach/Main, Germany, 2006).
31. A. Knoblauch, *On structural plasticity in neural associative networks.*, Internal Report HRI-EU 08-04, Honda Research Institute Europe GmbH (D-63073 Offenbach/Main, Germany, 2008).
32. A. Knoblauch, *SIAM Journal on Applied Mathematics* **69(1)**, 169 (2008).
33. A. Knoblauch, G. Palm and F. Sommer, *Neural Computation, manuscript under review* (2008).
34. L. Squire and P. Bayley, *Current Opinion in Neurobiology* **17**, 185 (2007).
35. D. Ji and M. Wilson, *Nature Neuroscience* **10(1)**, 100 (2007).
36. R. Ross and H. Eichenbaum, *The Journal of Neuroscience* **26(18)**, 4852 (2006).
37. G. Buzsaki, *Cerebral Cortex* **6**, 81 (1996).
38. R. French, *Trends in Cognitive Sciences* **3(4)**, 128 (1999).
39. A. Robins and S. McCallum, *Connection Science* **7**, 121 (1998).

40. A. Lee and M. Wilson, *Neuron* **36**, 1183 (2002).
41. H. Markram, J. Lübke, M. Frotscher, A. Roth and B. Sakmann, *Journal of Physiology* **500(Pt 2)**, 409 (1997).
42. P. Lennie, *Current Biology* **13**, 493 (2003).
43. S. Laughlin and T. Sejnowski, *Science* **301**, 1870 (2003).
44. D. Attwell and S. Laughlin, *Journal of Cerebral Blood Flow and Metabolism* **21**, 1133 (2001).
45. K. Steinbuch, *Kybernetik* **1**, 36 (1961).
46. E. Gardner and B. Derrida, *J.Phys. A: Math. Gen.* **21**, 271 (1988).
47. S. Zola, Amnesia I: Neuroanatomic and clinical issues., in *Patient-based approaches to cognitive neuroscience.*, eds. M. Farah and T. Feinberg (MIT-Press, Cambridge, MA, 2000) pp. 275–290.
48. A. Baddeley, *Human memory: theory and practice.* (Lawrence Erlbaum, Hillsdale, NJ, 1990).
49. T. Ribot, *Les maladies de la memoire.* (Germer Baillare, Paris, 1881).
50. A. Knoblauch, H. Markert and G. Palm, An associative model of cortical language and action processing., in *Modeling Language, Cognition and Action. Proceedings of the 9th Neural Computation and Psychology, Workshop University of Plymouth, UK, 8-10 September 2004 (NCPW9)*, eds. A. Cangelosi, G. Bugmann and R. Borisyuk (World Scientific Publishing, 2005) pp. 79–86.
51. A. Knoblauch, R. Kupper, M.-O. Gewaltig, U. Körner and E. Körner, *Neurocomputing* **70(10-12)**, 1838 (2007).
52. A. Knoblauch, *Neural associative networks with non-linear local learning.*, Internal Report HRI-EU 09-xy, Honda Research Institute Europe GmbH (D-63073 Offenbach/Main, Germany, in preparation).

CONTEXT AND SEMANTIC WORKING MEMORY IN SCHIZOPHRENIA: A COMPUTATIONAL AND EXPERIMENTAL INVESTIGATION

MARIUS USHER, EDDY J. DAVELAAR, ALLESSANDRA BERTELLE and SHOPNA SEEVARAJAH

School of Psychology, Birkbeck, University of London
London, WC1E 7HX, United Kingdom

We present a computational model for contextual deficits that underlie thought disorder in Schizophrenia. Predictions were obtained using a neurocomputational model in which lexical-semantic information is maintained in an activation buffer that can bias the interpretation of ambiguous information. Deficits in the capacity to maintain information in the buffer result in deficit in context maintenance. The predictions are shown to match results from an experimental study on Schizophrenia patients and matched controls.

1. Introduction

Since the earliest days of psychiatric research, language disorganization has been one of the cognitive hallmarks of Schizophrenia [1, 2]. This disorganization, resulting in speech that appears incoherent due to a pattern of derailment (loose associations) and tangentiality, is now recognized as one component (along with reality-distortion and with negative symptoms) within the heterogeneous Schizophrenic syndrome [3]. The nature of this deficit, also labeled as formal thought-disorder (FTD) has been the focus of intensive research, which has tried to explain its source as arising from deficits in one (or few) fundamental cognitive processes. One of the prominent theories for FTD proposed that the deficit is caused by an inability to maintain and use context [4, 5][*].

This theory was also developed into a quantitative neurocomputational model, which makes precise predictions explaining Schizophrenic deficits in a number of tasks. Cohen and colleagues showed that this theory accounts for contextual disambiguation deficits in Schizophrenia patients, as well as specific

[*]The role of a context maintenance deficit to thought-disordered speech is illustrated in the following extract reported by Bleuler from a letter a patient wrote to his mother "...I always liked geography. My last teacher in that subject was Professor August A. He was a man with black eyes. I also like black eyes. There are also blue and gray eyes and other sorts, too. I have heard it said that snakes have green eyes...". Note that although each sentence is clearly related to the preceding one, the across-sentence context is not being maintained.

patterns (regarding errors) in attentional context tasks, such as the AX-CPT (a contextual version of the continuous performance task, where participants have to respond to a target-X only if it follows a context-A) and Stroop. The way in which context is understood in the computational theory of Cohen and colleagues involves "information that must be actively held in mind in such a form that it can be used to mediate task appropriate behavior" [5, p. 120], and it is distinctive from the more traditional process of short-term memory (STM), the capacity of which is measured via word/digit span task and is not impaired in Schizophrenia patients.

Recent experimental and computational work in the neuropsychology of STM, has suggested however, that the traditional concept of a verbal STM, based on a purely phonological buffer [6] is over-restrictive. Neuropsychological findings support the existence of separate phonological and lexical-semantic STM buffers. In particular, STM-patients with more anterior lesions show semantic deficits, while those with posterior lesions show phonological deficits [7]. Using neurocomputational modeling, we have shown [8] that a lexical-semantic buffer, implemented as an activated part of a lexical-semantic representation, can explain a number of neuropsychological dissociations in free-recall tasks, and bias the way in which (semantic) information is processed [9], lending further support for the proposal that a deficit of the lexical-semantic STM may mediate deficient contextual processing.

The aim of the present study is twofold. First, we present a neurocomputational activation-buffer model of two tasks, one of semantic-STM and the other of contextual disambiguation, which makes detailed predictions on how a reduction in the capacity of the buffer (corresponding to reduced gain or neural loss in frontal areas in Schizophrenia) affects behavioral patterns in both tasks. Second, these predictions are tested in an experiment that administered the tasks to Schizophrenia patients and healthy matched controls.

2. Tasks: contextual-disambiguation and semantic-STM

2.1. *The missing-letter task*

We focus on a variant of the contextual disambiguation task, labeled as the "missing-letter-task" [5]. In this task, participants are presented with a missing-letter (ML) string, which consists of a word with one letter omitted (e.g., _ILK), and are required to produce the first word that comes to their mind, consistent with that string (i.e., to fill in the missing letter M or S). Assume that one of these two words in more frequent (MILK) and thus is likely to trigger a dominant response (most participants would choose it, most of the time). The task, however, manipulates the context (and its immediacy) in which the ML-string is presented. Preceding the ML-string the observer is presented with a sequence of three prime-words, one of which is associated with the nondominant word-completion (SILK). If participants are maintaining the meaning of the three primes in a semantic-STM buffer, this is likely to bias their choice for the ML-string, although they are instructed to respond with the first thing that comes to mind. We label such choices as "contextual" as opposed to "dominant/non-contextual". Responses to other possible word-completions (that are neither dominant nor associated with one of the prime-words, are labeled "unrelated" responses. It is expected that, as a result of a reduced capacity of the semantic-buffer, Schizophrenia patients would have a decreased number of contextual-responses (in particular for remote context; 1st or 2nd but not 3rd prime) and an increased number of unrelated responses.

2.2. *The semantic-STM task*

The semantic STM task, also labeled conceptual span in our previous work [10] presents participants with a sequence of 9 words, made out from 3 categories (3 words from each), in an unblocked way. At the end of the sequence, a category-probe is presented (one of the 3 categories used in that trial) and the participants are required to report all the words (maximum 3) they can remember from that trial that match the category. If deficits of context-maintenance are due to a reduced capacity of a lexical-semantic buffer, then Schizophrenic patients should show a deficit in this task, especially for items presented earlier in the list (performance is measured separately for the primacy 1-3, middle 4-6 and recency 7-9 positions). Note that, although the two tasks involve maintenance of information, they do this in different ways. While maintenance is an explicit requirement of the semantic-STM task, it is only implicit to the ML-task, where as in language, the maintenance and the use of context is thought to be automatic.

We now turn to the neurocomputational model that produced the predictions to be compared with the experimental tests. We present details about the experimental methods in Appendix B.

3. Modeling context maintenance and semantic-STM in Schizophrenia

The neurocomputational model used in our predictions of the ML and the semantic-STM task, is an activation buffer (Figure 1A) with localistic representations for lexical units (representing words), with recurrent excitation, which allows the units to remain active after stimulus offset, and global inhibition, which prevents an unbounded spread of activation and permits only a few items to be active simultaneously. Between semantically related units there is a weak excitatory connection, which partially offsets the global inhibition when both semantic associates are active simultaneously (for an investigation of semantic similarity effects, see [9]). As in buffer models such as SAM [11], later items tend to replace earlier items in the buffer (Figure 1C), resulting in a recency-biased probability function that an item resides in the buffer at any given moment (Figure 1B). Figure 1B shows serial positions curves for two values of self-recurrent excitation. With lower self-recurrency, and thus lower capacity, the model retains only the very last items. To account for the deficit in Schizophrenia, we assume that the recurrent excitation parameter in the model, is reduced in Schizophrenia, resulting in reduced buffer capacity [12]. This reduced recurrent excitation corresponds to either reduced neuromodulatory gain [4] or neural loss [13, 14]. The predictions of the model are based on 1000 simulation runs per task.

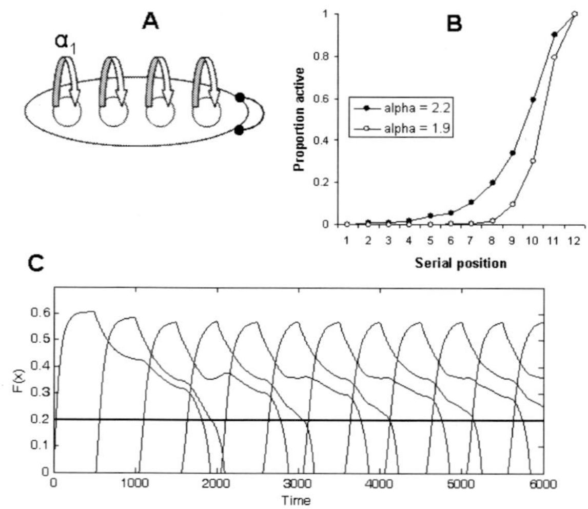

Figure 1. A. Buffer component used in the present simulations. Each unit receives self-recurrent excitation (arrows) and all units compete through global inhibition (denoted by the arrow with solid heads). B. Serial-position function showing the proportion of simulation runs that an item presented at a given input position is still active above threshold at the end of the sequence. Alpha refers to the amount of self-recurrent excitation. C. Activation trajectories of 12 sequentially activated buffer units, up to the moment when (in immediate free recall) a recall prompt is provided. The number of time steps is set on the abscissa, whereas the output activation value, F(x), is set on the ordinate. All units active above a certain memory threshold value (e.g., .2) are assumed to be accessible for subsequent recall from the buffer.

3.1. *Model for contextual disambiguation*

For the contextual disambiguation task, the model has eight units: three corresponding to the contextual words, three to their semantic associates (non-dominant units), one unit that forms the dominant choice for a given missing-letter cue and one unit that is unrelated to any of the other units. ML or category probes are assumed to provide input to related items in addition to the activation present in the buffer (see also [12]). At the end of the 3-word presentation, 3 of the units are still in active state (shaded units). When the ML-probe is presented, it activates a dominant non-contextual response (thick arrow corresponding to a strong connection) and a non-dominant response (thin arrow corresponding to weak link) to another item, which is also supported by context and, which due to this contextual bias, tends to be selected (the process is stochastic due to Gaussian noise in input to all units; see *Appendix A* for additional details).

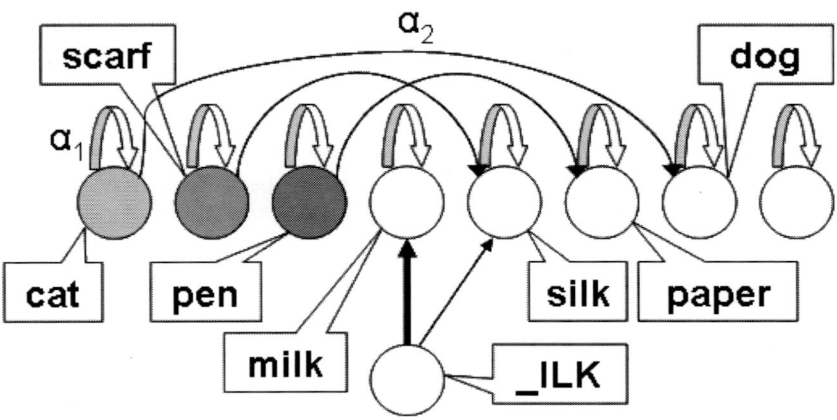

Figure 2. Illustration of the model's retrieval phase in the ML-task. The units in the upper layer correspond to the buffer lexical-semantic representations and the arrows to self-recurrent (α_1) and associative (α_2) excitation.

The three contextual words are presented sequentially for 1000 time-steps each, with an input strength of 0.33. After the offset of the final word, there is an empty interval of 500 iterations, followed by the activation of the dominant (with input = 0.35) and non-dominant (with input = 0.30) unit. Whenever any of the activations of the units reaches the response threshold of 0.60, an output is recorded. Trials in which the dominant unit (MILK) wins are labeled "dominant/non-contextual"; trials in which the contextual unit wins (SILK) are labeled "contextual", while trials in which other units win or no unit reaches the threshold within 1000 iterations are labeled "unrelated". The value for the self-recurrent excitation was varied at three-levels (2.3, 2.0 and 1.8) to a buffer capacity corresponding to normal controls and two types of patients (mild/severe), whereas the global inhibition was fixed at 0.15 and the standard deviation of the noise was set to 1.0.

In the experiments, we determined for each participant the dominant response and, in a separate session, we presented the ML-string following a sequence of 3 contextual words (e.g., cat, scarf, pen: scarf → silk), one of which was related to the non-dominant response (see *Appendix B)* of that participant.

3.2. *Results for contextual disambiguation*

The model predictions, together with the experimental results of normal controls and Schizophrenia patients in the contextual disambiguation task are shown in Figure 3. We observe that upon reduction of the recurrent excitation, we find a reduction of contextual-responses, in particular at early (non-immediate) context positions, in parallel with an increase in the faction of unrelated responses. As predicted by the model (left panel), we find in the contextual disambiguation task that the patients show an increased number of unrelated responses (patients: 1.94, controls: 0.59: t(18.5) = 2.66, p = .016) and a decreased number of non-dominant contextual responses, in particular when the context is presented as position-1 or at position-2 in the 3 item list (patients: 3.94, 4.25, 5.44, controls: 6.04, 5.41, 5.85) (sp1: t(41) = 2.61, p = .012, sp2: t(41) = 2.03, p = .049, sp3: t(41) = 0.50, p = .691). A group of 3 patients, who on the basis of type/token ratio [15] of recorded interview are categorized as being extreme thought-disordered, demonstrate an exaggerated pattern of these deficits.

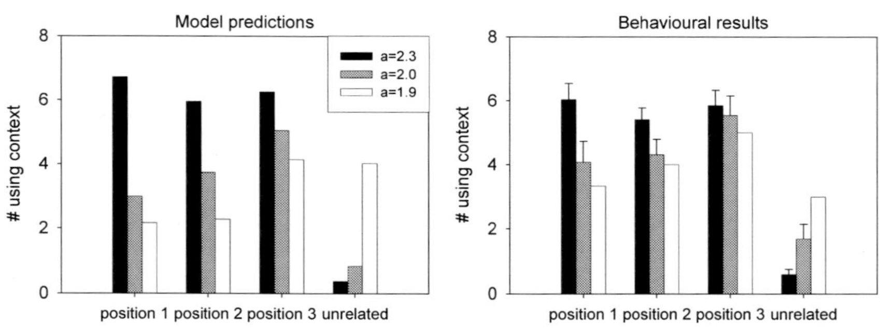

Figure 3. Model predictions (left) and experimental data (right) in the contextual disambiguation (ML) task. Three values of the recurrent-excitation parameter are used in the model reflecting the degree of TD deficit in patients.

3.3. *Model for semantic STM*

For the conceptual span task, the model has 20 units (previous work has shown that the capacity of the system is independent of the number of units in the system, [16]). During list presentation, nine units are sequentially activated for 1000 iterations each with an input strength of 0.33. After the offset of the final word, there is an empty interval of 500 iterations after which the first three, the middle three or the last three units are activated by the category-cue with an input of 0.16. Whenever any of the activations of the units reaches the response threshold of 0.50, an output is recorded. The simulation ended after 1000 iterations. The value for the self-recurrent excitation was varied with 3 levels (corresponding to controls, and mild/severe patients), whereas the global inhibition was fixed at 0.15 and the standard deviation of the noise was set to 1.0.

3.4. *Results for semantic STM*

The model predictions, together with the experimental results of normal controls and Schizophrenia patients in the semantic-STM task are shown in Figure 3. The model predicts that as a result of reduced recurrent excitation, there is a decrease in the ability to report items, in particular at early (primacy) positions. As predicted by the model (left panel), we find in the semantic STM task that the patients are able to report less words to the category probe, at all positions (patients: .22, .49, .61, controls: .45, .73, .83) (primacy: $t(41) = 4.01$, $p < .001$, middle: $t(41) = 3.83$, $p < .001$, recency: $t(41) = 4.66$, $p < .001$). The three extreme TD patients show an exaggerated deficit on the primacy items.

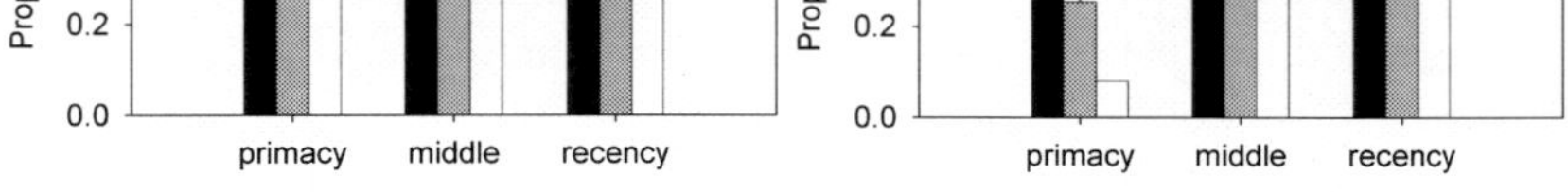

Figure 4. Model predictions (left) and experimental data (right) in the semantic-STM task. Three values of the recurrent-excitation parameter are used in the model reflecting the degree of TD deficit in patients.

4. Discussion

The aim of this study was to examine and to extend the context deficit hypothesis in Schizophrenia. This hypothesis has been developed within a formal computational theory by Cohen and colleagues [4, 5]. Within this theory, the processes involved in context maintenance are distinguished from those of STM. Here, we presented a computational model, in which an activated lexical-semantic buffer, of the type suggested by a number of neuropsychological dissociations, predicts deficits in both contextual disambiguation (the ML-task) and in a semantic STM task, as a result of changes in a single parameter that determines the buffer capacity. We interpret this parameter to correspond to either a reduced neuromodulatory gain [4] or to neural loss that affects cortical representations in Schizophrenia [13, 14]. As predicted by the model, the patients with Schizophrenia showed a deficit in reporting the words in the semantic-STM task and they made less contextual non-dominant responses, especially when the context was remote, than the controls. In particular, we find that as predicted by the model, the deficits in both tasks are exacerbated for items that are relatively remote from test (i.e., non-immediate).

It is important to note that, although, these two tasks have some common features (the need to respond to lexical-semantic probe) they also have important differences. While the semantic-STM task requires participants to remember the words presented in the last trial and to select for response the ones that match a category probe, no such requirement is made in the ML-task, where participants simply respond to the first word that comes to their mind. The use of context in this task is thus implicit as it is in language production, and thus it provides a stringent test for the hypothesis that language disorganization in Schizophrenia reflects a deficit in the maintenance of context. Finally, a correlational analysis on the experimental data, indicates a strong correlation [$r(56) = .44$, $p < .01$] between the participants' performance on these two tasks, supporting an overlap of the processes involved.

To dissociate between semantic and phonological STM, we have also administered (in all controls and patients) a digit-span test, which is associated with the traditional STM-span. Unlike in the semantic-STM and contextual disambiguation, the patients did not show significant deficits in the digit span [patients: 5.4; controls: 6.0: $t(41) = 1.85$, $p = .071$; the three severe patients had a score of 6.0, as for the controls], and there was a smaller correlation between context-use and digit-span [$r(56) = .39$, $p < .01$]. Once the overall memory ability (as measured by a separate memory test) and was controlled for, partial correlations showed a significant correlation between context-usage and conceptual span [$r(45) = .37$, $p = .01$], but not between context-usage and digit span [$r(45) = .15$, $p > .32$]. This supports the distinction between a phonological and a semantic buffer that is involved in the use of context [4, 17].

Although our present model explains the deficits we observed in terms of a simple buffer capacity, we want to emphasize that both the ML and the semantic-STM tasks also involves a selection requirement, which was recently suggested to be impaired in Schizophrenia [18]. Note however, that the model we presented, mediates selection as well as maintenance. Previously, we showed how the system that actively maintains a number of representations transforms into a system that selects among active representations through the modulatory effects of catecholamines, such as norepinephrine [12]. Future work is needed to contrast the selection and maintenance hypotheses in Schizophrenia.

Acknowledgments

We thank Dr Stephen Orleans Foli for access to patients.

Appendix A: Computational details

The activations of all units are updated in parallel according to:

$$x_i(t+1) = \lambda x_i(t) + (1 - \lambda)[\alpha_1 F(x_i(t)) - \beta \Sigma F(x_j(t)) + \alpha_2 F(x_i(t)) + I_i + \xi]$$

where the activation, $x_i(t)$, at time t depends on the activation in the previous time step, $x_i(t - 1)$; the recurrent self-excitation, $\alpha_1 F(x_i(t))$; the global inhibition, $\beta \Sigma F(x_j(t))$; the excitation from semantic associates, $\alpha_2 F(x_i(t))$, the sensory input, $I_i(t)$; and zero mean Gaussian noise, ξ, with standard deviation σ and the decay parameter λ ($0 < \lambda < 1$). The output activation function $F(x) = x/(1+x)$ (for $x > 0$, 0 otherwise) is threshold linear at low input and includes a saturation at high input (for discussion, see [11]).

Appendix B: Experimental methods

Sixteen inpatients with Schizophrenia from the acute ward at Charing Cross Hospital, Hammersmith and Fulham Mental Health Unit, London and 30 aged and socioecomically matched controls, took part in the experiment. The patients with Schizophrenia were diagnosed according to the DSM IV. The schizophrenic patients were interviewed and assessed for FTD, according to the SAPS [19] and the type/token ratio [15]. An additional group of 14 psychiatric patients (with a variety of disorders, including bipolar disorder) were tested to increase the statistical power of the correlational analyses between tasks. The mean patient age group was 36.7 years (SD = 10.9, range 19-57 years of age), while healthy controls had a mean age of 34.1 years (SD = 12.9, range 19-60 years of age). There were no statistical differences between groups. All the participants were fluent in English. Exclusion criteria for controls included history of schizophrenia or psychotic symptoms. All participants gave informed consent prior to their participation in the experiments and the participation of the patient population has received ethical approval of the ethical committee of the West London Mental Health NHS Trust, in accordance with the Helsinki protocol. All the patients were medicated at the time of test. For all tasks, stimuli were presented on a laptop computer. The experimenter used pen and paper to write down the participants' verbal responses. Participants were tested over the course of two 30-minutes sessions that were about one week apart.

The Conceptual Span task consisted of one practice trial and ten test trials. On each trial, participants were shown a randomized list of nine words (in lower case) drawn from three categories (three per category), at a rate of one word/second. After the final word, a category name (in upper case) was presented and participants were asked to recall aloud the words belonging to the cued category that were shown in the list in any order within one minute. For example, a sequence could be: lamp, pear, tiger, apple, grape, elephant, horse, fax, phone, FRUIT?.

The Contextual Disambiguation (Missing Letter) Test was used in the first session to determine the dominant response for each participant at each of the ML-words. Participants were given a sheet with a list of 36 words that was missing a single letter (e.g., _ILK) and were instructed to complete this with the first letter that comes to mind in order to form a meaningful word (e.g., MILK). This response was interpreted as that participant's dominant response to that ML-string. Based on the participant's response a 3-word sequence was created in which one of the words was semantically related to a non-dominant response of the ML-string (e.g., cat, scarf, pen: scarf → silk). In the second session, the task was presented on the computer and consisted of 36 trials. On each trial, participants were shown the constructed sequence of words at a rate of 4 seconds per word followed by a ML-string and were asked to read aloud each word, to think about each word and the usefulness of these words and say aloud a brief one or two words description of the word (e.g., for cat, a possible response was "pet"). Then participants were instructed to complete the missing letter word by saying the response out aloud for the experimenter to record manually. The word providing context ("scarf" in the above example) would appear in the first, second or third position of the 3-word sequence. The position of the contextual cue word was counterbalanced across participants. Responses to the missing letter word were classified as dominant (same as in the first session: milk), as non-dominant/contextual (related to the context word: silk) or as non-dominant/unrelated (e.g., bilk).

References

1. E. Bleuler, *Dementia praecox, or the group of schizophrenias* (New York: International Universities Press, 1911).
2. Kraeplin, *Dementia praecox and paraphrenia (J. Zinkin, Trans.).* (New York: International Universities Press, 1950).
3. P. F. Liddle, *British Journal of Psychiatry* 151, 145 (1987).
4. J. D. Cohen and D. Servan-Schreiber, *Psychological Review* 99, 45 (1992).
5. J. D. Cohen, D. M. Barch, C. Carter and D. Servan-Schreiber, *Journal of Abnormal Psychology* 108, 120 (1999).
6. A. D. Baddeley, (1986). *Working memory* (Oxford: Oxford University Press, 1986).
7. R. C. Martin, J. R. Shelton and L. S. Yaffee, *Journal of Memory and Language* 33, 83 (1994).
8. E. J. Davelaar, Y. Goshen-Gottstein, A. Ashkenazi, H. J. Haarmann and M. Usher, *Psychological Review* 112, 3 (2005).
9. E. J. Davelaar, H. J. Haarmann, Y. Goshen-Gottstein and M. Usher, *Memory & Cognition* 34, 323 (2006).
10. H. J. Haarmann, E. J. Davelaar and M. Usher, *Journal of Memory and Language* 48, 320 (2003).
11. J. G. W. Raaijmakers and R. M. Shiffrin, *Psychological Review* 88, 93 (1981).
12. M. Usher and E. J. Davelaar, *Neural Networks* 15, 635 (2002).
13. L. A. Flashman and M. F. Green (2004). *Psychiatric Clinics of North America* 27, 1 (2004).
14. W. Cahn, H. E. Hulshoff and M. Bongers, *British Journal of Psychiatry Supplement* 43, s66 (2002).
15. T. C. Manschreck, B. A. Maher, T. M. Hoover and D. Ames, *Psychological Medicine* 14, 151 (1984).
16. E. J. Davelaar, *PhD Dissertation* (University of London, 2003).
17. E. K. Miller and J. D. Cohen, *Annual Review of Neuroscience* 24, 167 (2001).
18. J. M. Gold, C. M. Wilk, R. P. McMahon, R. W. Buchanan and S. J. Luck, *Journal of Abnormal Psychology* 112, 61 (2003).
19. N. C. Andreasen, *Scale for the assessment of positive symptoms (SAPS)* (Iowa City: University of Iowa College of Medicine, 1984).

THE PERFORMANCE OF SPARSELY-CONNECTED 2D ASSOCIATIVE MEMORY MODELS WITH NON-RANDOM IMAGES

LEE CALCRAFT, ROD ADAMS and NEIL DAVEY

School of Computer Science, University of Hertfordshire
College Lane, Hatfield, Herts AL10 9AB, U.K.

A sparsely connected associative memory model is built with small-world connectivity, and trained on both random, and real-world image sets. It is found that pattern recall using real-world images can vary significantly from that of random images, and that the relationship between network wiring strategy and performance changes dramatically when training sets consist of certain types of real-world image.

1. Introduction

In any physically realised sparsely connected neural network such as the cortex, the structure of the interconnections between the component neurons will be critical to the functionality of the system [1]. And in modelling such a system it is found that the pattern-completion performance of a network, when used as an associative memory, is strongly influenced by the connection strategy employed in creating it [2, 3]. In this respect, locally-connected networks, in which the input of each node is connected to its k nearest neighbours, perform poorly, while randomly-connected networks perform the best [4].

a
b
c
d

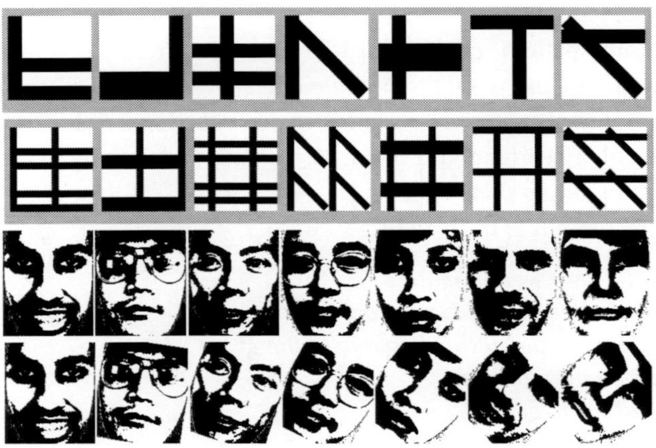

Figure 1. Samples from four of the image sets used: a. Shapes, b. Tiled shapes, c. Faces [5], d. Rotated faces. The image size used in all cases was 60 x 60 pixels.

These results are based on the use of randomly generated training patterns. If instead of using random pattern sets we build our input patterns from real-world images with more naturalistic distributions of pixels – see Figure 1, where all light coloured pixels are represented by a zero, and all dark pixels by a one, we obtain interesting results. When these real-world images are used to train an associative memory, the relationship between connection strategy and performance is dramatically altered in a way which is dependent on the type of pattern set used. In some cases randomly-connected networks can give poor results with naturalistic images, while the best performance occurs in networks built with a combination of local and distal connections. In the present work we explore this phenomenon.

2. Network Dynamics and Training

Each unit in our networks is a simple, bipolar, threshold device, summing its net input and firing deterministically. The net input, or *local field*, of a unit, is given by: $h_i = \sum_{j \neq i} w_{ij} S_j$ where $\mathbf{S}$ (± 1) is the current state and w_{ij} is the weight on the connection from unit j to unit i. The dynamics of the network is given by the standard update:

$$S_i' = \begin{cases} 1 & \text{if } h_i > 0 \\ -1 & \text{if } h_i < 0 \\ S_i & \text{if } h_i = 0 \end{cases} \quad \text{where } S_i' \text{ is the new state of } S_i$$

Unit states may be updated synchronously or asynchronously. Here we use asynchronous, random order updates.

If a training pattern, ξ^μ, is one of the fixed points of the network, then it is successfully stored and is said to be *a fundamental memory*. Given a training set $\{\xi^\mu\}$, the training algorithm is designed to drive the local fields of each unit the correct side of a learning threshold, T, for all the training patterns. This is equivalent to requiring that $\forall i, \mu \;\; h_i^\mu \xi_i^\mu \geq T$

So the learning rule is given by:

Begin with a zero weight matrix
Repeat until all local fields are correct
Set the state of the network to one of the ξ^μ
For each unit, i, in turn
Calculate $h_i^p \xi_i^p$.
If this is less than T then change the weights on connections into unit i according to:

$$\forall j \neq i \quad w'_{ij} = w_{ij} + C_{ij}\frac{\xi_i^p \xi_j^p}{k} \quad \text{where } \{C_{ij}\} \text{ is the connection matrix}$$

The form of the update is such that changes are only made on the weights that are actually present in the connectivity matrix $\{C_{ij}\}$ (where $C_{ij} = 1$ if w_{ij} is present, and 0 otherwise), and that the learning rate is inversely proportional to the number of connections per unit, k. Earlier work has established that a learning threshold $T = 10$ gives good results [6], and this is used throughout. Additionally we make no requirement that the connectivity matrix $\{C_{ij}\}$ should be symmetrical.

3. Measuring Performance

The ability to store patterns is not the only functional requirement of an associative memory: fundamental memories should also act as *attractors* in the state space of the dynamic system resulting from the recurrent connectivity of the network, so that pattern correction can take place.

To measure this we use the *Effective Capacity* of the network, *EC* [3]. The Effective Capacity of a network is a measure of the maximum number of patterns that can be stored in the network with *reasonable* pattern correction still taking place. We take a fairly arbitrary definition of *reasonable* as correcting the addition of 60% noise to within an overlap of 95% with the original fundamental memory. Varying these figures gives differing values for *EC* but the values with these settings are robust for comparison purposes. For large fully-connected networks the *EC* value is proportional to *N*, the total number of nodes in the network, and has a value of approximately 0.1 of the maximum theoretical capacity of the network. For large sparse locally-connected networks, *EC* is proportional to the number of connections per node, with the constant of proportionality dependent upon the actual connection matrix *C*.

The Effective Capacity of a particular network is determined as follows:

Initialise the number of patterns, P, to 0
Repeat
    Increment P
    Create a training set of P random patterns
    Train the network
    For each pattern in the training set
        Degrade the pattern randomly by adding 60% noise
        With this noisy pattern as the initial state, allow the network to converge
        Calculate the overlap of the final network state with the original pattern
    EndFor
    Calculate the mean pattern overlap over all final states
Until the mean pattern overlap is less than 95%

The Effective Capacity is P-1.

For the purposes of the present paper, our measurements are based on a more stringent variant of Effective Capacity, EC-100, which requires pattern completion to be 100% correct after the addition of 60% noise, rather than 95% correct. We are using this variant because in the case of non-random images, different images within the image set may on occasion have considerable overlap, and the 95% requirement may not always be sufficient to distinguish between similar completed patterns.

4. Network Topology

The networks discussed here are based largely on two-dimensional lattices of N nodes with periodic boundary conditions, though some phenomena have been verified using one-dimensional networks. The 1D networks take the form of a ring, and the 2D implementations that of a torus, thus avoiding boundary conditions. The networks are sparse, in which the input of each node is connected to a relatively small, but fixed number, k, of other nodes. The main 2D networks examined consist of 3600 nodes arranged in a 60 x 60 array, with 40 afferent (incoming) connections per node. The 1D networks consist of 1600 nodes, again with 40 connections per node. All references to spacing refer to the distance between nodes around the ring in the case of the 1D network, or across the surface of the torus in the 2D case (see Figure 2).

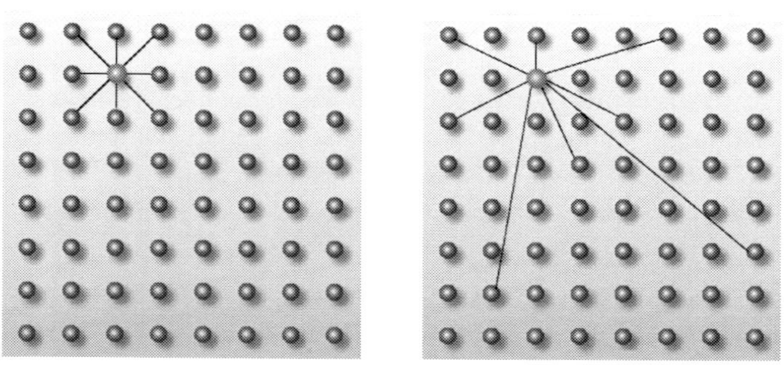

Figure 2. Two-dimensional sparsely-connected network with 64 nodes, and 8 connections per node, illustrating the connections to a single node: Left, locally-connected, right, after rewiring. Note that opposite edges are joined to form a toroidal surface.

It has been established for a 1D network trained with random patterns that purely local connectivity results in networks with low wiring length, but with poor pattern-completion performance, while randomly-connected networks perform well, but have high wiring costs [2, 4]. In searching for a compromise between these two extremes we will use the network connection strategy introduced by Watts and Strogatz [7] for generating small-world networks. This was applied to a one-dimensional associative memory by Bohland and Minai [4], and subsequently by Davey et al [8]. A locally-connected network is set up, and a fraction of the connections to each node is rewired to other randomly-selected nodes. By varying the proportion of connections which are rewired they were able to move incrementally between a network with local-only connections, and one whose connections were completely random.

5. Background and Motivation

In applying the small world principles of connectivity to associative memory models, Bohland and Minai [4] demonstrated that when progressively rewiring a one-dimensional locally connected network, its performance would improve as rewiring progressed, until a point was reached beyond which little or no further improvement would occur. In their network of 1000 nodes, this point was reached when 40% of local connections had been rewired. Repeating this experiment we found similar results (see Figure 3), though the point at which further increases in rewiring brought no further rewards ranged from 30-60% rewiring, depending on network size and sparsity of connections [3].

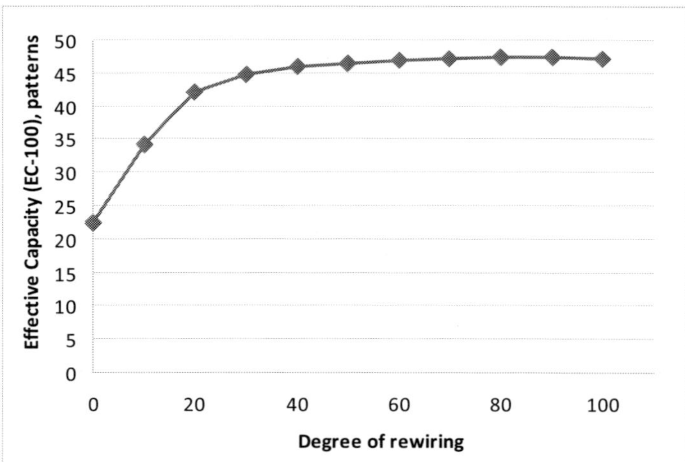

Figure 3. The Effective Capacity (EC-100) of a 1D network of 1000 units, with 150 connections per node, as a function of the degree of rewiring of the network, averaged over 100 runs. Performance improves as rewiring proceeds up to the point where the network is rewired by around 40%, after which further rewiring has little effect. This follows the experiment of Bholand and Minai [4], though we use a different measure of performance here.

The above work used training sets of uncorrelated random patterns. Turvey et al. [9] explored the performance of associative memory models built with local and with random connectivity, and tested with two naturalistic pattern sets. They measured performance by counting the number of nodes that failed to train under heavy pattern loadings, and found that locally connected networks performed better than networks with random connections. By way of explanation they posited that the locally connected network was better able to 'exploit the local correlation present in simple bitmap images'.

Our intention in the present work is to compare the performance of different pattern sets and different connection strategies, highlighting the types of images and connection strategies which yield the best performance. Our performance indicator will be EC-100, which measures pattern recall under noisy conditions, rather than simply measuring ability to train.

6. Results and Discussion

Our main experiments compare performance using three types of pattern sets: the first is based on purely random patterns (random arrangements of *on* and *off* pixels). The second is a set of 132 hand-generated shape patterns, illustrated in Figure 1a. These were designed as bold patterns with large contiguous areas of *on* or *off* pixels, with low correlation between individual patterns across the set. In contrast to this artificially created shapes set, the third set consisted of 40 digitised faces [5], each of a different individual, as illustrated in Figure 1c. The network under test has 3600 nodes, configured as a 60 x 60 two-dimensional associative memory. It is sparsely connected with 40 afferent connections per node.

In the first experiment the network initially has local-only connections. After performance measurements have been made by measuring EC-100, the network is rebuilt, but now 10% of connections are made to random locations. Measurements are again made, and the procedure is repeated in steps of 10% until rewiring reaches 100%. The results appear in Figure 4. The random images perform as expected, with a relatively low Effective Capacity (EC-100) of 6 when connections are purely local. This improves as the network is rewired, and once rewiring has reached around 60%, there is little further improvement in performance.

The shapes set, by contrast, continues to improve in performance as the network is rewired, peaking at a rewiring of 80% with an unexpectedly high Effective Capacity (EC-100) of 46. Pattern recall then drops dramatically, reaching an EC-100 of around 10 by the point at which the network is fully rewired (*i.e.* connectivity is random). The faces set shows a very different profile, increasing more slowly even than the random image set, and never reaching an EC-100 of more than about 15. We will discuss these results in more detail below, but before that we will briefly seek to verify the unexpected peak obtained with the shapes pattern set.

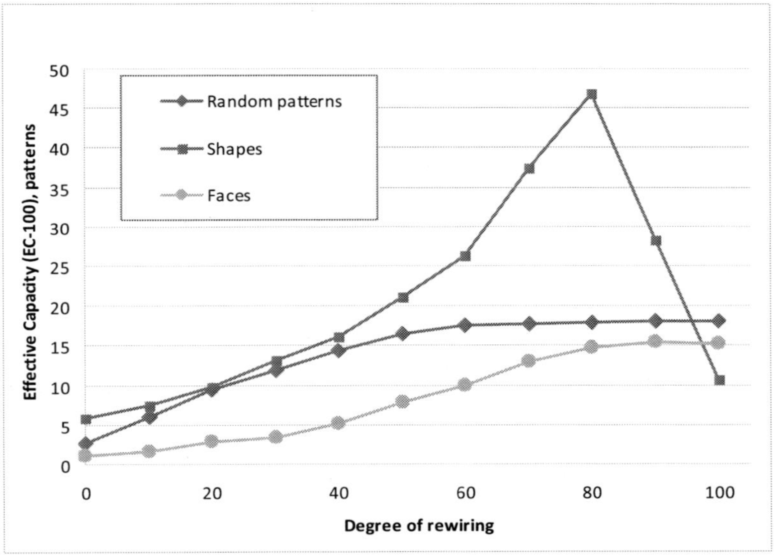

Figure 4. Effective Capacity (EC-100) as a function of the degree of rewirng of the network for the shapes, faces and random image sets. The two-dimensional network consists of 3600 nodes, with 40 connections per node. Results are averages over 30 runs.

6.1. *Verification*

Because of the unexpected nature of the peak with the shapes image set, we ran tests using a 1D network, measuring the mean radius of the basins of attraction [10]. Patterns were created with clustered sets of similar pixels around a ring. A network of 1600 units, each with 40 connections was used for this test. Our verification tests thus used a network of different size and dimensionality, a different means of measuring performance, and a different pattern set to the original experiment. The results appear in Figure 5. The degrees of clustering refer to the probability that adjacent pixels around the one-dimensional ring will be in the same state as each other (pixels can either be in an *on* or *off* state).

Although *R* measures the mean minimum radius of the basins of attraction, rather than the number of patterns which can be recalled by the network under noisy conditions, we obtain broadly similar results. With highly grouped patterns (cluster probability 0.95), the network performs slightly less well than with random patterns up to the point of 80% rewiring. The cluster pattern performance then peaks above that of the random patterns, and then falls back again at 100% rewiring in a similar way to that seen with the shapes image set in Figure 4 above. With lesser degrees of clustering the effect is less marked. This suggests that the unexpected peak in Figure 4 may be caused in a similar way.

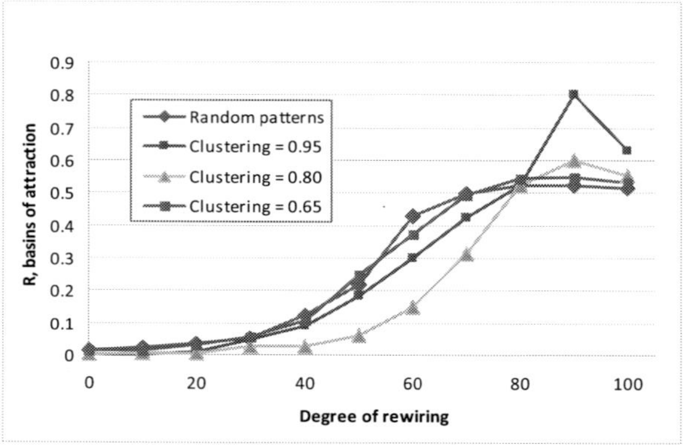

Figure 5. Mean radius of the basins of attraction as a function of the degree of rewiring of the network for random patterns, and patterns with varying degrees of pixel clustering, or local correlation, (a clustering of 0.95 means that there is a 95% chance that any two adjacent pixels will be of the same value - pixels may be *on* or *off*). The one-dimensional network consists of 1600 nodes, with 40 connections per node. The network was trained on 22 patterns, and the results averaged over 10 runs.

6.2. *How do different pattern sets affect memory recall?*

The fact that in the 1D tests, simply increasing the clustering of a set of random patterns produces a similar recall profile to that of the shapes pattern set in the 2D network (*cf* Figures 4 and 5) seems to indicate that the performance of

Table 1. Correlation and coherence of images within an image set for five different image sets. Correlation is the mean pixel-by-pixel correlation between similarly-positioned pairs of pixels across the image set. Coherence is the mean correlation between each pixel and its 8 nearest neighbours averaged across the image set.

Image type	Correlation	Coherence
Shapes	0.04	0.92
Shapes tiled	0.06	0.82
Faces	0.26	0.74
Faces rotated	0.10	0.76
Random	0.00	0.00

the 2D shapes set is due, at least in part, to the grouping or clustering of pixels in the image set. In order to confirm this, we ran a test where the shapes pattern set was tiled, so that each image was created by placing four smaller versions of the same shape adjacent to each other (see Figure 1b). The degree of clustering, or coherence, in each image of this image set would thus be less than that in the un-tiled shapes set. See Table 1, which shows values for the correlation between images in the image set, and the degree of coherence. This latter is simply the mean correlation between the value of each pixel in an image, and its 8 nearest neighbors. This is averaged over the pattern set. The tiled shapes set has a coherence of 0.82 compared to 0.92 for the non-tiled shapes set.

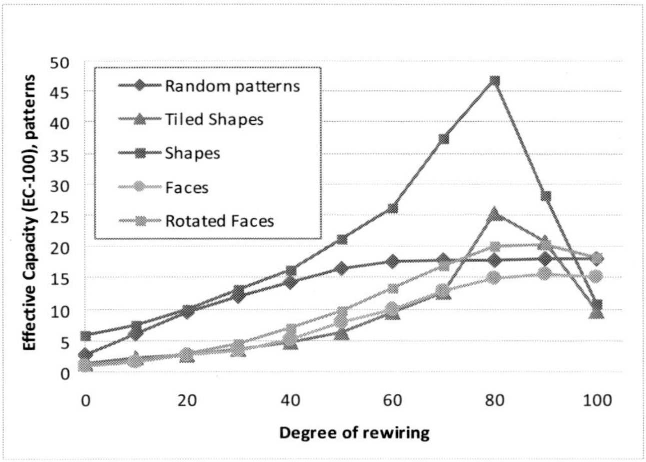

Figure 6. Effective Capaciy (EC-100) as a function of the degree of rewiring of the network for the shapes, tiled shapes, faces, rotated faces and random image sets. The two-dimensional network consists of 3600 nodes, with 40 connections per node. Results are averages over 30 runs.

The results for the simulation appear in Figure 6. As may be seen, the tiled shapes pattern set still has a peak at 80% rewiring, but the number of patterns recalled at each stage of rewiring is considerably less than that of the non-tiled shapes set. This adds support to the notion that the grouping or clustering of similar-valued pixels is a factor in the high performance of the shapes set.

We now turn our attention to the faces pattern set. This pattern set displays a greater degree of pixel clustering than the random images, yet performs significantly worse. Looking at the faces set, it can be seen that there is a certain degree of similarity between images within the set. The images tend to have groupings of pixels in similar areas, for example at the eyes, the noses and the mouths. This is borne out by the value of 0.26 for the correlation between images within the set (see Table 1). It is likely that the similar placing of areas of activity over the image set may make recall more difficult. To test this hypothesis, we created a new set of faces (see Figure 1d) in which each of the 40 faces in the set was rotated by a different amount (images were rotated in steps of 9 degrees to cover the full 360 degree range). In this way the coherence within each image remains largely unchanged, but the overlapping of one image with another is significantly reduced (correlation was reduced to 0.10 - see Table 1).

Figure 6 shows the results of the Effective Capacity run. Rotating the faces results in an improved performance, and a peak at around 80-90% rewiring which exceeds the best performance of the random image set. This supports the view that the relatively poor performance of the face set was due to the large overlap of the images within the set.

We now turn our attention to one final feature of the plots in Figures 4 - 6: the drop in performance as rewiring approaches 100%. This can be seen for all pattern sets except the random patterns. This is likely to be caused by the loss of local connectivity in the network at 100% rewiring. Once the network is fully rewired, there is only a very small proportion of local connections (bearing in mind that each node has only 40 connections, and that they will be distributed across the whole 3600 node network), so that when added noise causes local problems for a particular node, it no longer has the support of other local connections for correction purposes.

7. Conclusion

We have explored the performance of sparsely connected two-dimensional associative memories using different connection strategies, and different types of image sets. We found that a set of images containing bold shapes performed particularly well. With a progressively rewired network rewired by 80%, nearly three times as many shapes images could be recalled than random images. Once the shapes images were tiled so that each image consisted of four copies of a given shape, performance dropped considerably, suggesting that high pixel coherence (the grouping of large numbers of like pixels in an image) in the images of the training set improves pattern recall.

With a set of images consisting of digitised human faces, performance was considerably worse than that of the shapes set, and even worse than that recorded for completely random images. But once the facial images were each rotated by a different amount, in order to reduce the similarity between them, performance considerably improved. On the basis of this and other tests, we identified two factors affecting pattern correction ability: image correlation and image coherence. For good associative memory performance it is important that images in the training set should have a relatively low value of correlation, each being sufficiently different from each other. On the other hand, image coherence should be high: each image should have large contiguous areas of *on* or *off* pixels. The best two performers of our image sets were the shapes set and the rotated faces. Both have relatively low correlation and high coherence. The worst performers had low coherence (the random set), or high correlation (the faces set). It may be interesting to carry out similar tests on human subjects, studying the learning and recall of simple patterns (rather than faces, which are handled in a special way), where it seems possible that broadly similar results might be found, with high image coherence and low correlation between images giving rise to the best recall rates.

References

1. O. Sporns and J. D. Zwi, Neuroinformatics **2**, 145 (2004).
2. L. Calcraft, R. Adams, and N. Davey, Proceedings of ESANN 2006: 14th European Symposium on Artificial Neural Networks. Advances in Computational Intelligence and Learning, 617 (2006).
3. L. Calcraft, R. Adams, and N. Davey, Connection Science **19** (2007).
4. J. Bohland and A. Minai, Neurocomputing **38-40**, 489 (2001).
5. P. J. Phillips, H. Wechsler, J. Huang, et al., Image and Vision Computing **16**, 295 (1998).
6. N. Davey, S. P. Hunt, and R. G. Adams, Neurocomputing **62**, 459 (2004).
7. D. Watts and S. Strogatz, Nature **393**, 440 (1998).
8. N. Davey, B. Christianson, and R. Adams, Proceedings of the IEEE International Joint Conference on Neural Networks (2004).
9. S. P. Turvey, S. P. Hunt, R. J. Frank, et al., Proceedings of The Third IASTED International Conference on Artificial Intelligence and Applications (2003).
10. I. Kanter and H. Sompolinsky, Physical Review A **35**, 380 (1987).

Categorisation

IMAGE CATEGORIZATION AND RETRIEVAL

ANDRZEJ WICHERT

IST - Technical University of Lisboa,
2780 990 Porto Salvo, Portugal
andreas.wichert@tagus.ist.utl.pt
web.tagus.ist.utl.pt/~andreas.wichert/

Hubel and Wiesel's discoveries inspired several hierarchical models for pattern and image categorization. During the hierarchical categorization the neural network gradually reduces the information from the input layer through the output layer. The units of the output layer represent the categories .Local features are integrated into more global features in sequential transformations. In our proposed model the hierarchical neural network performs beside the categorization a similarity-based image or pattern retrieval by a backward operation. During similarity-based image retrieval, the search starts from the images represented by global features. In this representation, the set of all possible similar images is determined. In the next stage, additional information corresponding to the representation of more local feature is used to reduce this set represented by some triggered units. This procedure is repeated until the similar images can be determined.

Keywords: CBIR, Clustering, Hierarchical neural networks, Neocognitron, Visual System

1. Introduction

Hubel and Wiesel discovered that the mammalian visual system has a hierarchical structure.[1] This finding inspired the design of artificial hierarchical neural networks. It seems that the visual system is used as well for image retrieval from the memory during mental imagery.[2,3] Mental imagery is the mental invention or re-creation of an experience that at least in some respects resembles the experience of actually perceiving an object in the absence of direct sensory stimulation.[2] The imagery is formed through the construction of the represented object by the associative memory. The process involves information flow from the associative memory to and the visual cortex. During image retrieval in the hierarchical visual system the information flows in the opposite direction as in image recognition. We will examine the resulting consequences for such an inverse information flow.

2. Image Similarity

We examine gray images of fixed size 128×96 in which each gray level is represented by 8 bits. The image database consists of 1000 images with photos of landscapes and people, with several outliers consisting of drawings of dinosaurs or photos of flowers.[4] All images are represented by vectors of dimension 12288 each in which component has a value between 0 and 255. Two images $\vec{x}$ and $\vec{y}$ are similar if their Euclidian distance is smaller or equal to ϵ, $d(\vec{x}, \vec{y}) \leq \epsilon$. The result of a range query computed by this method is a set of images that have spatial gray characteristics that are similar to the query image. Let DB be a database of s gray images $\vec{x}^{(i)}$ represented by vectors of dimension m in which the index i is an explicit key identifying each image,

$$\{\vec{x}^{(i)} \in DB | i \in \{1..s\}\}. \tag{1}$$

The set DB can be ordered according to a given image $\vec{y}$ using an Euclidian distance function d. This is done by a monotone increasing sequence corresponding to the increasing distance of $\vec{y}$ to $\vec{x}^{(i)}$ with an explicit key that identifies each image indicated by the index i,

$$d[y]_n := \{d(x^{(i_n)}, y)_n \mid \forall n \in \{1..s\}, \forall i_n \in \{1..s\} : d(x^{(i_1)}, y)_1 \leq d(x^{(i_2)}, y)_2$$
$$\leq ... \leq d(x^{(i_n)}, y)_n .... \leq d(x^{(i_s)}, y)_s\} \tag{2}$$

if $\vec{y} \in DB$, then $d[y]_1 := 0$. The set of similar image in correspondence to $\vec{y}$, $DB[y]_\epsilon$, is the subset of DB, $DB[y]_\epsilon \subseteq DB$ with size $\sigma = |DB[y]_\epsilon|$, $\sigma \leq s$:

$$DB[y]_\epsilon := \{x^{(i)} \in DB \mid d[y]_n = d(x^{(i)}, y) \leq \epsilon\}. \tag{3}$$

In Figure 1 we see the ordered image test database DB for a given image $\vec{y}$ using the Euclidian distance function d.

3. Clustering

Lets suppose our hierarchical structure of the visual system has just one level. Such a structure can be simply modeled by a clustering algorithm, as for example k-means. We group the images into clusters represented by the cluster centers c_j. After the clustering cluster centers $c_1, c_2, c_3, ..., c_k$ with clusters $C_1, C_2, C_3, ..., C_k$ are present with:

$$C_j = \{x | d(x, c_j) = \min_i d(x, c_i)\} \tag{4}$$

$$c_j = \{\frac{1}{|C_j|} \sum_{x \in C_j} x\}. \tag{5}$$

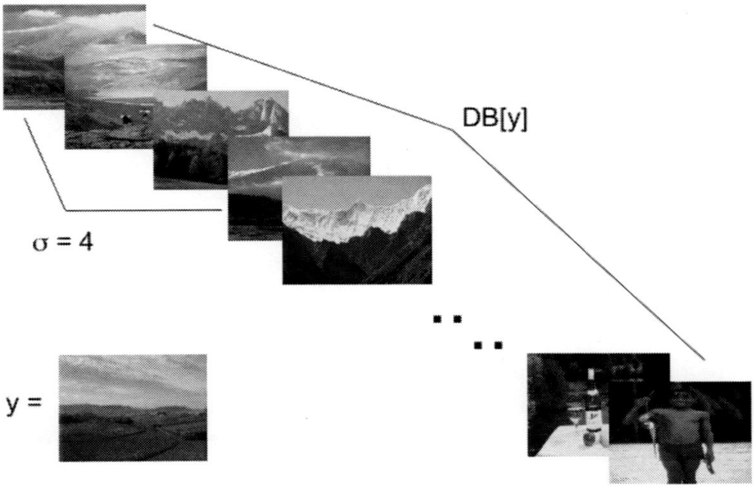

Fig. 1. Ordered image test database DB a given image $\vec{y}$ using the Euclidian distance function d. The size of the set of similar objects in correspondence to $\vec{y}$ is $4 = \sigma = |DB[y]_\epsilon$. The top level image is the most similar corresponding to the distance $d[y]_1$. The bottom image is the most dissimilar corresponding to $d[y]_s$.

During the categorization task to a given input image y the most similar cluster center c_i is determined representing the category. Does this simple model also work for image retrieval? Could we take advantage of the the grouping of the images into clusters? The idea would be to determine the most similar cluster center c_i which represents the most similar category. In the next step we would search for the most similar images $DB[y]_\epsilon$ only in this cluster C_i. By doing so we could save some considerable computation. Suppose $s = \min_i d(y, c_i)$ is the distance to the closest cluster center and r_{max} the maximal radius of all the clusters. Only if $s \geq \epsilon \geq r_{max}$ we are guaranteed to determine $DB[y]_\epsilon$. Otherwise we have to analyze other clusters as well. When a cluster with a minimum distance s was determined, we know that the images in this cluster have the distance between $s + r_{max}$ and $s - r_{max}$. Because of that we have to analyze additionally all the clusters with $\{\forall i | d(y, c_i) < (s +_r max)\}$. It means that in the worst case we have to analyze all the clusters. The worst case is present when the dimension of the images is high (like the size of an image $128 \times 96 = 12288$). High dimensional spaces (like for example dimensions > 100) have negative implications on the number of clusters we have to analyze. These negative effects are named as the "curse of dimensionality." Most problems arise from the fact that the volume of a sphere with the constant radius grows exponentially with increasing dimension. A nearest-neighbor query in a high dimensional space corresponds to a hyper-sphere with a huge radius which is mostly larger than the extension of the data space in most dimensions.[5] Based on the known GEMINI indexing approach and the hierarchical neural network architecture we will propose a solution to this problem.

4. GEMINI

The idea behind the generic multimedia indexing (GEMINI)[6,7] approaches is to find a feature extraction function that maps the high dimensional objects into a low dimensional space. In this low dimensional space, a so-called 'quick-and-dirty' test can discard the non-qualifying objects. Objects that are very dissimilar in the feature space are expected to be very dissimilar in the original space as well. Ideally, the feature map should preserve the exact distances. However, if the distances in the feature space are always smaller or equal than the distances in the original space, a bound which is valid in both spaces can be determined. The distance of similar objects is smaller or equal to ϵ in the original space and, consequently, it is smaller or equal to ϵ in the feature space as well. No object in the feature space will be missed (false dismissals) in the feature space. However, there will be some objects that are not similar in the original space (false hints/alarms). That means that we are guaranteed to have selected all the objects we wanted plus some additional false hits in the feature space. In the second step, false hits have to be filtered from the set of the selected objects through comparison in the original space.

The size of the collection in the feature space depends on ϵ and the proportion between both spaces may reach the size of the entire database if the feature space is not carefully chosen. The lemma which guarantees that no objects will be missed in the feature space is called the "lower bounding lemma and is expressed mathematically as follows;

Lemma 4.1. *Let O_1 and O_2 be two objects; $F()$, the mapping of objects into f dimensional space should satisfy the following formula for all objects, where d is a distance function in the original space and $d_{feature}$, in the feature space:*

$$d_{feature}(F(O_1), F(O_2)) \leq d(O_1, O_2). \tag{6}$$

In the first step, in the GEMINI approach, the distance function has to be defined. The second step consists in finding the feature extraction function $F()$ that satisfies the bounding lemma and determining it. $F()$ has to capture most of the characteristics of the objects in a low dimensional feature space. In most cases, the distance functions used in the original space and in the feature space are equal.

All images of the DB are mapped with $F()$, the mapping which satisfies the lower bounding lemma in f dimensional feature space,[8]

$$\{F(\vec{x})^{(i)} \in F(DB) | i \in \{1..s\}\}. \tag{7}$$

The set $F(DB)$ can be ordered in relation to a given image $F(\vec{y})$ and a distance function $d_{feature}$.

This is done by a monotone increasing sequence corresponding to the increasing distance of $F(\vec{y})$ to $F(\vec{x}^{(i)})$, with an explicit key identifying each object indicated by the index i,

$$d[F(y)])_n := \{d_{feature}(F(x^{(i)}), F(y)) \mid$$

$$\forall n \in \{1..s\} : d[F(y)]_n \leq d[F(y)]_s\} \tag{8}$$

The set of similar images in correspondence to $F(\vec{y})$, $F(DB[y])_\epsilon$ is the subset of $F(DB)$, $F(DB[y])_\epsilon \subseteq F(DB)$ with size $\hat{F}(\sigma) := |F(DB[y])_\epsilon|$, $\sigma \leq \hat{F}(\sigma) \leq s$:

$$F(DB[y])_\epsilon := \{F(x)_n^{(i)} \in F(DB) \mid d[F(y)]_n =$$

$$= d_{feature}(F(x)^{(i)}, F(y)) \leq \epsilon\}. \tag{9}$$

To determine $DB[y]_\epsilon$ through linear search, we need $s \cdot m$ computing steps, assuming that computation of distance between two m-dimensional vectors requires m computing steps. To determine $DB[y]_\epsilon$ when $F(DB[y])_\epsilon$ is present, we need $\hat{F}(\sigma) \cdot m$ steps; the false hits are separated from the selected objects through comparison in the original space. If no metric tree is used to index the feature space, the savings used result from the size of $F(DB[y])_\epsilon$ in proportion to the dimensions of both spaces $\frac{f}{m}$.

Corollary 4.1. *The computing time of $DB[y]_\epsilon$ is saved comparatively to linear matching in the original space if:*

$$s \cdot m > \hat{F}(\sigma) \cdot m + s \cdot f \tag{10}$$

$$\left\lfloor s \cdot (1 - \frac{f}{m}) \right\rfloor > \hat{F}(\sigma). \tag{11}$$

5. Hierarchical Neural Networks

Lets suppose our hierarchical structure of the visual system has several levels. Neocognitron[9–11] was one of the first of models of the visual system with several layers. However, Neocognitron has been referred to as being complex in structure and parametrization.[12] It is one of the most complicated neural networks. A less complex description was proposed in.[13–15] In our model we omit the shift invariance. The classification of our model begins with the input image of the first layer. The input image is tiled with a squared mask M of size $i \times i$ in which a corresponding class is determined. The class is determined through the use of the elements in each squared mask. Each sub-pattern in a mask is replaced by a number which indicates a corresponding class. Each mask corresponds to a $i \times i$ dimensional vector. The corresponding classes are learned by a simple clustering algorithm like k-means. However, if k-means is to be used, the number of classes k has to be determined through experiments. During the classification of a layer, the class which is most similar to each sub-pattern is determined. This is done by finding the cluster center (representing the class) which is most similar to the sub-pattern. In the corresponding layers, the process is repeated. Each stage acts as a filter which reduces the information. The reduced information is then passed to a simple classifier of the last layer which yields a classification for the input pattern.[15]

5.1. *Image retrieval by hierarchical neural networks*

During similarity-based image retrieval, the search starts from the images represented by global features. In this representation, the set of all possible similar images is determined. In the next stage, additional information corresponding to the representation of more local features is used to reduce this set represented by some triggered units. This procedure is repeated until the similar images can be determined. In our simplified model of the Neocognitron we have to distinguish between two different representations of the image during the hierarchical classification. The class space CU and the re-projection space RU. The class space of a layer is the representation sub-pattern in a mask by a number which indicates a corresponding class. The dimension of a class space is dependent on the size of the mask and the hierarchy. The re-projection space RU has the same dimension as the input image, it is the representation of the image by the corresponding features by a backward projection. Neocognitron uses only the class space.

The output of a layer is the class space which is the input of the following layer.

During image retrieval the space RU defines the similarity between the images and space CU the reduced representation. The image in the space RU is represented by the tiled masks M. Suppose a hierarchical neural network with one layer performs a reduction operation into the space CU. An image of the size 128×96 is tiled by 2×2 masks (see Figure 2). 256 different masks are used. The representation of this image in the class space CU is reduced to the size 64×48. To compute the distance between two images

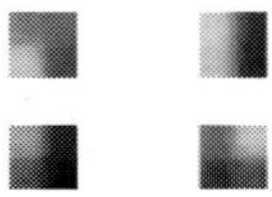

Fig. 2. Examples of two times two dimensional masks.

represented in space RU only 64×48 components need to be compared. To preform this computation we compute the distances between the 256 different masks and represent them in a table of the size 256×256. This table is later used for the computation of the Euclidian distances between two images in the space RU. We do not need to compute the distance by pixels. Instead we use the table with the pre computed values for each mask.

Generally each mask corresponds to a $i \times i$ dimensional vector learned by a simple clustering algorithm like k-means. That means that in the worst case we had to subtract r_{max} for each mask in the image before computing the Euclidian distance function. If we compute the Euclidian distance between all images and compare it to the Euclidian distance between images represented in the space RU, we find that the corresponding value is much lower. We can estimate the value by computing the Euclidian distance between a representative set of images and their representation in RU. We call the corresponding value *error* and define the following Equation. If O_1 and O_2 be two images; $RU()$ the representation in reprojection space RU, then

$$d^*(F(RU(O_1), RU(O_2)) := d(F(RU(O_1), RU(O_2)) - error$$
$$\leq d(O_1, O_2). \tag{12}$$

The Lemma 4.1 is valid. We can define a sequence of class spaces $CU_0, CU_1, CU_2, \ldots, CU_n$ with $CU_0 = RU_0$ the original space

$$dim(CU_0) > dim(CU_1) > dim(CU_2) \ldots > dim(CU_n).$$

The DB mapped by the first layer of the hierarchical neural network to RU_1 is indicated by $RU_1(DB)$. We introduce the following notation for the other hierarchies:

$$\{d[RU_k(y)]_n := \{d^*(RU_k(x^{(i)}), RU_k(y)) \ | $$

$$\forall n \in \{1..s\} : d^*[RU_k(y)]_n \leq d^*[RU_k(y)]_{n+1}\} \tag{13}$$

$$\{RU_k(DB[y])_\epsilon := \{RU_k(x)_n^{(i)} \in RU_k(DB) \ | $$

$$d[RU_k(y)]_n = d^*(RU_k(x)^{(i)}, RU_k(y)) \leq \epsilon\}, \tag{14}$$

with the size $RU_k(\sigma) = |RU_k(DB[y]_\epsilon)|$ and $RU_0(\sigma) < RU_1(\sigma) < \ldots < RU_{(n)}(\sigma) < s$.

Corollary 5.1. *Let be* $dim(RU_0) := m$, *the computing costs for image retrieval in a hierarchical neural network are*

$$\sum_{i=1}^{n} RU_i(\sigma) \cdot dim(CU_{(i-1)}) + s \cdot dim(CU_n). \tag{15}$$

5.2. *Class space as input space*

In our first experiment we implemented a two layered hierarchical model in which we used 256 masks M of size 2×2 . The masks were determined by k-means clustering. Each sub-pattern in a mask was replaced by a number which indicates a corresponding class. Because we used 256 classes we could represent them as gray values. By doing so we got a reduced representation of the image in the class space CU. From each reduced image we can reconstruct an image of the original size by a re-projection RU. We used a two layer hierarchical neural network which models the Neocognitron. However as we found out all the information about the original image is lost in the second layer. This is because the second layer uses the class space as the input, and the class space has no relation with the original space, the input space. Each sub-pattern in a mask is replaced by a number which indicates a corresponding class, and the number has no relation to the corresponding sub-pattern, see Figure 3.

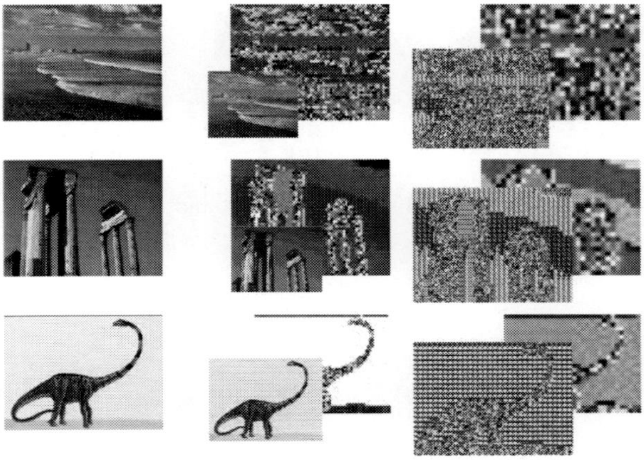

Fig. 3. A two layer hierarchical neural network which models a Neocognitron. On the left are the original images, following their representation in CU and their reprojection in RU (smaller images). The information about the original image is lost in the second layer, see the representation in RU_2.

The use of self organizing maps as suggested in[13] would reduce the error. However the resulting error can be large. A solution would be to use an orthogonal projection as described in the hierarchical linear subspace method.[8] An orthogonal projection would correspond to a mean value computation of the values inside the mask and seems less biologically plausible.

5.3. *Re-projection space as input space*

Instead of the class space we use the re-projection space of the proceding layer as the input for the following layer. To archive the computational saving we use masks of different size. In the first layer we use masks of the size 2×2, second 4×4 and the third 8×8, see Figure 2 and Figure 4. The masks are trained on the re-projection of the image for each layer. We used 256 different masks in each layer.

By the use of the re-projection space of each proceeding layer as the input of a layer minimal information about the image is lost, see Figure 5. The image is described with less accuracy, so that the following layers with bigger mask can learn the classes (without producing a big *error* value).

We determined the value of *error* by computing the Euclidian distance between all images and their representation in RU. Following *error* values were determined, for the first layer RU_1 the *error* is 300, for the second

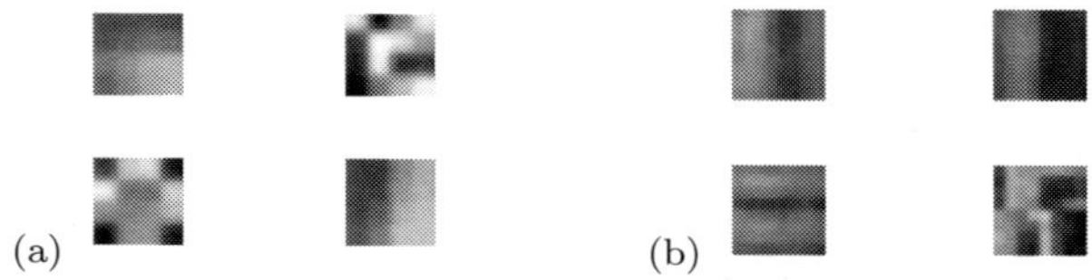

Fig. 4. Some masks of the second 4×4 and the third 8×8.

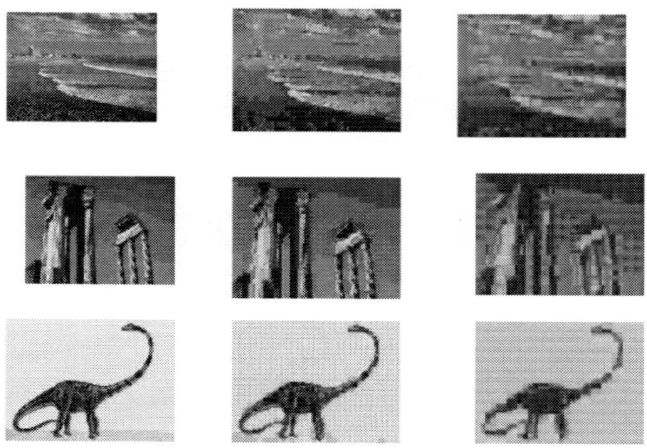

Fig. 5. Representation of the images of the Figure 3 in the space RU_1, RU_2 and RU_3 by three layered hierarchical neural network which uses as the input for each layer the reprojection space instead of the class space. By the use of the reprojection space of each proceeding layer as the input of a layer minimal information about the image is lost. The image is described with less accuracy.

layer RU_2 the *error* is 1050 and for layer three, RU_3 the *error* is 1997. To estimate ϵ and its dependency on $RU_k(\sigma)$, we define a mean sequence $d[RU_k(DB)]_n$ which describes the characteristics of an image database in our system:

$$d[RU_k(DB)]_n := \sum_{i=1}^{s} \frac{d[RU_k(x^{(i)})]_n}{s}. \tag{16}$$

In Figure 6 we see the corresponding characteristics.

To retrieve 24 most similar images the estimated ϵ value is 6623. We computed the mean value $RU_k(\overline{\sigma})$. For $\epsilon = 6623$ the values are $RU_0(\overline{\sigma}) = 24$, $RU_1(\overline{\sigma}) = 69$, $RU_2(\overline{\sigma}) = 228$, $RU_3(\overline{\sigma}) = 728$. To retrieve the 24 most similar images to a given query image of the image test database, the mean

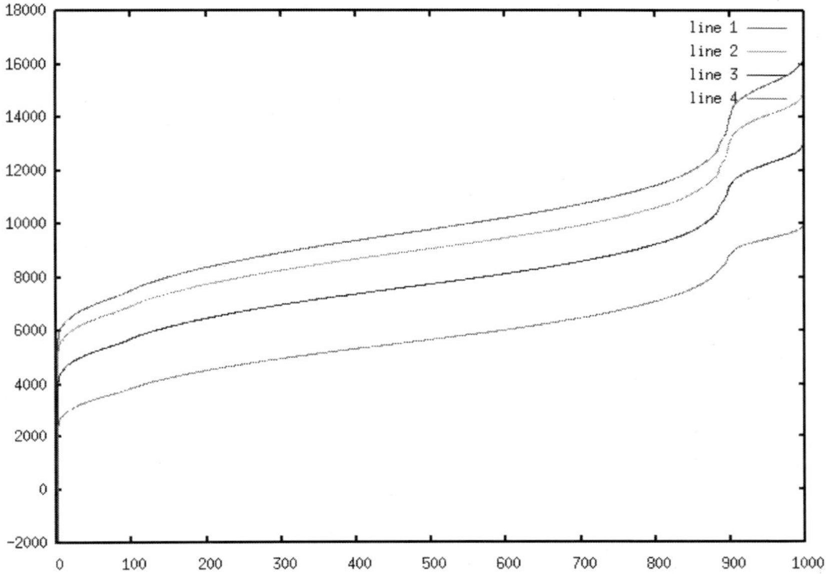

Fig. 6. Characteristics of $d[RU_0(DB)]_n$ = line 1, $d[RU_1(DB)]_n$ = line 2, $d[RU_2(DB)]_n$ = line 3 and $d[RU_3(DB)]_n$ = line 4.

computation costs are according to Equation 15:

$$(12288 \cdot 69 + 3072 \cdot 228 + 768 \cdot 728 + 192 \cdot 1000) = 2299392$$

which is 5.34 times less complex than a list matching which requires $12288 \cdot 1000$ operations.

6. Conclusion

We indicated a way how is the hierarchical structure of the visual system used during information retrieval. In our proposed model the hierarchical neural network performs beside the categorization a similarity-based image or pattern retrieval by a backward operation. Models like Neocognitron use the class space, a consequence is that the information about the original image is lost. This does not make much harm during the categorization if the number of images is small and simple (binary images). Instead of the class space hierarchical neuronal networks should use use the re-projection space of the preceding layer as the input for the following layer. We formulate the assumption that the visual system uses the same principle as our theoretical model. By doing so, less information is lost. During similarity-based image retrieval by such an hierarchical neuronal network, the search starts from the images represented by global features. In this representation, the set of all possible similar images is determined. In the next stage, additional information corresponding to the representation of more local features is used to reduce this set represented by some triggered units. The size of the receptive fields is proportional to the distance between the characteristics. This procedure is repeated until the similar images can be determined. The mean computation costs of 24 most similar images which should be retrieved were up to 5.34 times better compared to a simple list matching.

References

1. D. H. Hubel, *Eye, Brain, and Vision* (Scientific Ammerican Library, Oxford, England, 1988).
2. S. M. Kosslyn, *Image and Brain, The Resolution of the Imagery Debate* (The MIT Press, 1994).
3. A. Wichert, J. D. Pereira and P. Carreira, *Neurocomputing* **71**, 2806 (2008).
4. J. Wang, J. Li and G. Wiederhold, *IEEE Transactions on Pattern Analysis and Machine Intelligence* **23**, 947 (2001).
5. C. Böhm, S. Berchtold and A. K. Kei, D., *ACM Computing Surveys* **33**, 322 (2001).
6. C. Faloutsos, R. Barber, M. Flickner, J. Hafner, W. Niblack, D. Petkovic and W. Equitz, *Journal of Intelligent Information Systems* **3**, 231 (1994).
7. C. Faloutsos, Modern information retrieval, in *Modern Information Retrieval*, eds. R. Baeza-Yates and B. Ribeiro-Neto (Addison-Wesley, 1999) pp. 345–365.
8. A. Wichert, *Journal of Intelligent Information Systems* **31**, 85 (2008).
9. K. Fukushima, *Biological Cybernetics* **20**, 121 (1975).
10. K. Fukushima, *Biol Cybern* **36**, 193 (1980).
11. K. Fukushima, *Neural Networks* **2**, 413 (1989).
12. D. Lovell, D. Simon and A. Tsoi, Improving the performance of the neocognitron, in *Fourth Australian Conference on Neural Networks*, 1993.
13. A. Wichert, MTCn-nets, in *Proceedings World Congres on Neural Networks*, (Lawrence Erlbaum, 1993).
14. C. Kemke and W. A., Hierarchical self-organizing feature maps for speech recognition, in *Proceedings World Congres on Neural Networks*, (Lawrence Erlbaum, 1993).
15. Ângelo Cardoso, Delay neocognitron, Master's thesis, Universidade Técnica de Lisboa (1997).

TOWARDS A COMPETITIVE LEARNING MODEL OF MIRROR EFFECTS IN YES/NO RECOGNITION MEMORY TESTS

K. C. DIETZ*, H. BOWMAN and J. C. VAN HOOFF

Centre for Cognitive Neuroscience and Cognitive Systems, University of Kent, Canterbury, CT2 7NF, UK
**E-mail: kcd5@kent.ac.uk*
www.kent.ac.uk

Manipulations of encoding strength and stimulus class can lead to a simultaneous increase in hits and decrease in false alarms for a given condition in a yes/no recognition memory test. Based on signal detection theory, the strength-based 'mirror effect' is thought to involve a shift in response criterion/threshold (Type I), whereas the stimulus class effect derives from a specific ordering of the memory strength signals for presented items (Type II). We implemented both suggested mechanisms in a simple, competitive feed-forward neural network model with a learning rule related to Bayesian inference. In a single-process approach to recognition, the underlying decision axis as well as the response criteria/thresholds were derived from network activation. Initial results replicated findings in the literature and are a first step towards a more neurally explicit model of mirror effects in recognition memory tests.

1. Introduction

The accommodation of mirror effects in recognition tests has long posed a puzzle for memory researchers and has caused them to revise their assumptions of the underlying decision process (for a review, see Ref. 1). In a typical verbal yes/no recognition test, a list of individual words is presented during a study phase. In a subsequent test phase, the studied old words are randomly interleaved with new, not previously presented, words. For each test item, participants have to give a response, indicating whether they think it is old ('yes' response) or new ('no' response). The resulting decision matrix contains four possible outcomes: hits ('yes' responses to old items), misses ('no' responses to old items), false alarms ('yes' responses to new items) and correct rejections ('no' responses to new items).

A mirror effect occurs when there are two conditions that differ in their ease of recognition, and the easier condition shows not only a higher hit rate than the harder condition, but (perhaps surprisingly) also a lower false alarm rate.[2] While the generality of this effect has been questioned (*e.g.*

Ref. 3), it is generally accepted as a 'regularity of recognition memory' (*e.g.* Ref. 4, p.177).

We introduce theories that explain which mechanisms may give rise to mirror effects, and describe a preliminary neural network model implementing these in a biologically plausible way.

2. Signal detection theory and the mirror effect

Conventionally, recognition decisions are analyzed from a signal detection perspective (for a detailed introduction, see Ref. 5). Two underlying factors are assumed: the strength of the memory signal elicited by a test item[a], and its relation to the placement of the participant's response criterion/threshold.

Memory signals for old and new items are represented as two Gaussian distributions of unequal variance.[6] The variance of the old distribution exceeds that of the new distribution, as it reflects the variability of learning in the study phase in addition to noise.[7] The distance between the means of the old and new distributions (in units of standard deviation) determines the ease of discrimination and is termed d'.

The criterion/threshold can be thought of as a single point along the strength-of-evidence axis. Test items whose memory signal exceeds this criterion/threshold value receive a 'yes' response, resulting in hits for old items and false alarms for new items. An optimal decision criterion/threshold maximizes correct responses and would be placed at the point of intersection of the old and new distributions.

Based on this signal detection framework, it is thought that two mechanisms can give rise to a mirror effect: shifts in the absolute placement of the response criterion/threshold along the strength-of-evidence axis (Type I) and changes in the underlying distributions (Type II).[8]

2.1. *Type I mirror effects*

Type I mirror effects (see Fig. 1) are usually observed for strength manipulations of otherwise identical stimulus materials.[9] For example, repeating half of the items in the study phase will lead to more hits and fewer false alarms compared to items presented only once.

[a]Whether the signal is based on a single continuous variable, combines a continuous with a dichotomous variable or involves a second independent process, is beyond the scope of this paper.

Repetition has long been shown to lead to more accurate and robust encoding (*e.g.* Ref. 10), so that the mean of the strong old condition (repeat presentation) tends to be located further along the decision axis (further to the right) than that of the weak old condition (single presentation). This is also reflected by a larger d' value in the strong condition.

Assuming the mean signal of the new distribution remains constant, participants have to shift their decision criterion/threshold upwards (to the right) to maintain an optimal response strategy. This criterion/threshold shift accounts for fewer false alarms in the strong condition, while the simultaneous upwards (to the right) movement of the old distribution explains the increased hit rate. Note that there is only a single new distribution in a Type I mirror effect.

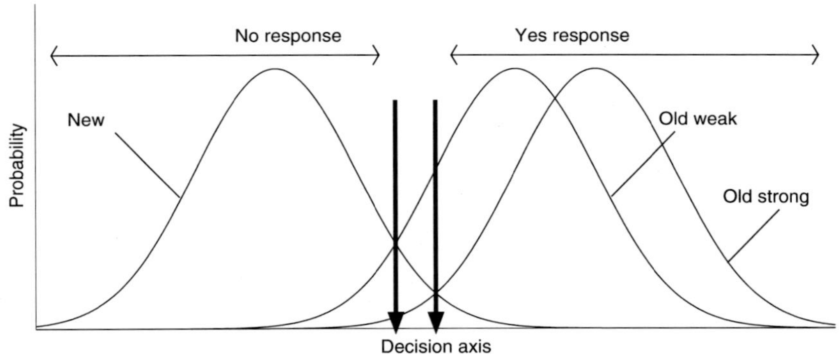

Fig. 1. Type I mirror effect: Underlying distributions and response criteria/thresholds.

2.2. *Type II mirror effects*

Type II mirror effects (see Fig. 1) are usually observed for manipulations of stimulus class, for example where high- and low frequency words are presented during both study and test. In this case, no criterion/threshold shift is observed even if explicit cues are provided about which items are of high- and low frequency;[8] yet the low frequency words consistently produce lower false alarm- and higher hit-rates. Given that low frequency words tend to have fewer definitions and are used in less varied contexts, they are thought to elicit a lower strength memory signal than high frequency items when new. By the same token, they are also more accurately encoded, explaining the advantage for recognition of low frequency old items.[11,12] It has also been proposed that due to their comparative 'novelty', low frequency words elicit increased attention and therefore more elaborative processing.[2,13] As a result of the increased separation of the old and new distribution for low-frequency words, d' is larger than for high-frequency words.

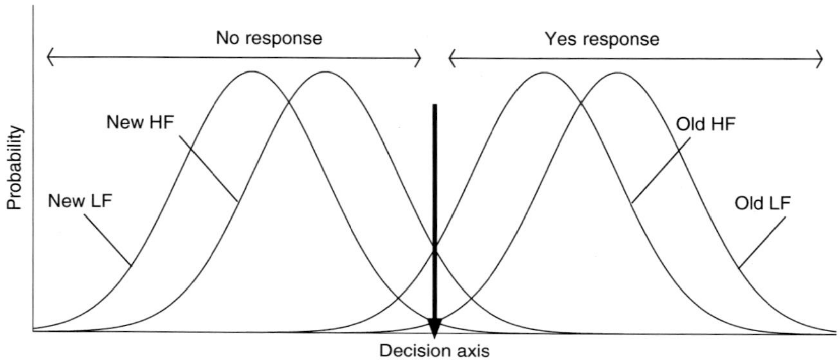

Fig. 2. Type II mirror effect: Underlying distributions and response criterion/threshold. LF = low frequency words, HF = high frequency words.

3. Our model

Although there are a large variety of single- and dual-process models of recognition (*e.g.* Ref. 14, 15, for a review, see Ref. 7), not all address mirror effects. Those that do are often single-process Bayesian models[9,12,16,17] (but see *e.g.* Ref. 18 for an exception). While theoretically pleasing, such Bayesian models largely ignore issues of neural implementation by using mathematical quantities without specifying how these might be calculated by the brain. In this paper, we present a first step towards a neurally more detailed model of the mirror effect in yes/no recognition memory tests.

We use McClelland and Chappell's subjective likelihood model[16] as a starting point, as it reproduces a wide variety of recognition memory phenomena. As in their model, each simulation run emulates a yes/no recognition test in which a participant is presented, one 'word' at a time, with a single, multi-item study list. Study items are learned, that is encoded into memory. In a subsequent test phase, (studied) old items are mixed with new, not previously presented, items. No learning occurs at test, but stored information about each presented item is retrieved and a yes/no decision is made according to its position relative to the response criterion/threshold.

We preserved a number of the implementation ideas but deviate from their key idea that the recognition decisions are based on a likelihood evaluation: in our model, the decision axis represents simple memory trace strength often termed 'familiarity'.

The model is a simple two-layer feed-forward network with a competitive Conditional Principal Component Analysis learning rule (CPCA, Ref. 19) using Winner-Takes-All (WTA). We use distributed representation of items on the input layer, but a localist representation on the output layer. Each item is a binary vector of 'features' (such as orthographic properties or semantic and contextual associations) across the 500 units of the input layer. Fifty randomly chosen features are active (1), all others are inactive (0), with the exception of low frequency items, which have one fewer active features. This reflects the previously mentioned property that low frequency items have fewer definitions and appear in fewer contexts. Each stimulus class comprises 30 such patterns. Initially, the output layer consists of 120 detectors. These are reduced to a maximum number of 60 (for 2 classes of 30 items) after learning, so that invariably, one detector comes to encode one item presented during the study phase (old items). The exact number is subject to constraints of the learning algorithm, which allows the possibility that a single detector comes to encode multiple items, but the initial weight settings keep the probability of this low.

In the study phase, items are presented in random order. In the simulation of a Type I mirror effect (strength-based), half of the items at study are presented twice whilst all other parameters are kept constant. In the simulation of a Type II mirror effect (frequency-based), half the presented patterns are of low frequency, with one less active input unit and a higher learning rate. The latter reflects the previously discussed increased attention to low frequency items. Weights between the input and output layer are initialized to random values in the range [0.45–0.55], which is the initial conditional probability that a given input unit is active for a specific detected item. When an input pattern is presented, competitive winner-takes-all learning takes place. The activation of each detector (denoted y_j) is calculated by feeding its summed, weighted and normalized net input (denoted η_j, Eq. 1) through a sigmoid function with a gain term $\lambda = 10$ and bias term $\beta = 0.5$ (Eq. 2), where N is the number of active units in an input pattern.

$$\eta_j = \frac{1}{N} \sum_i x_i \, w_{ij} \tag{1}$$

At this stage, Gaussian noise is added $G \sim N(0, 0.03^2)$.

$$y_j = G + \frac{1}{1 + e^{\lambda(-\eta_j + \beta)}} \tag{2}$$

Weights of the most active detector are adjusted using a CPCA Hebbian learning rule (Eq. 3, Ref. 19), bounded between [0–1]. Weights between active input units and detectors are increased and connections between active detectors and inactive input units are decreased. The rate of change is determined by the learning constant ϵ. (No change occurs for weights to inactive detectors, unlike for some other biologically plausible Hebbian learning rules.[b])

$$\Delta w_{ij} = \epsilon \; y_j(x_i - w_{ij}) \tag{3}$$

For each trial (that is, for each presented item in the study phase), the noisy activation of the winning detector is added to a weighted average (denoted avg_{max}). Relative proportions are determined by the time constant τ, which was set to 0.7, so that the current trial contributes 0.3 and the previous average 0.7.

$$avg_{max}(t) = \tau \; avg_{max} \; (t-1) + (1-\tau) \; y_j \tag{4}$$

In Equation 4, y_j denotes the activation of the winning detector and t indexes trials, *i.e.* patterns being presented to the network. This 'time averaging' is a simple and efficient method used by biological neurons for increasing the signal-to-noise ratio.[20] Initially, all time averages have a value of 0.5 to indicate that no information is known about the relationship between the detector activation and the input feature activation. In the Type I mirror effect simulations, time averages for weak *old* and strong *old* items are calculated throughout the study phase. These are based on the noisy activation value of the most active detector for a given pattern. In the Type II mirror effect simulation, a single time average for *old* items is calculated by collapsing across high and low frequency words.

On completion of the study phase, but before the test phase, thirty random *new* patterns are generated per condition (Type I simulation: new, Type II simulation: weak class new, strong class new). These are presented to the network using the fixed learned weights from the study phase. Time averages are calculated based on network activation as before (see Eq. 4). For the Type II simulation, the time average is collapsed across high and low frequency words to generate a single time average for *new* items.

---

[b]We would like to thank Max Garagnani for pointing this out.

Table 1. Model generated data for Type I and Type II mirror effects over 100 simulations. Hits and false alarms (FA) are shown in percentages. d' values reflect the ease of discrimination. Criteria/thresholds are based on *estimated* activation averages.

	Weak cond.	Strong cond.	High freq.	Low freq.
Hit	75.100	91.767	80.767	96.400
FA	7.000	2.900	16.400	1.1
d'	2.153	3.285	1.847	4.089
Criterion/Threshold	.541	.558	0.550	

In the test phase, previously presented items are mixed with an equal number of new items and presented in random order. Activation values are calculated as before. For simplicity, we assume an unbiased response criterion/threshold in each simulation, located half-way between the *estimated* average activation of the maximally active detector for old and new items (*i.e.* avg_{max}), both derived prior to the test phase (see Eq. 4). The criterion/threshold is based on *estimates* rather than actual values, as participants are assumed not to have access to this information.[21]

In the Type I mirror effect simulation (strength-based), two criteria/thresholds are used: one between new and weak old items (single presentation) and one between new and strong old items (repeat presentation). This represents the notion that on average, participants have a higher feeling of familiarity for repeated items and thus require a higher activation level before declaring these to be old. In contrast, weak old items elicited a lower level of memory activation, so that a less stringent criterion/threshold is adopted.[8]

In the Type II mirror effect simulation (stimulus class based), a single decision criterion/threshold is calculated, which collapses new and old items across low- and high frequency. This is based on the observation that participants do not appreciate that low frequency items are more memorable, but instead adopt a single response criterion/threshold, even if provided with explicit cues about the item type.[8]

4. Results

Results for 100 simulation runs of Type I and Type II mirror effects are given in Table 1 and depicted in Fig. 3 and Fig. 4. Distributions are plotted for the noisy activation values for the most active detector by item class. As previously suggested, criteria/thresholds were placed in an unbiased 'optimal' way, half-way between the *estimated* activation means for old and new items.

4.1. *Type I mirror effect*

In the Type I mirror effect simulation (strength-based), strong and weak old items differed only by the number of repetitions during the study/learning phase. Weak items were presented once, strong items twice, both with a learning constant $\epsilon = .05$. In line with empirical data, new items, whose representation did not differ, form a single distribution (see Fig. 3).

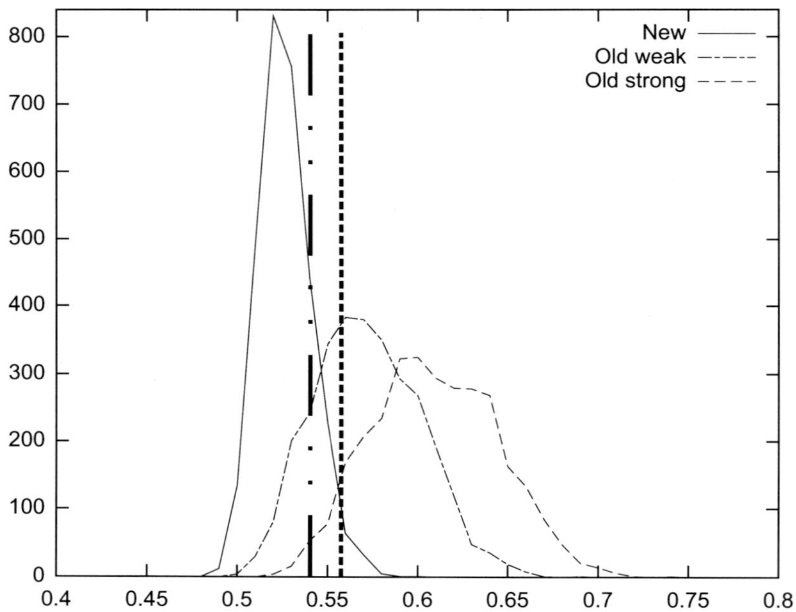

Fig. 3. Type I mirror effect simulations: Frequency (y-axis) distributions for actual maximal activation values (x-axis) per item type, based on 100 experimental runs. Response criteria/thresholds for weak old (dash-dot line) and strong old items (short-dashed line) are placed mid-way between new and old *estimated* maximal activation averages.

Distributions of weak and strong old items separate due to more accurate encoding of the latter, resulting in a larger d' in the strong condition. Old items have a larger variance than new items as they were also subject to variability during learning. The response criterion/threshold in the strong condition has shifted upward as a function of the higher estimated mean activation of strong old items. Hits and false alarms follow a mirror effect pattern (see Table 1).

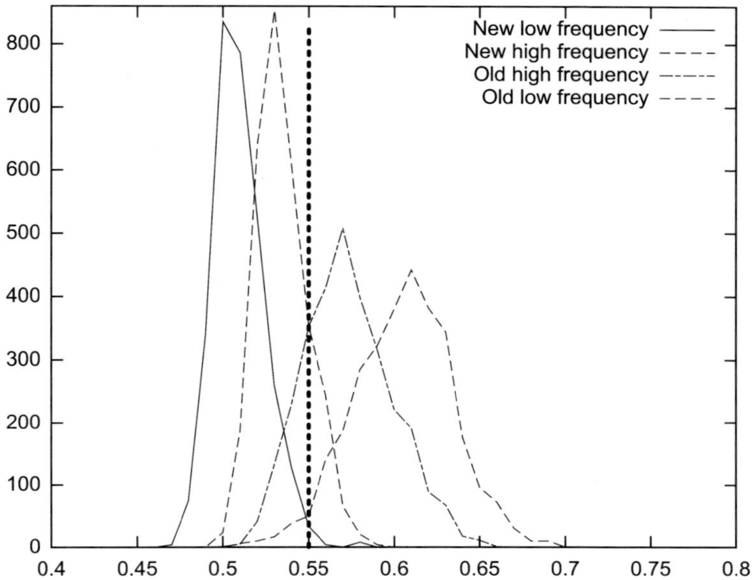

Fig. 4. Type II mirror effect simulations: Frequency (y-axis) distributions for actual maximal activation values (x-axis) per item type, based on 100 experimental runs. A single response criterion/threshold (short-dashed line) is used for high- and low frequency items and placed mid-way between collapsed new and old *estimated* maximal activation averages.

4.2. *Type II mirror effect*

In the Type II mirror effect (stimulus class based) simulation, low-frequency differed from high frequency items in two respects. They had one less active unit (49 compared to 50), which was meant to reflect the fact that low-frequency words tend to have fewer definitions and are thus used in less varied contexts.[11,12] They also had a higher learning rate η than high frequency items (0.09 compared to 0.04), simulating better encoding due to increased attention to their comparative 'novelty'.[2,13] Based on Stretch and Wixted's findings,[8] a single criterion/threshold was used for high- and low frequency items. The model reproduces a Type II mirror effect, with appropriate hits, false alarms and d' values (see Fig. 4 and Table 1).

5. Conclusions and further work

We have presented a neural network model of memory processes underlying yes/no decisions in a recognition memory test, which reproduces Type I and Type II mirror effects. The approach takes inspiration from Bayesian models of recognition memory, especially from McClelland and Chappell's subjective likelihood model.[16]

One of the most significant differences between the approach presented here and existing Bayesian models[8,12,16,17] is that we obtain a mirror effect without an explicit likelihood ratio calculation. We have shown here that the two basic classes of mirror effects can be generated from a simple, competitive learning neural network in which the values for the familiarity axis are directly generated from the activation of the winning detectors. The simplicity of this approach, which is based on a signal detection, single-process view of recognition memory, along with the direct calculation of the criterion/threshold from neural activation are the key benefits of the model we have introduced.

A limitation of our model concerns the treatment of low frequency words. In order to replicate Type II mirror effects, we had to combine two assumptions. Firstly, low frequency words elicited increased amounts of attention compared to high frequency words,[2,13] which was reflected by their higher learning rate. Secondly, low frequency words tend to have fewer definitions and are associated with fewer contexts, which was reflected by one less active input unit or 'feature' for this stimulus class.[11,12] Some competitor models distinguish low- and high frequency through just one manipulation.[2,11–13]

We further assume that neurons can perform a maximum-like operation (which results in an output signal that approximates the maximum among several input signals) to calculate response citeria/thresholds. This operation has been shown to be approximated by complex cells in the visual cortex of cats and neurons in Area V4 of macaques[22] and demonstrated in a neurophysiologically plausible way for feed-forward models.[23]

We also assume that humans are able to distinguish high-strength from low-strength stimuli, yet we do not implement how this might be achieved. Whilst this is not ideal, this assumption is common in the literature (*e.g.* Ref. 8).

Our model shares some similarities with Bogacz, Brown and Giraud-Carrier's familiarity discrimination model.[24] This model closely reproduces observed activation patterns of 'novelty' neurons in the perirhinal cortex with a two-phase three-layer network (binary input, familiarity discrimination, decision) with primarily feed-forward connections, biologically plausible parameters and Hebbian learning rules. While the authors did not use sparse coding, they demonstrated by simulation that the network's behaviour would essentially remain unchanged.

During the critical initial period (the familiarity discrimination phase), the Bogacz et al.[24] model's familiarity discrimination neurons (FDNs) are likely to become more active for familiar patterns than for novel ones. This is because Hebbian learning leads the synaptic weights to reflect the correlation between the active inputs for a given FDN. The number of FDNs that can become active for a given input are limited by fixed high synaptic weights between specific input and output units in combination with inhibition. Our implementation of a CPCA learning rule in combination with winner-takes-all achieves similar results, although we do not use homosynaptic long-term depression.

In comparison to Bogacz et al.,[24] we are less explicit in relating our model parameters back to functional neuroanatomy and we do not analyse our model storage capacity mathematically. However, the focus on modelling mirror effects and the use of a signal detection framework distinguishes our work.

For further work, we would like to use a principled approach (such as maximum likelihood estimation) for the setting of free parameters and extend the model to generate reaction time data. We want to move from qualitative to quantitative modeling. We aim to generalize the model to cases in which mirror effects are predicted but not observed and eventually to a broader range of recognition memory phenomena (*e.g.* the list length effect). Eventually, the model could be refined and extended to emulate known properties of functional neuroanatomy, like, for example, Norman and O'Reilly's model.[15]

Acknowledgements

We would like to thank our anonymous reviewers for their comments which helped to improve this paper.

References

1. R. Ratcliff and G. McKoon, *Oxford Handbook of Memory* (OUP: New York, 2000), ch. Memory models, pp. 571–582.
2. M. Glanzer and J. K. Adams, *Memory and Cognition* 8 (1985).
3. R. L. Greene, *The Foundations of Remembering: Essays in Honor of Henry L. Roediger, III* (Psychology Press: Hove, UK., 2007), ch. Foxes, Hedgehogs, and Mirror Effects: The Role of General Principles in Memory Research, pp. 53–66.
4. G. Stenberg, M. Johansson and I. Rosén, *Acta Psychologica* 174 (2006).
5. N. A. Macmillan and C. D. Creelman, *Detection Theory: A user's guide*, 2nd edn. (Psychology Press: Hove, UK., 2005).

6. R. Ratcliff, C. F. Sheu and S. D. Gronlund, *Psychological Review* **99**, 518 (1992).
7. J. T. Wixted, *Psychological Review* **114**, 152 (2007).
8. V. Stretch and J. T. Wixted, *Journal of Experimental Psychology: Learning, Memory and Cognition* **24**, 1379 (1998).
9. M. Glanzer, J. K. Adams, G. J. Iverson and K. Kim, *Psychological Review* **100**, 546 (1993).
10. A. M. Glenberg, *Memory and Cognition* **7**, 95 (1979).
11. M. Glanzer and N. Bowles, *Journal of Experimental Psychology: Human Learning and Memory* **2**, 21 (1976).
12. R. M. Shiffrin and M. Steyvers, *Psychonomic Bulletin and Review* **4**, 145 (1997).
13. M. Glanzer and J. K. Adams, *Journal of Experimental Psychology: Learning, Memory and Cognition* **16**, 5 (1990).
14. R. A. Diana, A. P. Yonelinas and C. Ranganath, *Trends in Cognitive Sciences* **11**, 379 (2007).
15. K. A. Norman and R. C. O'Reilly, *Psychological Review* **110**, 611 (2003).
16. J. L. McClelland and M. Chappell, *Psychological Review* **105**, 724 (1998).
17. M. Murdock, *Psychonomic Bulletin and Review* **10**, 570 (2003).
18. M. Cary and L. M. Reder, *Journal of Memory and Language* **49**, 231 (2003).
19. R. C. O'Reilly and Y. Munakata, *Computational Explorations in Cognitive Neuroscience: Understanding the Mind by Simulating the Brain* (Cambridge: MIT Press, 2000).
20. J. L. McClelland, *Psychological Review* **86**, 287 (1979).
21. D. L. Hintzman, *Journal of Experimental Psychology: Learning, Memory and Cognition* **20**, 201 (1994).
22. M. A. Giese and T. Poggio, *Nature Reviews Neuroscience* **4**, 179 (2003).
23. T. Serre, M. Kouh, C. Cadieu, U. Knoblich, G. Kreiman and T. Poggio, *A theory of object recognition: computations and circuits in the feedforward path of the ventral stream in primate visual cortex*, tech. rep., MIT: Cambridge, MA (2005), CBCL Paper 259/AI Memo 2005-036.
24. R. Bogacz, M. W. Brown and C. Giraud-Carrier, *Journal of Computational Neuroscience* **10**, 5 (2001).

REPRESENTATION AND CLASSIFICATION OF FACIAL EXPRESSION IN A MODULAR COMPUTATIONAL MODEL

ARUNA SHENOY[1]
TIM GALE[1,2]
RAY FRANK[1]
NEIL DAVEY[1]

[1]*Department of Computer Science, University of Hertfordshire, College Lane, Hatfield, AL10 9AB, UK*

[2]*Department of Psychiatry, QEII Hospital, Welwyn Garden City, AL7 4HQ, UK*

Recognizing expressions is a key part of human social interaction; processing of facial expression information is largely automatic in humans, but it is a non-trivial task for a computational system. The purpose of this work is to develop computational models capable of differentiating between a range of human facial expressions. Here we use two sets of images, namely: Angry and Neutral. Raw face images are examples of high dimensional data, so here we use some dimensionality reduction techniques: Principal Component Analysis and Curvilinear Component Analysis. We preprocess the images with a bank of Gabor filters, so that important features in the face images are identified. Subsequently the faces are classified using a Support Vector Machine. We also find the effect size of the pixels for the Angry and Neutral faces. We show that it is possible to differentiate faces with a neutral expression from those with an angry expression with high accuracy. Moreover we can achieve this with data that has been massively reduced in size: in the best case the original images are reduced to just 6 dimensions.

1. Introduction

According to Ekman and Friesen [1] there are six easily discernible facial expressions: anger, happiness(smile), fear, surprise, disgust and sadness. Moreover these are readily and consistently recognized across different cultures [2]. In the work reported here we show how a computational model can identify facial expressions from simple facial images. Specifically we investigate the differentiation of angry from neutral faces. In particular we show how angry faces and neutral faces can be differentiated.

Data presentation plays an important role in any type of recognition. High dimensional data is normally reduced to a manageable low dimensional data set. We perform dimensionality reduction using Principal Component Analysis (PCA) and Curvilinear Component Analysis (CCA). PCA is a linear projection technique and it may be more appropriate to use a non linear Curvilinear

Component Analysis (CCA) [3]. The Intrinsic Dimension (ID) [4], which is the true dimension of the data, is often much less than the original dimension of the data. To use this efficiently, the actual (Intrinsic) dimension of the data must be estimated. We use the Correlation Dimension to estimate the Intrinsic Dimension and is explained in later section. We compare the classification results of these methods with raw face images and of Gabor Pre-processed images [5, 6]. The features of the face (or any object for that matter) may be aligned at any angle. Using a suitable Gabor filter at the required orientation, certain features can be given high importance and other features less importance. Usually, a bank of such filters is used with different parameters and later the resultant image is a *L2 max* norm(at every pixel the maximum of feature vector obtained from the filter bank) superposition of the outputs from the filter bank.

2. Background

We basically perform an experiment to classify two expressions: neutral and Angry. We do pre-processing by Gabor filters and dimensionality reduction by techniques, namely, Principal Component Analysis and Curvilinear Component Analysis followed by a Support Vector Machine (SVM) [7] based classification technique and these are described below.

2.1. *Gabor Filters*

A Gabor filter can be applied to images to extract features aligned at particular orientations. Gabor filters possess the optimal localization properties in both spatial and frequency domains, and they have been successfully used in many applications [8]. A Gabor filter is a function obtained by modulating a sinusoidal with a Gaussian function. The useful parameters of a Gabor filter are orientation and frequency. The Gabor filter is thought to mimic the simple cells in the visual cortex. The various 2D receptive field profiles encountered in populations of simple cells in the visual cortex are well described by an optimal family of 2D filters [9]. In our case a Gabor filter bank is implemented on face images with 8 different orientations and 5 different frequencies.

Recent studies on modeling of visual cortical cells [10] suggest a tuned band pass filter bank structure. Formally, the Gabor filter is a Gaussian (with variances S_x and S_y along x and y-axes respectively) modulated by a complex sinusoid (with centre frequencies U and V along x and y-axes respectively) and is described by the Equation 1:-

$$g(x,y) = \frac{\exp\left[-\frac{1}{2}\left\{\left(\frac{x}{S_x}\right)^2 + \left(\frac{y}{S_y}\right)^2\right\} + 2\pi j(Ux+Vy)\right]}{2\pi S_x S_y} \tag{1}$$

The variance terms S_x and S_y dictates the spread of the band pass filter centered at the frequencies U and V in the frequency domain. This filter is complex in nature.

A Gabor filter can be described by the following parameters: The S_x and S_y of the Gaussian explain the shape of the base (circle or ellipse), frequency (f) of the sinusoid, orientation (Θ) of the applied sinusoid. Figure 1 shows examples of various Gabor filters. Figure 2 b) shows the effect of applying a variety of Gabor filters shown in Figure 1 to the sample image shown in Figure 2 a). Note how the features at particular orientations are exaggerated.

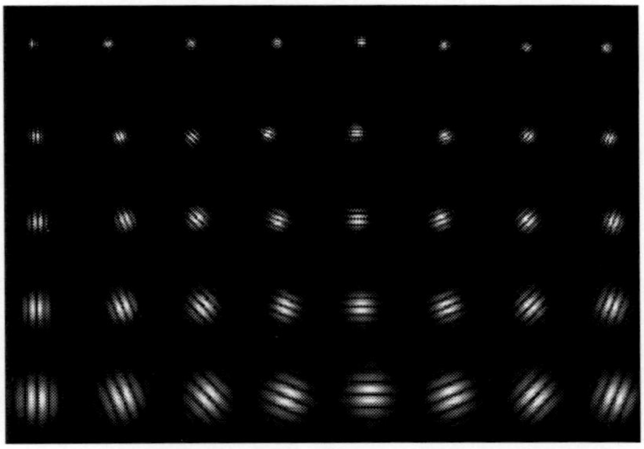

Figure 1: Gabor filters: Real part of the Gabor kernels at five scales and eight orientations.

An augmented Gabor feature vector is created of a size far greater than the original data for the image. Every pixel is then represented by a vector of size 40 and demands dimensionality reduction before further processing. So a 63 × 63 image is transformed to size 63 × 63 × 5 × 8. Thus, the feature vector consists of all useful information extracted from different frequencies, orientations and from all locations, and hence is very useful for expression recognition.

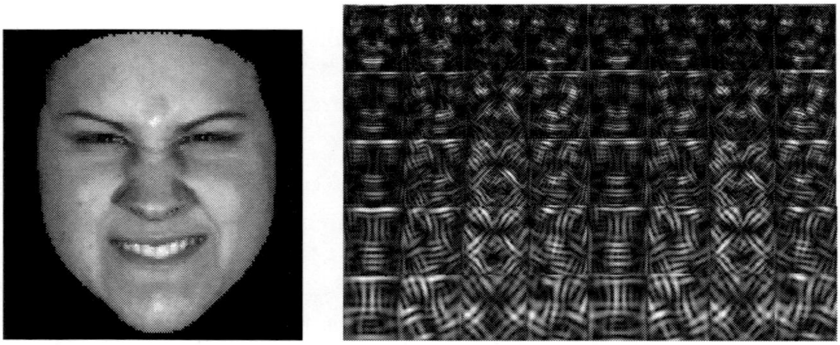

(a) (b)

Figure 2: a) Original face image. b) Forty Convolution outputs of Gabor: The rows correspond to decreasing frequency (from top to bottom) and columns represent various orientation.

Once the feature vector is obtained, it can be handled in various ways. We simply take the *L2 max* norm for each pixel in the feature vector. So that the final value of a pixel is the maximum value found by any of the filters for that pixel. The *L2 max* norm Superposition principle is used on the outputs of the filter bank and the Figure 3 b) shows the output for the original image of Figure 3 a).

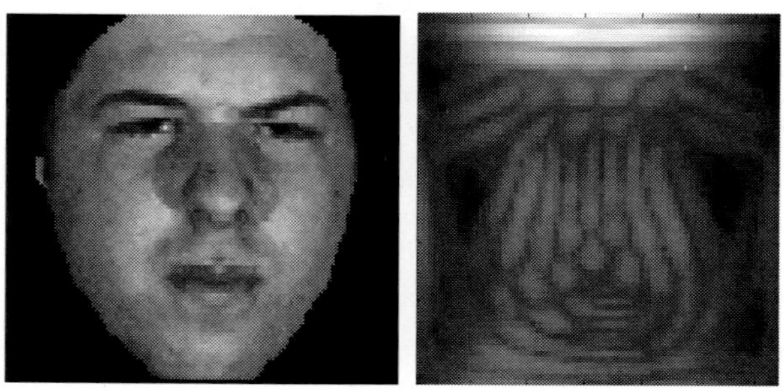

(a) (b)

Figure 3: a) Original Image used for the Filter bank. b) Superposition output (*L2 max* norm).

2.2. *Principal Component Analysis*

Principal Component Analysis (PCA) transforms higher dimensional datasets into lower dimensional uncorrelated outputs by capturing linear correlations among the data, and preserving as much information as possible in the data. PCA transforms data from the original coordinate system to the principal axes coordinate system such that the principal axis passes through the maximum possible variance in the data. The second principal axis passes through the next largest possible variance and this is orthogonal to the first axis. This is repeated for the next largest possible variances and so on. All these axes are orthogonal to each other. On performing this PCA on the high dimensional data, Eigenvalues or principal components are thus obtained [11]. The required dimensionality reduction is obtained by retaining only the first few principal components. Figure 4 shows the first two principal components.

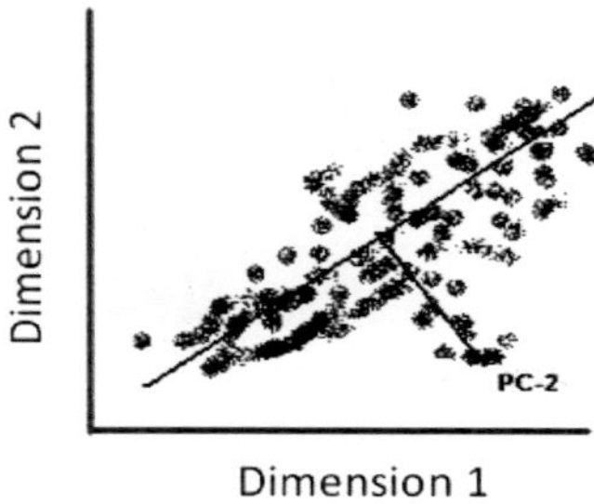

Figure 4: The first two consecutive principal components are shown.

2.3. *Curvilinear Component Analysis*

Curvilinear Component Analysis (CCA) is a non-linear projection method that preserves distance relationships in both input and output spaces. CCA is a useful method for redundant and non linear data structure representation and can be used in dimensionality reduction. CCA is useful with highly non-linear data, where PCA or any other linear method fails to give suitable information [3]. The D-dimensional input X should be mapped onto the output P-dimensional space Y, where $P<<D$. Their P-dimensional output vectors $\{y_i\}$ should reflect the topology of the inputs $\{x_i\}$. In order to do that, Euclidean distances between the x_i's are considered.

Corresponding distances in the output space y_i's is calculated such that the distance relationship between the data points is maintained. CCA puts more emphasis on maintaining the short distances than the longer ones. Formally, this reasoning leads to the following error function:

$$E = \frac{1}{2}\sum_{i=1}^{N}\sum_{j=1}^{N}(d_{i,j}^{X} - d_{i,j}^{Y})^2 F_\lambda(d_{i,j}^{Y}) \quad \forall j \neq i \tag{2}$$

where $d^x_{i,j}$ and $d^Y_{i,j}$ are the Euclidean distances between the points i and j in the input space X and the projected output space Y respectively and N is the number of data points. $F(d^Y_{i,j})$ is the neighbourhood function, a monotonically decreasing function of distance. In order to check that the relationship is maintained a plot of the distances in the input space and the output space ($dy - dx$ plot) is produced. For a well maintained topology, dy should be proportional to the value of dx at least for small values of dy's. Figure 5 shows CCA projections for the 3D data horse shoe data. The $dy - dx$ plot shown is good in the sense that the smaller distances are very well matched [3].

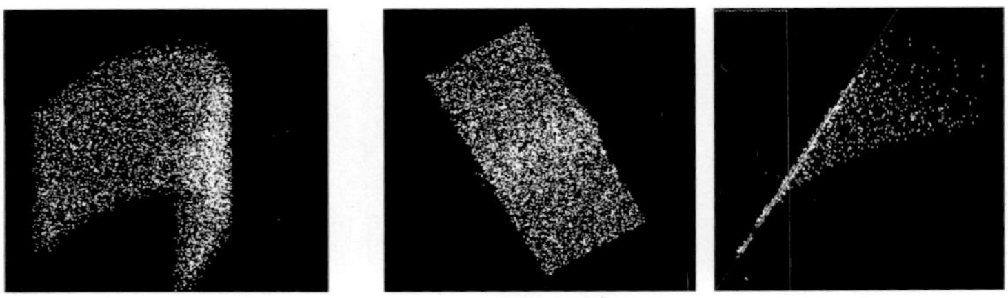

(a) (b) (c)

Figure 5: (a) 3D horse shoe dataset. (b) 2D CCA projection. (c) $dy - dx$ plot.

2.4. *Intrinsic Dimension*

One problem with CCA is deciding how many dimensions the projected space should occupy, and one way of obtaining this is to use the intrinsic dimension of the data manifold. The Intrinsic Dimension (ID) can be defined as the minimum number of free variables required to define data without any significant information loss. Due to the possibility of correlations among the data, both linear and nonlinear, a D-dimensional dataset may actually lie on a P-dimensional manifold ($D \geq P$). The ID of such data is then said to be P. There are various methods of calculating the ID; here we use the correlation Dimension [8] to calculate the ID of face image dataset.

2.5. *Encoding Face*

'Effect Size' is a way of expressing the difference between two groups. Here two groups: Angry and Neutral are used. Cohen [12] defined d as the difference between the means, $M_1 - M_2$, divided by standard deviation, σ of either group.

$$d = \frac{M_1 - M_2}{\sigma} \tag{3}$$

M_1 and M_2 are the means of two groups and σ is the standard deviation and it is calculated by Equation 4.

$$\sigma = \sqrt{\frac{(\sigma_1^2 + \sigma_2^2)}{N}} \tag{4}$$

σ_1 and σ_2 are the standard deviation of the two classes, Angry and Neutral respectively and N is the total number of samples. 'Encoding face' is obtained by finding the Effect size of each pixel in an image. In other words it shows which pixels discriminate most between Angry and Neutral faces.

2.6. *Classification Using Support Vector Machines*

A number of classifiers can be used in the final stage for classification. We have concentrated on the Support Vector Machine. Support Vector Machine (SVM) is a set of related supervised learning methods used for classification and regression. SVM's are used extensively for many classification tasks such as: handwritten digit recognition [13] or Object Recognition [14]. A SVM implicitly transforms the data into a higher dimensional data space (determined by the kernel) which allows the classification to be accomplished more easily. We have used the LIBSVM tool [7] for SVM classification.

3. Experiments and Results

We experimented on 200 faces (112 female and 88 male) each with two classes, namely: *Neutral* and *Angry* (100 faces for each expression). The images are from the BINGHAMTON dataset [15] and some examples are shown in Figure 6.

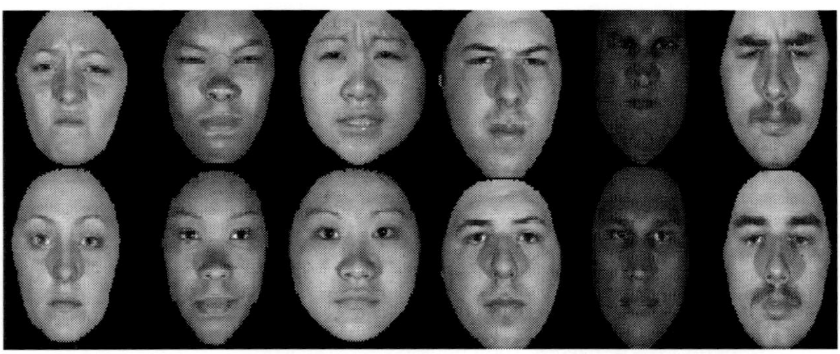

Figure 6: Examples of BINGHAMTON images used in our experiments was converted to gray scale and then reduced to size 63 × 63 for all experiments.

The training set had 160 faces (with 46 female, 34 male and equal numbers of them with neutral and angry expression). The original 128 × 128 image was reduced to 63 × 63. The test set consists of 40 faces (10 female, 10 male and equally balanced number of expression).

For PCA reduction we use the first few principal components which account for 95% of the total variance of the data, and project the data onto these principal components. This resulted in using 105 components of the raw dataset and 22 components in the Gabor pre-processed dataset. As CCA is a highly non-linear dimensionality reduction technique, we use the intrinsic dimensionality technique and reduce the components to its Intrinsic Dimension. The Intrinsic Dimension of the raw faces was approximated as 10 and that of Gabor pre-processed images was 6. The SVM classification results are shown in Table 1. Figure 7 shows the Eigen faces obtained by performing the PCA on the data set. Figure 8 shows the ***dy-dx*** plot of the CCA projection for the data set.

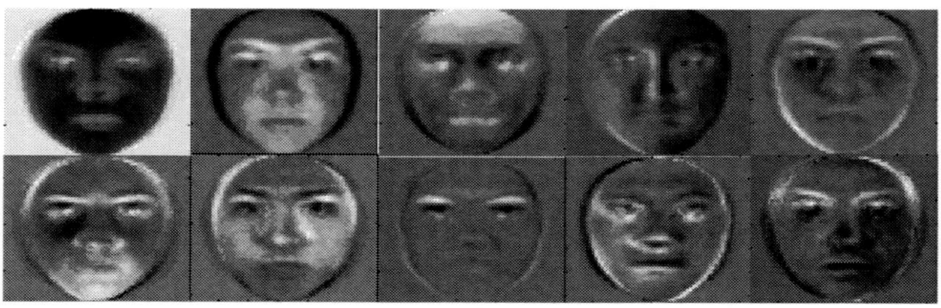

Figure 7: First ten Eigen faces of the dataset with two classes namely, Neutral and Angry.

The SVM was trained in the following way:

1) Transform the data to a format required for using the SVM software package - LIBSVM -2.86 [7].
2) Perform simple scaling on the data so that all the features or attributes are in the range [-1, +1].
3) Choose a kernel. We used the RBF kernel, $k(x,y)=e^{-\gamma|x-y|^2}$.
4) Perform fivefold cross validation with the specified kernel to find the best values of the cost parameter C and γ.
5) Using the best value of C and γ, train the model and finally evaluate the trained classifier using the test sets.

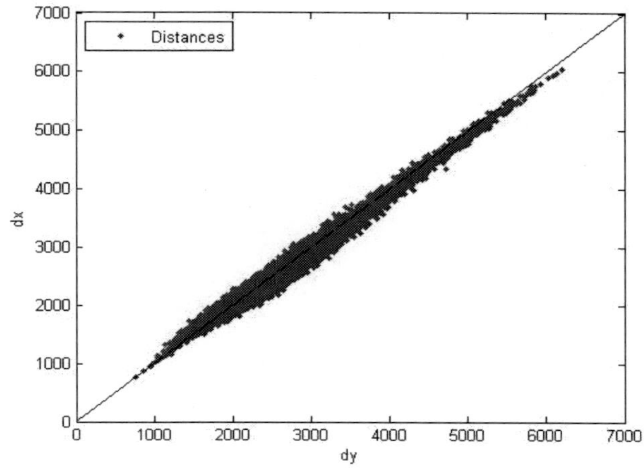

Figure 8: The ***dy-dx*** plot of the CCA projection for the raw data set. If there is a good matching between input and output spaces and the data is linear, then all the distances would be on the line ***dy = dx*** line. Here the original 3969 dimensions have been reduced to just 10 components by CCA.

Table 1. SVM Classification accuracy of raw faces and Gabor pre-processed images with PCA and CCA dimensionality reduction techniques.

% SVM Accuracy	Testset (40 images)
Raw faces	37 (92.5%)
Raw with PCA105	27 (67.5%)
Raw with CCA10	31 (77.5%)
Gabor pre-processed faces	29 (72.5%)
Gabor with PCA22	30 (75%)
Gabor with CCA6	28 (70%)

The Encoding Angry face, the image where pixels which discriminate most between Angry and Neutral faces, is shown in Figure 9. The eyebrows are pulled together and down to form vertical wrinkles between the eyebrows in the forehead which is diagnostic of angry faces and can be seen clearly in the image. The glaring stare which is caused by the tightening of the muscles around the eyelids can also be somewhat seen [16]. The flaring of the nostrils and the clenching of jaws [17] may also be an important indicator, though to a lesser extent.

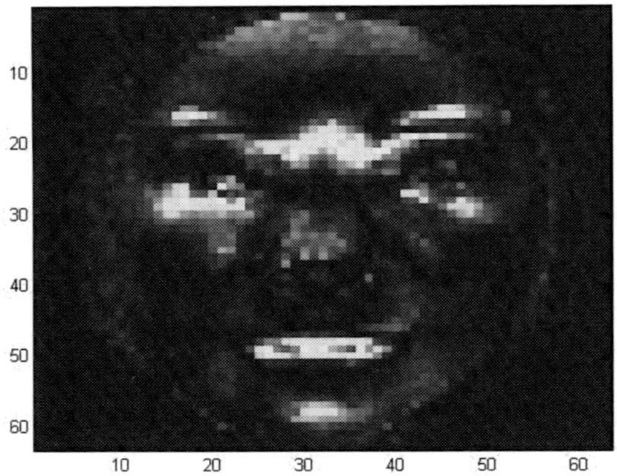

Figure 9: Encoding face: for Angry and Neutral.

4. Conclusions

Identifying facial expressions is a challenging and interesting task. Our experiment shows that identification from raw images can be performed very well. However, with a larger data set, it may be computationally intractable to use the raw images. It is therefore important to reduce the dimensionality of the data. The experiments so far have shown that Gabor pre-processed images, with dimensionality reduced by CCA to just 6 components, offer a promising approach for investigation. In order to examine the consistency of the different models, further experiments need to be run with larger datasets and with other expression categories. The Similarities and differences in these results may be useful and informative in developing a better computational model and may contribute to our understanding of human processing of face expressions. Also, the performance of the computational model will have to be compared with the performance accuracy of human subjects with respect to a range of expressions.

References

1. Ekman, P. and W.V. Friesen, *Constants across cultures in the face of the emotion.* Journal of Personality and Social Psychology, 1971. **17**.
2. Batty, B., M.J. Taylor, and *Early processing of the six basic facial emotional expressions.* Cognitive Brain Research, 2003. **17**.
3. Demartines, P. and d.J. Hérault, *Curvilinear component analysis: A self-organizing neural network for nonlinear mapping of data sets* IEEE Transactions on Neural Networks, 1997. **8**(1): p. 148-154.

4. Grassberger, P. and I. Proccacia, *Measuring the strangeness of strange attractors.* Physica D, 1983. **9**.
5. Jain, A.K. and F. Farrokhnia, *Unsupervised texture segmentation using Gabor filters.* Pattern Recognition, 1991. **24**(12).
6. Movellan, J.R., *Tutorial on Gabor Filters.* 2002.
7. Chang, C.-C. and Chih-Jen Lin *LIBSVM: a library for support vector machines.* 2001.
8. Zheng, D., Y. Zhao, and J. Wang, *Features Extraction using A Gabor Filter Family.* Proceedings of the sixth Lasted International conference, Signal and Image processing, Hawaii, 2004.
9. Daugman, J.G., *Uncertainty relation for resolution in space, spatial frequency and orientation optimized by two dimensional visual cortical filters.* Journal of Optical.Society of .America .A, 1985. **2**(7).
10. Kulikowski, *Theory of spatial position and spatial frequency relations in the receptive fields of simple cells in the visual cortex.* Biological Cybernetics 1982. **43**(3): p. 187-198.
11. Smith, L.I., *Tutorial on Principal Component Analysis.* 2002.
12. Cohen, J., ed. *Statistical power analysis for the behavioural sciences.* 1988, Lawrence Earlbaum Associates.: Hillsdale, New Jersey, .
13. Cortes, C. and V. Vapnik, *Support Vector Networks.* Machine Learning, 1995. **20**: p. 273-297.
14. Blanz, V., et al., *Comparison of view-based object recognition algorithms using realistic 3D models.* Proc. Int. Conf. on Artificial Neural Networks 1996: p. 251-256.
15. Yin, L., Wei, X., Sun, Y., Wang, J. & Rosato, M. J. , *A 3D Facial Expression Database For Facial Behavior Research.* 7th International Conference on Automatic Face and Gesture Recognition (FGR06), 2006
16. Hager, J.C. *Data Face*. 2003 [cited; Available from: http://www.face-and-emotion.com/dataface/expression/interpretations.html.
17. Novaco, R.W., *Anger.* Encyclopedia of Psychology. 2000: Oxford University Press.

MODELLING THE TRANSITION FROM PERCEPTUAL TO CONCEPTUAL ORGANIZATION

GERT WESTERMANN

Department of Psychology, Oxford Brookes University, Oxford OX3 0BP, UK

DENIS MARESCHAL

Centre for Brain and Cognitive Development, Birkbeck, University of London, London WC1E 7HX, UK

We present a neural network model of the transition from early, perceptually-based category formation to conceptual categorization based on the learning of category labels. The model investigates the interactions between category structure and labelling success in terms of category compactness, between-category similarity, frequency of labelling and prelinguistic object knowledge. By providing accounts both of the effect of category structure on word learning and of word learning on category structure the model presents the first step of a unified account of category and word learning.

1. Introduction

An extensive body of research has shown that even young infants can form perceptual categories on the basis of exposure to a sequence of pictures or objects from that category (e.g., [1-3]). Much of this work is based on the familiarization-novelty preference procedure which relies on the fact that infants tend to spend more time looking towards novel than towards familiar stimuli. In a typical study infants are familiarized to a sequence of objects from a single category and are then tested with two new objects, one from the familiarized category and one from a different category. When infants show a looking preference to the object from the new category it can be concluded that during familiarization they have formed a category that includes the new within-category object but excludes the object from the different category. For example, in a seminal study Quinn et al. [1] familiarized 3-4 month old infants on a sequence of cat pictures and found that in the test phase they looked longer at pictures of dogs, horses and humans than at pictures of novel cats.

Once infants begin to learn and use words the question arises how word learning and category knowledge interact. The study of word learning has proceeded along several strands. In one, researchers are interested in how and when children learn words, how these words are used and extended to novel objects, how much exposure to a word is necessary to link it with an object, and what errors children make in labelling objects. This approach has helped to identify constraints on lexical development that are characteristic of children's early word learning such as a whole object constraint (the bias that a new label refers to a whole object rather than to its parts), a shape bias (a bias to expect that objects that are referred to by a label are defined by shape similarity), mutual exclusivity (the notion that one object can only have one label), and a taxonomic constraint that biases children to assume that a learned label for an object generalizes to all members of the object's category (see [4, 5] for overview). Research in this framework has also maintained that word-label associations might be learned after a single exposure but that repeated exposure is necessary to fine-tune the association [6], and that vocabulary growth accelerates after around 18 months of age.

Another strand of research, usually focusing on younger children, has examined how knowledge of a label (or co-exposure to an object and a label) affects the processing of the labelled object and the formation of categories. There has been considerable debate on this question: whereas some have claimed that labels serve to highlight commonalities between objects sharing the same label and thus serve as invitations to form categories [7, 8] or that labels can have a constructive role in category formation [9], others have maintained that acoustic information interferes with visual information and disrupts category formation [10, 11].

Despite their obvious close relation there has been little interaction between these two research strands. In this paper we make an attempt to remedy this situation by presenting a computational model based on a model of early categorization that aims to provide an integrated account of word and category learning, and of the transition from perceptual to conceptual, language based categorization.

Previous models of infant categorization have employed so-called auto-encoder neural networks (e.g., [12, 13]). These are three-layer models usually trained with the backpropagation algorithm in which input and target are the same so that the model has to learn to recreate its input on the output layer. Since the hidden layer of these models is usually smaller than both input and output layers the model need to learn to effectively compress and decompress information as it flows through the network. The error produced by an auto-encoder for a specific object can be seen as analogous to the looking time of an infant to that object (see [12] for details). These models have been used to provide a mechanistic account of looking time differences in infant studies across stimuli and across ages [12, 13]. Here we use an extension of the auto-encoder modelling paradigm to simulate the transition from pre-linguistic to linguistic categorization and to generate predictions for word learning experiments under a variety of conditions.

2. The Model

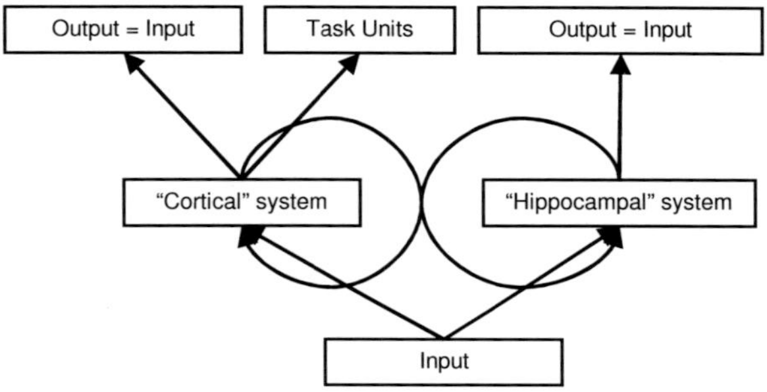

Figure 1: The categorization/word learning model. Input and Output layers had 18 units each, and hidden layers had 15 units. The task layer had 4 or 26 units, depending on the task (global level or basic level categorization, respectively). Learning rate in the hippocampal system was 0.2 and in the cortical system, 0.01.

The model (Fig. 1) is an extension of a dual-memory model of early categorization [14, 15]. It is based on the idea that conflicting results from the infant categorization literature can be reconciled by considering the unfolding interactions between two memory systems: an early, fast system based on the hippocampus/striatum in which information is acquired rapidly and that can be examined through studying looking preferences, and a slower memory system that is cortically based and that regulates more complex interactions with objects such as touching, examining or naming. Based on research on early memory development [16] the idea is that preferential looking studies tap into the hippocampal system whereas sequential touching and object examination tasks recruit cortical representations. The fact that different methods utilize different representations can explain why results showing the ages at which categories are formed differ substantially depending on the methodology used to assess categorization.

In the model each memory system is implemented by an auto-encoder network, and interactions between the systems are modelled through uni-directional connections between the hidden layers of the networks. Both systems differ only in their learning rate, that is, the rate at which weights are adapted in response to exposure to objects. This model has previously been shown to capture a range of phenomena such as the development of perceptual categorization and the effect of background knowledge on preferential-looking behaviour. Here the model is extended with *task units* linked to the slow memory system. The task units can encode a variety of functions such as representing specific ways of interactions with objects, knowledge of hidden properties, or, in the present case, object labels.

2.1. *Stimuli*

In order to model the development of basic and global level categories under varying labelling conditions, 10 photographs each of objects from 26 basic level categories were chosen. The object categories were man, woman, dog, cat, rabbit, horse, elephant, giraffe, cow, squirrel, fish, eagle, songbird, duck, bicycle, forklift, bus, car, plane, ship, desk, table, bed, sofa, chest of drawers and chair. They fell into four global-level categories (humans, animals, vehicles, furniture) that have all been previously used to test infant category formation [17] and varied in their within-category perceptual similarities.

Each of these 260 objects was represented by 18 general (geometric) and object-specific (facial) features: maximal height, minimal height, maximal width, minimal width, minimal width of base, number of protrusions, maximal length/width of left, right, lower and upper protrusion, minimal width of lower protrusion, texture, eye separation, face length and face width. Feature values were scaled between 0 and 1. For each basic level category a prototypical object was created by averaging the feature values of all of its members.

In order to simulate an infant's experience with the world, objects were presented to the model in random order for random exposure lengths (between 1 and 1,000 epochs). In simulations that explored the effect of labelling, each object had a 50% chance of being labelled. In these cases the object label was presented on the task layer and the hidden layer-task layer connections were updated. When no label was presented these connections were not updated. In the present simulations object labels were represented by a single active unit on the task layer. Before the onset of labelling the model was always trained without labels to develop an initial category structure. Training the model on an object proceeded as follows: the object was presented to the input layer and activation propagated to the hidden layers. Activation then flowed between the hidden layers until they settled in a stable state. Next, hidden activations flowed to the output and, if applicable, task layers. Output values were compared with target values (the input values for the output layers and the correct label for the task layer) and error was propagated backwards through the connections, leading to weight updating. Weights were updated at each presentation of an object (online learning).

3. Results

3.1. *Effect of labels on cortical representations*

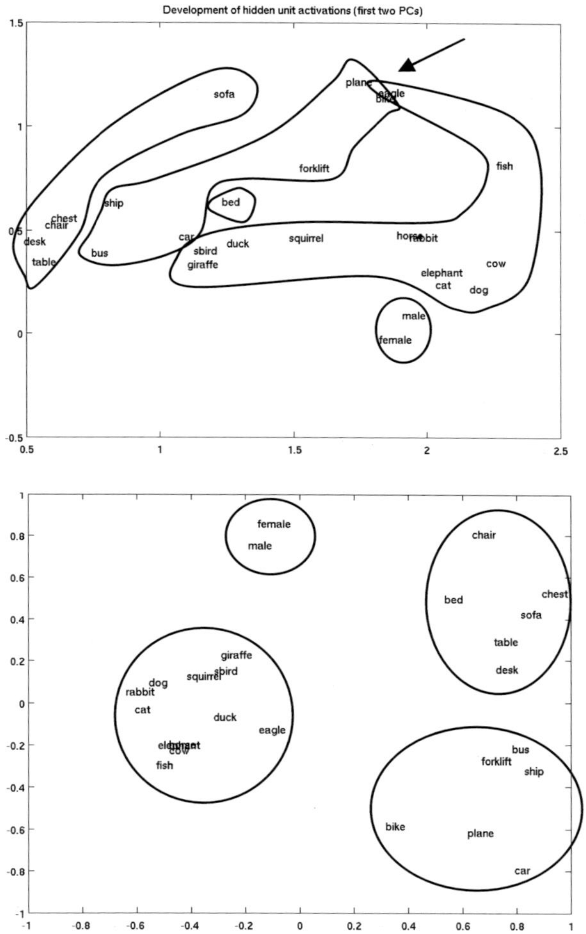

Figure 2: Developed hidden representations of the object prototypes after training on 2,500 objects without labels (top) and after total training on 3,500 objects including 450 global category labelling events (bottom). Representations are plotted in terms of their first two principal components.

Figure 2 shows the developing hidden representations (the modelled cortical memory representations) without (top) and with (bottom) labelling of global categories. Without labelling the representations clustered on the basis of the objects' perceptual similarities with a reasonable, but not perfect separation of global level categories. Idiosyncratic clusters such as that of plane, bicycle and eagle (see arrow) can be explained by the feature encoding (in this case, each object being characterized by two long, thin protrusions: wings and handlebars). While therefore perceptual similarity seems to be a good first step in separating categories, a clear separation of global level categories was achieved when objects were labelled with their global category label (human, animal, vehicle, furniture). Learning the objects' labels warped the cortical representational space to reflect both perceptual similarity and the membership in different global categories (Fig. 2 bottom).

3.2. *Vocabulary spurt and overextension of labels*

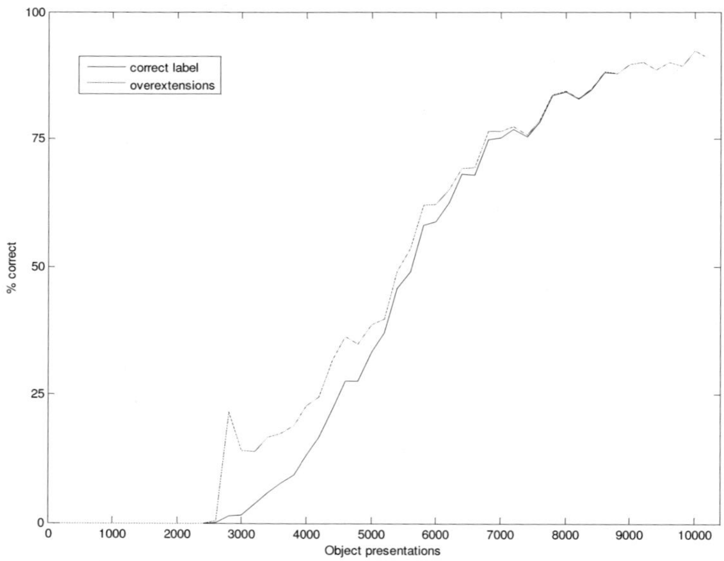

Figure 3: Correct label usage and label overextensions.

In infants early vocabulary growth is quite slow (one or two new words per week between 12 and 18 months of age) but then accelerates considerably. Some researchers have claimed that this so-called vocabulary spurt signifies a qualitatively new process of word learning such as referential language use [18], emerging constraints on lexical acquisition [4] or the emerging ability to categorize concepts [19] whereas others have explained it with the nonlinear properties of a connectionist learning system [20]. Here we examined vocabulary expansion by labelling objects with their basic level name, again by presenting objects with a 50% chance of being labelled.

Figure 3 shows the developing ability of the model to generate the correct label for a presented object after a pre-labelling phase of 2,500 object presentations. Without a qualitative change in the word learning mechanism the model nevertheless displayed a vocabulary spurt: after an initial slow increase in correct labels, from around 4,000 object presentation onwards the rate of correct labelling rapidly increased.

Young children sometimes apply a learned word to a member of another category, e.g., calling a horse a dog when they have learned the label 'dog'. One explanation for such overextensions has been the perceptual overlap between the objects [21]. Figure 3 also shows the rate at which known labels are over-extended to the members of other categories. Initially the rate of over-extension is high but decreases with growing vocabulary size. In the model, overextensions were largely restricted to perceptually similar objects: when the 26 basic level category labels were learned, over 80% of over- extensions occurred for members of the same global category as the object label (Fig. 4).

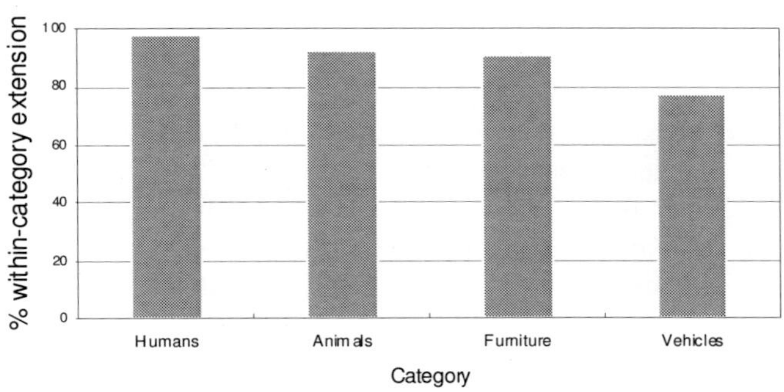

Figure 4: Percentage of overextended basic level labels that were misapplied within the same global category.

The taxonomic constraint [4] leads children to assume that a learned name for an object applies to all other members of the object category. However, infants' categories are different from those of adults, and therefore labels can be misapplied to objects from other categories. While there is debate on whether over-extensions really indicate that infants believe that a mislabelled object is a member of the labelled category (e.g., whether an infant naming a horse a 'dog' really believes that the horse is a dog), over-extensions occur frequently to objects that share perceptual features with the original object [21].

3.3. *Statistical effects on word learning*

Not all words are learned with equal ease (for example, nouns seem to be acquired more easily than verbs [22]). However, there has been little investigation into the role of statistical factors of categories on the acquisition of category names. Here we examined the effect of distributional factors of objects on labelling success in the model. Figure 5 (top) shows an example simulation of the development of correct labelling of objects from 8 basic level categories. Correct labelling shows considerable variation between objects. Whereas the labels *bike, bed*, *chair* and *car* are used correctly early on, the labels *dog*, *man* and *woman* are learned late.

In a first simulation we examined the effect of label frequency on learning its correct use. For this purpose, the usually late-learned labels *dog, man* and *woman* were now presented every time one of these objects was trained while all other objects were labelled only in 50% of occurrences as before. The result of this manipulation is shown in Figure 5 (bottom). While *dog* had previously not been consistently applied correctly before 10,000 object presentations, now it was used correctly in 100% of cases after 7,000 object presentations. The usage of *man* and *woman* likewise improved with frequency of labelling, from an average of 40% correct to 80% correct. Thus, perhaps unsurprisingly this simulation showed that more experience with a specific object label increases its correct use and reduces over-extensions.

We further investigated the role of similarity between members of a specific category (i.e., category compactness) on the speed with which the label for this category was acquired. The 26 basic level categories had different compactness. For example, the *chair* category was the most compact with a mean Euclidean distance between its members of 0.22. The broadest category was *eagle*, comprising photographs of sitting and flying eagles from a variety of perspectives (and thus very different measurements), with a mean distance between category members of 1.3.

During the first 1,200 labelling events there was a positive correlation between compactness and label correctness (mean $r = .62$, $p < .004$), indicating that the labels for broad categories with perceptually different members were initially learned better. This counterintuitive result can be explained with broad categories forming larger 'attractor basins' and therefore facilitating acquisition of the corresponding label. After more than 1,200 labelling events, no further correlation between category broadness and label correctness was found. Furthermore, there was no correlation between category broadness and over-extensions. In sum, these results indicate that labels for categories with perceptually diverse members are initially learned better, but are no more overextended to other categories than the labels of perceptually similar objects.

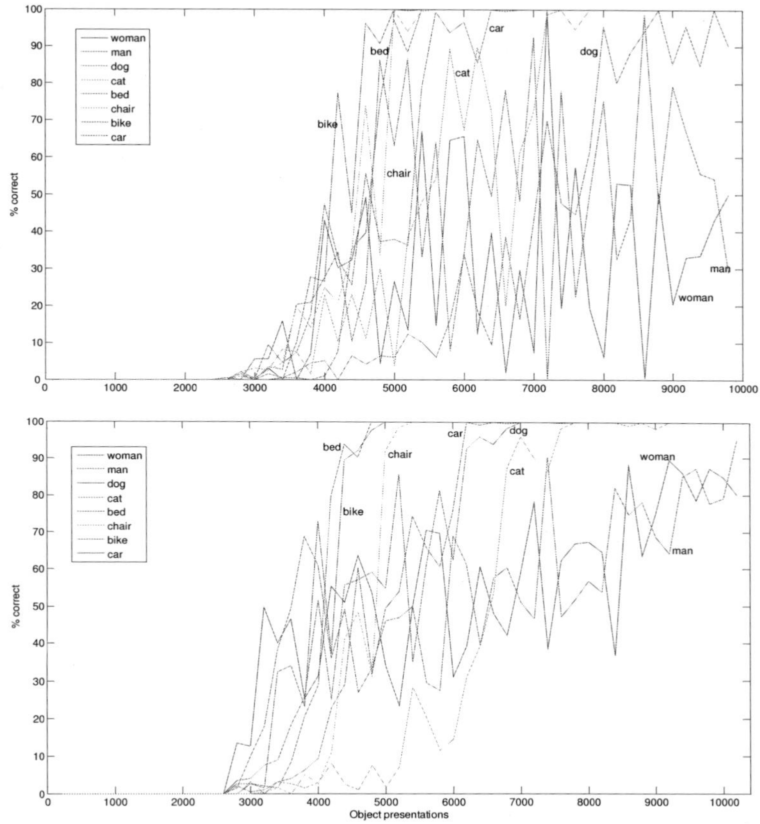

Figure 5: Development of correct labelling of different categories when all objects were labelled with 50% probability (top) and when *man*, *woman* and *dog* were labelled in 100% of cases (bottom).

For a final simulation investigating the effects of category distribution on word learning we created a semi-artificial stimulus set in which all categories had the same compactness to control for the reported effect of compactness on word learning. For this purpose, for each category 10 artificial members were created by adding random Gaussian noise (width 0.1) to the feature values of the category prototype. Ten models were then trained as before, but now only on the artificial category members. Then we computed correlations between correct label usage and a category's mean distance to all other categories, and to its distance to its nearest-neighbour category. The same correlations were computed for label over-extensions (Table 1).

These correlations indicate that labels are learned best for categories that are perceptually different (on average) from all other categories and that have no close nearest neighbour. Category labels are particularly prone to over-extensions if there is a perceptually highly similar neighbour category and no other similar categories. This result can be understood by considering that two perceptually highly similar categories with no other neighbours will be hard to discriminate and labels will be overextended to the respective other category. The same will be true for three or more highly similar categories, but as each label will be overextended in this case the overextension rate of a particular label will decrease.

Table 1. Correlations between label usage and distance relationships between categories.

	Mean distance to all other categories	Distance to nearest neighbour category
Correct label use for a basic level category	$r = 0.41$, $p = .0384$	$r = 0.82$, $p < .0001$
Label over-extension to a basic level category	$r = 0.63$, $p < .001$	$r = -.48$, $p = .0128$

3.4. *Effect of word knowledge on object familiarization*

Familiarization-preferential-looking studies have been widely used to investigate category formation in young infants, yet little is known about the effect of an infant's background knowledge on familiarization time. One study has shown that previous knowledge with a category facilitates familiarization [23]. In categorization tasks with adults it has been found that knowing a label for a novel object likewise facilitates categorization [24]. Here we investigated the effect of prior experience with category members and labels on familiarization in the model. For background knowledge in the model to have an effect on familiarization time, representations from the cortical component have to interact with the hippocampal representations when familiarization stimuli are presented. Depending on the developed structure of cortical representations these could affect hippocampal processing in different ways.

We trained three models in different environments. The first model was not given experience with any background knowledge. The second model was trained on all objects from the 26 categories, but only 2 of the 10 rabbits were used, and no object was labelled. The third model was trained like the second, but this time 50% of all objects were labelled. After training these models for 4,000 object presentations, they were familiarized on the remaining 8 rabbits.

This was done by presenting each of the rabbits to the model repeatedly until the output error of the hippocampal system fell below criterion. The results of this simulation are shown in Figure 6. Familiarization time to the rabbit category was significantly shorter when the model had previous experience with objects (including other rabbits) than when it did not. Importantly, when objects were labelled familiarization time was again significantly shorter than when they were merely presented without labels. This result predicts that infants will familiarize faster to objects for which they know the label.

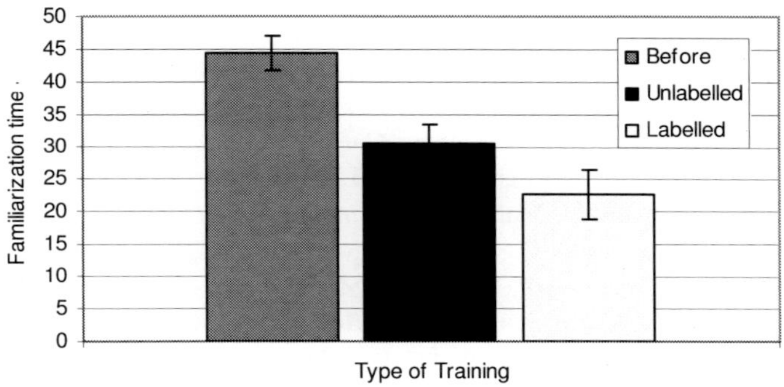

Figure 6: The effect of prior knowledge on object familiarization time (number of object presentation before output error < 0.01).

4. Discussion

In this paper we have extended a previous model of preverbal infant categorization to a model of word learning. This model was able to account for two sets of data: first, the structure of world knowledge affects how fast and how accurate words are learned. Second, learning words warps developed cortical representations to reflect both perceptual similarity and category structure. Through interactions between cortical and hippocampal memory systems, prior knowledge of objects and labels can affect on-line category formation. The precise ways in which perceptual and labelling information interact depends on prior knowledge as well as on distributional properties of the objects in category space. The presented connectionist model represents a starting point to untangle this complex relationship between world knowledge and word learning.

References

1. P.C. Quinn, P.D. Eimas, and S.L. Rosenkrantz, *Perception*. **22**, 463 (1993).
2. B. Younger, *Child Development*. **56**, 1574 (1985).

3. D. Mareschal, R.M. French, and P.C. Quinn, *Developmental Psychology*. **36**, 635 (2000).
4. E.M. Markman, *Categorization and Naming in Children*, Cambridge, MA: MIT Press (1989).
5. W.E. Merriman and L.L. Bowman, *Monogr Soc Res Child Dev*. **54**, 1 (1989).
6. J.S. Horst and L.K. Samuelson. *In 15th Biennial International Conference on Infant Studies*. Kyoto, Japan (2006).
7. M.T. Balaban and S.R. Waxman, *Journal of Experimental Child Psychology*. **64**, 3 (1997).
8. A.L. Fulkerson and R.A. Haaf, *First Language*. **26**, 347 (2006).
9. K. Plunkett, J.F. Hu, and L.B. Cohen, *Cognition*. **106**, 665 (2008).
10. C.W. Robinson and V.M. Sloutsky, *Infancy*. **11**, 233 (2007).
11. V.M. Sloutsky and C.W. Robinson, *Cognitive Science*. **32**, 342 (2008).
12. D. Mareschal and R. French, *Infancy*. **1**, 59 (2000).
13. G. Westermann and D. Mareschal, *Infancy*. **5**, 131 (2004).
14. G. Westermann and D. Mareschal, In *From Associations to Rules: Connectionist Models of Behavior and Cognition*, R.M. French and E. Thomas, (Eds.), World Scientific: London, 127 (2008).
15. D. Mareschal and G. Westermann, In *Neoconstructivism: The New Science of Cognitive Development*, S.P. Johnson, (Ed.), Oxford University Press: New York, (in press).
16. C.A. Nelson, *Developmental Psychology*. **31**, 723 (1995).
17. P.C. Quinn and P.D. Eimas, In *Advances in Infancy Research*, Rovee-Collier and L. C.Lipsitt, (Eds.), 1 (1996).
18. T. Nazzi and J. Bertoncini, *Developmental Science*. **6**, 136 (2003).
19. A. Gopnik and A.N. Meltzoff, *Child Development*. **63**, 1091 (1992).
20. K. Plunkett, C. Sinha, M.F. Møller, and O. Strandsby, *Connection Science*. **4**, 293 (1992).
21. M. Bowerman, In *The development of communication*, N. Waterson and C. Snow, (Eds.), Wiley: New York, 263 (1978).
22. D. Gentner, In *Language development: Vol. 2. Language, thought and culture*, S.A. Kuczaj, (Ed.), Erlbaum: Hillsdale, NJ, 301 (1982).
23. K.A. Kovack-Lesh, J.S. Horst, and L.M. Oakes, *Infancy*. **13**, 285 (2008).
24. G. Lupyan, D.H. Rakison, and J.L. McClelland, *Psychological Science*. **18**, 1077 (2007).

Temporal Aspects of Cognition

DETECTION OF IRREGULARITIES IN AUDITORY SEQUENCES: A NEURAL-NETWORK APPROACH TO TEMPORAL PROCESSING*

JOACHIM HAß[1,2†], STEFAN BLASCHKE[1,2], THOMAS RAMMSAYER[1,3] and J. MICHAEL HERRMANN[1,4]

[1] *Bernstein Center for Computational Neuroscience Göttingen, Germany;*
[2] *University of Göttingen, Göttingen, Germany;*
[3] *University of Bern, Bern, Switzerland;*
[4] *University of Edinburgh, Edinburgh, UK*
† *E-mail: joachim@nld.ds.mpg.de*

Combining experiments and modeling, we study how the discrimination of time intervals depends both on the interval duration and on contextual stimuli. Participants had to judge the temporal regularity of a sequence of standard intervals that contained a deviant interval. We find that the performance to detect the deviant increases with the number of standards preceeding the deviant and decreases with the duration of the standard. While the effect of the standard duration can be explained by an neural network model that realizes the concept of multiple synfire chains, the position effect is incorporated into the model by an in-situ averaging process. Furthermore, experiments are discussed that are critical for the predictions of the model.

Keywords: time perception; sequence experiment; synfire chains; adaptation; serial memory system.

1. Introduction

Whenever we listen to somebody talking, or to a piece of music, we are presented with a sequence of stimuli that contain information in their duration and timing. For instance, the phonemes /ba/ and /pa/ differ by only 25 to 50 ms in their onset time but can still be reliably discriminated. This discrimination is even better when the phonemes are embedded in a sequence that forms natural speech.

While speech is a quite complex example of a sequence including semantic information, the neural mechanisms that enable discrimination of interval durations are not well understood even for much simpler sequences

*This study was supported by a grant from the BMBF in the framework of the Bernstein Center for Computational Neuroscience Göttingen, grant number 01GQ0432.

with purely temporal context, or even single intervals. Despite of numerous experimental and theoretical studies on the topic,[1–3] many ambiguities even about the psychophysical regularities remain. For instance, it is established that variability of time estimates σ_T increases as the intervals T to be estimated get longer,[1] but it is debated whether this increase is linear in T (Weber's law),[4] even steeper[5] or less steep than linear.[6] Similarly, for the question of whether context information enhance discrimination performance, there is both supporting[7,8] and contradicting evidence.[9,10]

We approach these two questions with an experimental paradigm (Sec. 2) where participants discriminate the duration of a variable interval from the constant standard durations of a number of previously presented intervals. The more standards are presented before the variable interval, the more context information is available. Varying the standard duration between blocks, we can simultaneously assess the decrease of discrimination performance with the interval duration. This experiment can be seen as a critical test between two classes of models: Static models like the classical pacemaker-accumulator system[11] predict no context effects at all, while dynamic models such as the multiple look model[7] predict an improved performance with increasing context information. Our results support the latter class, as performance increases at later positions of the variable interval.

In Sec. 3, we formalize the concept of the multiple look model[7] that improved performance results from averaging previous temporal information to reduce discrimination errors. The model provides a statistical framework for perception of both single intervals and sequences of intervals, as judgements about sequences are based on comparison of the individual intervals it is composed of. The model can be readily extended to account for more complex aspects of time perception and has partly been implemented as a biological neural network.[12] This implementation is based on general connection principles in the neocortex and does not depend on any modality-specific properties. Finally, Sec. 4 discusses the results and gives an outlook on further experiments.

2. Sequence experiment

2.1. *Method*

23 psychology undergraduates (mean age 23 years, 17 female) participated in the experiment for partial fullfillment of course requirements. They were naive to the purpose of the experiment, but were debriefed afterwards,

including feedback about their performance. In each trial, a sequence of seven intervals filled with white noise was presented via headphones. Six of these intervals were standard intervals (STI) with a constant duration, while the seventh was a variable interval (VTI). All intervals were separated by an inter-stimulus interval (ISI) with a duration identical to the STI. Participants were instructed that a deviating interval could be presented at any of the seven positions in the sequence and that if there was a deviating interval in the sequence, it would be the only one. The task was to decide whether the presented sequence was regular or irregular. As independent variables, we used the position of the VTI within the sequence (position 1 to position 7), which was randomized from trial to trial, and three different STI durations (50 ms, 150 ms and 250 ms), which were tested in separate blocks. The duration of the VTI was adjusted by a weighted up-down method.[13] Starting from an initial value, the duration was increased (step-up) if the participant had judged the sequence as "regular" and decreased (step-down) after an "irregular" judgment. The adjustments were done independently for each position of the variable interval. We chose the step sizes such that the VTI converged to the .75 percentile of the answer "irregular". As the dependent variable, we used the 75% detection threshold V_{75}, which can be computed from the percentile by subtracting the respective standard duration. The smaller the threshold, the better is the performance in detecting a deviant interval.

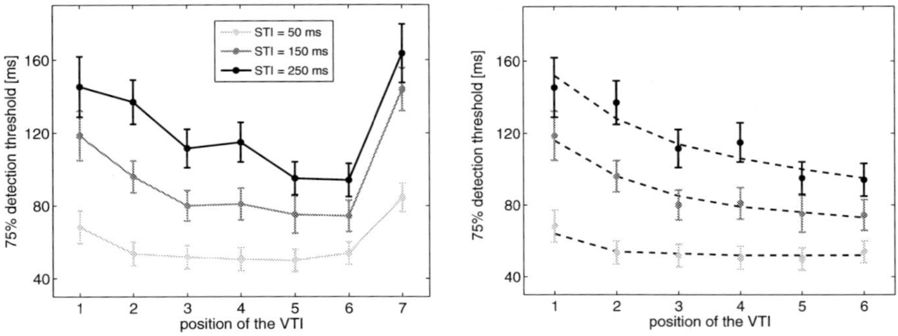

Fig. 1. 75% detection thresholds as a function of the position of the variable interval for three standard durations. The dots are means over participants with standard error bars. (Left) Data for all seven positions. (Right) Data for position one to six. The lines are fits of this data to Eqn. 6 (see Sec. 3.2.4). The color map is the same in both figures.

2.2. *Results*

Fig. 1 shows the mean values of V_{75} as a function of both the position of deviant and the duration of the STI. Three effects are apparent: The threshold increases with the standard duration, decreases from position one to six, and finally, increases again at the last position. To confirm these effects statistically, we performed a two-way ANOVA with the factors position and standard duration (levels as indicated above). The ANOVA showed highly significant effects for both factors, $F(6, 132) = 35.61$, $p < .001$, $\eta = 0.62$ and $F(2, 44) = 68.97$, $p < .001$, $\eta = 0.76$, respectively, and also an interaction, $F(12, 264) = 8.02$, $p < .001$, $\eta = .27$ (η is short for partial eta-squared). These results did not qualitatively change when the seventh position was excluded from the analysis (data not shown).

To further analyse the increase of V_{75} with the STI duration, we take the mean over all seven positions within an STI duration and calculate the Weber fraction $\bar{V}_{75}/STI$ for each STI duration. The values were 1.18, 0.64 and 0.49 for $S = 50$ ms, 150 ms and 250 ms, respectively. Decreasing Weber fractions are in accordance with standard theories of temporal perception[1] within this range of relatively short durations.

The significant decrease of the detection threshold from position one to six established that the number of STIs presented before a VTI indeed improves the performance to detect the deviant. This rules out static models of time perception[11] that would predict no such effect. However, also adaptive models that predict improved performance with increasing number of standards do not predict the decrease in performance at the final position.

3. Serial memory model

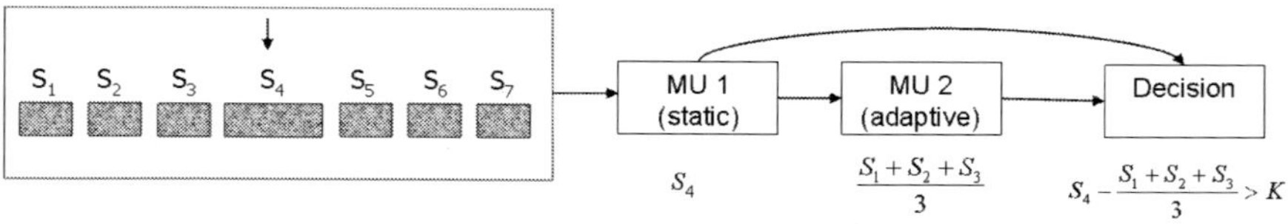

Fig. 2. Illustration of the model structure.

We now develop a model that aims to explain the findings in the present experiment. The model composes the representation of a temporal sequence from the representations of the individual intervals. The basic structure of this model (Fig. 2) is similar to the classical pacemaker-accumulator system,[11] although its elements include mechanisms of adaptivity. Each interval is first encoded in a single-interval representation. We proposed a neural model for this encoding,[12] which we briefly present in the next section.

The second stage in the model is a memory system with two units (MU). These units also exist in the original model, but we make two modifications. First, the units are arranged in serial, e.g. the representation of interval one is first stored in MU1, but as the second interval is encoded, interval one is shifted to MU2 and interval two is stored in MU1 and so on (cf. Fig. 2). And second, while MU1 always contains a representation of the individual intervals, in MU2 the representations of all presented intervals are *averaged* to decrease variability.

Finally, in the third stage, the intervals represented in the two units are compared, and whenever the difference between the two exceeds a certain criterion, a deviant interval is detected. In this respect, the framework is similar to classical signal detection theory.

3.1. *Single interval representations by synfire chains*

A neural correlate of an interval representation should consist of a neural network that is able to store a wide range of time intervals with high precision. A neural structure that fullfills these requirements is the synfire chain,[14] a layered network of spiking neurons with feed-forward connectivity. This type of network has been shown to enable stable propagation of neuronal activity: If a sufficient number of neurons in the first layer is activated, neurons in the second layer also start spiking after some time, and this activation in turn is transmitted to the third pool, and so on. It has been shown that under broad conditions on the strength and timing of the initial activation[15,16] and the model parameters,[12] this propagation is stable, and activity travels along the layers like a wave. The propagation is linear in time and the temporal spread σ_L of the wave at each layer converges to a constant fixed point value in the range of milliseconds,[15,16] even in the presence of synaptic background noise. Therefore, the system is able to translate temporal information into a precise quasi-spatial code: The time elapsed since the initiation of the wave is represented in the position of the layer that is currently most active.[12]

Variability in the representation arises from the remaining temporal spread σ_L in the spikes. This constant error in each layer accumulates to smear the arrival time T of the wave at layer i to a standard deviation σ_T

proportional to the square root of i. Therefore, the Weber fraction σ_T/T decreases with the interval length like $1/\sqrt{T}$, consistent with the results of our experiment.

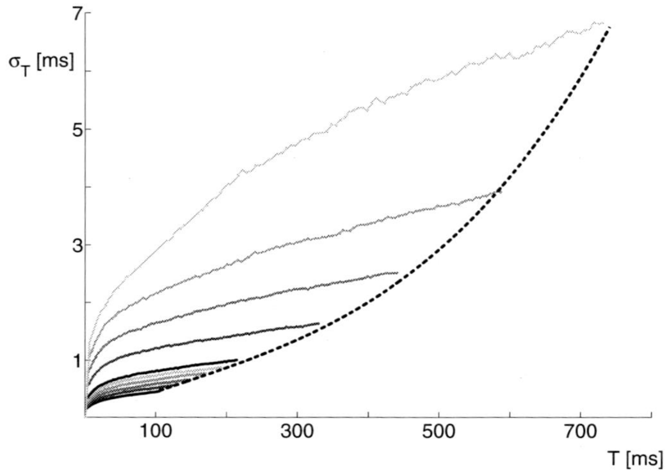

Fig. 3. Timing error, e.g. standard deviation σ_T of the total runtime of an activity wave as a function of time T for various transmission speeds of the chains. The solid curves depict simulation data and the dotted line represents the optimal timing error $\sigma_T^*(T)$ from Eqn. 1. It is close to the lower envelope of the simulation data.

For short intervals up to a few hundred milliseconds, this result of a decreasing Weber fraction has also been found previous experiments.[1,6] However, the steeper increase found at longer intervals (linear or even superlinear with duration[1,3–5]) is not easily reconciled with the accumulation of neuronal noise. For the steeper increase at longer intervals, there must be an additional constraint. In a synfire chain, the most obvious of such constraints is a finite chain length L. With a given mean transmission delay Δt from one pool to the next, the maximal interval to be represented is $T = \Delta t \cdot L$. For longer intervals, a chain with a higher value of Δt must be used. We could show that the speed of the activity wave can be manipulated by various model parameters,[12] but that any change in the synfire model that increases Δt also increases the spread of the spike times σ_L and thus, results in a larger timing error σ_T (Fig. 3).[12] From Fig. 3, it is also apparent that there exists an optimal chain for each interval of time to be encoded, meaning that the timing error σ_T is minimal. As the increase of this error with Δt is much larger (order 3) than the increase along the layers (order 1/2), it is always optimal to use the entire length of the chain with the lowest ΔT that is able to encode the current interval. The form of the optimal timing error is[12]

$$\sigma^*_T(T) = \begin{cases} \sigma_{\min(\Delta t)} \cdot \sqrt{T} + D & \text{for } T \leq \min(\Delta t) \cdot L \\ AT^3 + BT^2 + CT + D & \text{otherwise,} \end{cases} \tag{1}$$

where $\sigma^2_{\min(\Delta t)}$ is the variance of the minimal transmission delay Δt. The dotted line in Fig. 3 shows a fit of the simulated data to Eqn. 1, which is close to the lower envelope of all chains.

The data in our experiment shows a decreasing Weber fraction, so all intervals can be assumed to be encoded by the fastest synfire chain available. We thus use the first column of Eqn. 1 to fit the data, resulting in values of $\sigma_{\min(\Delta t)} = 7.13$ ms and $D = 6.87$ ms. The fit gives a very good description of the data averaged over participants (97.5% of variance explained).

3.2. *Memory and decision stage*

3.2.1. *Stochastic framework*

We now formalize the adaptation in the serial memory system as an information processing model. A neural implementation of this system is in progress. The central stochastic variable is the difference $X_i(I)$ between the contents of the first and the second unit, where I is the time index of the intervals and i is the position of the deviant interval within the sequence. We use a general number of N intervals (set to seven to fit the present data). The intervals are presented during the first N time steps, while the computation of the difference $X_i(I)$ starts with the arrival of the second interval ($I = 2$) and is finished after $I = N + 1$ to complete a total of N comparisons.

Each interval represented by the spike patterns of the synfire chains is denoted by S_i and can be considered as a Gaussian random variable with the actual interval duration as the mean and the variance determined by the timing error σ_T (cf. Sec. 3.1). Assuming the same σ_T for both standard and deviant interval, the VTI is given by

$$S_i = S_v = \mathcal{N}(\bar{S}_v, \sigma^2_T) \tag{2}$$

and the STI is

$$S_j = S_s = \mathcal{N}(\bar{S}_s, \sigma^2_T), \qquad j \neq i. \tag{3}$$

With these definitions, we can write $X_i(I)$ in the general form

$$X_i(I) = S_I - \sum_{j=1}^{I} \frac{S_j}{I}. \tag{4}$$

The first term is the content of MU1 (the interval presented at position I), and the second term is the average in MU2 over all intervals presented before position I.

The difference $X_i(I)$ between the two units can now be used to evaluate the current interval in MU1 based on the information accumulated in MU2: If the difference exceeds a decision criterion K, the interval is judged to be irregular, otherwise it is judged to be regular. The probability for an "irregular" judgment is thus given by

$$P(X_i(I) > K) = \Phi\left(\frac{\bar{X}_i(I) - K}{\sqrt{\mathrm{Var}(X_i(I))}}\right), \tag{5}$$

where Φ is the standard normal distribution function and $\bar{X}_i(I)$ and $\mathrm{Var}(X_i(I))$ are the mean and the variance of $X_i(I)$, respectively.

In the framework of signal detection theory, the probability of a "irregular" response given the VTI in MU1 would correspond to the hit rate, while the probability of the same response, given an STI in MU1 would be the false positive rate. However, we are more interested in the joint probability to judge the entire sequence of N intervals as "irregular", since this response determines the 75% detection thresholds $\bar{S}_v$ in the experiment. This probability is given by

$$P(\text{“irreg''}) = 1 - P\left(\bigcap_{I=2}^{N+1} (X_i(I) < K)\right) = 1 - \prod_{I=2}^{N+1} P\left(X_i(I) < K\right). \tag{6}$$

The second equality holds under the assumption that all events are statistically independent. Note that Eqn. 6 gives an implicit equation for the 75% detection thresholds $\bar{S}_v$ at each of the positions of the VTI, given the probability $P(\text{“irreg''})$, and the set of parameters$\{\sigma_T, K\}$. $P(\text{“irreg''})$ is set to 0.75 in the current experiment, and the parameter set $\{\sigma_T, K\}$ can be used to fit the model to the experimental data.

3.2.2. *Results*

To use Eqn. 6 for determining the $\bar{S}_v$ values, we must calculate the probabilities $P(X_i(I) > K)$ for each value of i and I, and thus, the means and variances of the respective variables $X_i(I)$. However, we can divide all possible combinations of i and I in three groups, each of which have the same mean and variance for all its respective members:

1) The VTI has not yet been presented at position I ($i > I$). In this case, both MU1 and MU2 contain only STIs. Thus,

$$X_i^{(1)}(I) = S_s - \sum_{j=1}^{I} \frac{S_s}{I}; \qquad \bar{X}_i^{(1)}(I) = 0. \tag{7}$$

2) The VTI is presented at time I ($i = I$). Now MU1 contains the VTI, while MU2 is the same as in 1):

$$X_i^{(2)}(I) = S_v - \sum_{j=1}^{I} \frac{S_s}{I}; \qquad \bar{X}_i^{(2)}(I) = \bar{S}_v - \bar{S}_s. \tag{8}$$

3) The VTI has already been presented at an earlier position than I ($i < I$). MU1 contains an STI, again, but one of the intervals in MU2 is the VTI. Thus,

$$X_i^{(3)}(I) = S_s - \sum_{j=1}^{I} \frac{S_s}{I} - \frac{S_v}{I}; \qquad \bar{X}_i^{(2)}(I) = \frac{\bar{S}_s - \bar{S}_v}{I}. \tag{9}$$

The variance of the $X_i(I)$ does is the same in all three cases, because the variance σ_T does not differ for the STIs and the VTI:

$$\text{Var}(X_i^{(1)}(I)) = \text{Var}(X_i^{(2)}(I)) = \text{Var}(X_i^{(3)}(I)) = \sigma_T \frac{I^2 + I}{I^2}. \tag{10}$$

Additionally, it must be noted that the criterion K can not be entirely freely chosen. Specifically, it must be ensured that the probability of an "irregular" judgment is below the defined $P(\text{"irreg"})$ if the sequence does not contain a deviant interval, or $\bar{S}_s - \bar{S}_v = 0$. Otherwise, the adaptive method would make the detection thresholds converge to zero, as a sequence of regular intervals would be sufficient to elicit "irregular" responses with the defined probability. Together with Eqn. 5 and 7, this requirement results in the following condition on K:

$$K > \sigma_T \left(1 - P(\text{"irreg"})\right)^{1/N} \approx 0.915\, \sigma_T, \tag{11}$$

where the second equality holds for $P(\text{"irreg"}) = 0.75$ and $N = 7$.

3.2.3. *Approximation*

Plugging the results Eqn. 7, 8, 9 and 10 into Eqn. 6 yields an equation that only depends on σ_T, K and the detection thresholds $\bar{S}_v - \bar{S}_s$. This equation can be used to fit σ_T and K to the experimentally obtained thresholds. However, the relative contributions of the two parameters to the data will not be apparent in these equations. Here, we derive an approximation where these contributions can be more clearly seen.

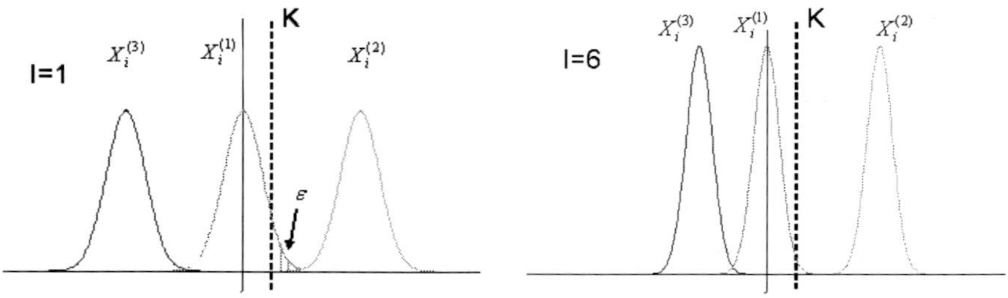

Fig. 4. Distributions of $X_i(I)$ for the three cases (see text) and two values of I.

Fig. 4 illustrates the three distributions of differences $X_i(I)$ for two values of I. All distributions become more peaked for later Is as a result of the averaging process. Furthermore, the mean value of $X_i^{(2)}$ always reflects the actual difference between the VTI and the STI, while the mean of $X_i^{(3)}$ is the negative of this difference for $I = 1$ and decreases in its absolute value for later I. Therefore, it is apparent that the false positive rate $\epsilon = P(X_i(I) < K \mid S_i = S_s)$ (shaded area in Fig. 4) is maximal for $X_i^{(1)}$.

Now assume that we have chosen the criterion K such that ϵ never exceeds a certain value ϵ^* for $X_i^{(1)}$. Then, from the above observations, we see that ϵ^* is also the upper bound for the false positive rate for $X_i^{(3)}$, so we can consider $\epsilon \leq \epsilon^*$ for all $N-1$ false positive cases and approximate Eqn. 6 by

$$P(\text{“irreg”}) \geq 1 - (1-\epsilon^*)^{N-1}\left(1 - \Phi\left(\frac{\bar{S}_v - \bar{S}_s - K}{\sigma_T(I)}\right)\right), \tag{12}$$

where $\sigma_T^2(I)$ is the position-dependent variance common to all three cases, as given in Eqn. 10. Thus, the detection threshold is given for each i by

$$\bar{S}_v - \bar{S}_s \geq \Phi^{-1}\left(1 - \frac{1 - P(\text{“irreg”})}{(1-\epsilon^*)^{N-1}}\right)\sigma_T\sqrt{\frac{I^2 + I}{I^2}} + K. \tag{13}$$

From this equation, one can see that the threshold decreases with I like $\sqrt{1+1/T}$, while the steepness of the decrease is governed by σ_T and a factor depending on ϵ^*, $P(\text{"irreg"})$ and the number of intervals N. Additionally, there is an offset that is equal to the criterion K.

3.2.4. *Fit to data*

We use Eqn. 6 together with the results on mean and variance Eqn. 7, 8, 9 and 10 and the constraint on K, Eqn. 11 to fit the parameters σ_T and K to the data set of the three different standard durations. The fits are depicted as solid lines in Fig. 1. The model gives a good description of the data averaged over participants. (see Tab. 1).

Table 1. Fit parameters for Eqn. 6 (and others, see text).

STI duration [ms]	σ_T [ms]	K/σ_T	variance explained [%]
50	45	0.923	87
150	90	0.965	97
250	110	1.0	89

4. Discussion

We presented a model that can explain context effects on interval discrimination performance that we observed in a sequence experiment, and also the decrease of performance with increasing standard interval durations. Apart from the indivdiual effects, the model also explains the interaction of the two: σ_T increases with the STI durations and enters as a factor in Eqn. 13. Thus, longer STI durations increase the steepness of the adaptation curve, and thus enhances the position effect.

Fitting Eqn. 1 to the data suggested a very high temporal spread, $\sigma_{\min(\Delta t)} = 7.13$ ms. This is about one order of magnitude higher than the values that we found to be realistic.[12] However, this may be a specificity of sequence experiments, as the Weber fractions (0.49 to 1.18) are also very high compared to interval discrimination, where fractions between 0.05 and 0.2 are typical. A possible explanation lies in the rapid presentation of the stimuli: The ISI of maximally 250 ms might not be long enough to allow the intervals to be completely processed, causing an additional error.

The detection thresholds decrease with the position I of the variable interval like $\sqrt{1+1/I}$. Therefore, even for very long sequences, the variablity will not be eliminated, but only decreased to a value close to σ_T (cf. Eqn. 13), the variability of a single interval. Therefore, the model could be falsified by data showing a drastically different form of decrease, e.g. linear or superlinear. Moreover, the model predicts that i) the saturation of the detection threshold should be apparent in longer sequences, and ii) that there should only be a limited effect in single-interval task such as interval production. We already confirmed the first prediction in an experiment with nine intervals.[17]

On the other hand, the model is not directly falsified by the fact that it does not explain the end effect. Like other more complex effects,[17] this could be included by introducing a decay of the representations in the MUs. At the final time step, no new interval is represented in MU1, so the comparison has to rely on the partly decayed memory trace of the second-to-last interval. Because of the decay, the variability of this representation will be increased, which explains the poor discrimination performance at the final position.

References

1. S. Grondin, *Psych Bull* **127**, 22 (2001).
2. J. Gibbon, C. Malapani, C. L. Dale and C. R. Gallistel, *Curr Opin Neuro* **7**, 170 (1997).
3. T. H. Rammsayer and S. Grondin, *Psychophysics of human timing*, in *Time and the brain*, ed. R. Miller (Harwood Academic, 2000), pp. 157–167.
4. J. Gibbon, *Psychol Rev* **84**, 279 (1977).
5. L. A. Bizo, J. Y. Chua, F. Sanabria and P. R. Killeen, *Behav Process* **71**, 201 (2006).
6. D. J. Getty, *Perception and Psychophysics* **20**, 191 (1976).
7. C. Drake and M.-C. Botte, *Perception and Psychophysics* **54**, 277 (1993).
8. R. B. Ivry and E. Hazeltine, *J Exp Psychol [Hum Percept]* **21**, 3 (1995).
9. G. ten Hoopen, R. Hartsuiker, T. Sasaki, Y. Nakajima, M. Tanaka and T. Tsumura, *Perception* **24**, 577 (1995).
10. H. Pashler, *J Exp Psychol [Hum Percept]* **27**, 485 (2001).
11. C. D. Creelman, *J Acoust Soc Am* **34**, 582 (1962).
12. J. Haß, S. Blaschke, T. Rammsayer and J. M. Herrmann, *J Comput Neurosci* **25**, 449 (2008).
13. C. Kaernbach, *Perception and Psychophysics* **49**, 227 (1991).
14. M. Abeles, *Corticonics: Neural circuits of the cerebral cortex* (Cambridge University Press, 1991).
15. J. M. Herrmann, J. A. Hertz and A. Prügel-Bennet, *Network-Comp Neural* **6**, 403 (1995).
16. M. Diesmann, M.-O. Gewaltig and A. Aertsen, *Nature* **402**, 529 (1999).
17. S. Blaschke, J. Haß, J. M. Herrmann and T. H. Rammsayer, *submitted* (2008).

INFORMATION DYNAMICS AND THE PERCEPTION OF TEMPORAL STRUCTURE

S. A. ABDALLAH* and M. D. PLUMBLEY

Centre for Digital Music,
Queen Mary, University of London,
London, E1 4NS, UK.
**E-mail: samer.abdallah@elec.qmul.ac.uk*

In this paper we describe how information theoretic methods can be used in the context of time-varying subjective probability models in order to quantify such notions as uncertainty and surprisingness as experienced by a hypothetical observer exposed to sequences of symbolic stimuli, in particular, musical patterns. Novel measures of predictive information and predictive information rate, introduced in previous work[1] as a potential model for 'interestingness' or formal aesthetic value, are extended to account for adaptation in the observer's probability model on repeated exposure to a pattern. The system is applied to minimalist music and compared with results from previous rule-based systems of music analysis.

Keywords: information theory; expectation; surprise; subjective probability; Bayesian inference; Markov chain; music

1. Expectation and surprise in music

It has often been observed[2,3] that, in music, an important part of the experience is to do with the way the listener's expectations are manipulated as the music unfolds: in a suitably acculturated listener, certain passages create strong or weak expectations which may be fulfilled or confounded by the subsequent development. This landscape of varying expectancy, uncertainty and surprise is thought to characterise the significant temporal structure of the piece and be a major determinant of the listener's overall response.[4]

Prediction and expectation are essentially probabilistic concepts and can be modelled mathematically using probability theory. In particular, Shannon's *information theory*[5] provides us with a number of measures, such as entropy and mutual information, which are suitable for quantifying states of uncertainty and surprise, and thus could potentially enable us to build quantitative models of the listening process described above. They are what Berlyne[6] called 'collative variables' since they are to do with patterns of occurrence rather than medium-specific details. Berlyne sought to show that the collative variables are closely related to perceptual qualities like complexity, tension, interestingness, and even aesthetic value, not just in music, but in other temporal or visual media. The relevance of information theory to music and art has also been addressed by researchers from the 50s onwards.[2,7–10]

Our work continues this thread, but in a framework that explicitly considers the observer's role in perception. Specifically, collative variables such as entropy are not properties of the stimulus alone, but of the stimulus *and* the probabilities assigned by the observer as it attempts to predict future events. These probabilities depend on the observer's particular model of the process under observation and are therefore *subjective* in an essential way. Studies such as those by Saffran *at al*[11,12] have shown that human listeners are indeed sensitive to statistical regularities and are able to use them to parse and categorise sequences of sounds. We focus on how (a) these ideas can be implemented in simple probabilistic models of discrete processes (b) which information-theoretic variables can usefully be computed; and (c) on how these might relate to subjective experiences in human listeners.

As a demonstration of how the approach performs on a piece of music, a Markov chain model is used to analyse two pieces by composer Philip Glass: *Two Pages* (1969) and *Gradus* (1968), yielding structural analyses with many points of correspondence with those of an expert listener.

2. Information theory in sequences

2.1. *Entropy and information*

Entropy is a measure of the uncertainty represented by a probability distribution. If $p(x)$ is a distribution over possible observations x of a random variable X, then the entropy of the random variable is $H(X) = \mathrm{E} - \log p(X)$. One can consider $-\log p(x)$ to be a measure of the 'surprisingness' of a observing x, tending to infinity as the $p(x)$ approaches zero, which case, the entropy is the 'expected surprisingness'.

We consider the 'belief state' of an intelligent observer to consist of probability distributions over quantities of interest to the observer. In this case, 'information' is that which reduces uncertainty and hence involves a change of belief state. If $\mathcal{D}$ represents new evidence relevant to a variable X and $\mathcal{B}$ background knowledge avalaible before the new evidence is observed, then the information in $\mathcal{D}$ about X is quantified as the Kullback-Leibler

(KL) divergence between the prior and posterior distributions $p(x|\mathcal{B})$ and $p(x|\mathcal{D},\mathcal{B})$:

$$\mathcal{I} = D_{kl}(p_{X|\mathcal{D},\mathcal{B}}||p_{X|\mathcal{B}}) = \mathrm{E}_{X|\mathcal{D},\mathcal{B}} \log \frac{p(X|\mathcal{D},\mathcal{B})}{p(X|\mathcal{B})}, \tag{1}$$

If we take two variables which the observer believes to be dependent, then learning the value of X will alter the observer's beliefs about Y. The mutual information is the expected information in X about Y:

$$I(X;Y) = H(Y) - H(Y|X) = H(X) - H(X|Y), \tag{2}$$

where the background knowledge is now implicit in the definitions of the entropies. Note the symmetry of the definition and its interpretation as the expected change in entropy of one variable on learning the other. Further details can be found in any textbook on information theory.[13]

2.2. *Random sequences*

Now consider the observation of a random sequence $S_1, S_2, \ldots$. At any time there is an observed past, a 'now', and an unobserved future. Eg, at time $t = 4$, we have the situation depicted in fig. 1. As each element of the sequence is observed in turn, the observer can maintain a dynamically evolving belief state based on a probabilistic model of the sequence, $p(\text{Future}|\text{Past})$.

What we are calling 'information dynamics' is the analysis of how various time-varying information-theoretic quantities develop as the sequence unfolds. We consider the following quantities defined in terms of entropies and KL divergences (see fig. 1):

- Predictive uncertainty: $H(X|Z)$.
- Surprisingness: $-\log p(X|Z)$.
- Predictive information: $D_{kl}(p_{Y|X,Z}||p_{Y,Z})$.
- Predictive information rate: $I(X;Y|Z) = H(Y|Z) - H(Y|X,Z)$.
- Information arriving about any model parameters θ: $D_{kl}(p_{\theta|X,Z}||p_{\theta|Z})$.

2.3. *Predictive information and the Wundt curve*

Previous work on information theory and aesthetics[6,14] looked into the relationship between perceived value ('pleasingness','hedonic value' etc.) and the randomness or complexity of stimuli as quantified by some objective entropy or entropy rate. In many cases, an inverted 'U' shaped curve was

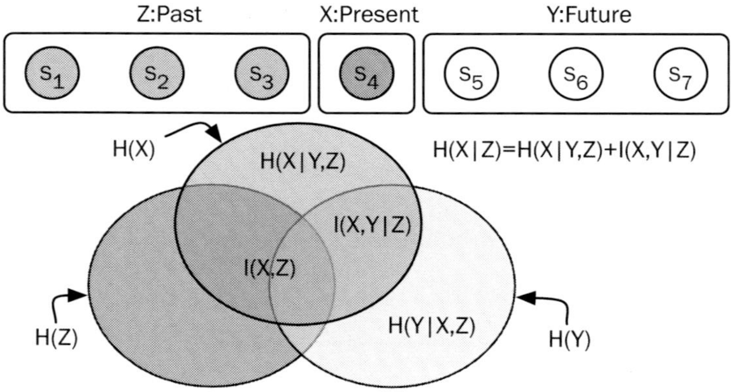

Fig. 1. Random variables and information theoretic quantities involved in observing a random sequence. If X, Y and Z stand for the present, infinite future and infinite past respectively, then $H(X|Z)$ is the entropy rate and $I(X,Y|Z)$ is the predictive information rate.

found, similar to that observed by Wundt[15] and illustrated in fig. 2, where optimal value was attached to stimuli of intermediate randomness; intuitively, those which are neither too deterministic (predictable, boring) nor too random (unstructured, noise-like).

There are two problems with this approach. Firstly, the notion that observers can assess any kind of 'objective' entropy measure is questionable: much more relevant is the *subjective* assessment each observer makes based its prior experience and on the information available to it. Secondly, the discovery of a 'U' shaped curve does not explain the position of the optimum, which leads us to ask if there is any theoretical quantity which is maximal when aesthetic value is maximal?

An interesting property of the the predictive information rate (PIR) as defined above is that it has an upper bound which displays a similar inverted 'U' relationship with the entropy rate, with a natural optimum at intermediate entropy rates. Consider a process which is perfectly predictable given the observed past. In this case, both the entropy rate and the PIR are zero because there is no uncertainty about the next observation and therefore no new information when that observation is made. One would expect such a process to be, or rapidly become, boring. At the other extreme, consider a maximally random process with no temporal dependencies (like white noise). The lack of temporal dependence means each symbol carries no information about any other; once the observer has learned this, then its

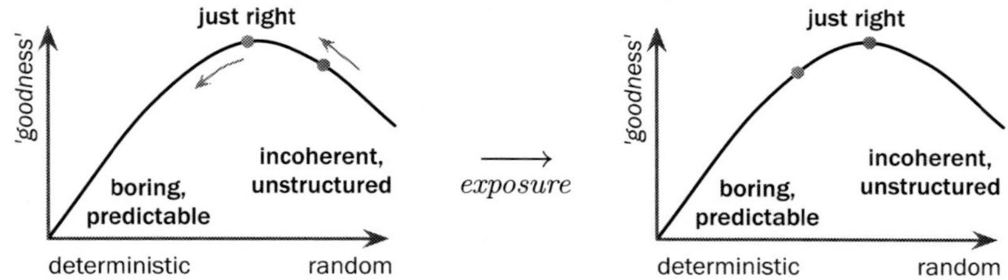

Fig. 2. The Wundt curve relating randomness/complexity with perceived value. Repeated exposure sometimes results in a move to the left along the curve.[6]

subjective predictive information rate will again be zero even thought the entropy rate may be large. Thus to achieve a large predictive information rate, there must be randomness but also structure.

2.4. *Summary of central hypothesis*

As we listen to a piece of music, we continually assimilate new data in order to maintain a dynamically evolving picture of the expected evolution. If this belief state is represented in terms of probability distributions over possible futures, we can judge uncertainty, surprisingness, and information gain using the tools of information theory.

By tracing the evolution of a few such information measures, we obtain a low-dimensional description that summarises probabilistic structure at a level of abstraction removed from the details of the sensory experience. The approach is also quite general in that it can, in principle, be applied to any sensory modality using whatever probabilistic models are appropriate, available, or tractable. Finally, it incorporates the notion of subjectivity in a fundamental way, since the analysis depends on the probabilistic machinery that a particular observer can bring to bear at a particular time, and is thus dependent on observer's prior experience and ability to learn.

Our aim is to find out if information dynamics can explain the human percetion of temporal structure in music and potentially in other domains.

3. Information dynamics in Markov chains

One of the simplest models of temporal dependence is the Markov chain, for which various information dynamic quantities can be derived exactly. Assume we have a stationary Markov chain with transition matrix $\mathbf{T}$ such that $p(S_{t+1} = i|S_t = j) = T_{ij}$. Let $\mathcal{H}(\mathbf{T})$ be the entropy rate, which,

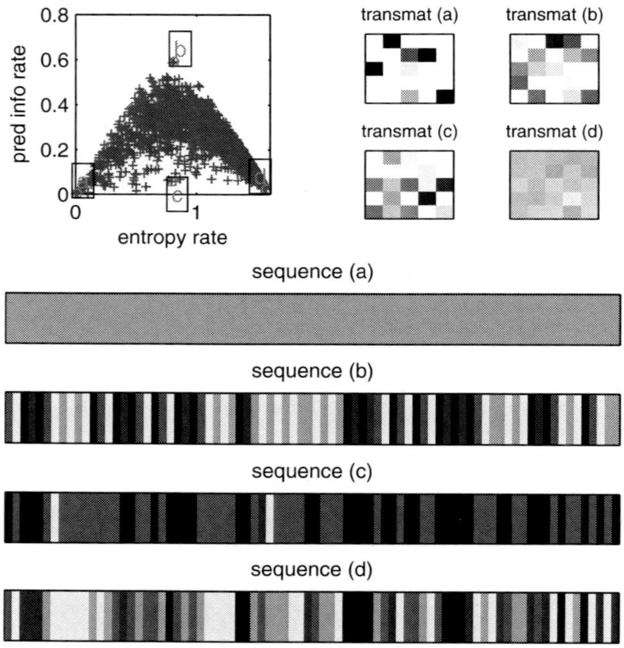

Fig. 3. The space of 5-by-5 Markov chains and 4 examples with different information dynamic properties. Each point in the scatter plot represents one stationary Markov chain (i.e., one transition matrix).

for a stationary Markov chain, is equivalent to the conditional entropy $H(S_{t+1}|S_t)$ and is independent of t. In this case, the predictive information rate is easily found to be $\mathcal{I}_1(\mathbf{T}) = \mathcal{H}(\mathbf{T}^2) - \mathcal{H}(\mathbf{T})$.

We can explore the space of transition matrices by generating them at random and plotting the entropy rate against PIR, as shown in fig. 3. We can also optimise the PIR directly using general purpose optimiser with numerical gradients. We observe empirically (see fig. 4) that relatively sparse transition matrices maximise the PIR, and that the maximal PIR for each size of transition matrix over a wide range appears to be approximately half the maximal entropy rate (plot not shown due to lack of space).

4. Learning and subjective information

Theoretical development so far relies on observer knowing the 'true' model. In practise, there may be no 'true' model, only some, usually finite, amount of data, and observer must estimate a model to fit it. In the case of the

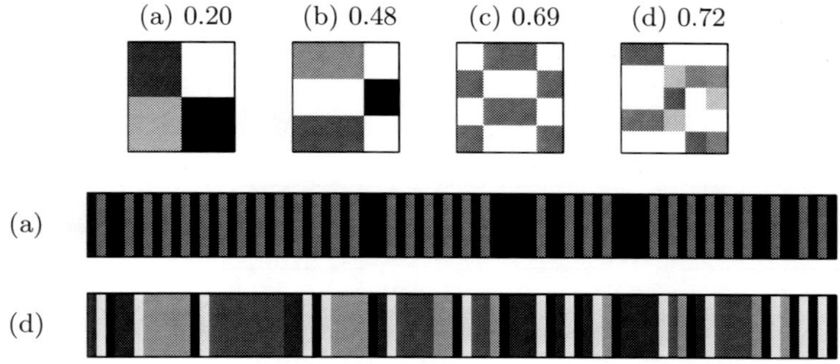

Fig. 4. Four examples of transition matrices with maximal PIR, and sequence sampled from matrices (a) and (d).

Markov chain model, we can generalise the analysis to examine what happens if a long sequence is sampled from a known generative transition matrix, but is processed by an observer assuming a different transition matrix. We can also compute how the observer's assessment of the process changes if it gradually adapts its transition matrix to better fit the data.

We find that while the observer's subjective entropy rate generally decreases as it learns about the statistical stucture of the process, its subjective predictive information rate can go up or down depending the process under observation and the initial state of the observer. This could provide an explanation for the phenomenon illustrated in fig. 2, but suggests that it is more complex than a simple migration along the Wundt curve. The results are summarised in fig. 5.

5. An analysis of minimalist music

We used the adaptive Markov chain model to analyse *Two pages* by minimalist composer Philip Glass, a piece of music which is well suited to the model since it is monophonic and consists of a steady stream of notes with no rhythmic variation. Hence, it is composed of very simple elements but is still 'real' music. We compared the results with the six 'most surprising' moments chosen by an expert listener (Keith Potter, Goldsmiths, Univ. of London) and the rule-based Local Boundary Detection Model.[16] The results can be seen in fig. 6. Note how the major and minor structural boundaries are reasonably well captured by the surprise and information signals, and how the model information rate (information in observations about the transition matrix) agrees quite well with the six most surprising

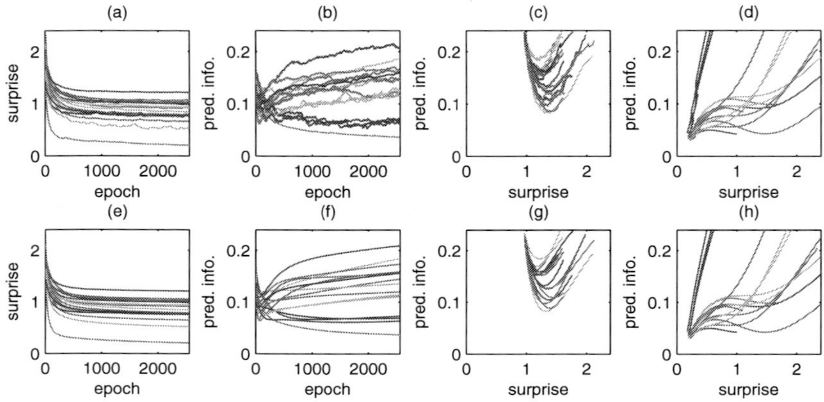

Fig. 5. Learning dynamics in an adaptive Markov chain model. The upper row shows the actual stochastic learning while the lower shows the idealised deterministic learning. Plots (a/b/e/f) show multiple runs starting from the same initial condition but using different generative transition matrices. Plots (c/d/g/h) show multiple runs starting from different initial conditions and converging on two transition matrices with (c/g) high or (d/h) low PIR respectively.
In (a/e), subjective surprisingness tends to decrease, since this the objective of learning. In (b/f), subjective predictive information rate, after initial transient phase, can go up or down depending on the generative system. The two target systems in (c/g) and (d/h) correspond to the highest and lowest lines in (a/b/e/f).

moments. The rule-based analysis, in contrast, reflects the structure, but without a clear interpretation in terms of major and minor boundaries.

We applied same analysis to *Gradus*, also by Glass. This piece uses a wider pitch range, is more tonal, and is less systematically structured. The results are harder to interpret, but comparison with a detailed musicalogical analysis of the piece[17] shows many points of correspondence, include several which are not captured by the rule-based analysis.

In addition to an event-by-event comparison, we also investigated whether or not the metrical structure (that is, an implied regular pattern of strong and weak beats) of the piece was revealed by the information dynamic analysis. We averaged the various information measures over events at equivalent metrical positions assuming bar lengths of 32, 64, and 128 notes (which are all quavers in this piece) to see if there was any systematic variation. For example, we computed the average surprisingness of the first note in each bar, the second note in each bar etc. bar (the notated bar length is 32 quavers). We found that the first note of each bar was con-

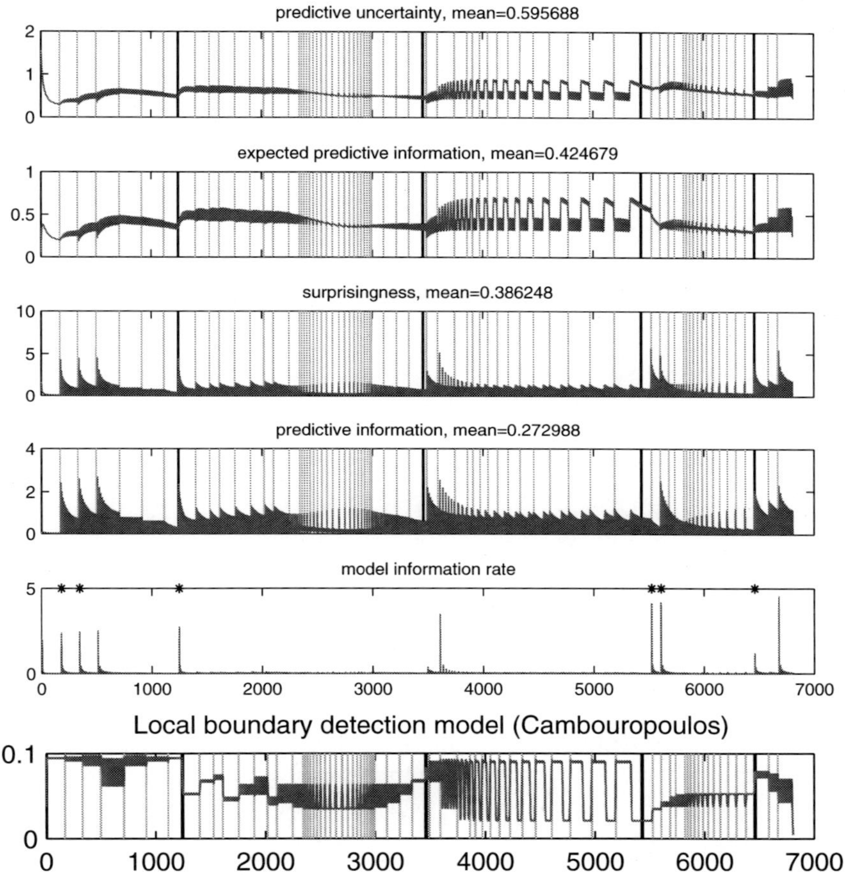

Fig. 6. Analysis of *Two Pages*. The thick vertical lines are the part boundaries as indicated in the score by the composer. The thin grey lines indicate changes in the melodic 'figures' of which the piece is constructed. In the 'model information rate' panel, the black asterisks mark the six most surprising moments selected by Keith Potter. The bottom panel shows a rule-based boundary strength analysis computed using Cambouropoulos' LBDM. All information measures are in nats and time is in notes.

sistently more surprising and informative than the others (see fig. 8) and also that the first note of every 2-bar segment (i.e. every 64 quavers) was more surprising and informative still, suggesting the presence of a 64-quaver hyper-metrical structure. However, there was no evidence of a 128-quaver metre.

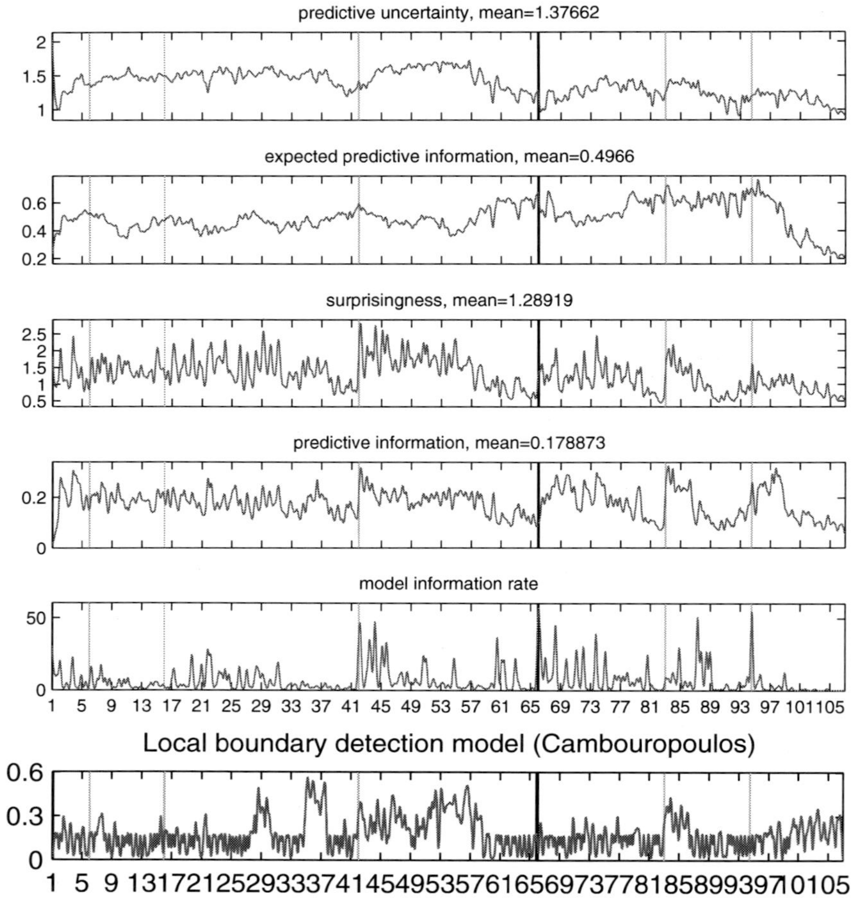

Fig. 7. Analysis of *Gradus*. The thick black vertical lines indicate the part boundaries as indicated in the score by the composer. The thin grey lines indicate a segmentation given by Keith Potter. Note that the traces were smoothed with a Gaussian window about 12 events wide to make them more legible. The top five panels show the information dynamic analysis while the bottom panel shows a rule-based boundary strength analysis using using Cambouropoulos' LBDM. Time is in bars.

6. Conclusions and future work

In this paper, we have described an approach to the analysis of temporal structure based on an information-theoretic assessment made from the point of view of an observer with a dynamic, subjective probability model of

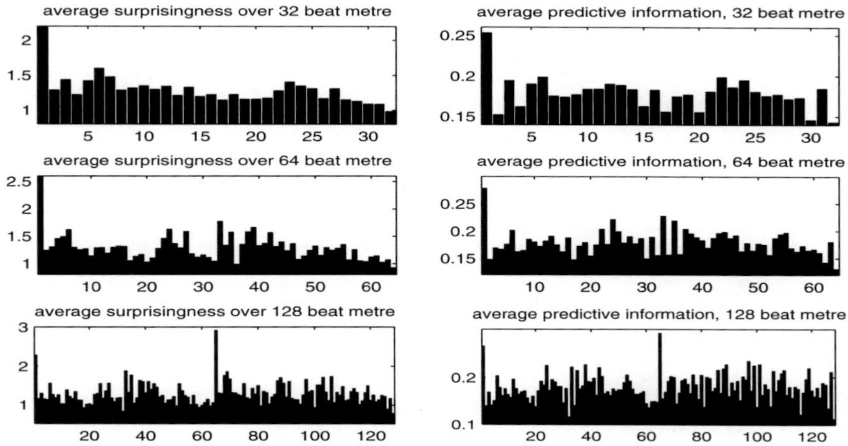

Fig. 8. Metrical analysis by computing average surprisingness and informative of notes at different periodicities (i.e. hypothetical bar lengths) and phases (i.e. positions within a bar).

the sequences of observations. When applied to minimalist music, using an extremely simple model with no specifically musical features, this produces a structural analysis that corresponds quite well with the known structure of the pieces and an analysis by a human listener, and in some ways is an improvement on analyses using a rule-based designed specifically for music (though not for minimalist music).

The theoretical analysis of information dynamics in Markov chains reveals some phenomena which may be relevant to modelling aesthetic perception, in particular, the Wundt-curve like behaviour of the predictive information and the effects of learning on the predictive information rate.

The results so far are suggestive but require further investigation, especially with regard to their relavance to cognitive processes in humans. Hence, we plan to look for physiological and neurological correlates of the theoretic quantities computed using our model, and also examine a possible relationship between predictive information and perceptions of aesthetic goodness or interestingness.

On the theoretical side, possible avenues for further work include application to other probabilistic models (such as hidden Markov models, Gaussian processes and so on) and models that combine short-term learning of a particular piece with long-term learning of general styles. One fundamental theoretical aspect we have yet to address is the effect of variabilities in event durations: in music, time spent waiting for the next event provides information relevant to predicting the times of future events. Predictive information in patterns of duration may shed light on the perception of rhythm and metre.

Acknowledgments

This research was supported by EPSRC grant GR/S82213/01 and EPSRC Platform Grant EP/E045235/1. Thanks are also due to to Keith Potter and Geraint Wiggins (Goldsmiths, University of London) for providing musicological analyeses of *Two Pages* and *Gradus*, and to Marcus Pearce (Goldsmiths, University of London) for providing the rule-based analyses of both pieces.

References

1. S. A. Abdallah and M. D. Plumbley, Information dynamics and the perception of temporal structure in music, in *Proc. NIPS 2007 Workshop on Music, Brain and Cognition*, (Vancouver, Canada, 2007).
2. L. B. Meyer, *Music, the arts and ideas: Patterns and Predictions in Twentieth-century culture* (University of Chicago Press, 1967).
3. E. Narmour, *Beyond Schenkerism* (University of Chicago Press, 1977).
4. D. Huron, *Sweet Expectations* (MIT Press, 2006).
5. C. E. Shannon, *The Bell System Technical Journal* **27**, 379 (1948).
6. D. E. Berlyne, *Aesthetics and Psychobiology* (Appleton Century Crofts, New York, 1971).
7. J. E. Youngblood, *Journal of Music Theory* **2**, 24 (1958).
8. E. Coons and D. Kraehenbuehl, *Journal of Music Theory* **2**, 127 (1958).
9. J. E. Cohen, *Behavioral Science* **7**, 137 (1962).
10. A. Moles, *Information Theory and Esthetic Perception* (University of Illinois Press, 1966).
11. J. R. Saffran, E. K. Johnson, R. N. Aslin and E. L. Newport, *Cognition* **70**, 27 (1999).
12. P. Loui and D. Wessel, Acquiring new musical grammars — a statistical learning approach, in *International Conference on Music Perception and Cognition (ICMPC9)*, 2006.
13. T. M. Cover and J. A. Thomas, *Elements of Information Theory* (John Wiley and Sons, New York, 1991).
14. D. E. Berlyne (ed.), *Studies in the New Experimental Aesthetics: Steps towards an objective psychology of aesthetic appreciation* (Hemisphere, Washington D.C., 1974).
15. W. Wundt, *Outlines of Psychology* (Englemann, Lepzig, 1897).
16. E. Cambouropoulos, Towards a general computational theory of musical structure, PhD thesis, University of Edinburgh1998.
17. K. Potter, G. A. Wiggins and M. T. Pearce, *Musicae Scientiae* **11**, 295 (2007).

Concepts and High-Level Cognition

COMBINING SELF-ORGANIZING AND BAYESIAN MODELS OF CONCEPT FORMATION

TIINA LINDH-KNUUTILA*, JUHA RAITIO and TIMO HONKELA

Adaptive Informatics Research Centre
Helsinki University of Technology P.O. Box 5400
FI-02015 TKK, Espoo, Finland
**E-mail: tiina.lindh-knuutila@tkk.fi*
http://www.cis.hut.fi/research/cog

In this article, we consider contemporary theories of concepts, and Bayesian and self-organizing models of concept formation. After introducing the different models, we present our own experiment. It utilizes a multi-agent simulation framework, in which the emergence of a common vocabulary can be studied. In the experiment, we use jointly the self-organizing maps and probabilistic modeling of concept naming. The results of the experiments show that a common vocabulary to denote prototypical colors emerges in the agent population.

Keywords: concept, concept formation, self-organization, Bayesian inference, multi-agent simulation, language game

1. Introduction

Concept learning is an essential task in any real life machine learning and artificial intelligence application. In this paper, we contrast self-organized with Bayesian approaches in concept formation learning, also considering the different background assumptions. First, we will characterize concepts through a short introduction to the contemporary theories, followed by examination of the process of concept formation as modelled by studies in self-organized and Bayesian fields. After contrasting these approaches, we present our own model that combines probabilistic modeling of concept naming with the self-organization of the underlying conceptual space.

2. Concepts

In our view, a concept is the mediating level between the perception and language (Fig. 1). We require concepts to be grounded. There are several different views on the grounding problem.[1] We see grounding as the process of transfering sensory perceptions into non-symbolic (connectionist)

representations. A concept can also be grounded through its relation to other concepts. Concept as such, does not suppose the existence of a linguistic label, but this label emerges through its function in communication. The *meaning* of a label is established in its association to a concept.

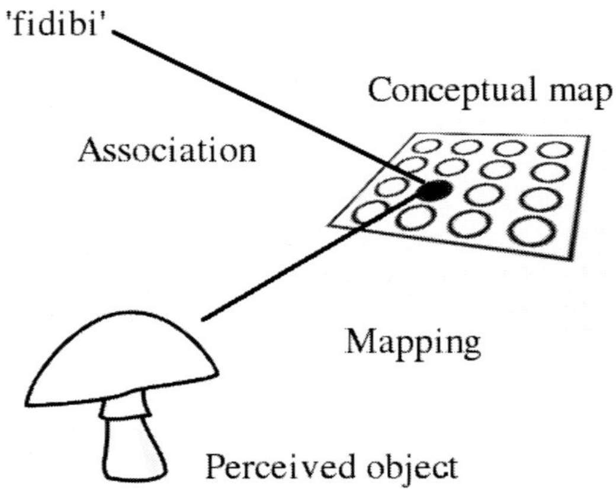

Fig. 1. The three level model of perceptions, concepts and language.

2.1. *Historical theories*

The classical, Aristotelean view sees concepts as a set of necessary and sufficient definitions (e.g bird has wings, beak etc.). This kind of view has a long history in philosophy.[2,3]

The prototype theory emerged in the 1970s as an alternative to the classical theory of concepts. The main idea was to include the experimental findings of typicality effects,[2,4] which means that some instances are better examples of a category than others (e.g. 'robin' is considered a better example of category *bird* than 'penguin'). According to the prototype theory, most lexical concepts are complex representations, whose structure encodes a statistical analysis of the properties their members tend to have: Categories have graded memberships around a certain prototype.

Since 1980s, there has also been a significant amount of research building on artificial neural network models with the aim of connecting the neural and symbolic levels (cf. e.g. the work by P.M. Churchland[5] and P.S. Churchland[6] as early influential accounts).

2.2. *Theory of conceptual spaces*

Theory of conceptual spaces[7] was developed to model conceptual representations in a cognitive framework. A conceptual space is built upon geometrical structures based on a number of quality dimensions. Concepts are not independent of each other but can be structured into domains, e.g., concepts for colors in one domain, spatial concepts in the other domain.

Categories are seen as convex regions in a conceptual space. The concepts are learned from a limited number of examples and by generalizing from them. The similarity of two objects can be defined as a distance between their representation points in the conceptual space, which can then be used, e.g., for categorization: The perceived item belongs to the category whose prototype is the nearest to the mapping of the item in conceptual space. The prototype effects can also be explained in the conceptual spaces. The prototypes are simply those instances of the category that are located in the central parts of these regions.

In general, the theory of conceptual spaces proposes a medium to get from the continuous space of sensory information to a higher conceptual level, where concepts could be associated to discrete symbols. It has been proposed[7] that for example multi-dimensional scaling (MDS) and self-organizing maps (SOM) could be used to model a domain in a conceptual space.

3. Models of concept formation

We adopt the position that concepts are learned, and they adapt. In the process of concept formation, mental constructs are developed based on sensory experience. Concept formation figures prominently in cognitive development (see e.g. Ref. 8). As a concept emerges, it becomes subject to testing. Consideration of a wide range of possibilities e.g. through playing games, contributes to this process.

3.1. *Self-organization*

The basic principle of the self-organized representations is that internal relations of categories may be derivable from the mutual relations and roles of the data in an unsupervised way.[9]

3.1.1. *The self-organizing map*

The self-organizing map (SOM) is a neural network model developed in the early 1980s.[10,11] It produces a topographic mapping the input space into an array of nodes. Perhaps the most typical notion of the SOM is to consider it as an artificial neural network model of the brain,[12] especially of the experimentally found ordered cortical "maps".

Each node of the SOM consists of a prototype vector of the same dimension as the input vectors. The SOM is trained according to a competitive learning principle. When an input vector is fed into the system, a prototype vector with the smallest distance to the input (the best-matching unit, BMU) vector is selected. In the adaptation process, the BMU and its neighbors in the topological ordering are moved toward this input in the space. The degree of adaptation depends on the learning function $m_i(t+1) = m_i(t) + h_{ci}(t)[x(t) - m_i(t)]$, where $h_{ci}(t)$ is the neighborhood function defining how large the neighborhood is, m_i is the ith map unit, $x(t)$ the input vector, and t is the discrete time coordinate.

A detailed description about the selection of the parameters, variants of the map, and many other aspects have been covered in Ref. 11. In this work, we have used the classical SOM architecture due to its reasonably high validity as a neuro-cognitive model. A well motivated alternative in this particular case would also be the Bayesian version of the SOM, i.e. the Generative Topographic Map (GTM).[13]

3.1.2. *Models using self-organization*

Ritter and Kohonen made first experiments of concept learning with the SOM.[9] In the experiment, contextual information for words (preceding and following word of the target word) based on generated three-word sentences was fed to the SOM. Later, Honkela[14] conducted an extended study in the same subject which used the Grimm's tales in English as data. The experiments show that based on the contextual information the target words were indeed organized in a SOM in a way that seems meaningful — nouns in one group, verbs in another. Words with similar usage (e.g., verbs with past tense, nouns describing animate or inanimate objects) could also be found in smaller subgroups.

Schyns[15] demonstrated how simple concepts could be learned with a modular neural network model. The model has two modules, one for categorizing the input in an unsupervised manner and another module for learning the names for the categories in a supervised mode. The input for the SOM, which was used as a categorization module, was pictorial image data varied around 'prototypes' in such a way that the prototypes were never directly shown to the SOM. Instead, the map was fed distortions around these prototypes. In a sense, this image data could then correspond to certain 'sensory data'. The result of this experiment was that the map learned to represent the prototypes. Schyns sees that the categorization module fills the definitions of the prototype theory. In the second phase, the names for these categories were learned in a supervised manner.

Other examples of SOM applied to symbol processing include Ref. 16, where the representations emerging from color spectrum input and their association to color names were studied. In Ref. 17, a multi-agent simulation of a simple language emergence was conducted. The agents learned very simple concepts in the color domain using SOM as a model for the conceptual memory. In the course of the simulation, symbols emerged, and were associated with areas on the conceptual map, and as a result a simple, shared vocabulary emerged.

The self-organizing models of concept formation often use real-world data, either in textual form or fairly simple data from one conceptual domain. The approach is bottom up, and the learning is self-organizing and unsupervised. The representations obtained are pattern-like, and the inference between concepts is similarity based. It seems, though, that a single SOM cannot be used for representation for a complete set of concepts, but rather, various SOMs are needed for different domains. Additionally, a system to produce the per-concept feature selection for more complex concepts would be needed. See more detailed discussion on this in Ref. 18.

3.2. *Bayesian modeling*

3.2.1. *Bayesian inference*

Bayesian models are very commonly used in modern research in several fields. Bayesian inference utilizes the Bayes' theorem, $P(h|x) = \frac{P(x|h)P(h)}{P(x)}$, where $P(h|x)$ is the posterior probability of a hypothesis h given observation x, $P(x|h)$ the conditional probability (likelihood) of observing x under the hypothesis h, $P(x)$ the probability of the observation, and $P(h)$ the a priori probability of the hypothesis. In Bayesian inference, observations are used to infer the probability that a hypothesis may be true. New observations update this probability.

3.2.2. *Models using Bayesian inference*

There are several researchers who use Bayesian inference as a tool for modeling some cognitive phenomenon. We will briefly describe some of the research relevant to this article. Bayesian modeling of concept learning has been considered e.g. in Tenenbaum's model[19,20] which is based on the following basic building blocks: (1) A constrained hypothesis space of possible extensions of a concept, (2) a prior distribution over the hypothesis space reflecting the learner's relevant background knowledge, (3) the size principle for scoring the likelihood of hypothesis, favoring smaller consistent hypotheses, and (4) hypotheses averaging: integrating the predictions of multiple consistent hypotheses.

More specifically, the task of learning simple concepts was defined as the task of learning axis-parallel rectangles, based on a small number of positive examples only. The likelihood $p(x|h)$ was computed based on the background assumption of randomly sampled positive examples (strong sampling criterion[20]) $P(x|h) = \begin{cases} \frac{1}{|h|} & \text{if } x \in h \\ 0 & \text{otherwise} \end{cases}$, where h indicates the size of the region. This leads to the *size principle*: smaller hypothesis that just cover the observed samples become more likely than larger ones. They define the purpose of concept learning to help in the decision making: As an example, they give a doctor who needs to learn a doctor to learn which levels of cholesterol can be considered healthy[19] or a baby bird that needs to learn which worms are edible edible based on the worm color shades.

Dowman studies the Bayesian concept learning principle in the color domain,[21,22] using the Bayesian approach described earlier. His work does not consider the pre-linguistic categorization, instead phenomenological color space consisting only of the hue of color is assumed to be the representational level for colors. A further assumption is that all humans are able to produce a representation of the color space in a similar way and that there is a 'correct' denotation of the color term and color association as a norm of the speech community as a whole. It does not make a distinction between color words and color categories which is often made e.g. in Ref. 23, but simply names a range of colors directly without any reference to a prelinguistic category.

3.3. *Combining self-organizing and Bayesian models*

The self-organizing models assume a prototype or conceptual spaces theory of concepts. The main purpose of these models is in transferring sensory percepts in some way to the conceptual level. The Bayesian models studied here are based on classical and prototype theory and these models assume that the conceptual representations are the same for each learner, which makes a crucial difference to the self-organizing approach presented later in this paper. Though the extent of the area each term occupies in the representational space can vary as in Refs. 21, 22, the underlying representations for the conceptual color domain are the same.

In the following, we employ the self-organizing map for representing color perceptions and combine it with probabilistic modeling of concept naming.

4. Experiment in the color domain

As a basis of the language emergence, we use language games introduced by Wittgenstein.[24] We implemented a version of the naming game[23] using the SOM. The setup follows closely an earlier the multi-agent simulation framework,[17] where a SOM is used as a model of the conceptual memory of an agent. We use data from the color domain which is often used used[16,21,22] since the data is simple and easily obtained. Following the conceptual spaces theory, we are then treating one domain of integrated dimensions, the color space. For practical reasons, we use the RGB color space, even though any other color space should be equally good.

Each agent thus has a conceptual map which is based on a SOM. Prior to simulation, each of these maps is trained with color data. The training data sets for agents share similarities, but are not the same, yielding individual (albeit similar) conceptual memories for each agent. After the initial training, which takes place before the simulated naming games, the SOMs are not changed. Similarly, an additional set of color vectors is created to serve as the topics of the naming games. In the simulation, agents play naming games, which proceed as follows:

1. Two agents are randomly selected from the population. They are assigned the tasks of the speaker, and the hearer, respectively. Similarly, a topic vector is randomly selected.
2. Both agents map the topic to their conceptual memories. In the SOM, this corresponds to finding the BMU in the map.
3. The speaker searches for a word that could best match the given topic. If no word is found, a new word is invented and communicated to the hearer. The decision making process is described in more detail in the following.
4. The hearer also searches for the words that best match the given topic.
5. If the word the speaker communicates is among the words the hearer found, the game is a success, otherwise the game fails.
6. In case of a success, both the speaker and the hearer increase the counter for that word-node association by one.

7. In case of failure, counters are not updated, except when the word was not known beforehand. In that case, the word is added to the lexicon with an initial counter value of 1.

This algorithm results in the agents selecting the term to denote a given topic based on the maximum likelihood, $\max P(C|T)$, which is estimated as the number of successful uses of the term for that BMU, proportional to all of the successful uses of all the terms in that node. The likelihood is estimated for all the terms associated with the BMU and for those nodes adjacent to it, and the term with the highest likelihood is selected and uttered. If no term is found to be associated with the color or the neighborhood, a new term is invented. The hearer estimates the likelihood $P(C|T)$ in the same fashion for the BMU and the neighborhood in its own SOM finding the preferred terms (in order) for the given color.

We use the likelihood instead of a posterior probability since taking into account the a priori probability, the most frequent terms would always be preferred - regardless of the color they have been associated with before. In earlier work,[17,23] the associations between color terms and the map nodes were employed differently: Each color term – map node pair had an association weight which was changed according to the outcome of the language game: increased if the game was successful and decreased if the game was unsuccessful.

To evaluate the degree to which a language has emerged in the process, we define communication success ratio[23] (CS) as a measure which tells how often the communication is successful. It is given as the average number of successfully played games in 100 previous language games (or less, if 100 games have not been played yet).

4.1. *Experimental setup*

We implemented the simulation framework described earlier and conducted two experiments using different population sizes. In our experiments, each agent had a conceptual memory based on a self-organizing map. The size of the maps was 96 nodes. The neighborhood used was hexagonal and the maps were initialized randomly.

The maps were trained separately for each agent with different data sets, which were data taken from generated color pictures. The training data contained RGB values of eight different prototypical colors: black, blue, green, cyan, red, magenta, yellow and white. To make the distributions for each color less spiky, uniform noise was added independently to each of the color channels. The noise level was set to 20%. The total length of the training data was 10,000 samples. The training data sets for each agent were slightly different, but generated in the same way. (See also Figure 3 where conceptual memories of two agents are shown.) A set of 400 color samples, created similarly to the training data, was used as the language game topics. These topics were not part of the training data. The emerging words were created in the simulation in the same way as in Ref. 17 and the set of words in the simulation can be considered open.

We ran three sets of experiments all of which consisted of 10,000 language games and 10 repetitions. In the first experiment, the population size was fixed to $N = 2$, and in the second experiment to $N = 4$. To experiment with a larger population size, we also did the similar simulation runs for agent population of $N = 10$. In these experiments, a game was considered a success if the word uttered by the speaker was also considered the best word by the hearer.

4.2. *Results*

Figure 2 shows the communication success for two, four and ten agents, each averaged over 10 simulation runs. In the two-agent case, the communication success rises rapidly to $CS = 0.8$ and then steadily up to $CS = 0.95$ during the 10,000 simulated games. The communication success for four agents grows slower than in the previous experiment, but still increases up to $CS = 0.86$, where it seems to settle. The bigger population size, in the ten-agent case yields into considerably slower convergence, reaching approximately $CS = 0.8$ in 10,000 games.

All the language games are played pair-wise, i.e. only two agents of the whole population participate in each game, and other agents have access to the words only through subsequent language games with the same topic. This means that when the population size grows, the convergence to common vocabulary is considerably slower. More competing words for a given topic emerge, and it simply takes longer for each agent to see a representative subset of the topics.

Figure 3 shows the conceptual maps of the two agents in the first experiment. The colors denote the converged RGB values of the prototype vectors of the map. The map has organized well and transformations from one color to other are smooth. The eight prototypical colors used are more prominent, since they are represented more in the data than the intermediate colors that have resulted from added noise.

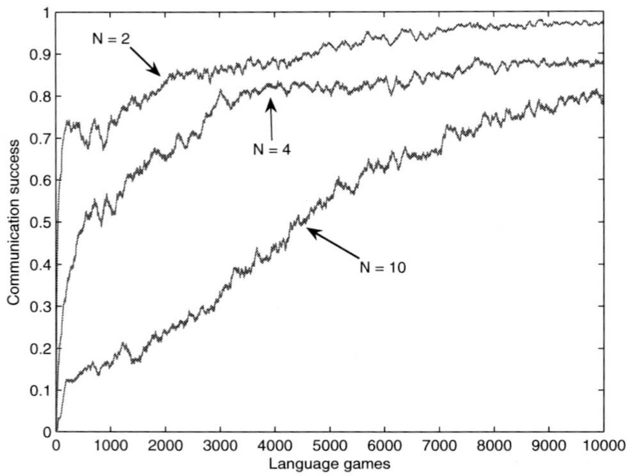

Fig. 2. Communication success for $N = 2$, $N = 4$ and $N = 10$ agents in the population.

When comparing the figures, it is evident that for most prototypical colors there are one or two words that are preferred: *deci* is preferred for black or dark, *hihi* for blue, *fehe* for green, *hebe* for cyan, *defebe* and *gahefa* for red, *cede* for magenta, and *babi* and *dabide* for yellow. For white, the most common word used is *gedi*, but there are also competing labels for bluish white, pinkish white and so on because white covers a larger area in the space. The conceptual memories support the conclusion already visible in the communication success ratio – that a common vocabulary for the agents has emerged.

5. Conclusions and discussion

In this article, we have contrasted the self-organizing and Bayesian approaches to concept formation. We analyzed the approaches taking into account what assumptions are made, what the representation of concepts is like, what kind of inference takes place, and whether symbol grounding is addressed or not. We also built a model of our own for concept formation in a naming game as a combination of the approaches. In our experiments, a common vocabulary emerges in a population of agents using the probabilistic concept naming model based on likelihood.

This work employs a different model for the concept naming than earlier,[17] and presents the preliminary experiments. Future work includes more detailed study of the process of language convergence and more rigorous

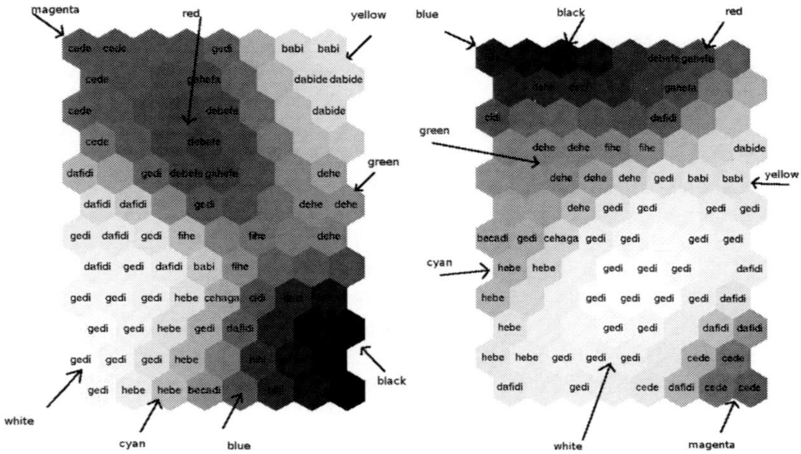

Fig. 3. The conceptual memories of the agents in the two-agent simulation. Only the most probable label for each node is shown.

study of the characteristics of the emerging vocabulary: how coherent is the language use and in which degree polysemous and synonymous terms exist. Also, employing the GTM approach as an alternative to the SOM will be considered.

Acknowledgments

This work was supported by the Academy of Finland through the Finnish Centre of Excellence programme and the Finnish Graduate School of Language Technology. We also thank the anonymous reviewers for their invaluable comments.

References

1. L. Steels, Perceptually grounded meaning creation, in *ICMAS96*, ed. M. Tokoro (AAAI Press, 1996).
2. S. Laurence and E. Margolis, Concepts and cognitive science, in *Concepts: Core Readings*, eds. E. Margolis and S. Laurence (MIT Press, Cambridge, MA, 1999)
3. J. Locke, *An essay concerning human understanding* (Oxford University Press, 1690/1975).
4. E. Rosch, Principles of categorization, in *Cognition and Categorization*, (Lawrence Erlbaum Associates, 1978) pp. 27–48.
5. P. M. Churchland, *A neurocomputational perspective: the nature of mind and the structure of science* (MIT Press, Cambridge, MA, USA, 1989).

6. P. S. Churchland and T. J. Sejnowski, *The Computational Brain* (MIT Press, Cambridge, MA, USA, 1992).
7. P. Gärdenfors, *Conceptual spaces: The Geometry of Thought* (MIT Press, 2000).
8. J. Piaget, *Child's conception of the world* (Routledge and Kegan Paul, 1928).
9. H. Ritter and T. Kohonen, *Biological Cybernetics* **61**, 241 (1989).
10. T. Kohonen, *Biological Cybernetics* **43**, 59 (1982).
11. T. Kohonen, *Self-Organizing Maps*, Series in Information Sciences, Vol. 30, 3rd. edn. (Springer, 2001).
12. T. Kohonen and R. Hari, *Trends Neurosci.* **22**, 135 (1999).
13. C. M. Bishop and C. K. I. Williams, *Neural Computation* **10**, 215 (1998).
14. T. Honkela, V. Pulkki and T. Kohonen, Contextual relations of words in grimm tales analyzed by self-organizing map, in *Proceedings of International Conference on Artificial Neural Networks, ICANN-95*, (EC2 et Cie, 1995).
15. P. Schyns, *Cognitive Science* **15**, 461 (1991).
16. J. Raitio, R. Vigário, J. Särelä and T. Honkela, Assessing similarity of emergent representations based on unsupervised learning, in *Proceedings of IJCNN 2004)*, (Budapest, Hungary, 2004).
17. T. Lindh-Knuutila, T. Honkela and K. Lagus, Simulating meaning negotiation using observational language games, in *Symbol grounding and beyond*, , Lecture Notes in Computer Science Vol. 4211 (Springer Berlin/Heidelberg, 2006).
18. T. Honkela, K. Hynnä, K. Lagus and J. Särelä, *Adaptive and Statistical Approaches in Conceptual Modeling*, Publications in Computer and Information Science A75, Helsinki University of Technology (2005).
19. J. Tenenbaum, Bayesian modeling of human concept learning, in *Advances in Neural Information Processing systems 11*, (MIT Press, 1999).
20. J. Tenenbaum and T. Griffiths, *Behavioral and brain sciences* **24**, 629 (2001).
21. M. Dowman, *A Bayesian Approach to Color Term Semantics*, Technical Report 528, Basser Department of Computer Science, University of Sydney (2001).
22. M. Dowman, *Cognitive Science* **31**, 99 (2007).
23. L. Steels and P. Vogt, Grounding adaptive language games in robotic agents, in *Proceedings of the Fourth European conference on Artificial Life*, (MIT Press, Camridge, MA and London, 1997).
24. L. Wittgenstein, *Philosophical Investigations* (Macmillan, 1963).

TOWARDS THE INTEGRATION OF LINGUISTIC AND NON-LINGUISTIC SPATIAL COGNITION: A DYNAMIC FIELD THEORY APPROACH*

JOHN LIPINSKI†

Institut für Neuroinformatik, Ruhr-Universität-Bochum
Universitätsstr. 150, Gebäude ND, Raum 04/583
44801 Bochum, Germany

JOHN P. SPENCER

Department of Psychology
University of Iowa
Iowa City, IA 52242

LARISSA K. SAMUELSON

Department of Psychology
University of Iowa
Iowa City, IA 52242

We present empirical results and an implemented computational model grounded in the Dynamic Field Theory [1] that directly addresses the second-to-second dynamics governing the integration of linguistic and non-linguistic spatial systems. Results from two experiments show activating a spatial term can differentially bias location memories in the direction of the spatial term prototype. Subsequent simulations from a hybrid Dynamic Field Theory-connectionist model capture the observed term-dependent modulation of those biases. Together, our simulations and results provide strong evidence that a formalized, dynamic framework directly linked to observable behavior can facilitate the theoretical integration of linguistic and non-linguistic spatial systems.

1. Introduction

Spatial language often refers to remembered rather than visible object relations. Because this remembered information is typically based on non-linguistic experience, a key challenge in the domain of spatial language is to produce a

*This work was supported by an NRSA pre-doctoral fellowship (NIMH 1 F31 MH072133-01A1) awarded to John Lipinski and by grants from the National Institutes of Mental Health (NIMH RO1 MH62480) and the National Science Foundation (NSF BCS 00-91757; NSF HSD 0527698) awarded to John P. Spencer

† Corresponding author: 2johnlipinski@gmail.com

dynamically sensitive, neurally-grounded theory that integrates such linguistic and non-linguistic spatial processes. To this end, it is important to development a detailed, empirical foundation around which such models can be tested and developed. In service of this goal, we first present two experiments asking how spatial term activation influences spatial working memory. Given the frequent dependence of spatial language on remembered relations, we hypothesize that spatial term semantic structures are dynamically integrated into the non-linguistic spatial memory system. To preview our results, we find that spatial term activation systematically shifts memory biases towards the presumed spatial term prototype. These findings provide an empirical foundation for tests of our model integrating linguistic and non-linguistic spatial cognition.

2. Experiment 1

The goal of Experiment 1 is to determine how directionally-specific spatial term activation influences spatial working memory performance. Based on the observed behavioral link between spatial language and non-linguistic memory, we hypothesize that spatial semantics and spatial working memory are dynamically integrated. We therefore predict that spatial term activation will modulate the canonical target location memory biases away from the vertical axis [2,3,4] in the direction of the spatial term prototype. An alternative hypothesis, however, predicts that non-linguistic spatial memory processes operate independently of explicit linguistic categorization processes [2] and thus no differential biases.

2.1. *Methods*

2.1.1. *Participants*

Thirty-three students from the University of Iowa participated in Experiment 1. All reported to be native speakers of English with normal hearing and normal or corrected-to-normal vision.

2.1.2. *Procedure*

Participants sat at a large table with a homogeneous surface. A single referent disk appeared along the vertical axis (30cm) and was visible throughout each trial. A small, spaceship-shaped target then appeared on the screen for two seconds. Five-hundred milliseconds after the termination of the spaceship stimulus, individuals were asked to respond "Yes" or "No" to one of three possible statements spoken by the computer: "The ship is to the left of/ above/ to the right of/ the dot." Participants responded "Yes" or "No" by pressing either "1" or "3" on a numeric keypad (counterbalanced) within the 2000ms response window. After the response, participants looked up from the table during a 10s delay. Participants then heard a response cue at which point they looked back at the reference dot and moved the mouse cursor to the remembered location.

2.1.3. *Design*

There were three experimental trial blocks. In each block, targets were presented six times to each of the following locations: ±60°, ±50°, ±40°, ±30°. These locations corresponded with the most semantically ambiguous locations and were thus the only locations analyzed. For each of these targets, participants were asked to respond Yes/No twice to "Above", twice to "Right", and twice to "Left". Participants were not expected to provide "Yes" responses for "Left" statements to targets to the right side of the vertical axis (and analogously for "Right"), but these trials were included to reduce "yes" response biases. Targets were also presented three times in each block at ±100°, ±80°, and ±10° to more evenly balance the spread of target locations. These locations were excluded from analyses, however, because they strongly correspond to only a single term.

2.1.4. *Method of Analysis*

The critical prediction of Experiment 1 is that delayed location memory response errors made after "Above" confirmations will exhibit reduced delay-dependent drift relative to memory performance for the same target locations made after confirmation of a "Left" or "Right" relationship. For this reason, only "Yes" responses to valid location-word matches at the ±30° - ±60° targets were analyzed. Each participant was required to have at least two "Yes" responses to each of the valid word-location matches for each of the analyzed target locations (±30° - ±60°). Six participants failed to meet this criterion and were eliminated. Six additional participants were also eliminated because they consistently failed to provide a Yes/No response within the allotted time. One additional participant failed to attend to the task and was also eliminated.

Directional memory errors (in degrees) were calculated by comparing the vector from the reference disc to the response with the vector from the reference disc to the actual location of the target. Positive errors reflect errors in the direction away from the vertical axis and negative errors reflect errors towards the vertical axis. Outliers (2.7%), defined as any directional errors exceeding the target group mean by 2 standard deviations or more, were removed.

2.2. *Results and Discussion*

Directional errors from the Mouse task were analyzed in a 3-way ANOVA with Target (±30°-±60°), Term ("Above" vs. "Left/Right"), and Side (targets to the left of vertical, targets to the right of vertical) as within-subjects factors. Results from the 3-way within-subjects ANOVA yielded a main effect of both Target, $F(3,57)=6.59$, $p=.001$, and Term, $F(1,19)=5.25$, $p=.034$. No other effects were significant. The Target effect (not shown) indicated that Mouse memory errors were largest for locations closest to the vertical axis, consistent with previous results [3]. Critically, the Term effect (Figure 1A) shows that directional errors were significantly smaller after responding "Yes" to the "Above" query relative to Yes-Right and Yes-Left trials. Comparison of mean errors for the Yes-Above trials ($M=2.7$) with the Yes-Left/Right trials ($M=3.4$) reveals a 21% error reduction across the conditions. These results indicate that categorical spatial language modulates location memory biases towards the spatial term prototype.

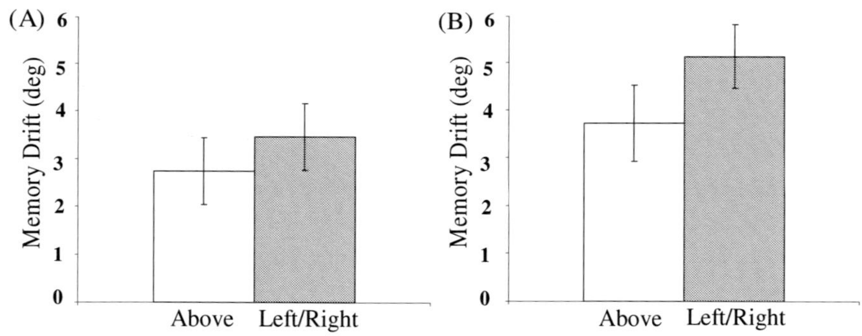

Figure 1. Results from Experiment 1 (A) and Experiment 2 (B) comparing working memory drift away from the vertical axis. The error bars represent standard errors.

3. Experiment 2

Experiment 1 established that spatial term activation can differentially bias non-linguistic location memories towards the spatial term prototype, contra Huttenlocher et al. [2]. However, it is not clear whether these effects generalize to cases without an explicit link between the linguistic and non-linguistic tasks. To answer this question, Experiment 2 employs a same/different spatial language comparison task in which participants compare the spatial relations presented in two sentences (e.g. "The shoe is to the right of the lamp" v. "The ball is above is the key"). Critically, they provide a location memory response after hearing the spatial relation in the first sentence. If the differential biasing observed in Experiment 1 does not depend on an explicit task link, the spatial relation in the first sentence should again modulate memory performance.

3.1. *Methods*

3.1.1. *Participants*

Eighteen students from the University of Iowa participated in Experiment 2. All reported to be native speakers of English with normal hearing and normal or corrected-to-normal vision.

3.1.2. *Materials*

Each spatial relation sentence was formed by concatenating three individual sound files using the following form: (1) "The object 1 is", (2) "to the right of/above/to the left of", (3) "the object 2". The objects were selected from a list of 17 possible single syllable words, each with a concreteness measure of 550 or higher [4] and beginning with a different consonant.

3.1.3. *Procedure*

The Experiment 2 procedure followed that of Experiment 1 with the exception of the spatial language task. In Experiment 2, we presented a sentence describing the spatial relation between two objects 500ms after the termination of the ship stimulus. After an additional 7000ms delay, participants provided a spatial working memory response. Participants then heard a second sentence describing the relation between two different objects and responded whether the spatial relations they heard in the two sentences were the same or different by pressing either a "1" or "3" (counterbalanced).

3.1.4. *Design*

As in Experiment 1, each participant received three blocks of experimental trials. In each block, targets were presented six times to each of the following locations: ±60º, ±50º, ±40º, ±30º. Only these locations were included in the analyses. For each of these targets, participants were asked to make a Same/Different response by comparing the spatial relations presented in the first sentence with that presented in the second sentence following the memory response. Each target location was therefore associated with six sentence pairs (1 pair/ trial X 6 trials). Of the six sentences heard first for each target, two contained an "Above" relation, two contained a "Right" relation, and two contained a "Left" relation. In accord with Experiment 1, the spatial term in the first sentence therefore corresponded to the target location on 4 of the 6 trials. Half the trials were randomly assigned to the "Same" condition. For the "Different" trials, the spatial relation in the second sentence was determined by randomly selecting one of the two remaining relations. Objects were selected randomly such that they could not be repeated within the same trial or on consecutive trials.

The following targets were also presented three times in each block: ±100°, ±80°, and ±10°. Each of these target locations was therefore associated with three sentence pairs (1 pair / trial X 3 trials). For the three sentences heard first at each of these targets, one contained an "Above" relation, one a "Right" relation, and one a "Left" relation. As with Experiment 1, these locations were not analyzed but were nonetheless included to more evenly balance the spread of target locations.

3.1.5. *Methods of Analysis*

Similar to Experiment 1, each participant was required to have a minimum of two correct Same/Different responses to each of the valid word-location matches for each of the analyzed target locations (±30° - ±60°). Three participants failed to meet this criterion and were excluded. Memory errors and outliers (3.5%) were calculated according to the methods described in Experiment 1.

3.2. *Results and Discussion*

Mean directional errors from the Mouse task were analyzed in a 3-way ANOVA with Target (±30°-±60°), Term ("Above" vs. "Left/Right"), and Side (targets to the left of vertical, targets to the right of vertical) as within-subjects factors. Results from the 3-way within-subjects ANOVA yielded a main effect of both Target, $F(3,42)=7.35$, $p<.001$, and Term, $F(1,14)=18.57$, $p=.001$, consistent with Experiment 1. No other effects were significant. The Target effect (not displayed) again indicated that memory errors were largest for locations closest to the vertical axis. Critically, the replication of the Term effect (Figure 1B) indicates that the mean memory errors for responses following "Above" relation trials (M=3.8) were significantly smaller than those following "Left" or "Right" trials (M=5.1), a 28% reduction in error across the conditions. These results indicate that term-dependent spatial working memory biases generalize to cases without an explicit link between the linguistic and non-linguistic spatial tasks.

4. SPAM-Ling: An Intergrative Dynamic Field Theory Model

Experiments 1 and 2 provide novel empirical evidence that spatial term semantic structures are dynamically integrated into the non-linguistic spatial memory system. Building on these results, we here present simulations from the hybrid Spatial Planning And Memory with Linguistic processes model (SPAM-Ling). This model integrates a Dynamic Field Theory approach to spatial working memory [5] with a competitive, connectionist-style spatial semantic network. The resulting simulations show that SPAM-Ling can qualitatively capture the demonstrated empirical modulation of memory biases.

4.1. *Introduction to Dynamic Fields*

The principle building block of the SPAM-Ling model is the dynamic field (see Figure 2). Dynamic fields are based on the theory of nonlinear dynamical systems and emphasize attractor states and bifurcations within continuous, sub-symbolic activation distributions [1, 6]. These activation distributions are defined over a topographically organized set "neurons" or nodes (see Figure 2A, X axis) that collectively represent the value(s) of a continuous behavioral or perceptual parameter (e.g. reaching amplitude, heading direction, color). Each node within the field represents a single value of the selected parameter and provides maximal activation (Figure 2A, Y axis) in the presence of information corresponding to that "preferred" value.

The critical feature of a dynamic field is that node activations evolve continuously in time according to a nonlinear local excitation/lateral inhibition function [see 1]. Local excitation refers the ability of an active node to excite (i.e. increase the activation) other nodes in the region that code for a similar parameter value. Lateral inhibition, on the other hand, leads to the inhibition of nodes that code for more distant values in the parameter space. Collectively, these

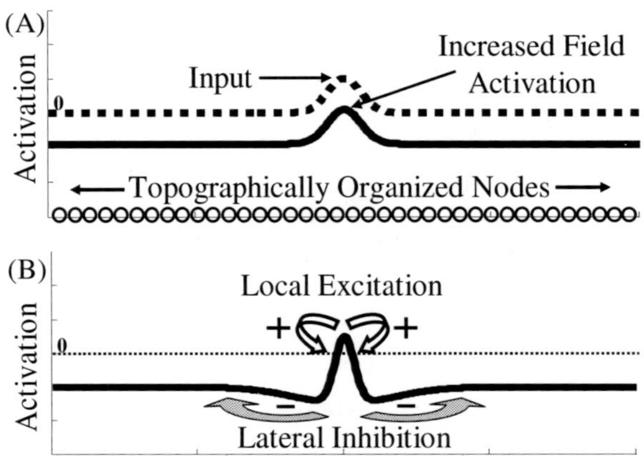

Figure 2. Dynamic field with (A) an input-driven activation increase and (B) a self-sustaining peak.

interactions provide a means for generating a self-sustaining activation peak in the field even after the initial stimulus is removed. Such self-sustaining peaks thus provide a form of working memory (Figure 2B; for similar dynamics see [9],[10])

4.2. *SPAM-Ling: Integrating Non-Linguistic and Linguistic Spatial Cognition*

The SPAM-Ling model (see Figure 3) incorporates the same core characteristics of the basic dynamic field but implements it within a three-layer architecture inspired by the cytoarchitecture of visual cortex [see 7]. The X axis in each layer represents location in angular deviation. The top layer is the Perceptual field. Excitation in this field reflects perceived events in the task space (e.g. appearance of stimuli) as well as stable perceptual cues such as the visible borders or the symmetry axes of the task space. In the top layer of Figure 3, for example, there are two hillocks of activation. The first (and larger) of the two represents the target object to the left (-30°) of the midline symmetry axis of the task space. The second, smaller hillock (0°) represents the perceived midline symmetry axis of the task space itself. This activation in the Perceptual layer is then propagated to the remaining two layers. One of these layers is the Spatial Working Memory field (SWM; see Figure 3). This field receives input from the Perceptual field and is primarily responsible for maintaining a memory of the target location through self-sustaining activation—a neurally plausible mechanism for the maintenance of information in neuronal populations [see 8, 9-11]. The local excitatory interactions supporting such sustained activation arise from the nodes in the SWM field

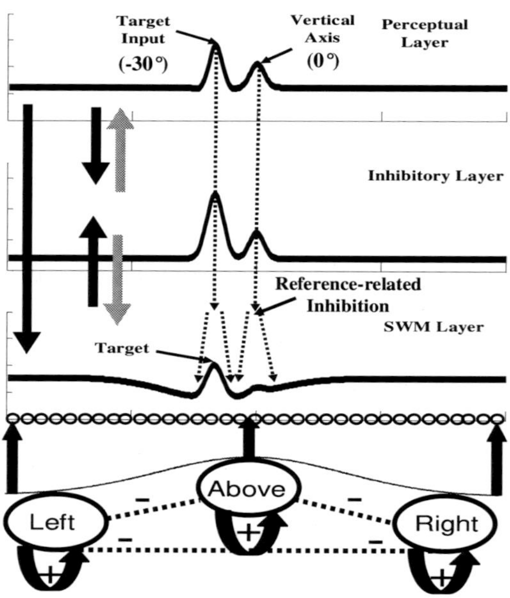

Figure 3. The SPAM-Ling model. See text for details.

itself. The lateral inhibition, on the other hand, comes from the shared Inhibitory layer (see Figure 3). Activation in this Inhibitory layer arises from activation input coming from both the Perceptual and the Spatial Working Memory layers. The emerging activation in the Inhibitory layer then projects inhibition broadly *back* to both of the layers (see gray arrows, Figure 3). Putting it all together then, the excitatory interactions sustain the activation in the SWM field associated with the target location while the broad inhibitory input keeps this activation peak from continually spreading and eventually exploding.

4.3. *Spatial Language Semantic Network*

To model both linguistic and non-linguistic spatial behaviors, SPAM-Ling incorporates a bank of competitive, localist representations for Above, Left, and Right (see Figure 4). Although the current model uses only three terms, this model can be easily expanded to include other axially-based projective terms (e.g. below, over, under, front, back). Each node has a self-excitatory connection and can also receive excitatory input from external speech. Each node is also reciprocally coupled to the SWM field through a set of spatially-specific connection weights centered on the prototypical location for that word (see "Above" node Gaussian, Figure 3). Thus in the case of 'Above', the weight strengths linking the 'Above' node to the field nodes are highest for nodes near the prototypical 'Above' location along the vertically extended midline of the task space (0°). The weight strengths for the remaining nodes then systematically decline as the node locations shift further away from this prototypical 'Above' region. The connection weights for the remaining terms are structured analogously.

As a consequence of this node-field coupling, the nodes receive input from SWM field activation and can therefore generate an appropriately descriptive spatial term (e.g. 'Above' for a target at 0°) if the node exceeds the activation threshold (set here to 0). Conversely, activation of a spatial term through "speech" input (implemented here as a brief increase in node activation) can lead to spatially-specific input in the SWM field. The spatial term network is thus reciprocally and dynamically integrated with the SWM field. The complete model, combining the three-layer architecture and the spatial term nodes, is distinguished from other spatial language models [e.g. 12, 13] through its grounding in the non-linear dynamics of non-linguistic spatial representation.

4.4. *Spatial Working Memory Drift in the Dynamic Field Theory*

The DFT accounts for the canonical memory drift effect through inhibition grounded in the perceptual reference frames of the task space. In simplest terms, the vertical symmetry axis of the task space provides a consistent source of input into the Perceptual field (see Figure 3). Although this reference-related input contributes activation into the Spatial Working Memory field, it also leads to a broad inhibitory distribution in the shared Inhibitory layer (see Figure 3) that is then propagated into the SWM field. As a result, target locations to the immediate right or left of the vertical axis (0°) encounter greater inhibition than target locations further away from the axis. Nodes on the side of the peak closer to the axis therefore receive more inhibition than those nodes on the other side of the peak. This differential inhibition between the sides of the memory peak shifts the balance of peak activation away from the axis over time, thus leading to the memory drift effect.

4.5. *Term-Dependent Memory Drift in SPAM-Ling*

In the SPAM-Ling model, each spatial term has a set of Gaussian-weighted connections that are dynamically and reciprocally linked to the SWM field. Because these Gaussian-weighted connections are centered at the prototypes, spatial term activation leads to a spatially-specific activation boost in the SWM field region overlapping with the term. If a memory peak overlaps with this boosted region, then this spatially-specific spatial term boost should bias the peak towards the spatial term prototype over time. As a result, peaks that overlap with the "Left" (or "Right") node activation boost should be pulled further to the left (or right) and thus exhibit greater drift away from the vertical axis relative to peaks overlapping with the "Above" activation profile.

4.6. *Simulations*

Two SPAM-Ling simulations of an Experiment 2 trial at the -30° target location demonstrate this functionality. Within these simulations, one timestep corresponds to 4.5 ms of an experimental trial. The timing of the simulated stimulus and response events thus corresponded precisely to the experimental trials. The first simulation shows the effect of "Left" node activation on memory peak drift, the second the effect of "Above" node activation. In the "Left" node simulation (Figure 4A, left side), activation of the "Left" spatial term node leads to a localized boost in the SWM field that overlaps with the peak at the -30° target location when the spatial term is presented. This pulls the peak to the left, thus increasing the drift away from the vertical axis. In contrast, when this same target peak is instead paired with "Above" activation, the spatially-specific boost provides additional activation favoring the "Above" prototype location centered at the vertical axis (Figure 4A, right side). The "Above" boost does not

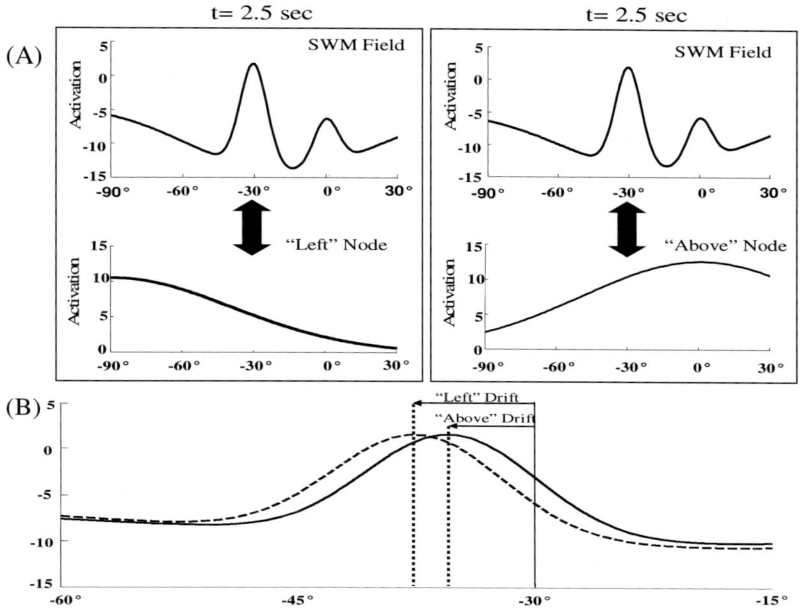

Figure 4. (A) Localized spatial term input into the SWM field for the Left and Above nodes at when the term is first presented for the -30° target (B) Comparison of differential memory drift for Left and Above node activation at the end of the trial simulations.

overwhelm the reference-related inhibition that drives memory drift so the peak still drifts over the delay. Nevertheless, this memory peak exhibits 2.1° less drift away from the original -30° target location relative to the "Left" trial (see Figure 4B). This reduction is comparable to the empirical 2.3° difference observed at the +/-30° targets in Experiment 2.

5. Conclusion

Theoretical models to date have failed to consider the second-to-second dynamics governing the integration of linguistic and non-linguistic spatial systems. To close this theoretical gap, we first presented new experimental results showing that spatial term activation modulates spatial working memory in the direction of the spatial term prototype. These results, coupled with our simulations of these effects, provide strong evidence that formalized, dynamic frameworks linked to observable behavior such as SPAM-Ling can enhance our understanding of linguistic and non-linguistic spatial integration.

References

[1] W. Erlhagen and G. Schöner, Psychological Review 109 (2002) 545.

[2] J. Huttenlocher, L. Hedges, B. Corrigan, and L. E. Crawford, Cognition 93 (2004) 75.

[3] J. Lipinski, J. P. Spencer, and L. K. Samuelson, in The spatial foundations of language (L. B. Smith, M. Gasser, and K. Mix, eds.), Oxford University Press, in press.

[4] M. D. Wilson, Behavioural Research Methods, Instruments and Computers 20 (1988) 6.

[5] J. P. Spencer, V. S. Simmering, A. R. Schutte, and G. Schöner, in Emerging landscapes of mind (J. M. Plumert and J. P. Spencer, eds.), Oxford University Press, Oxford, 2007, p. 320.

[6] S. Amari, Biological Cybernetics 27 (1977) 77.

[7] R. Douglas, H. Markham, and K. Martin, in The Synaptic Organization of the Brain (G. M. Shepherd, ed.), Oxford University Press, Oxford, 2004.

[8] T. P. Trappenberg, M. C. Dorris, D. P. Munoz, and R. M. Klein, Journal of Cognitive Neuroscience 13 (2001) 256.

[9] A. Compte, N. Brunel, P. S. Goldman-Rakic, and X.-J. Wang, Cerebral Cortex 10 (2000) 910.

[10] S. Amari and M. A. Arbib, in Systems Neuroscience (J. Metzler, ed.), Academic Press, New York, 1977, p. 119.

[11] S. Amari, in Dynamic Interactions in Neural Networks: Models and Data (M. A. Arbib and S. Amari, eds.), Springer, New York, NY, 1989, p. 15.

[12] T. Regier and L. Carlson, Journal of Experimental Psychology: General 130 (2001) 273.

[13] K. R. Coventry, A. Cangelosi, R. Rajapakse, A. Bacon, S. Newstead, D. Joyce, and L. V. Richards, in Spatial Cognition IV, Vol. LNAI 3343 (C. Freksa, ed.), Springer-Verlag, Heidelberg, 2005, p. 98.

INVESTIGATING SYSTEMATICITY IN THE LINEAR RAAM NEURAL NETWORK

I. FARKAŠ* and M. POKORNÝ

Comenius University
Mlynská dolina, 84248 Bratislava, Slovak Republic
**E-mail: farkas@ii.fmph.uniba.sk*

Processing structured data is a continuing challenge for connectionist models that aim at becoming a plausible explanation of human cognition. The recently proposed linear Recursive Auto-Associative Memory (RAAM) model was shown to have a much higher encoding capacity and not to be subject to overtraining compared to classical RAAM. We assess the effect of terminal encoding on the performance of linear RAAM in case of encoding trees of ternary semantic propositions and we show that the highest representation capacity is achieved with (sparse) binary WordNet-based codes, compared to (symbolic) neutral and to (distributed) word co-occurrence based codes. Only with WordNet codes the model could generalize to processing structures that contain known words at new syntactic positions or contain novel words, as long as these shared semantic features with the words from the training set.

Keywords: Syntactic systematicity; Linear recursive autoassociative memory; Neural network; Word features

1. Introduction

In their fundamental criticism in 1988, Fodor and Pylyshyn[1] expressed their serious doubts regarding connectionist models of that time; namely, whether they could account for generativity and systematicity observed in mental representations without merely implementing symbolic systems. Generativity expresses the idea that mental representations can be generated in an unlimited way, by combinatorial manipulations of atoms. Systematicity refers to the mental property that understanding certain sentences (e.g. `John loves Mary`) inherently implies understanding of related sentences (such as `Mary loves John`). This concept was more clearly defined by Hadley[2] who proposed that systematic behaviour in a connectionist network was a matter of learning and generalization. Hadley distinguished three levels of systematicity: weak, quasi-, and strong. Niklasson & van Gelder[3] subsequently proposed a more comprehensive and more detailed taxonomy (levels 0 through 5, with increasing "degree" of novelty in testing sentences), having loose correspondence to Hadley's three levels. Connectionist models, as a qualitatively different cognitive architecture, were challenged in showing they could represent structured data without pointers or logical addresses (natural part of symbolic systems), using vectors of fixed dimension. Since 1990 we have witnessed a number of connectionist attempts to handle systematicity,[22] out of which Recursive Auto-Associative Memory[5] appearantly attracted most attention, reflected in a variety of applications and modifications of the original RAAM.[3,6–8,10,11,13] The RAAM, as a recursive auto-encoder trained by error backprogation, learns the compressed (reduced) representations at its hidden layer. Despite its widespread use among connectionists, RAAM is known to have a number of drawbacks: the difficulty to train, sensitivity to noise and a rather poor generalization, to name a few.[9] The most recent alternative to the original model – linear RAAM by Voegtlin and Dominey (henceforth, V&D),[14] was reported to achieve a much better generalization performance and to avoid the problem of overtraining. In this paper, we examine the linear RAAM and illustrate its properties in the context of testing its systematicity in processing linguistic structures using various encoding schemes of terminals (words).

2. Linear RAAM

The recently proposed linear RAAM[14] differs from original RAAM[5] in three points: (1) it uses neurons with linear activation function (identity mapping), as opposed to sigmoidal neurons, (2) it uses unsupervised Oja's rule for updating weights, unlike supervised error backpropagation, and (3) it uses the same weight matrix for both encoding and decoding structures (thanks to linearity). Like RAAM, linear RAAM is a three-layer neural network with nk-k-nk units (Figure 1) that learns to encode n-ary trees. The tree encoding proceeds recursively bottom-up and left-right which is illustrated for a binary tree in Figure 2a. First, we take the pair `(A B)` as an input and store its reduced representations computed at the middle layer (MID) in a stack. [a] Next, we put the pair `(C D)` to the left group of inputs (LI). Then, the compressed representation of `(C D)` is moved via (one-to-one) recurrent links from MID to LI. The right group of inputs (RI) reads the symbol `E`, and the mapping yields the representation of the subtree `((C D) E)`. The last step consists in copying it to RI and reading the previously obtained representation of `(A B)` to LI. The activity of MID will then correspond to the reduced representation of the whole tree.

[a] a conventional storage space used in algorithms

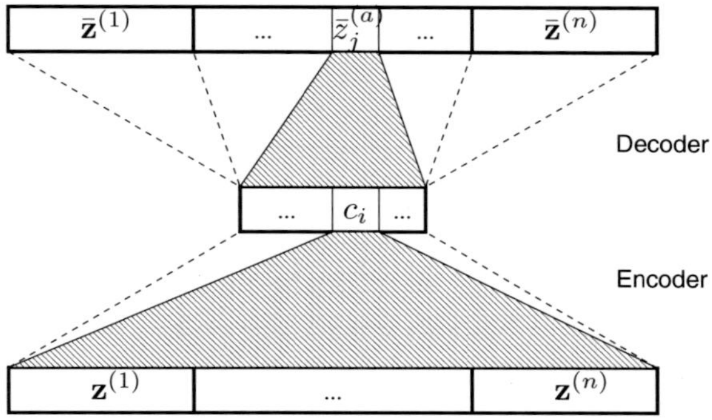

Fig. 1. Sketch of the n-ary linear RAAM. See the text for activation computation.

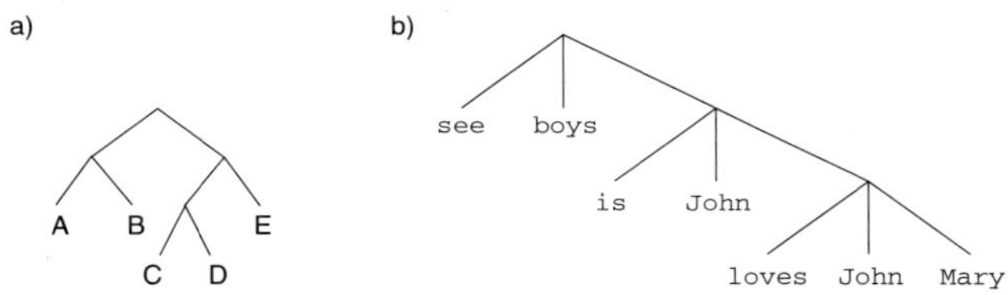

Fig. 2. Example of (a) binary and (b) ternary tree structure. The binary tree has leaves (terminals) without any meaning. Terminals on the right are words that bear linguistic meaning, which can encoded in the terminal representations.

If we denote $z_j^{(a)}$ the activity of neuron j from the group a (out of n) in the input layer, c_i the activity of the neuron i of the compressing layer, and $w_{ij}^{(a)}$ the synaptic weight between these two neurons, then we can express encoded activations as

$$c_i = \sum_{a=1}^{n} \sum_{j=1}^{k} w_{ij}^{(a)} z_j^{(a)}$$

or, in the vector form as $\mathbf{c} = \mathbf{W}^{(1)}\mathbf{z}^{(1)} + \mathbf{W}^{(2)}\mathbf{z}^{(2)} + \ldots + \mathbf{W}^{(n)}\mathbf{z}^{(n)} = \mathbf{Wz}$, where $\mathbf{z}^{(a)}$ is a k-dimensional column vector representing neuron activations in input group a, $\mathbf{c}$ is the activation vector of MID and $\mathbf{W}^{(a)} = \|w_{ij}^{(a)}\|_{k \times k}$ is the weight matrix between a-th group of inputs and MID. Then, the whole weight matrix $\mathbf{W} = [\mathbf{W}^{(1)}; \mathbf{W}^{(2)}; \ldots \mathbf{W}^{(n)}] \in \mathbb{R}^{k \times nk}$, and $\mathbf{z} = [\mathbf{z}^{(1)^T}; \mathbf{z}^{(2)^T}; \ldots; \mathbf{z}^{(n)^T}]^T \in \mathbb{R}^{nk \times 1}$ is the vector of input activations.

2.1. *Decoding process*

Reconstruction of the original tree also proceeds recursively, but in top-down fashion which is illustrated using the ternary structure in Figure 2b. First, we copy the representation of the whole tree (corresponding to the sentence `boys see John who loves Mary`) to MID. As a result of its decomposition we obtain the representation of the terminal `see` in LI and the representation of the terminal `boys` in the middle group of inputs (MI). The activation pattern in RI does not correspond to any of the terminals, so its content is copied to MID and decoded. As a result, now we get in LI and MI the representations of terminals `is` and `John`, respectively. Since the content of RI does not correspond to any of the terminals, it is copied to MID and decoded, which results in decoded representations of all three terminals at the correponding groups of inputs, namely, `loves`, `John` and `Mary`. In general, trees can have at certain depth more vertices that are not leaves. For example, both children of the root in Figure 2a are not leaves. In this case, during encoding we must store the obtained subtree representation in a stack, later retrieve and use it as an input, after we have obtained the representations of the remaining subtrees. Analogical use of the stack is available during the decoding of the structure. For decoding of the group activity we use the same weight matrix, i.e. $\bar{\mathbf{z}}^{(a)} = \mathbf{W}^{(a)^T}\mathbf{c}$ and the overall mapping from MID to the output layer is $\bar{\mathbf{z}} = \mathbf{W}^T\mathbf{c}$. However, the decoding process is rarely ideal in a sense that the reconstructed images $\bar{\mathbf{z}}$ would exactly match the originals. [b] Therefore, we need a terminal test that could help us decide whether the obtained representation is to be considered a terminal or it should be further decoded.

2.2. *Terminal test*

In the terminal test used by Pollack[5] the reconstructed vector was considered a terminal, if all its elements differed by less than τ from the required values, where he used $\tau = 0.2$. V&D[14] used the Euclidean distance instead, and a decoded vector was considered to encode a terminal if and only if the Euclidean distance to the vector encoding this terminal was below a *reconstruction threshold* θ. We need to specify what we mean by successful

[b]Formation of reduced representations involves dimensionality reduction. The rank of the matrix $\mathbf{P} = \mathbf{W}^T\mathbf{W}$ is $rank(\mathbf{P}) \leq k$, whereas the dimension of input vectors is nk. Therefore, if the input contains more than k linearly independent vectors, their reconstructions (using mapping defined by $\mathbf{P}$) will be linearly dependent vectors and will hence differ from the originals.

decoding. Even though we can allow certain inaccuracies during decoding while applying the terminal test, we may not succeed in reconstructing the original structure. The following cases can result: (i) ambiguous case – if for chosen θ, the reconstructed vector could represent more than one terminal; (ii) unrecognized terminal – if the reconstructed structure should yield a terminal but it does not (which could lead to infinite loops in the decoding); (iii) terminating non-terminal – if at certain position we decode a terminal but the original structure contains a subtree at that position; (iv) wrong terminal decoded – if that differs from the required terminal. We will consider *decoding the structure* successful, if none of the above cases occurs. Such a structure is then encodable (representable) by the network.

2.3. *Training the network*

The network is trained as an autoassociator. Minimization of the quadratic error between input (target) $\mathbf{z}$ and its reconstruction $\bar{\mathbf{z}}$ yields the stochastic rule for weight modification

$$\begin{array}{l}\forall 1 \le i, j \le k \\ \forall 1 \le a \le n\end{array} \qquad \Delta w_{ij}^{(a)} = \eta\, c_i \left(z_j^{(a)} - \sum_{r=1}^{k} w_{rj}^{(a)} c_r \right) \tag{1}$$

where η is the learning rate. This corresponds to Oja's constrained Hebbian learning rule,[15] which is known to find the linear subspace spanned by k principal components of the distribution of an input vector. Principal Components Analysis allows one to linearly transform data from high-dimensional input space to the feature space of lower dimension. It consists in finding orthogonal vectors corresponding to the directions with the highest variance. The linear RAAM performs a more complex operation than does PCA, because the input vector $\mathbf{z}(t)$ depends on reduced representation $\mathbf{c}(t-1)$, which in turn depends on previous input $\mathbf{z}(t-1)$. Hence, the distribution of a vector $\mathbf{z}$ is not defined a priori, but it results from the internal representation devised by the network. This type of learning is called a *moving target problem.*

The adaptation runs recursively bottom up. First, the network is presented only parts of the structure that contain leaves. We always remember the representation of the presented subtree and modify weights according to Eq. 1. In the next steps, we process those parts of the structure that contain a subtree as well. This process is illustrated in Table 1 referring to the tree in Figure 2a.

Table 1. The order of training inputs for the structure in Figure 2a.

Input $\mathbf{z}$		Reduced repr.		Output $\bar{\mathbf{z}}$
(A B)	$\longrightarrow$	$R_{AB}(t_1)$	$\longrightarrow$	($\bar{A}$ $\bar{B}$)
(C D)	$\longrightarrow$	$R_{CD}(t_2)$	$\longrightarrow$	($\bar{C}$ $\bar{D}$)
($R_{CD}(t_2)$ E)	$\longrightarrow$	$R_{CDE}(t_3)$	$\longrightarrow$	($\bar{R}_{CD}(t_2)$ $\bar{E}$)
($R_{AB}(t_1)$ $R_{CDE}(t_3)$)	$\longrightarrow$	$R_{ABCDE}(t_4)$	$\longrightarrow$	($\bar{R}_{AB}(t_1)$ $\bar{R}_{CDE}(t_3)$)

Table 2. Examples of simpler generated sentences and their translations.

Steve walks	(walks Steve NULL)
women see boys	(see women boys)
dogs who_pl see girl bark	(bark (are dogs (see dogs girl)) NULL)
boy feeds cat who John sees	(feeds boy (is cat (sees John cat)))

Note: For a sentence with embedding of depth n, the tree depth is $2n + 1$.

3. Simulation experiment

3.1. *Encoding schemes for terminals*

To assess the effect of terminal encoding on network performance, we tested the model in the linguistic domain which nicely lends itself to structured data. We compared three types of features for the terminals – words in our task: (a) the (symbolic) neutral code, (b) word encoding derived from word co-occurrences, and (c) word encoding containing WordNet-based features. These encodings can be seen as examples of qualitatively different classes of representation (Section 3.2). For input data we generated English sentences based on specified probabilistic context-free grammar, using semantic constraints.[17] 300 sentences, based on the lexicon of 50 words, were transformed into ternary trees of propositions. Table 2 shows a few examples of simpler generated sentences and their translations. [c] In sentence translation, we tried to preserve, following Pollack, the recursive order (ACTION AGENT OBJECT), where these categories correspond to verb, subject, and object, respectively. In sentences with the missing object, we used a new terminal `NULL`. Note that ternary structures do not include words `who` and `who_pl`.

3.2. *Generation of word features*

The neutral codes implied 50-dimensional localist (one-hot) word representations, and the special symbol `NULL` was representated by the zero vector.

[c]Symbol who_pl was introduced for translation purposes, to differentiate between the singular and the plural.

Neutral codes are symbolic so they do not convey any information about what they stand for. Hence, the distance between any two meaningful terminals was $\sqrt{2}$, but the distance between `NULL` and any of these terminals was 1. Therefore, the optimal $\theta_{opt} > 0.5$.

Word co-occurrence-based word encoding were created using the a special recurrent neural network – word co-occurrence detector (WCD) that learns the lexical co-occurrence constraints of words.[18,19] WCD reads through a stream of input sentences (one word at a time) and learns the transitional probabilities between words (the window size can be modulated and in this work we considered two nearest neighbors on either side) which it represents as a matrix of weights. Given a total lexicon of size N, all word co-occurrences can be represented by an $N \times N$ contingency table, where the representation for the ith word is formed by concatenation of ith column and ith row vectors from the table. For symbols `is` and `are` we used WCD codes of `who` and `who_pl`, respectively. Investigation of the WCD data revealed that the minimal distance betwen two words was $d_{min} < 0.05$. To enhance word discrimination, we rescaled the vectors such that its maximum component reached activation one. Since the largest vector component for some words was almost 0.5, the rescaling of the vector components was done using factor of two. In this case we estimated the optimal $\theta_{opt} \in (0.05, 0.1)$. These representations can also be seen as "relational" since they refer one word to all other words.

WordNet-based word features were obtained from a feature generation system[20] that can produce a (smaller) set of binary features for each word. Harm's software incorporates semantic features mainly from WordNet,[21] but it did not provide features for all words so we generated those manually. Altogether, we had 41 features for all 50 words, so the word representations could be were 41-dimensional. Each word (except `NULL`) had 1 to 6 features. For this encoding, the minimum Euclidean distance of two words was $d_{min} = 1$, so the optimal threshold $\theta_{opt} > 0.5$.

The minimum network size that would accommodate all three types of word representation would be $k = 100$ (for neutral and WordNet codes the remaining bits would be padded with zeros). Preliminary simulations showed, however, that the network capacity could be increased if we provided extra room for encoding structures, so we used $k = 150$. For training, we generated 100 sentences, resulting in the overall amount of 325 ternary structures. In order to achieve successful training, we had to use a rather small learning η between 10^{-6} and 10^{-7} (for larger η, the weights diverged). As an undesirable consequence, the training time became rather extensive, especially for WCD codes, because even after 200000 iterations, the weights were still not converged.

Table 3. Levels of systematicity tested with linear RAAM.

Level	Description of the test set
0	No novelty (training data used)
1	Novel sentences (novel word combinations)
2	Novel positions (of at least one atom)
3	Novel atoms (at least one atom never appeared in training)
4	Novel complexity (of test sentences compared to training)
5	Novel atoms and novel complexity (combination of 3 and 4)

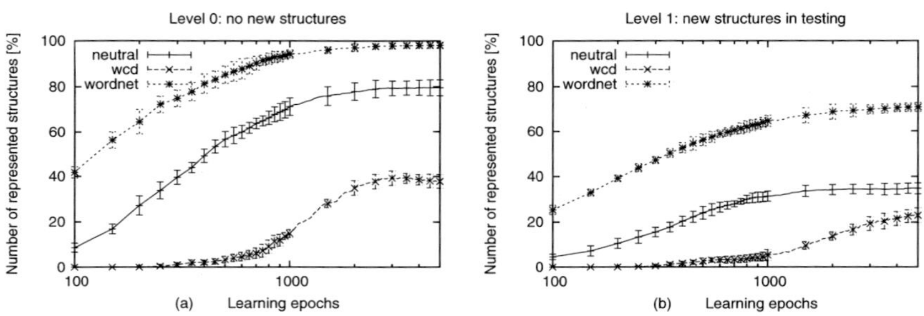

Fig. 3. Systematicity performance for (a) the training set (b) the testing set (level 1).

3.3. *Levels of systematicity*

In the original paper of Fodor and Pylyshyn, the use of concept of systematicity was rather vague, so it was difficult to test it in connectionist models. In our experiments, we followed the taxonomy proposed by Niklasson & van Gelder,[3] shown in Table 3. For training we used in all experiments 150 structures from the base, but the actual selection of training sentences depended on the level of systematicity being tested. In the subsequent plot, we show results averaged over 7 runs. For each run, the weights were initialized to small values randomly chosen $[-0.1; 0.1]$. For neutral and WordNet codes we set $\eta = 0.001$ and for WCD codes $\eta = 005$. In search for optimal reconstruction, we set $\theta_{\text{neutral}} = 0.55$, $\theta_{\text{WCD}} = 0.1$, and $\theta_{\text{WordNet}} = 0.7$. In all cases, the training was stopped after 5000 epochs.

Figure 3a shows the results regarding systematicity level 0, i.e. using training data. In case of WordNet code, the network could represent almost all 150 structures from the training set, in case of neutral code it was approximately 80% and in case of WCD code somewhat below 40%.

As a next step, the networks were presented novel structures from the test set (level 1). Results are in Figure 3b. In case of neutral code, the network performance dropped to roughly 40% of novel structures in the test set (from 80% in the training set). If we assume that the network capacity is sufficient for representing 120 structures (which is 80% out of 150), then the network learnt only a half of novel structures. Analogical argument in case of WCD and WordNet codes leads to the conclusion that the network only learnt to exploit roughly 75% of its representational capacity.

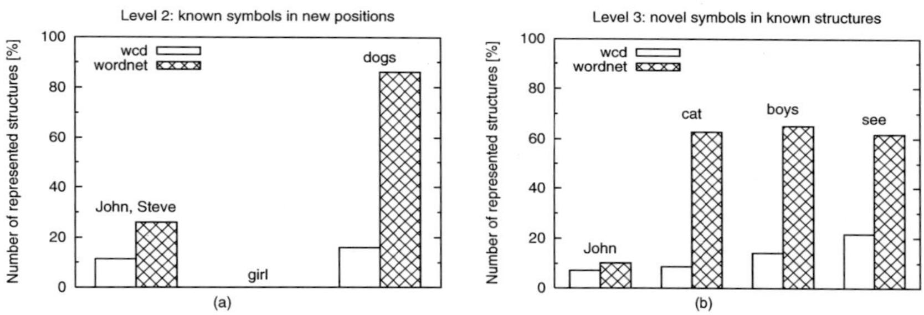

Fig. 4. Test results for higher levels of systematicity.

For testing level 2 we correspondingly selected propositions for the test set: Since only nouns can occur at more than one syntactic position in our propositions, we excluded a few of these from the object position: `John` and `Steve`, singular `girl`, and plural `dogs`. The results are shown in Figure 4a. With the neutral code (not shown), the network failed to represent a single novel structure. For WCD and WordNet codes, the network achieved a certain degree of systematicity, albeit not impressive and highly atom-dependent. The best result was observed for structures containing the atom `dogs` in the object position. In case of `John` and `Steve` we had to use a different thresholds ($\theta_{\mathrm{WCD}} = 0.07$, $\theta_{\mathrm{WordNet}} = 0.9$) to achieve the accuracy shown in Figure 4a. Finally, in case of `girl` the network failed to represent a single novel structure, irrespective of the word codes. The reasons for differences in behavior can be found in the test set itself. The test set for case `girl` only contained this atom at the lowest levels (at least 3) of the trees, so one could expect that the error during reconstructing the novel word will be higher compared to other words that appeared at the same positions in both training and test sets. If the word appeared at larger depth, the error is accumulated in reduced representations of corresponding superstructures. At the same time, each additional level probably increases the inaccuracy in decoding a superstructure. Therefore, we got zero performance in case of `girl`. This hypothesis is supported by the existence of represented structures in case of `John` and `Steve`: these atoms always occurred at depth 1.

For testing level 3, we prepared four data sets for training (and testing), each having one word (noun or verb) excluded from all training structures, but contained in all test structures. These words were: `John`, `cat`, `boys` and `see`. The average results are displayed in Figure 4b. For `John` we used $\theta_{\text{WCD}} = 0.07$ and $\theta_{\text{WordNet}} = 0.9$. To make the network able to represent structures containing a novel word there must exist a "very similar" word to it (in terms of Euclidean distance) in the training set. Hence, in case of neutral code we got zero performance for this level, whereas in case of WordNet code there exist pairs of words differing only in one feature, such as `cat` and `cats`. Note that in case of WordNet code, the performance for `John` is much worse compared to other words. The reason is that its closest neighbor, `Steve` (distance $\sqrt{2}$), only occurred in 10 out of 150 structures from the training set, so `John`, unlike other three cases (`cat`, `boys` and `see`) did not have "sufficient training" to become represented during testing. Finally, regarding the level 4 we found that the network was unable to represent deeper structures, irrespective of the three word encodings used. We assumed that level 5 would also be beyond the representatinal capacity of the linear RAAM.

To summarize, the linear RAAM using neutral code can only satisfy level 1 systematicity, which is similar to what was concluded by V&D [14, sec. 6.5]. In case of WCD and WordNet codes we could observe a certain degree (higher for WordNet) of systematic behavior at levels 2 and 3, which depends on two factors: First, due to expected inaccuracy in reconstructing the word, i.e. during testing novel word [d], the reconstruction error is more problematic if the word lies at larger depth within a structure. Second, if the training set contains a word with a code similar (in terms of Euclidean distance) to the novel word, then the trained network is capable of also representing structures containing that novel word, thanks to exploiting shared word features.

---

[d] such as being a known atom at novel position (level 2), or as a completely novel atom (level 3)

4. Conclusion

Our experiments with the recently proposed linear RAAM[14] shed some light on the network learning and representation properties. We investigated the effect of terminal encoding by comparing neutral code with two types of semantic features expecting that these would boost the representation capacity of the network. One type of features involved word encoding extracted from word co-occurrences within the English-like text corpus (context-free grammar with superimposed semantic constraints), the other was based on WordNet database. In the task of encoding trees of ternary semantic propositions, we observed that clearly the highest representation capacity was achieved with (sparse) binary WordNet codes. On the other hand, despite the appeal of word co-occurence models in linguistic modeling,[23] the word co-occurrence features did not work well in our task, because although this approach displayed the lowest reconstruction error, the real-valued features led to a high number of confusions in decoding, given the considered Euclidean metrics. In the context of testing levels of systematicity in the linear RAAM, according to taxonomy proposed by Niklasson & van Gelder,[3] we showed that the network with WordNet-based terminal encoding accomplished to a certain degree the third level of systematicity, i.e. it could generalize to processing structures that contained known words at new syntactic positions or contained novel words, as long as these shared semantic features with the words from the training set. In summary, these results suggest that the linear RAAM has certain generalization properties, and that connectionist representing symbolic structures (i.e. using neutral code) has its soft limits. In language domain, the linear RAAM was shown to benefit from exploiting appropriate binary semantic features of terminals in the process of generalization.

Acknowledgments

Suported by Slovak Grant Agency for Science (VEGA, no. 1/0361/08).

References

1. J. Fodor and Z. Pylyshyn. Connectionism and cognitive architecture: A critical analysis. *Cognition*, 28:3–71, 1988.
2. R. Hadley. Systematicity in connectionist language learning. *Mind and Language*, 9(3):247–272, 1994.
3. L. Niklasson and T. van Gelder. On being systematically connectionist. *Mind and Language*, 9(3):288–302, 1994.
4. G. Hinton. Mapping part-whole hierarchies into connectionist networks. *Artificial Intelligence*, 46(1-2):47–75, 1990.

5. J. Pollack. Recursive distributed representations. *Artificial Intelligence*, 46(1-2):77–105, 1990.
6. D. Chalmers. Syntactic transformations on distributed representations. *Connection Science*, pages 46–55, 1990.
7. L. Chrisman. Learning recursive distributed representations for holistic computation. *Connection Science*, 3:345–366, 1991.
8. R. Miikkulainen. Subsymbolic case-role analysis of sentences with embedded clauses. *Cognitive Science*, 20:47–73, 1996.
9. D. Blank, L. Meeden, and J. Marshall. Exploring the symbolic/subsymbolic continuum: A case study of RAAM. In J. Dinsmore, editor, *Closing the gap: symbolism vs. connectionism*, pages 113–148. LEA, Hillsdale, NJ, 1992.
10. A. Sperduti. Labeling RAAM. *Connection Science*, 6(4):429–459, 1994.
11. S. Kwasny and B. Kalman. Tail-recursive distributed representations and simple recurrent networks. *Connection Science*, 7(1):61–80, 1995.
12. S. Levy and J. Pollack. Infinite RAAM: A principled connectionist substrate for cognitive modeling. In *Int. Conf. on Cognitive Modeling*. LEA, 2001.
13. M. Adamson and R. Damper. B-RAAM: A connectionist model which develops holistic internal representations of symbolic structures. *Connection Science*, 11(1):41–71, 1999.
14. T. Voegtlin and P.F. Dominey. Linear recursive distributed representations. *Neural Networks*, 18:878–895, 2005.
15. E. Oja. Neural networks, principal components, and subspaces. *International Journal on Neural Systems*, 1:61–68, 1989.
16. M. Bodén and L. Niklasson. Semantic systematicity and context in connectionist networks. *Connection Science*, 12(2):111–142, 2000.
17. D. Rohde. The simple language generator: Encoding complex languages with simple grammars. Technical Report CMU-CS-99-123, Carnegie Mellon University, Pittsburg, PA, 1999.
18. P. Li, I. Farkaš, and B. MacWhinney. Early lexical development in a self-organizing neural network. *Neural Networks*, 17(8-9):1345–1362, 2004.
19. I. Farkaš and P. Li. Modeling the development of lexicon with a growing self-organizing map. In H. Caulfield et al., editor, *Proc. of the 6th Joint Conf. on Information Sciences*, pages 553–556, Research Triangle Park, NC, 2002.
20. M. Harm. Building large scale distributed semantic feature sets with WordNet. Technical Report PDP.CNS.02.1, Carnegie Mellon University, Pittsburg, PA, 2002.
21. G.A. Miller. WordNet: An on-line lexical database. *International Journal of Lexicography*, pages 235–312, 1990.
22. R. Hadley. Systematicity of generalizations in connectionist networks. In Arbib M., editor, *The Handbook of Brain Theory and Neural Networks*, 2nd edition, pages 1151–1156. The MIT Press, 2003.
23. J. Bullinaria. Extracting semantic representations from word co-occurrence statistics: A computational study. *Behavioral Research Methods*, 39:510–526, 2007.

ON THE PSYCHOLOGY AND MODELLING OF SELF-CONTROL*

ARISTODEMOS CLEANTHOUS† and CHRIS CHRISTODOULOU

Department of Computer Science, University of Cyprus, 75 Kallipoleos Avenue, P. O. Box 20537, 1678 Nicosia, Cyprus

Self-control can be defined as choosing a large delayed reward over a small immediate reward, while *precommitment* is the making of a choice with the specific aim of denying oneself future choices [10]. The *self* can be viewed as a goal directed hierarchical system, where goals are internally specified according to value systems that are developed through experience [14]. Given a situation, the presence of more than one established value system can give rise to interpersonal conflicts. Such conflicts can refer to self-control problems where people might attempt to overcome them by applying precommitment [1, 11]. A computational model of interpersonal conflict is proposed where we implement two spiking neural networks as two players, learning simultaneously but independently, competing in the Iterated Prisoner's Dilemma (IPD) game. Learning links behaviour to the synaptic level by reinforcing stochastic synaptic transmission [15]. An interpretation of the IPD is that it demonstrates interpersonal conflict [5]. It is possible, Kavka suggests, that such inner conflicts are resolved as if they were a result of strategic interaction among rational subagents [5]. The structure of the sub-agents' value systems is investigated with respect to the cooperative outcome of the game, which corresponds to the self controlled behaviour. The results seem to suggest that the degree of cooperation in the IPD depends on the structure of the payoff matrix. The relationship between precommitment behaviour and the value systems is also investigated and compared to our previous work [3]. In fact, with a technique resembling the precommitment effect, whereby the payoffs for the dilemma cases in the IPD payoff matrix are differentially biased (increased or decreased) [3], cooperation seems to be enhanced as the differential bias is increased.

1. Introduction

The current work implements to the best of our knowledge for the first time in a multiagent learning setting a game theoretical view of self control based on conflicting internal agents [5] through a computational system that learns through a biologically plausible algorithm [15]. The study confirms that an optimal neuronal system can be composed of conflicting "selfish" agents [7] by implementing the optimum in a strategic interaction and also suggests that self-

*This work is supported by a University of Cyprus Small Size Internal Research Programme grant.

†Corresponding author, aris@cs.ucy.ac.cy

control behaviour is a strategy adopted by an "optimal" brain in the presence of conflicting agents.

The current work perceives the *self* as a goal directed hierarchical system, where goals are internally specified according to value systems [14]. However, the presence of more than one established value systems can divide the interest within a single individual and give rise to interpersonal conflict. Self-control behaviour can be employed in such situations and could be justified as one's desire to maximise long term reward. Self-control can be broadly defined as choosing a large delayed reward (with smaller present value) over a small immediate reward (with greater present value) [11]. According to Ariely [1], and Rachlin [11], we recognize that we have self-control problems and try to solve them by *precommitment* behaviour. Precommitment behaviour can be seen as a desire by people to protect themselves against a future lack of willpower. *Precommitment* is more formally defined as making a choice now with the specific aim of denying (or at least restricting) oneself future choices [10]. A typical example of precommitment is putting an alarm clock away from your bed, to force you to get up to turn it off.

However, self-control problems arise because human nature is not always rational as perceived in the context of economic theory (rational utility agents), otherwise the large delayed reward choice would have always been practiced. It is more appropriate to refer to human nature as multi-rational in the sense that the brain, in the interpersonal conflict case, can be viewed as a society of conflicting subagents [8], each one of them selfishly seeking reward accumulation.

For the purpose of an example consider the following case of conflicting value systems. A student faces a dilemma whether he or she should stay at home and finish a project that is to be submitted the following morning or go to the pub and celebrate a friend's birthday. Possible options can be:

a. Go to the pub and have fun.

b. Go to the pub for a quick drink and go back home and study.

c. Stay home and study.

d. Do something different. Possible *d* outcomes could be staying at home but not be able to study or go to the pub and having a miserable time because of guilty feelings.

Now assume that the student's academic-conscious agent orders these options according to their value as $c>b>d>a$, whereas the fun-conscious agent values them as $a>b>d>c$. Although the underline mechanisms performed in the student's real brain are highly complex and the knowledge about them is incomplete, the final decision of the student depends crucially on these assigned values. A realistic approach would be to suggest that such inner conflicts are resolved as if they were a result of strategic interaction among goal directed subagents [5].

According to Kavka [5], in situations of interpersonal conflict, each of the subagents can either insist on getting their way or compromise to a choice that benefits the organism as a whole. According to our example, their interaction can be analysed and represented by theoretical games as in Table 1.

Table 1. Game theoretical representation of strategic interaction between subagents with conflicting value systems. Each agent can either "Compromise" (C) or "Insist" (I). There are four possible outcomes *a, b, c* and *d* or CI, CC, IC, II respectively, that result from the agents' combined choices.

		Academic Agent	
Fun Agent		Compromise	Insist
	Compromise	b	c
	Insist	a	d

The academic-conscious subagent can insist on staying at home and studying throughout the night or compromise to a choice involving less studying. On the other hand, the fun-conscious subagent can insist on partying throughout the night or compromise to a less fun outcome. If both agents decide to "Compromise" then the student goes to the pub for a quick drink and then goes back home and studies. This corresponds to the *b* outcome which is the second best outcome for both agents and represents the case where the student exhibited self-control. However if any of them decides to "Insist" in order to pursue its most preferred outcome (*a* for the fun agent and *c* for the academic agent), then there is the risk of ending up in the worse situation *d* if the other agent also decides to "Insist". Finally if one decides to "Compromise" in order to achieve its second best outcome *b*, it also has to bear in mind that if the other agent chooses to "Insist" then the outcome will be the least preferred (*c* for the fun agent and *a* for the academic agent). The formal analysis of the game specifies that the *d* outcome is the only Nash equilibrium [9] of the game, so both agents will receive the inferior value of the *d* outcome whereas they could have achieved a superior in value *b* outcome, if they both "Compromised". Therefore, if the student's agents were faced by this dilemma for only one time and knew that this is the only time they would interact, they would have both "Insisted" and the student would "Do something different".

Moreover, consider the payoff matrix of Table 2 where the four outcomes are replaced by the values that each subagent assigns to each outcome. The analysis remains the same. In addition, these values are not absolute in the sense that a different set of subagents might apply different values to the same outcomes thus the payoff matrix of Table 2 is just one of infinite possible matrices. However, the structure of the payoffs of any given matrix should preserve the agents' outcomes ordering.

Table 2. The payoff matrix of the interaction. Payoff for the fun agent is shown first. Notice that the outcome ordering for each agent is preserved as c (5) > b (4) > d (-2) > a (-3) for the academic agent and a (5) > b (4) > d (-2) > c (-3) for the fun agent.

	Academic Agent		
		Compromise	Insist
Fun Agent	Compromise	4, 4	-3, 5
	Insist	5, -3	-2, -2

This specific payoff matrix structure is a well studied theoretical game known as the Prisoner's Dilemma [12] which has been used to model human cooperation [2] as well as interpersonal conflict [5]. In the latter interpretation, the "Compromise"-"Compromise" (CC) outcome corresponds to the self-control outcome which is the best for the organism (if we add up the two values) and the second best for each agent. Apart from the payoff structure, the game specifies that one round of the game consists of the two players (agents) choosing their action simultaneously and independently and then informed about the outcome. It also prerequisites that the two players are rational in the sense that each player wants to maximize his or her own payoff. For the purposes of the current work we model the infinitely iterated version of the game where the same game is repeated for an unspecified amount of rounds. The infinitely repeated version suits the interpretation of interpersonal conflict more realistically as the two internal agents compete with each other for more than one time and additionally they do not have any valid reason to believe that the next time they come into conflict would be the last time they will ever compete with each other. The formal analysis of the infinitely iterated version shows that there are multiple equilibria including the CC (self-control) outcome which now constitutes the best possible long-term outcome both for the organism and the agents individually. The latter is true because the possible outcome where one agent always "Insists" and the other "Compromises" can never be sustained. The only extra rule imposed on the outcomes' values for the iterated version is that

$2b>a+c$ which guarantees that the agents are not collectively better off by having each player alternate between "Compromise" and "Insist". The current model investigates whether the *self* can achieve its best in the presence of conflicting subagents that have a capability of learning.

As already explained, precommitment is an exercised behaviour where an individual makes a choice at a point in time in order to deny himself or herself future actions. Precommitment requires that people know which of the alternatives is best for them in the long run so that they precommit to the one with the highest payoff. The brain's ability to recognise or predict future rewards is built in according to experiments by Richmond et al. [13] and past experience enhances this ability.

In order to model the *effect* of precommitment in our computational model, it is assumed that the agent knows the long term payoffs that result from the different outcomes. In our example, this would mean that the student knows the long term payoffs of all a to d outcomes and additionally we make the assumption that the long term payoff of submitting his or her work is greater than going to the pub (long term payoff from c is greater than long term payoff from a). This latter knowledge could have been acquired by the student by experiencing the satisfaction of earning good grades through studying and not going to the pub and the consequences of not submitting his or her work and going to the pub at similar occasions. Therefore if Table 2 corresponds to the original payoff matrix (before experience) where both a and c outcomes are expected to yield the same total payoff, then the payoff matrix of Table 3 corresponds to the payoff matrix that develops through experience [3].

Table 3. The differential payoff $\psi>0$ is added to both payoffs of the outcome that is believed to yield a greater long term value and subtracted from both payoffs of the outcome that is believed to yield a smaller long term value.

		Academic Agent	
		Compromise	Insist
Fun Agent	Compromise	4, 4	$-3+\psi$, $5+\psi$
	Insist	$5-\psi$, $-3-\psi$	-2, -2

The effect or outcome of precommitment is that if it is exercised (at an earlier point in time) it ensures or at least increases the probability of the action (at a future point in time) that results to the same outcome as the one that would have been obtained by exercising self control (at the same future point in time). Therefore we make the hypothesis that the payoff matrix with the differential payoff (ψ) should induce a similar effect to that of precommitment, which is the choice of the action that corresponds to the self-controlled behaviour i.e. the choice of a more compromising behaviour by both agents in the game.

2. Methods

In order to model interpersonal conflict we have developed two artificial agents that compete in the Iterated Prisoner's Dilemma (IPD) where the two agents are implemented by two spiking neural networks. The networks' architecture is depicted in Figure 1.

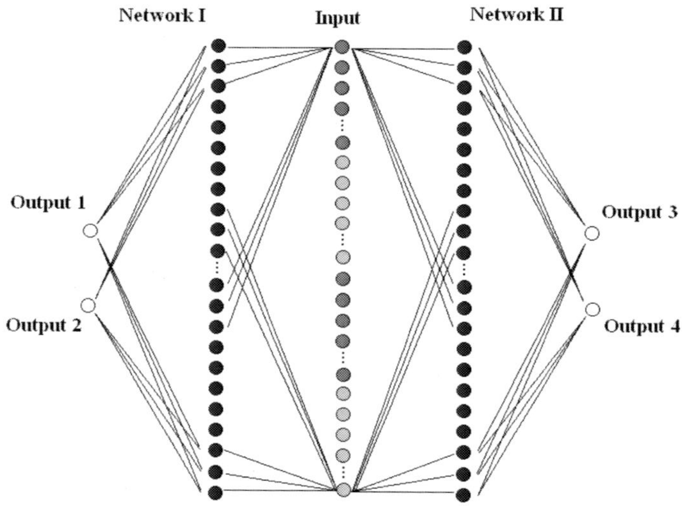

Figure 1. Two Spiking Neural Networks of Hedonistic Synapses Compete in the IPD. Two individual networks with multilayer perceptron type architecture receive a common input by 60 neurons, depicted in the middle of the figure. Each network (left and right) has two layers of hedonistic synapses that make feed forward connections between three layers of neurons; the 60 input neurons, 60 leaky integrate-and-fire hidden neurons and 2 leaky integrate-and-fire output neurons. The networks have full connectivity, though only some connections are shown for clarity. Neurons are randomly chosen to be either excitatory or inhibitory. The two networks simulate the corresponding two players of the game.

The networks receive a common input of 60 Poisson spike trains grouped in four neural populations. Each network has a hidden layer of 60 neurons and an output layer of 2 neurons, all modelled with the leaky integrate-and-fire equation:

$$C\frac{dV_i}{dt} = -g_L(V_i - V_L) - \sum_j G_{ij}(V_i - E_{ij}) \tag{1}$$

where V_L= -74 mV, g_L= 25 nS and C= 500 pF giving a membrane time constant τ= 20ms. The differential equations are integrated using an exponential Euler update with a 0.5 ms time step. When the membrane potential V_i reaches the threshold value of -54 mV, it is reset to -60mV (values as in the numerical simulations by Seung [15]. The reversal potential E_{ij} of the synapse from neuron j to neuron i is set to either 0 or -70 mV, depending on whether the synapse is excitatory or inhibitory. The synaptic conductances are updated via $\Delta G_{ij}= W_{ij}\, r_{ij}$ where r_{ij} is the neurotransmitter release variable that takes the value of 1 with probability equal to the probability that the synapse from neuron j to i releases a neurotransmitter (when j spikes) and 0 otherwise [15]. In the absence of presynaptic spikes G_{ij} decays exponentially with time constant τ_s = 5 ms. W_{ij} are the "weights" which do not change over time and are chosen randomly from an exponential distribution with mean 14nS for excitatory synapses and 45nS for inhibitory synapses.

The networks learn simultaneously but separately where each network seeks to maximize its own accumulated reward over a number of rounds. Learning is implemented through reinforcement of stochastic synaptic transmission [15]. Seung [15], makes the hypothesis that microscopic randomness is harnessed by the brain for the purposes of learning. The model of the hedonistic synapse is developed by Seung [15] along this hypothesis (all details can be found therein) where the reward system is built into the synapses. Briefly, within the framework of the model, each synapse acts as an agent who pursues reward maximisation. Upon arrival of a presynaptic spike, a synapse can take two possible actions with complementary probabilities; release a neurotransmitter with probability p or fail to release with probability 1- p. The release parameter q is monotonically related to p by the sigmoidal function given by:

$$p = \frac{1}{1+e^{-q}} \qquad (2)$$

Each synapse keeps a record of its recent actions through a dynamical variable, the eligibility trace ($\bar{e}$) [6]. It increases by 1- p with every release and decreases by $-p$ with every failure. Otherwise it decays exponentially with a given time constant. In order to differentiate the way the two networks integrate time related events, network *I* has an eligibility trace time constant equal to 2 ms and network *II* equal to 20 ms. This is because we make the hypothesis that two internal agents do not necessarily rely on past experience with the same degree. For example, the fun agent might rely less on past experience than the academic one. When a global reinforcement signal (h) is given to the network, it is subsequently communicated to each synapse which modifies its release probability according to the nature of the signal (reward or penalty) and its recent releases and failures. Learning is driven by modifying q according to the rule given by:

$$\Delta q = \eta \times h \times \bar{e} \tag{3}$$

where η is the learning rate. Synapses effectively learn by computing a stochastic approximation to the gradient of average reward. Moreover, if each synapse behaves hedonistically then the network as a whole behaves hedonistically, pursuing reward maximisation.

The input to the network during each learning round, encodes the decisions the two networks had at the previous round. For example, if at a given round network *I* chooses to "Insist" (I) and network *II* to "Compromise" (C), then during the next round the networks will receive input that encodes the "Insist"-"Compromise" (IC) outcome. One can identify here a cyclic procedure which starts when the networks decide, continues by feeding this information to the networks during which learning takes place and ends by a new decision. The input presentation and learning round last for 500 ms. The decision of each network is encoded in the input by the firing rate of two groups of Poisson spike trains. The first group will fire at 40Hz if the network "Compromised" and at 0Hz otherwise. The second group will fire at 40Hz if the network "Insisted" and at 0Hz otherwise. Consequently, the total input to the networks during each round is represented by four groups of Poisson neurons, two groups for each network, where each group fires at 40Hz or 0Hz accordingly. For any given round there are always two groups of 40Hz Poisson spike trains, preserving thus a balance at the firing rates of the output neurons at the beginning of learning. Any significant difference in the firing rate of the output neurons at any time should be induced only by learning and not due to differences in the firing rates of the driving input.

At the end of each learning round the networks decide whether to "Compromise" or "Insist" for the next round of the game. Decisions are carried out according to the value that each network assigns to the two actions, and these values are reflected by the firing rates of the output neurons at the end of each learning round. The value of the action "Compromise" for network *I* and *II* is taken to be proportional to the firing rate of output neurons *1* and *3* respectively. Similarly, the value of the action "Insist" for network *I* and *II* is taken to be proportional to the firing rate of output neurons *2* and *4* respectively. At the end of each learning round the firing rates of the competing output neurons are compared, for each network separately, and the decisions are drawn.

When the two networks decide their play for the next round of the IPD, they each receive a distinct payoff given their actions and according to the payoff matrix of the game (Table 2). The same payoff that each network receives as a result of their combined actions at the previous round of the game is also the global reinforcement signal that will train the networks during the next learning round and thus guide the networks to their next decisions. For example, if the outcome of the previous round was a CI then according to the payoff matrix (with differential payoff equal to 0) network *I* should receive a payoff of -3 for compromising and network *II* a payoff of +5 for insisting. During the next learning round network *I* receives a penalty of -3 and network *II* a reward of +5. Each network is reinforced for every spike of their output neuron that was "responsible" for the decision at the last round and therefore for the payoff received. Hence in the CI case, network *I* would receive a penalty of -3 for every spike of output neuron *1* (remember that the firing rate of output neuron *1* reflects the value that network *I* assigns for the action "Compromise") and network *II* would receive a reward of +5 for every spike of output neuron *4* (remember that the firing rate of output neuron *4* reflects the value that network II assigns for the action "Insist"). The networks therefore learn through global reinforcement signals which strengthen the value of an action that elicited reward and weaken the value of an action that resulted to a penalty.

In order to introduce competition between output neurons during a learning round, additional global reinforcement signals are administered to the networks for every spike of the output neurons that were not "responsible" for the decision at the last round [4]. For example, in the CI case, an additional reward of +1.5 is provided to network *I* for every spike of output neuron *2* and an additional penalty of -1.5 is provided to network *II* for every spike of output neuron *3*. The value of the action that was not chosen by each network is therefore also updated, by an opposite in sign reinforcement signal. The value of 1.5 is chosen to be small enough such that this complementary reinforcement signal would not cause a violation of the payoff rules that should govern the IPD. Overall during a learning round, each network receives global, opposite in sign reinforcements for spikes of both of its output neurons. One of the two signals is due to the payoff matrix of the game and its purpose is to "encourage" or "discourage" the action that elicited reward or penalty and the other signal is complementary and is purpose is to "encourage" or "discourage" the action that could have elicited reward or penalty if had been chosen in the previous round of the game. The overall reinforcement signals are presented in the Appendix.

3. Results and Discussion

Given the system configuration described in the Methods section, the two artificial agents compete in the IPD. Each game consists of 100 rounds during which the two networks seek to maximize their individual accumulated payoff by compromising or insisting at every round of the game. The table in the Appendix is used to administer reinforcement to each network at every round of the game. The system's payoff for each round is taken to be the addition of the two networks' payoffs. During the simulations, a strong self-controlled behaviour was established. This is depicted in Figure 2A which demonstrates a high accumulated average payoff as a result of a strong CC outcome. In fact, during the 100 rounds, the average number of the CC outcome was 75.44 whereas the other outcomes had averages 7.33 (CI), 13.33 (IC) and 3.9 (II). It is noted that the self-control outcome not only persisted during the final rounds of the games but it could also not change after the 100th round due to the system's dynamics that were evolved by that point in time in such a way to produce the self-control outcome consistently. This reveals that after a certain point the agents learned that is for their own benefit to compromise in order to maximize their reward. Moreover, as a result of the agents' behaviour, the system also ended up in maximizing payoff. The results comply with the theory that an optimal brain can be composed of conflicting "selfish" agents [7], and also suggest that self-control behaviour is a strategy adopted by an optimal brain in the presence of conflicting agents. At the same time, it raises the question whether the disability of some people to exhibit self control is due to the disability of their internal agents to maximize reward, reflecting a non optimizing brain.

In order to investigate how precommitment can influence the cases where self-control behaviour cannot be as strongly exhibited, the IPD simulation was repeated for the cases where the CC outcome that was obtained was the lowest. Figure 2B shows how ψ influences a particular case where the CC outcome was obtained only 65 times compared to 80 which was the best individual result. It is shown that the total accumulated payoff rises from 554 to 620 and most importantly the CC outcome rises from 65 to 76 which is the average. These findings are similar to our results produced with non-spiking neural networks and standard reinforcement learning algorithms [3]. Effectively, the use of ψ alters the payoff matrix of the game and therefore the values that each player assigns to the altered outcomes of the game.

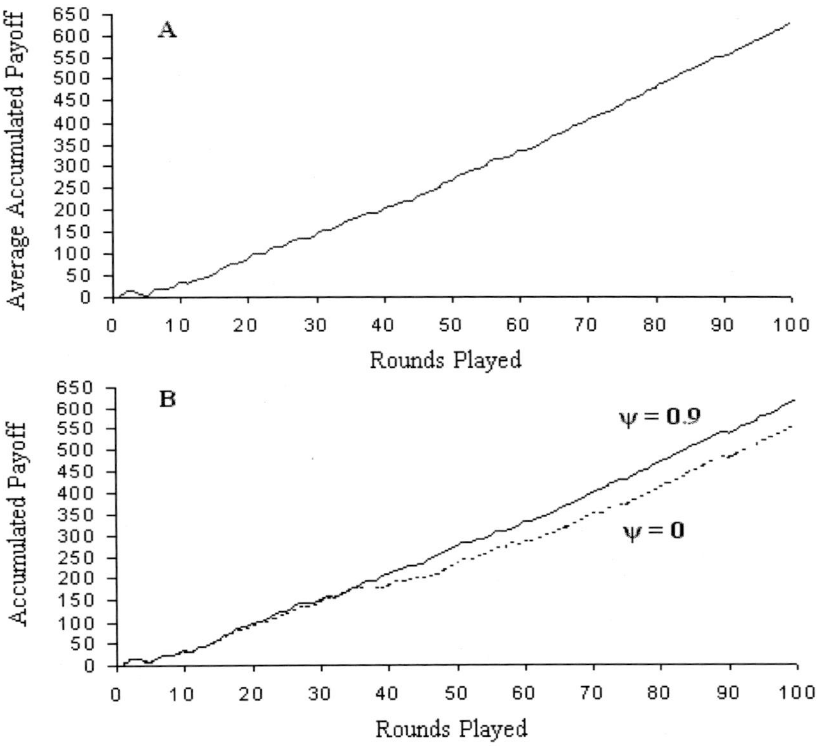

Figure 2. **A**. The average accumulated reward, gained by both networks during the IPD. **B**. The effect of differential payoff (ψ) at a particular case where the CC outcome with ψ=0 was substantially lower than the average (65).

The results demonstrate that learning promotes cooperation between the agents and thus leads to greater self-control. In addition, individual simulations suggest that increasing the precommitment effect (through increasing ψ) increases the probability of compromising with oneself in the future. Further investigation into these preliminary findings is required in order to verify its robustness.

Appendix

This table is an overview of the reinforcement signals that the networks receive during a learning round according to all possible outcomes of the previous round of the game. Reinforcement is administered for every spike of output neurons *1* to *4*.

	Output 1	Output 2	Output 3	Output 4
CC	+4	-1.5	+4	-1.5
CI	-3	+1.5	-1.5	+5
IC	+5	-1.5	-3	+1.5
II	+1.5	-2	+1.5	-2

References

1. D. Ariely, *Procrastination, Deadlines and Performance: Self-Control by Precommitment*. MIT Press, Cambridge, MA (2002).
2. R. Axelrod and W.D Hamilton, The Evolution of Cooperation. *Science* **211**, 1390-1396 (1981)
3. C. Christodoulou, G Banfield and A. Cleanthous, Self-Control with spiking and non-spiking neural networks playing games. *Journal of Physiology (Paris)* (under review) (2008).
4. A. Cleanthous and C. Christodoulou, Can Networks of Leaky Integrate-and-Fire Neurons with Spike-based Reinforcement Learning Play Games? Workshop for Spiking Networks and Reinforcement Learning, Utah, USA, March 2008 (available at URL: cosyne.org/wiki/Workshop_speaker _Aristodemos_Cleanthous).
5. G. Kavka, Is Individual Choice Less Problematic than Collective Choice? *Economics and Philosophy*, **7**, 291-310 (1991).
6. A. H. Klopf, *The Hedonistic Neuron: A Theory of Memory, Learning, and Intelligence.* Hemisphere Publishing, Washington, D.C. (1982).
7. A. Livnat, and N. Pippenger, An Optimal Brain Can Be Composed of Conflicting Agents. *Proc. of the National Academy of Sciences,USA*, **103**, 3198-3202 (2006).
8. M. Minsky, *The Society of Mind.* Simon and Schuster, New York, NY (1985).
9. J. F. Nash, Equilibrium Points in N-person Games. *Proc. of the National Academy of Sciences, USA*, **36**, 48-49 (1950).
10. H. Rachlin, Self-Control: Beyond Commitment. *Behaviour and Brain Sciences*, **18**, 109-159 (1995).
11. H. Rachlin, *The Science of Self-Control.* Harvard University Press, Cambridge, MA (2000).
12. A. Rappoport and A. M. Chammah, *Prisoner's Dilemma.* University of Michigan Press, Ann Arbor, MI (1965).
13. B. J. Richmond, Z. Liu and M. Shidara, Predicting future rewards. *Science*, **31**, 179-180 (2003).
14. M. R. Scheier and C. S. Carver, C. S., A model of behavioral self-regulation: Translating intention into action. In L. Berkowitz (Ed.), *Advances in Experimental Social Psychology*, Vol. 21, pp. 303-339, Academic Press, San Diego, CA (1988).
15. H. S. Seung, Learning in Spiking Neural Networks by Reinforcement of Stochastic Synaptic Transmission. *Neuron*, **40**, 1063-1073 (2003).

CONFLICT-MONITORING AND (META)COGNITIVE CONTROL

EDDY J. DAVELAAR
School of Psychology, Birkbeck, University of London
London, WC1E 7HX, United Kingdom

According to an influential theory of cognitive control, conflict between competing responses is monitored and used to exert control over information processing. In this paper, I shy away from debates in the literature and ask whether there are other uses for monitored conflict. I present simulation results showing that conflict can be used to (1) produce retrospective confidence judgements, (2) dynamically adjust the response threshold, and (3) modulate stimulus-response learning. Although predictions need to be tested, the general conclusion is that conflict can be involved in metacognitive control.

1. Introduction

According to an influential theory of cognitive control [1] performance on cognitive tasks is controlled by brain systems that detect conflict between response channels and use this conflict signal to bias the attention to task-relevant information. This particular theory makes the strong prediction that conflict monitored on trial n – 1 leads to better (faster or more accurate) responses on trial n. These sequential effects have, as predicted by the conflict/control-loop theory, been found across a range of so-called conflict tasks; tasks that are characterized by presenting a participant with conflicting stimulus information with the requirement to pay attention (and respond) to only the task-relevant information. For example, in the Eriksen flanker task [2], a central target character may be associated with a left or a right button press. On congruent trials, the target is flanked by distractor characters that are associated with the same response as the target. On incongruent trials, however, the flankers are associated with the opposite response. The standard finding is that reaction times (RTs) are slower for incongruent compared to congruent trials. This RT-difference is called the flanker effect and is shown to be smaller when the preceding trial was an incongruent trial compared to when the preceding trial was a congruent trial. This interaction between the previous trial-type and the current trial-type is called the Gratton effect and has featured in an ongoing debate on the accuracy of the conflict/control-loop theory. The strongest contender theory assumes that the Gratton effect is due to repetitions of stimulus-response associations. Although this debate is strongly polarized, alternative theories are being proposed, bridging the competing theories [3,4,5]. Apart from the sequential effects, other aspects that are the subject of intense research are the time-course (between- vs. within-trials) and domain-specificity of conflict-induced control (response- vs. stimulus-conflict; [6], for a review see [7]).

In this paper, I will expand the focus and relate conflict to retrospective metacognitive judgments through illustrative simulation models of two-choice decisions (section 3.1). I will then present two further proposals: (1) conflict can be used to adjust the response threshold (section 3.2), and (2) conflict can be used to modulate the amount of associative learning between stimulus and response (section 3.3). The paper will shy away from the ongoing debates and instead present a case for exploring the utility of conflict, as measured through competition between alternatives. This will necessarily lead to yet-to-be-tested predictions that an empirical researcher might like to explore.

2. Generic model

2.1. *Model architecture*

In order to address the various proposals for the utility of conflict, the architecture for the model needs to be selected. Two considerations led me to choose a two-layer feedforward localistic network with two competing representations in each layer (Figure 1). The first was the logical problem of using conflict measured at the response units to modulate the threshold of those same units. The second consideration was of an empirical nature. In an experiment, we tested twelve participants on a flanker task to look at sequential effects. On 75% of the trials, the participant responded as quickly as possible to a stimulus consisting of arrowheads (e.g., <<<<< or >><>>). On 25% of the trials, participants would withhold a response when a beep sounded (after 100 or 200 msec). We replicated the finding that the Gratton effect was only observed when the target/response repeats across trials [4,8,9]. Interestingly, the same pattern was observed for trials that followed a correctly withheld stop-signal trial (dotted lines in Figure 2). Irrespective of the interpretation of this triple interaction (between previous trial-type, current trial-type, and target/response repetition), the fact that the stop-signal did not alter the interaction, suggests that the stop-signal affects a processing stage that comes *after* the conflict monitoring stage.

Here, we focus on a two-layer model of perceptual choice (cf. [10). The first layer represents the decision layer and is presumed to be located in prefrontal areas that are involved in making a selection between competing information that are fed forward from posterior areas (not modeled). The second layer represents the execution layer and is presumed to relate to the output of the basal ganglia. The direct connections between the decision and execution layers are thus a short-hand for the response disinhibition through the basal ganglia. A detailed model of the basal ganglia could replace these connections, allowing further examinations of the proposals put forward in the next sections.

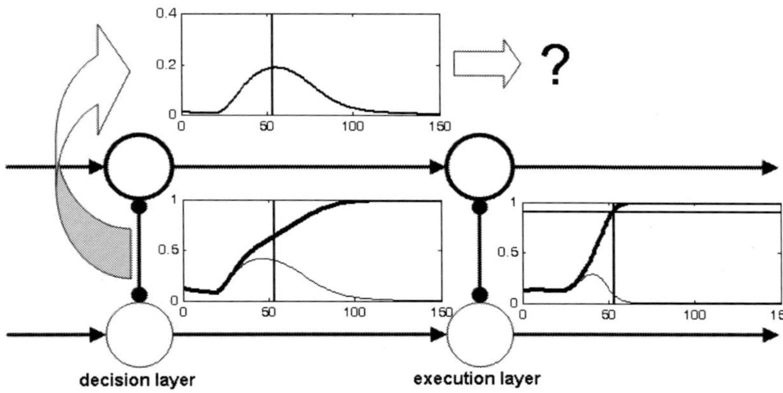

Figure 1. Architecture of the model used in the simulations. Conflict is monitored at the decision layer and a response is made (at t = 53) when one of the execution units reaches a threshold (horizontal line). Activation trajectories are presented for each layer and conflict. The bold trajectories are from the bold-outlined units. The question mark indicates the focus of this paper, i.e., what can the conflict-signal be used for?

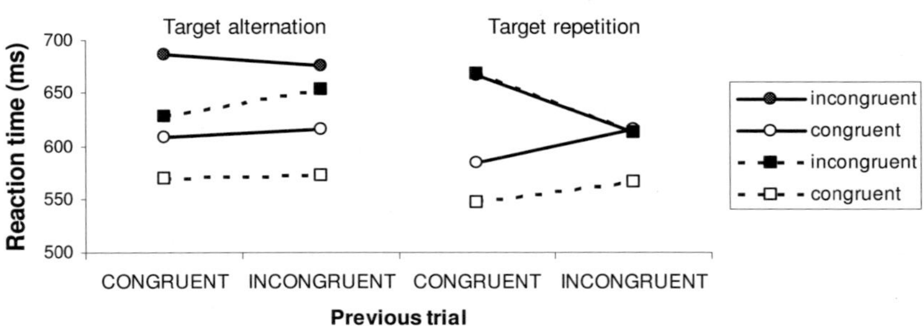

Figure 2. Results of a flanker study, showing that the triple interaction seen for the control trials (solid lines) is also obtained for trials following a correct stop-signal trial (dotted lines). The incongruent trials for the target repetition condition are the same after stop-signal and normal trials.

2.2. *Information processing in the model*

Each processing layer is a module exhibiting mutual inhibition with leakage. Each decision unit receives input, I_i, from earlier (not modeled) processing layers. Each unit, u_i, in the network has a sigmoidal output activation function, y_i, with slope = 4 and bias = 0.5. The decision units, u_1 and u_2, compete through lateral inhibition, w = 0.75, and send activation to the execution units, u_3 and u_4, that also exhibit mutual competition and leakage, k = 0.2. Activation accumulates in the execution units until one of the units reach a response threshold (= 0.9). At that time a (correct or error) response is recorded.

The activation in the units is updated in parallel with $dt_d = 0.1$, $dt_e = 0.2$, and the standard deviation of zero-mean white noise, cdW at 0.1.

$$dx_1 = (-kx_1 - wy_2 + I_1)dt_d + cdW_1$$
$$dx_2 = (-kx_2 - wy_1 + I_2)dt_d + cdW_2$$
$$dx_3 = (-kx_3 - wy_4 + y_1)dt_e + cdW_3$$
$$dx_4 = (-kx_4 - wy_3 + y_2)dt_e + cdW_4$$

$$y_i = 1/(1 + e^{-4(xi - 0.5)})$$

Following [1] and [10], conflict is calculated as the product of the output activations of the two decision units and the lateral inhibition, wy_1y_2. In all simulations in the next sections, this was done for 100 iterations after one of the execution units reached the response threshold. Each simulation is based on 10000 trials. During model exploration, it was found that noise in the execution units is necessary in order to obtain the appropriate right-skewed RT-distributions. This means that dynamic behavior at the execution level can not be fully predicted from the dynamics at the decision level and thus the use of a two-layer network does not involve redundancy.

3. The utility of conflict in metacognitive control

3.1. *Decision conflict and retrospective confidence judgments*

The term "conflict" in the context of decision-making brings with it the image of uncertainty. In this section, we explore the hypothesis that retrospective confidence judgments can be modeled by using post-response conflict. In situations where there is a clear answer, participants are able to make retrospective confidence judgments that show different distributions for error and correct trials. Specifically, the distribution of confidence judgments for error trials is a monotonic decreasing function with the peak over the lowest confidence judgment. The distribution of confidence judgments for correct trials is the mirror image of the incorrect distribution [11].

Previous work on conflict monitoring [1,12] has shown that post-response conflict is postdictive of an error response, with high conflict following an erroneous response and low conflict following a correct response. A simulation was run to obtain a distribution of conflict values (over 100 iterations, post-response). As can be seen in Figure 3, the distribution of post-response conflict of correct trials has a lower mean and standard deviation than the distribution of post-response conflict of error trials. In order to get a useful metric for confidence rating (between 0 and 1 and then categorized into six bins), the responses were transformed using a sigmoidal function. The choice for the sigmoidal function is compatible with the idea that conflict is an input to the brain area that monitors conflict and has a sigmoidal output activation function, y_c. How conflict-monitoring is actually implemented in the brain is still an open question. Any function that saturates with large input values should produce the same qualitative pattern. Figure 3 shows how the raw distributions of post-response conflict are transformed and how this produces distributions of confidence ratings that are comparable with empirical findings [11].

It is important to note that the slope (= 6) and threshold (= 0.5) of the sigmoid that transforms the conflict signal strongly influence the distribution of confidence. Therefore if these parameters can be regarded as governing the sensitivity of the conflict-monitoring system, the efficacy of this system governs metacognitive abilities.

The simulation provides all the "behavioral" results needed to apply signal-detection theoretic analyses. Figure 3 also presents receiver operator characteristics (ROC). As can be seen, the model produces standard ROC curves and the corresponding z-transformed ROC curves with the curves becoming more distant from the diagonal with increases in signal strength (I = 0.5, 0.51, 0.52, 0.53). This extra positive feature of the model could be used to investigate the relation between decision conflict and retrospective confidence judgements.

An obvious prediction here is that the error-related negativity (ERN) should be related to subjective confidence judgments. Some indication of this was found by [13], who found in one experiment that a conservative criterion setting produced stronger ERNs and in another experiment that it produced lower confidence (as shown by more frequent changes to the initial response) than a liberal criterion setting. Further studies are needed to directly test the predictions.

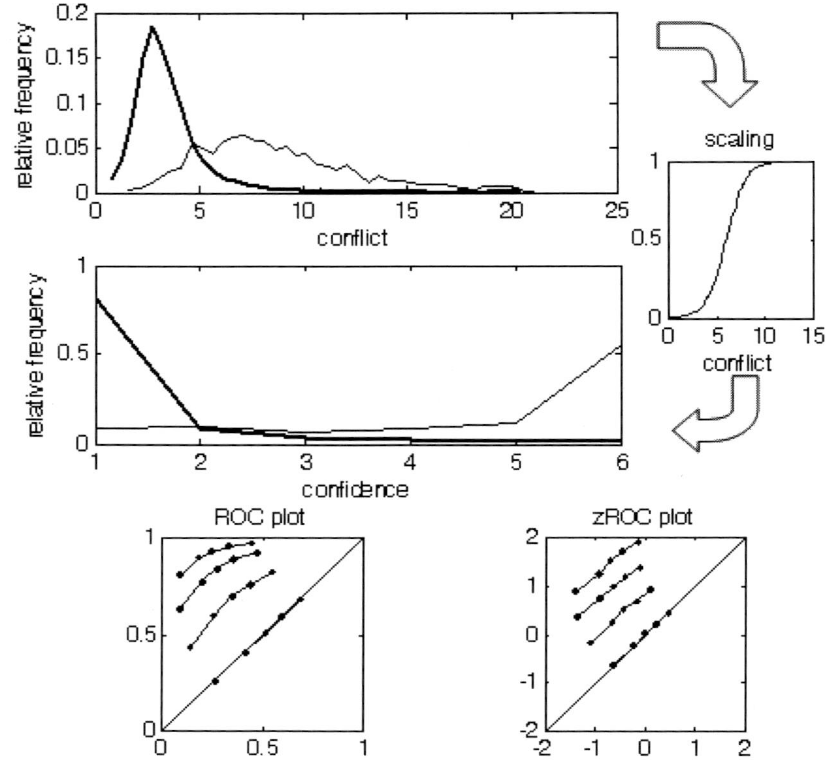

Figure 3. Simulation results showing the distribution of conflict (for I = 0.53) that is transformed using a sigmoidal function into confidence ratings (1: 1 – 5/6, 2: 5/6 – 4/6, 3: 4/6 – 3/6, 4: 3/6 – 2/6, 5: 2/6 -1/6, 6: 1/6 – 0). Bold lines are for correct responses, showing the postdictive nature of post-response conflict. The bottom two panels show ROC and zROC curves for four levels of difficulty.

3.2. *Cognitive control through within-trial dynamic threshold setting*

The conflict/control loop theory [1] proposes that conflict between competing response channels is monitored by the anterior cingulate cortex and used to tighten the control exerted by the prefrontal cortex. Using computational methods, they observe that the conflict signal has a particular time-course that maps well on findings obtained from electrophysiological studies.

Studies using electroencephalography (EEG) have shown that prior to a response, a negative deflection is observed that is larger for incongruent than congruent trials. This response-locked signal, called the N2-component, has a central topography and is believed to be produced by the same neural network that monitors conflict [12]. Yeung et al. [12] proposed that the N2-component reflect pre-response conflict. The functional view of the N2-component advanced here is inspired by other computational work [14,15]. In the area of optimal decision-making, Bogacz [14] proposed that the striatal and sub-thalamic pathways subserve two important functional roles. In the striatal pathway, the evidence for individual competing actions is presented for selection, whereas in the sub-thalamic pathway, conflict between competing actions is used to prevent premature responding. This resonates with the role of the subthalamic nucleus (STN) as a brake on responding as featured in the computational model by Frank [15]. In that model, the STN inhibits responding. This inhibition is similar to increasing the response threshold. Thus an emergent view from this work is that pre-response conflict can be used to increase the response threshold by inhibiting the execution units.

A different, but not incompatible, view of dynamic threshold setting is through across-trial adaptation to maximize reward [16]. However, in this section the focus is on *within-trial* dynamic threshold setting. To understand the benefit of such an approach, consider Figure 4, which shows the activation function of two decision units. Before $t = t_1$, the peak, the system does not exhibit full selection and behaves similar to a horse-race model, where two response channels race until one reaches the finish line. After $t = t_2$, the system behaves as a strong competition model, where on every iteration an increase for one unit means a decrease in the other unit. The transition from horse-race to strong-competition model, $t_1 < t < t_2$, has interesting properties regarding Weber's law [17]. For optimal responding, the threshold should be such that the response happens after the system has made a selection, i.e., after t_1 (for fast correct RT), and possibly after t_2 (to increase accuracy). However, due to noise in the system, the exact values of t_1 and t_2 change considerably. Nevertheless, the level of conflict is similar in the region between t_1 and t_2. Adjusting the threshold (by adding the conflict-signal to the threshold) influences response execution, leading to correct selection at the decision level. This should increase the accuracy given a particular RT.

In order to test the usefulness of within-trial adjustment of response threshold (through inhibition of execution units), a simulation was run with and without threshold adjustment. Figure 5 summarizes the results. The model is more accurate across the whole range of RT when the threshold gets adjusted, as shown by the cumulative distribution of hit rates (the overall hit rate was the same for each simulation).

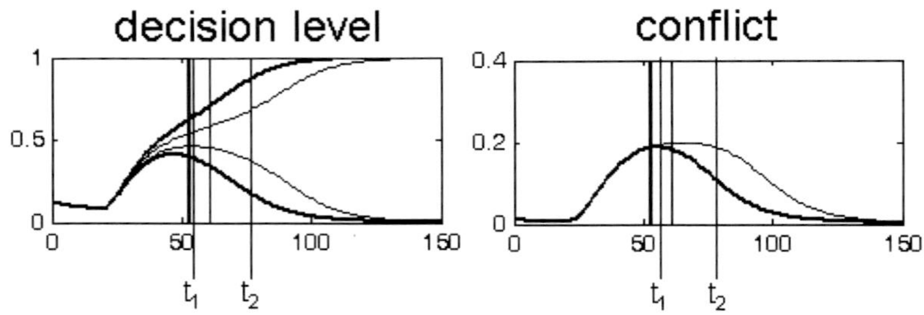

Figure 4. Two examples of activation trajectories (without threshold adjustment) for decision units (left panel) and corresponding conflict (right panel). The vertical lines with t_1 and t_2 are for the simulation producing the thin activation trajectories. The vertical lines without labels are the times at which each simulation produced a response.

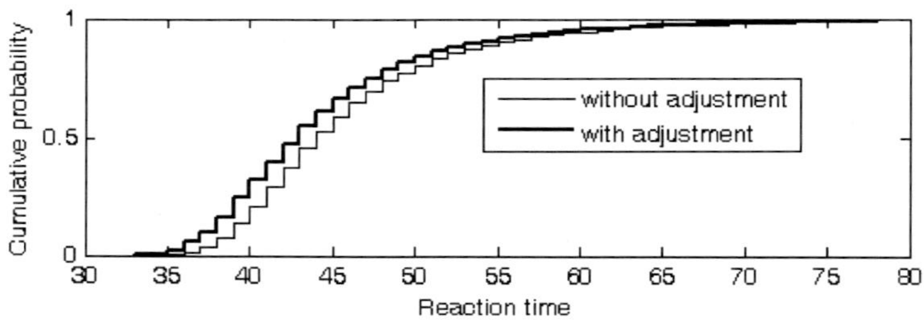

Figure 5. Cumulative distribution of hit rates (against RT) for a simulation without (thin line) and with (thick line) conflict-modulated threshold adjustment.

This simulation shows an important potential for modelling micro-adjustments to maintain optimal performance in the presence of noisy decision accumulators. A prediction would be that the N2-component should be predictive of optimal responding and interference at any stage from conflict-detection, transformation, and inhibition of execution units should directly affect optimality.

3.3. *Conflict-modulated learning of stimulus-response associations*

In the domain of attentional control, the debate regarding the explanatory power of the conflict/control loop theory has been challenged by the observation that the so-called Gratton effect – the effect that after an incongruent trial, the interference effect is smaller due to conflict-induced increase in attentional control – is obtained only when the same stimulus repeats across trials [8,9]. An alternative, non-conflict-based, explanation is that the Gratton effect reflects the result of learning an association between stimulus and response on trial n – 1 and using this association on trial n. This explanation received empirical support in a study using appropriate baseline conditions [4]. However, this study also revealed that the magnitude of the learning effect depended on the presence of conflict on the previous trial. This finding led to the proposal that conflict-related control is not necessarily through increase in attentional gain, but through modulating the learning of stimulus-response associations ([4]; see also [3,5]).

The view that conflict modulates learning is reminiscent of the large literature on reinforcement learning and therefore this learning rule will not be explained in too much detail here. The basic idea is simply that the associative strength between units in the input and in the decision layer is updated after every trial in a normal Hebbian fashion, i.e., amount of weight-change equals the product of activations of sending and receiving units and a learning rate parameter. The proposal here is that the learning rate parameter is a function of monitored conflict. For the present simulation, we use post-response conflict, as it has the attractive feature of being postdictive of errors. The importance of that feature will become clear in what follows.

To get an intuition for the dynamics consider the following scenario. On trial n – 1, the system is presented with stimulus-A, which requires response-X. After a correct response, the post-response conflict is small and thus any change in associative strength is small too. After an incorrect response, the post-response conflict is large and thus the weight update will also be large. With the sign of the change dependent on the accuracy of the trial, such a scheme makes small positive changes and large negative changes. However, the just-described scenario is one where feedback about the accuracy of the response is given: supervised learning. By using the feature that post-response conflict is postdictive of errors, an unsupervised learning rule can be developed that compares the post-response conflict to a criterion. When the conflict is larger or smaller than this criterion (= 7), the stimulus-response association will be decreased or increased, respectively.

In the final simulation, the decision units receive input such that without any change in connection strength, the accuracy stays around 63%. Figure 6 shows accuracy, RT, and post-response conflict over 100 blocks of 100 trials. The values are z-scores obtained by comparing the condition with learning with the baseline condition of no learning. Note that feedback about the accuracy is *absent* for all simulations. Therefore the increase in accuracy, decrease in reaction time and decrease in post-response conflict is all due to unsupervised conflict-modulated learning. Further developments are needed to obtain suitable algorithms for setting the conflict-criterion.

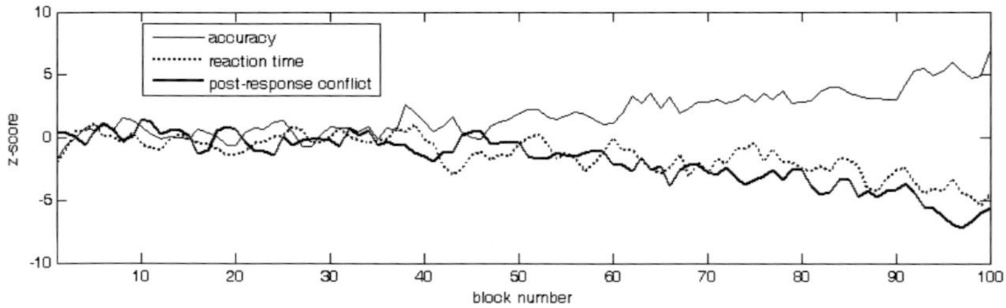

Figure 6. Results of conflict-modulated Hebbian learning. Despite the absence of feedback, the feature that post-response conflict postdicts error can be used to enhance performance.

4. General discussion

In this paper, I presented three proposals for the use of monitored conflict in a two-choice task. The first simulation showed that post-response conflict can be used to obtain an indication of retrospective confidence, which can also be used to create ROC-curves. The second simulation showed that pre-response conflict can be used to adjust response threshold, thereby increasing optimal responding. The third simulation showed that post-response conflict can be used to increase performance through modulating the learning of stimulus-response associations. When applying the results of the three simulations to humans, the strong assumption is that conflict is monitored by humans and used in the ways presented above. When these neural computations are taken outside of the domain of psychology, the simulations present pointers for new developments in different areas.

A number of interesting connections remain. First is the relation to detailed models of confidence judgments [18,19,20]. This issue has been left out, as a full discussion requires not only outlining relations among confidence, reaction time, and accuracy, but also how signal-detection theory maps onto neural computation. The second is the relation to post-error slowing, where within the presented framework, the post-error conflict is not only used as signal for confidence judgments, but also to increase the response threshold on subsequent trials. Finally, there is the question of whether the conflict-modulated Hebbian learning is optimal. This requires a mathematical analysis of the learning rule and benchmark rules and problems. In addition, the relation to infant categorization is only too obvious, but again this literature is vast. Despite the relations to these interesting topics, the work presented here shows the potential of using conflict-monitoring in other domains. A full investigation of these aspects is left for the future.

In this paper, I tried to convince the reader that going beyond useful and informative debates about the fundamental questions in basic research on conflict-monitoring, interesting applications can be developed from the partial answers that may form the basis of solutions in their own right. Future research in various disciplines may reveal how successful these applications of conflict-monitoring will be in reality.

Acknowledgments

I thank Ana Devenish for collecting the data shown in Figure 2 and Michael Dougherty, Eli Katsiri, Yoonhee Jang, and Adam Sanborn for discussions on various aspects at the early stages of this work.

References

1. M. M. Botvinick, T. S. Braver, D. M. Barch, C. S. Carter and J. D. Cohen, *Psychological Review* 108, 624 (2001).
2. B. A. Eriksen and C. W. Eriksen, *Perception & Psychophysics* 16, 134 (1974).
3. C. Blais, S. Robidoux, E. F. Risko and D. Besner, *Psychological Review* 114, 1076 (2007).
4. E. J. Davelaar and J. Stevens, *Psychonomic Bulletin & Review* (in press).
5. T. Verguts and W. Notebaert, (2008). *Psychological Review* 115, 518 (2008).
6. E. J. Davelaar, *Brain Research* 1202, 109 (2008).
7. T. Egner, *Trends in Cognitive Sciences* 10, 374 (2008).
8. U. Mayr, E. Awh and P. Laurey, *Nature Neuroscience* 6, 450 (2003).
9. S. Nieuwenhuis, J. F. Stins, D. Posthuma, T. J. C. Polderman, D. I. Boomsma and E. J. De Geus, *Memory & Cognition* 34, 1260 (2006).
10. A. D. Jones, R. Y. Cho, L. E. Nystrom, J. D. Cohen and T. S. Braver, *Cognitive, Affective, & Behavioral Neuroscience* 2, 300 (2002).
11. M. R. Dougherty, P. Scheck, T. O. Nelson and L. Narens, *Memory & Cognition* 33, 1096 (2005).
12. N. Yeung, M. M. Botvinick and J. D. Cohen, *Psychological Review* 111, 931 (2004).
13. T. Curran, C. DeBuse and P. A. Leynes, *Journal of Experimental Psychology: Learning, Memory, and Cognition* 33, 2 (2007).
14. R. Bogacz, *Trends in Cognitive Sciences* 11, 118 (2007).
15. M. J. Frank, *Neural Networks* 19, 1120 (2006).
16. P. Simen, J. D. Cohen and P. Holmes, *Neural Networks* 19, 1013 (2006).
17. G. Deco, L. Scarano and S. Soto-Faraco, *Journal of Neuroscience* 27, 11192 (2007).

18. E. C. Merkle and T. Van Zandt, *Journal of Experimental Psychology: General* 135, 391 (2006).
19. T. J. Pleskac and J. Busemeyer, In *Proceedings of the 29th Annual Cognitive Science Society* 563 (2007).
20. R. Ratcliff and J. J. Starns, J. J., *Psychological Review* (in press).

REPRESENTATION THEORY MEETS ANATOMY: FACTOR LEARNING IN THE HIPPOCAMPAL FORMATION*

ANDRÁS LŐRINCZ

Department of Information Systems, Eötvös Loránd University, Pázmány sétány 1/C Budapest 1117 Hungary

GÁBOR SZIRTES

Department of Cognitive Psychology, Eötvös Loránd University, Izabella u. 46 Budapest 1064 Hungary

In this paper we argue that computational issues like complexity, memory requirements and training time impose strong constraints on learning in any goal-oriented system. Along these constraints we derive a particular architecture that learns representations for optimizing plans e.g., trajectory planning. To comply with biological constraints as well, the resulting encoding mechanism is translated into a connectionist network. We argue that the goal-oriented framework implies distinct representations of place and direction in the hippocampal formation responsible for spatial navigation in mammals.

1. Introduction

Ample clinical evidence demonstrates the central role of the hippocampal region (HR) in forming long-term memories see, e.g. [1]. The complex structure of this brain region has inspired a plethora of models aiming to correlate its functioning with the peculiarities of the structure. One common view [2] in many models is that memory systems maintain representations (that is models) shaped to help executive control, because associative mapping of immediate stimuli to responses is insufficient to reflect the reward structure of the environment. Granted this assumption, computational constraints regarding speed and complexity on forming representations for control and desired goals should be applied on any model of memory. In this paper we focus on how these constraints may restrict potential models. In a general goal-oriented system

*This research has been supported by the EC NEST PERCEPT' Grant FP6-043261 and Air Force Grant FA8655-07-1-3077. Any opinions, findings and conclusions or recommendations expressed in this material are those of the authors and do not necessarily reflect the views of the European Commission, European Office of Aerospace Research and Development, Air Force Office of Scientific Research, Air Force Research Laboratory. G. Sz. has been supported by the Zoltán Magyary Fellowship. We are grateful for the anonym reviewer for his/her useful remarks.

learning has two stages; (i) the adaptation of the internal model, i.e., shaping of the *representations* and (ii) the optimization of sequential decision making, i.e., the state→desired state plans, to maximize the expectation value of discounted and cumulated long-term rewards. Sequential decision making may be treated within the framework of reinforcement learning (RL) and Markov decision process (MDP) can be used as its mathematical model motivated by psychology and neuroscience as well [3]. While the original MDP scales badly with the number of variables, its factored version (fMDP) [4] can avoid such complexity issues by assuming that dependencies among variables can be factored – under certain circumstances – to several components (see e.g. [5]). However, these factors should first be appropriately extracted and represented.

In what follows, we review the central notion of factors and how it implies the concept of independent process analysis (Section 2). The theoretical results are translated into a neural network architecture featuring Hebbian learning (Section 3). In Section 4 we show the close similarity between the derived architecture and the hippocampal region (HR). We shortly discuss how our model has evolved since the proposal of [17] in Section 5.

2. Factors and independent processes

We take navigation as an example to illustrate our ideas. The state of the animal is characterized by two independent factors, position and speed, according to Newton's second law. Acceleration depends on the net force g and the mass (m). Newton's equation $md^2s/dt^2 = g$ –where d^2s/dt^2 denotes the second temporal derivative of position s– can be discretized and for short time steps we get

$$s(t+1)=g(t)/m - 2s(t)+ s(t-1) \qquad (1)$$

This equation may be interpreted as an autoregressive process *driven by* $g(t)/m$. What makes this problem hard is that this simple form is typically hidden as observations are filtered through, for example, visual, olfactory or proprioceptive sensors thus providing a distorted function of the original process. Distortions may be caused by delays or by including differently transformed echoes (called moving averages, MA) of the same driving forces. The recovery of the hidden factors then includes the following steps: (i) translation of the problem into hidden autoregressive moving average (ARMA) processes, (ii) removal of both the AR and MA contributions, (iii) extraction of the hidden driving noises (or causes, e.g., the forces, or their immediate consequences; the changes of the trajectory) and (iv) identification of their relation. Recent advances on hidden ARMA models enable the recovery of the hidden processes as well as the hidden causes from the observations up to certain forms of invariance provided that multi-dimensional components of the hidden driving noise can be assumed *independent* (see [6] and the cited references). Loosely speaking, in contrast to simple decorrelation, independence implies that second *and* higher order correlations between the multi-dimensional components can be neglected.

We restrict our considerations to first order AR processes that assume the following form

$$h(t+1) = Gh(t) + f(t+1) \tag{2}$$

$$x(t) = Ah(t). \tag{3}$$

where matrix $G \in R^{k \times k}$ represents the dynamics of the system, vector $h(t) \in R^k$ is the hidden state or hidden process at time t, $f(t) \in R^k$ is the hidden driving noise process, $A \in R^{k \times k}$ is the mixing matrix that prohibits direct observation, and $x(t) \in R^k$ is the observation at time t (from now on, capital letters denote matrices, lower case letters denote vectors). We also assume that matrix A is invertible. The goal is to compute the estimations, $\hat{h}(t)$ for $h(t)$, $e(t)$ for $f(t)$, and the so called separation matrix W for A^{-1}. Within this setup it also makes sense to distinguish *independent processes* (time series) $h_i(t)$ in the sense that they do not mix: F may assume block structure. ARMA process with independence assumption on the noise will be referred to as ARMA-IPA model, where IPA stands for Independent Process Analysis.

3. A connectionist network for identifying ARMA-IPA models

Let us remark first that the observation of Eq. (3) is also an AR process, as substituting (2) in (3) yields:

$$x(t+1) = \mathcal{M}\, x(t) + n(t+1) \tag{4}$$

According to the central limit theorem, $n(t+1)=Af(t+1)$ is approximately Gaussian and thus matrix $\mathcal{M} = AFA^{-1}$ and noise $n(t+1)$ can be estimated by least-mean square methods, i.e. the cost function can be read as:

$$J(M) = ½\, \Sigma_t\, |x(t+1) - M\, x(t)|^2, \tag{5}$$

where M is the estimation of $\mathcal{M}$ yielding the following estimation of the observation noise: $\varepsilon(t)= x(t+1)-Mx(t)$. Because of the independence assumption on $f(t)$, term $\varepsilon(t)$ can now be analyzed by Independent Subspace Analysis (ISA, [7, 8]) techniques to estimate W, which then leads to the estimations of the hidden causes $f(t)$, the hidden state $h(t)$, and hidden dynamics G. (On the peculiarities of the special combination of ISA and ARMA models, see [6, 9].) ISA is a generalization of the Independent Component Analysis (ICA) methods in that it assumes multi-dimensional hidden sources and its solution can be decomposed into two subtasks: 1, on an ICA *separation* step (yielding more or less independent *one-dimensional* components) and then 2, a *clustering* of these components into independent subspaces. ISA, alike other ICA derivatives, is speeded up considerably if data is decorrelated (whitened) before the actual separation. ISA also inherits ambiguities of the ICA methods: components are not ordered, and their sign and scale may also vary. Furthermore, the ISA solution is ambiguous up to orthogonal transformations within the recovered subspaces.

Having identified the most important algorithmic components (namely, identification of an AR process, whitening, ICA separation, and clustering) now we are in the position to derive a connectionist network featuring local (i.e. Hebbian) interactions only. Inter- and intralayer synaptic weights or connections are denoted by matrices, while activity of a given layer is defined by a vector. The derived architecture will be mapped onto the neural substrate in the next section, but fine details like temporal characteristics, spike generation sparse coding and others will be omitted. For simplicity, rate coding (manifesting analogue values) and mixed weights (that contradict Dale's Principle) are assumed throughout the derivations, but the proposed functioning can in principle be also realized by using either positive coding [10] or homogenous connection systems [11]. Inhibitions (or subtractions) are manifested by separate inhibitory populations within a layer using feedback or feed-forward inhibition.

3.1. *Identification of the AR predictive matrix*

The following online and local learning rule for matrix M can be derived from the cost function of Eq. (5) by computing its negative gradient according to matrix M:

$$\Delta M(t+1) \sim \varepsilon(t+1)x(t)^T \tag{6}$$

This rule already has an effect on the construction of the network.

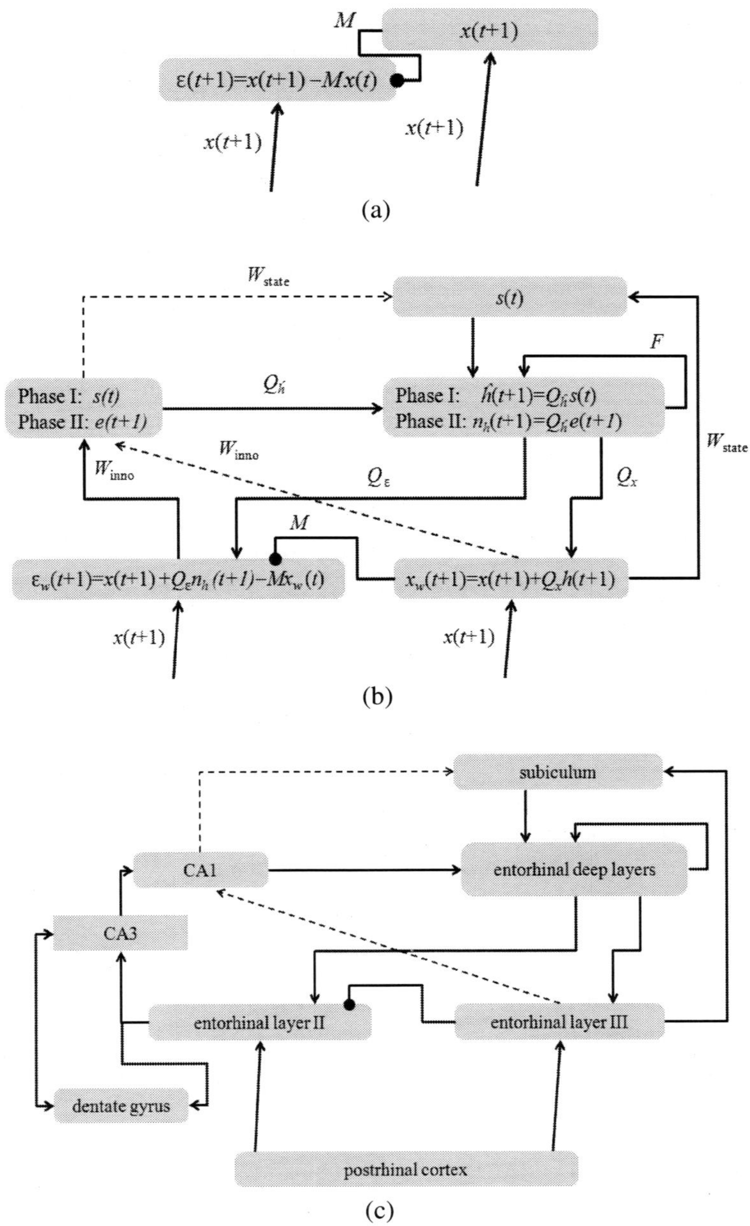

Figure 1. See p. 258 for the Caption.

Caption for Figure 1. Hebbian network of the hippocampal region. (a): a network that can extract the noise of the observed input: t time index, x input, ε estimated noise, *M:* estimated AR matrix. Open (circle) arrows: excitatory (inhibitory) connections. (b) Computational architecture. Q_x, Q_ε, $Q_{\hat{h}}$: whitening transformations targeting x, ε, $\hat{h}$, respectively. W_{state}, W_{inno}: separation matrices extracting state and innovation, respectively, s estimated independent components of the state, e estimated hidden independent components. ε_w and x_w whitened estimation of innovation and input, respectively. Estimated hidden dynamics: F, corresponding estimated state and noise $\hat{h}$ and n_h, respectively. Phase I and II refer to positive and negative phases of the theta oscillation, respectively. Straight lines: mainly proximal projections, dotted lines: mainly distal projections. (c): Most important connections in the hippocampal formation. CA3 subfield and dentate gyrus eliminate moving averages, or echoes, detailed in [16, 17, 18]. For more details, see text.

First, two distinct layers are required to sustain a term analogue to the estimated noise and the observed signal. The simplest construction depicted on Fig. 1(a) assumes two layers with a delayed feed-forward and mostly inhibitory connection system representing predictive matrix M. If the predictive connections are properly tuned, then activity of one layer represents the observed process, whereas activity of the other layer represents the observation noise.

3.2. *Whitening*

As we already noted, decorrelation is a necessary step prior to extracting the wanted independent components. Due to the special form (see below) of the remarkable online learning rule of [12], we need to introduce an additional layer whose activity is denoted by $\hat{h}(t)$ (and will be referred to as the 'internal model'), see Fig 1(b). Its role is quite central in our discussion, but for now it is enough to assume that it is already decorrelated and is projected through the linear connections Q_x and Q_ε onto layers holding $x(t)$ and $\varepsilon(t)$, respectively. Let us denote the modified observed signal by $x_w(t)=Q_x\hat{h}(t)+x(t)$, implying that $x_w(t)$ is still a linear function of $x(t)$. Decorrelation of $x_w(t)$ may be accomplished if tuning of Q_x is as follows:

$$\Delta Q_x(t+1) \sim Q_x(t) - x_w(t)x_w(t)^T Q_x(t) = Q_x(t) - x_w(t)\hat{h}(t)^T \qquad (7)$$

The second form is clearly Hebbian and it follows from the decorrelation assumption on $\hat{h}(t)$ and the fact that $Q_x=Q_x^T$. Whitening of the observation noise may follow similar principles in that the modified noise is $\varepsilon_w(t)= Q_\varepsilon n_h(t)+ x(t+1)$

$-Mx_w(t)$, where $n_h(t)$ is the noise of the internal 'model'. Tuning of Q_ε is also Hebbian:

$$\Delta Q_\varepsilon(t+1) \sim Q_\varepsilon(t) - \varepsilon_w(t) n_h(t)^T \qquad (8)$$

In turn, transformation M extracts the deterministic part from ε, whereas Q_ε decorrelates it yielding ε_w.

3.3. *Separation*

Whitening allows for separation of the hidden, independent sources from the observation noise. An additional layer needs to be introduced to represent the emerging independent components. Along the logic presented so far, we are looking for an online learning rule that complies with Hebbian constraints and yields the proper components. Interestingly, as it was shown in [13], a rule very similar to those defined by Eqs. (7-8) can be used to tune the transformation matrix between the layers representing the decorrelated and the independent components:

$$\Delta W_{inno}(t+1) \sim W_{inno}(t) - f(e(t))e(t)^T W_{inno}(t) = W_{inno}(t) - f(e(t))\,(W_{inno}{}^T e_w(t))^T \qquad (9)$$

Where $f(\cdot)$ denotes an almost arbitrary component-wise nonlinear transformation. Although W_{inno} is not symmetric, the second form of Eq. (9) is again Hebbian if signal backpropagation ($W_{inno}{}^T\ e(t)$) controls learning [14, 15]. Note that whitening may also be promoted by signal backpropagation.

The correctly tuned W_{inno} (as it approximates the inverse of the hidden mixing matrix, A) yields the estimation of the hidden driving sources, $e(t)$. However, as Eqs. (4) and (3) show, the *very same* transformation should be carried on to yield the hidden states $s(t)$ from the decorrelated observation ($x_w(t)$). In turn, an additional layer targeted by the layer of $x_w(t)$ seems to be in need to be introduced to represent $s(t)$ (see Fig. 1(b)). While the mathematics requiring the double application of separation is simple, a truly connectionist or neuronal implementation is not straightforward and impose strong architectural and functioning constraints besides the Hebbian nature of the interactions. Some consequences and putative mechanisms of such 'transformation adjustments' for different pathways will be discussed later.

3.4. *Remark on ARMA processes of higher order*

Although we assumed first order dynamics in the derivations above (Eqs. (2-5)), many real problems are prevailed by higher order dynamics. Sensory stimuli, for example, become higher order due to echoes (reflections) and delays (multi-modal integration, synaptic delays, etc.). As recent results show, even for hidden *integrated* [6] as well as *non-linear* hidden ARMA processes [16] can be recovered using ideas similar to what has been presented. Cancelling the distortions should take place before attempting separation, so the network derived so far should be extended with a separate subsystem that handles delays prior to the actual separation process. As delays are ignored in the present study, we do not discuss the implementation nor the mapping of this subsystem. For more details on the implementation and the mapping, see our supplementary material [17] and [18], respectively.

4. Mapping the network onto the hippocampal region

Due to the space limit we only sketch a possible functional mapping onto the hippocampal region and highlight some relevant supporting physiological and anatomical properties (for terminology, see [19] and for a detailed enumeration of the supporting anatomical findings, see [18]). Despite some differences in the connectivity structure, the common view is that mammalian HR-s share the same gross anatomy as well as functionality, so we refer to findings on rats as well as monkeys. The resulting mapping is depicted on Fig. 1(b)-(c). First, it is known that the superficial layers of the entorhinal cortex (denoted by EC II and EC III) are the main recipients of the cortical inputs. Since the exact nature of these incoming signals is not known we assume they share the same input. While they both have excitatory recurrent connections, an important difference is that EC II has a widespread inhibitory circuitry, too. Excitatory projections from EC III to EC II in part form a unique feed-forward inhibitory system interpreted here as the operation of 'subtraction'. This special connection may allow for the comparison needed to represent the observation noise. The emerging activity in EC II is then assumed to represent the observation noise and is projected onto sub-region CA3 and the dentate gyrus. The latter part of HR is known to have tuneable recurrent connections with extreme long time delays thus being able to diminish the distorting effects caused by larger order delays and reflections (see Subsection 3.4). CA3, on the other hand, is known to develop the so called 'place cells' (cells which are active only if the animal is at a given location ('place field' of the cell), like near the feeding place in the maze or at the centre). It also has a very extensive recurrent collateral system, which, however, is mostly active only at one phase of the characteristic theta oscillation of the hippocampal formation [20, 21]. What it implies is that if approximate independence of the place cells is the end result of a separation process then separation can only take place when these recurrent connections are turned off so interference can be avoided. CA3 projects onto CA1 which also features place cells showing even stronger independence. However, place field activity in CA1 can also be seen when only the direct connections from EC III are present, implying that these connections should also be able to form independent components. Subiculum shares many similarities with CA1, but instead of having place cells, it features the so called head direction cells which are active when the animal's head assumes a given relative direction. It is the major projection area of CA1, but it also receives input directly from EC III. An important finding [22] is that information flows from EC III and CA1 are specially crossed in the subiculum, that is, distinct loops are maintained carrying different bits of the flow of the same origin. Following the logic that requires separate representation of the factors, we conjecture that subicular activity represents the *ongoing* independent *processes* in synchrony with the independent driving sources represented by CA1. Intuitively, directional information would be such an independent process for navigational tasks. In order to be able to recombine the factors, an additional layer is needed, which is targeted by both components. The wiring diagram suggests that the wanted area should be the deep layers of EC which are also connected to the input layers of EC. As we noted earlier, separation can be greatly facilitated if decorrelation takes place first. To get a properly decorrelated estimated noise, activity at both EC II and EC III should be decorrelated. If the cortical input is not decorrelated, connections from the deep layers of EC should carry on this transformation. Furthermore the algorithmic derivations show that activity at EC V should also be decorrelated. To meet this requirement, we conjecture that projections from both CA1 and subiculum are tuned to help decorrelate the activity at the 'model' layer EC V. In this way the loop is closed and the information may go around till the right representations of the two factors, namely the position and the direction, are formed. For more information, see the supplementary material [17].

4.1. *Dynamics of the network*

Functional mapping would consist of description of the dynamics at two time scales: tuning (learning) of the synaptic weights and the working (information processing) of the whole system. Space limitations allow for discussing only some of the most intriguing characteristics but see [17].

4.1.1. *Co-learning in the parallel systems*

We have seen that the *very same transformation* (denoted by W_{inno}) is needed to recover the hidden driving sources, $e(t)$ and the hidden processes, $s(t)$. Due to ambiguities of the ICA solution, like the undetermined order of components (see, e.g., [8]), the emerging components of the different factors should be put in register, otherwise the integrating model ($h(t)$) would result in distorted estimation of the incoming inputs. While it is easy to realize two identical matrices on a computer, neuronal implementation of such 'transformation adjustments' should be explicitly treated.

In our model, CA1 is the focal area that sub-serves the matching of indices in the whole network. This area is unique from the point of view of the anatomy as it has no excitatory recurrent collateral system and so intra-areal mixing is limited. Accordingly, CA1 is also central to our model; the 'transformation adjustments' of the matrices should be arranged by its activity. Although network level synchronizations unique to the HR and the parallel routes described above may allow for different schemes, experimental evidences about the exact nature of information flow through the two pathways are insufficient or controversial. In turn, we only propose some potential mechanism by which the required registration may be implemented.

It is likely [26] that the pace maker theta oscillation can differentiate the inputs projected onto CA1. We speculate that transformation along both pathways could be driven by the input statistics. In our scheme, however, ICA learning depends on output activity and the backpropagated signals it gives rise to. Learning may be coupled in turn, because signal backpropagation may effect both pathways. However, there is another condition for learning: synapses should be activated by the *proper* bottom-up signals that (could have) produce(d) the outputs. By assuming an interlaced signalling mechanism, it may be possible that at one pace the trisynaptic pathway is tuned in an unsupervised manner driven by the observation noise. At the next pace both channels may transmit signals proportional to the observed input and the resulting activity at CA1 constrained by the trisynaptic signals reshapes the direct pathway via signal backpropagation. An additional option is that the recurrent connection system of CA3 may in principle be able to integrate the observation noise represented by EC II and thus its output is proportional to the observation. This scenario implies that 1, the observation noise should be sustained long enough to be the input to CA1 at one pace and drive the activity in CA3 at the next one; 2, the recurrent connections of CA3 should be turned off when integration is not needed and 3, pair pulsed facilitation is required at CA1 so the corresponding components of $s(t)$ and $e(t)$ can be put in register. Interestingly, there are findings indicating that all these requirements are actually met [26, 27, 28].

4.1.2. *The subiculum*

The intriguing 'cross-wired' topographical projections from CA1 and EC to the subiculum, i.e., that proximal parts of CA1 project onto the distal side of subiculum [23], may allow for separate channelling of noise and state related information. On the ground of the similarities between the wiring diagrams of the CA1 and the subiculum [22] we may conjecture that subiculum also realizes a double encoding mechanism carrying representations of the moving averages of the *independent processes* and the related innovations, i.e., the changes between these processes, respectively. In navigational tasks, running in different directions may appear as an averaged process while a change of this process occurs when the animal stops, so positional information may be seen as the related innovation. In turn, CA1 is responsible to transfer the estimated independent driving sources while subiculum maintains the representations of the independent processes. These signals may then be integrated in the internal model maintained by the deep layers of EC. The mechanism of this integration remains to be answered.

5. Discussion

Lack of space only allows for a short account on how our model has evolved since an early proposal of [18]. Excellent reviews on other computational models can, for example, be found in [24, 25] and [17] discusses how our models fares against some of the main ideas found in other models.

In the work of [18], (i) subiculum was not modelled, (ii) decorrelation or whitening was the putative role of CA3. Since 2000, considerable amount of information has emerged about the HR, including the time sharing mode of CA1 during the positive and the negative theta phases [23]. In addition, theoretical advances [6, 18] extended independent component analysis to independent process analysis and it has also been shown that Hebbian learning is potentially feasible [9]. In the present work we have built on these results and derived a more detailed model of the hippocampal region.

There are three particular points of our work: (i) on the ground of computational considerations on goal-oriented systems we argued that forming representations is linked to the problem of independent process analysis (ii) we speculate that supervised aspects of signal backpropagation guided training 'adjusting the transformations' of two parallel pathways may indeed be realized in the hippocampal region through the activity of CA1 (iii) our construction may shed light on the role of the subiculum in forming representations for navigation. Supporting numerical simulations can be found in [17].

References

1. L. R. Squire and S. Zola-Morgan, *Science* **253**, 1380 (1991).
2. G. L. Chadderdon, *J. of Cogn. Neurosci.* **18**, 242 (2006).
3. W. Schultz, *Neuron* **36**, 241 (2002).
4. C. Boutilier, R. Dearden and M. Goldszmidt, *Artif. Intell.* **121**, 1104 (2000).
5. I. Szita and A. Lőrincz, *Acta Cybern* (in press).
6. B. Póczos, Z. Szabó, M. Kiszlinger and A. Lőrincz, *Lect. Notes in Comp. Sci.* **4666**, 252 (2007).
7. J. F. Cardoso. *In Proc. of ICASSP*, **4**, 1941 (1998).
8. B. Póczos and A. Lőrincz. *In Proc. of ICML*, 673 (2005).
9. A. Lőrincz and Z. Szabó. *Neurocomputing*, **70**, 1569 (2007).
10. M. Plumbey, *IEEE Signal Proc. Lett.* **9**, 177 (2002).
11. C. Parisien, C. H. Anderson and C. Eliasmith. *Neural Comp.*, **20**, 1473 (2008).
12. J.-F. Cardoso and B. H. Laheld. *IEEE Tr. Signal Proc.*, **40**, 3017 (1996).
13. S. Amari, A. Cichocki, and H. H. Yang, *Adv. in NIPS*, **8**, 757 (1996).
14. Gy. Buzsáki, M. Penttonen, Z. Nádasdy, A. Bragin, *PNAS.*, **90**, 9921 (1996).
15. G. Chechik. *Neural Computation*, **15**, 1481 (2003).
16. Z. Szabó, B. Póczos, G. Szirtes, and A. Lőrincz. *Lect. Notes in Comp. Sci.* **4668**, 677 (2007).
17. A. Lőrincz, M. Kiszlinger, and G. Szirtes. http://arxiv.org/abs/0804.3176, (2008).
18. A. Lőrincz and Gy. Buzsáki. *Annals New York Acad Sci.* **911**, 83 (2000).
19. M. P. Witter and D. G. Amaral. In: *The Rat Nervous System* 635 (2004).
20. M. E. Hasselmo and C. Bodelon and B. Wyble (2002) *Neural Comp.*, **14**, 793 (2002).
21. Gy. Buzsáki, Rythms of the Brain, *Oxford Univ. Press* (2006).
22. J. Gigg. *Behavioural Brain Research*, **174**, 265 (2006).
23. G. Dragoi and Gy. Buzsáki. *Neuron*, **50**, 145 (2006).
24. L. R. Squire, *Psych. Rev.* **99**, 195 (1992).
25. P. Andersen, R. Morris, D. Amaral T. Bliss, and J. O'Keefe (Eds.) *Oxford Univ. Press* (2007).
26. J. R. Manns, E. A. Zilli, K. C. Ong, M. E. Hasselmo and H. Eichenbaum, *Neurobiol. of Learn. and Mem.*, **87**, 9 (2007).
27. D. M. Villarreal, A. L. Gross, and B. E. Derrick, *J. of Neurosci.*, **27**, 49 (2007).
28. T. Klausberger and P. Somogyi, *Science*, **321**, 53 (2008).

WHAT USE ARE COMPUTATIONAL MODELS OF COGNITIVE PROCESSES?

T. STAFFORD

Department of Psychology, University of Sheffield, Sheffield, S7 1HL, UK
E-mail: t.stafford@shef.ac.uk

Computational modellers are not always explicit about their motivations for constructing models, nor are they always explicit about the theoretical implications of their models once constructed. Perhaps in part due to this, models have been criticised as "black-box" exercises which can play little or no role in scientific explanation. This paper argues that models are useful, and that the motivations for constructing computational models can be made clear by considering the roles that tautologies can play in the development of explanatory theories. From this, additionally, I propose that although there are diverse benefits of model building, only one class of benefits — those which relate to explanation — can provide justification for the activity.

Keywords: Computational modelling; models; explanation; cognition; philosophy of science.

1. What use are models?

What kind of object are computational models, and how are they scientifically useful? Among the modelling community there is little in depth discussion of these issues. This is partly, we may suppose, because among the converted there is little need to rehearse doctrine. But even in textbooks the philosophical status of modelling *per se* takes second place to details of specific models and some introductory discussion of specific issues such as level of representation.[1–3] This can give the impression that the nature of modelling with regard to scientific explanation is well understood. As modellers we *know* that models are useful; indeed, our work is based on this assumption. However, not everyone shares this feeling, nor agrees with this position. In fact there have been sustained debates over the proper use and purposes of modelling.[4–6]

One point of contention, which this article will use as a starting point, is that computational models (henceforth 'models') are defined in mathematical terms and so can appear to share with mathematics the property of being tautological. This has led some to suggest that models cannot tell us anything new about the world.[7] Models, it is claimed, can make predictions but this is their only role in the scientific process. They cannot ever be part of a "test of how humans actually work" nor can they "provide new information about brain organisation or function".[7] An important related idea is that computational models can be uninterpretable black boxes — a-theoretical objects which may match human performance or structure but which do not provide any additional information, precisely because a model could have been built which would match any pattern of data, not just this specific one.[8] The claim is that, because the workings of a model are unintepretable or irrelevant to psychology or neuroscience, their only use is to make predictions which *can* be compared to psychology or neuroscience. Models, in this view, are in no way analogous to real theories of psychology or neuroscience (which are verbally or logically defined).

Beyond this, there has also been criticism of the 'glamour' of computational modelling. Nobel laureate Francis Crick was extremely sceptical of the early Parallel Distributed Processing[9] movement:

> "I also suspect that within most modellers a frustrated mathematician is trying to unfold his wings. It is not enough to make something that works. How much better if it can be shown to embody some powerful general principle for handling information, expressible in a deep mathematical form, if only to give an air of intellectual respectability to an otherwise rather low-brow enterprise." [10]

The implication is that modelling persists in recruiting practitioners and advocates because it has an air of mathematical rigour and complexity, while actually this disguises what is no more than a kind of grubby *ad-hoc*ism — some spur-of-the-moment engineering solutions motivated merely by fitting the data. And, worse than this, Crick suggests, modelling is a particularly non-informative kind of *ad-hoc*ism.

Clearly the utility of modelling is not as well established as you might suppose from attending a gathering of modellers, such as one of the Neural Computation and Psychology Workshops, or from reading a proceedings such as this one.

This article is underpinned by the belief that it is a lack of understanding of the nature of models and modelling that leads to confusion over their scientific value. Since models undeniably involve mathematical tautologies, and since this tautological nature has been leveled as a criticism against modelling, I will use the analogy of a tautology to explore the possible benefits of doing computational modelling. Through this I hope to clarify what theoretical work modelling can hope to do.

2. A very simple tautology

The code that runs a model can be expressed in mathematical equations, and it is mathematical element that makes a model tautological. However, the heart of any model is the effort to establish a correspondence between parts of the system being modelled and the parts of the model. As Kenneth Craik, a prescient theorist of cognitive science, said

> "By model we thus mean any physical or chemical structure system which has a similar relation-structure to that of the processes it imitates" [11]

Models will necessarily be tautological with respect to their component parts. Because it is possible to reduce a model to a set of mathematical equations this must be true. But our scientific interest in a model lies not merely in the equations as such, but in the relation of the component parts of the model to component parts of the world. Models are formally specified by their equations, but they are also comprised of a set of model-world relations. Because of this they are more than "black-boxes" and so can inform our theories of the world in deeper and more complex ways than merely making predictions.

As a vehicle to explore the different ways in which tautology can, in fact, inform us about the world, let us begin by taking a very simple tautology: that $1 + 2 = 3$. Model simulations only differ from this tautology in their degree of complexity, and their consequent opacity. This article will hope to use the very simplicity of this particular tautology to illustrate the value of models-as-tautologies in general.

3. The importance of tautology

So, let us begin to consider the possible ways in which a tautology can inform a scientific theory.

3.1. *Sufficiency*

The first way is the demonstration of sufficiency. Imagine that '3' in $1 + 2 = 3$ is a known real-world phenomenon. The model can demonstrate that other phenomena ('1' and '2') and known causal laws ('+') are sufficient to produce it.

Whether or not this is interesting theoretical work depends on the current beliefs of theorists about how '3' arises. When the existence of the result ('3') is uncontroversial but the ingredients are uncertain, we have provided a theoretical option, a possibility - the status of which depends on research into whether the ingredients exist, and on the number of other candidate theories there are for producing this result. An example of this kind of work is Linsker's [12] demonstration that self-organisation according to the Hebb rule can produce cells with receptive field properties like those found in the visual system. This model does not tell us whether the modelled dynamics actually are responsible for the receptive field properties of visual system neurons. It merely demonstrates rigourously that this possibility exists, and consequently, raises our assessment of the likelihood of this hypothesis being true.

3.2. *Prediction*

If the presence of the ingredient elements ('1 + 2') is uncontroversial but the result ('3') is either not known or not commonly associated with these ingredients, then the model makes a prediction: that the result element will arise from the ingredients. An example of this is McClelland & Rumelhart's[13] predictions concerning the effect of word context on letter recognition. These predictions were experimentally confirmed by Rumelhart & McClelland.[14] This ability to make predictions which can be confirmed or falsified is obviously a core part of the scientific process,[15] and is often offered as a major motivation for building models. The issue is discussed further below in relation to the desirability of cumulative modelling programmes.

3.3. *Existence proof*

Even if all the elements in the models are uncontroversial, then modelling can still provide an informative result by establishing a possible connection between the ingredients and the results. This is a variety of what is known as an existence proof. An example is Plaut & Shallice's [16] demonstration that attractor dynamics in the orthography-semantics mapping can produce the pattern of errors found in patients with deep dyslexia. The existence of attractor dynamics is not controversial, nor is the pattern of errors found in deep dyslexics. What the model established was that attractor dynamics could be the source of the pattern of errors, a possibility that was hitherto not regarded as a plausible hypothesis.

An existence proof style model does nor prove what *is* happening, merely what *could be* happening. Once an existence proof is offered the processes which do in fact cause some result still need to be investigated. How scientifically interesting an existence proof is depends on the current opinion about the mechanism illustrated. If it is controversial or novel the model is obviously more interesting.

3.4. *Insufficiency*

Equally useful, but less common than the purposes discussed above, is the demonstration of insufficiency. Consider again our tautology '1 + 2 = 3'. An implication of this tautology is that '1 + 2' equals 3 and no more than 3. In the case that some other result ('4') is known to exist, the model demonstrates the insufficiency of the hypothesized ingredients to produce it, and thus provokes a search for the additional factor which must be present, given that the ingredient elements have been shown to be insufficient alone. An apocryphal example (perhaps arising from [17]) is the story told of AI pioneer Marvin Minksy assigning 'vision' to a graduate student as a summer project. The point of the story is to illustrate how mistaken the scientific community was about the difficulty of vision as a problem. It was through a generation of researchers in AI attempting to build models which could recognise what they saw, and thus discovering that all known methods were insufficient to achieve this, that it was realised how hard the problem of vision really is. The demonstration of insufficiency is also important in establishing what results would contradict or falsify a model.[5]

4. Models as theories, theories as explanations

The above framework should make clear that the importance of models resides not in their formal structure alone, but in their purported correspondence to certain features of the world. The usefulness of a model lies in how it informs us about the potential relationships between features of the world.

An informal survey of modelling work presented at the 11th Neural Computation and Psychology Workshop (Oxford, July 2008) suggests that the most common purpose for which models are constructed — or at least the most common justification offered for their construction which falls within the current framework — is that of sufficiency: the demonstration that a certain set of ingredients is capable of producing a certain outcome. A danger of this kind of work is that, as previously noted, models may, if insufficiently constrained, match any possible outcome. Roberts & Pashler [5] have argued convincingly that the value of a model can only truly be assessed when that data which is *cannot* fit is also made clear. This relates to the idea of insufficiency in the current article.

This framework also helps draw out why realism *per se* is not the only metric on which models should be compared. The virtue of a model lies not in the number of biological details it contains, as such, but rather in its accuracy of correspondence with phenomenon at the level of description that it is trying to model. Indeed, one core motivation for modelling in the first place is to develop useful abstractions. Al Wilhite (personal communication) made this point eloquently by modifying a quote from Guy de Maupassant's essay 'The Novel', replacing the word 'artist' with that of 'theorist':

> "The [theorist] will endeavour not to show us a commonplace photograph of life, but to give us a presentment of it which shall be more complete, more striking, more cogent than reality itself. To tell everything is out of the question"

It is for this reason that more details are not necessarily better; sometimes models can be improved by including less detail rather than more. This point is a fundamental one when considering the choice between competing theories, going back to William of Ockham (c. 1288 - c. 1348), through to modern information theoretic formulations of criteria for model comparison (for an introduction, see chapter 28 of [18]). Nonetheless it is a point that still needs to be made concerning the modelling of cognition.[19] Obviously readers will have their own beliefs about the difficulties and benefits of modelling at different levels of description. There is a strong case to make that since one great strength of computational modelling is to connect psychological and neuroscientific levels of explanation, more biological detail will frequency yield models with greater explanatory powers, but this debate is beyond the scope of the current article.

If we accept that models are more than their mathematical constitution and are also comprised of assertions about the correspondence between their parts and the world, then we must acknowledge that models are more than mere black-boxes. In fact, models are theoretical entities, albeit with more formal constraints and distractions that verbally specified theories, and with the proviso that models are underdetermined by theories (analogously to the way that theories are underdetermined by data — any theory will have a family of modelling implementations). By making connections between known and proposed entities, models do the work of theories. If this is accepted then, like theories, models provide explanations. Furthermore their explanation-providing capacity is inextricably linked to their tautological nature.

There are deep and sustained issues concerning the philosophy of explanation.[20] The framework above is an attempt to illustrate the important theoretical work that can be done by models as tautologies. A similar, but far more thorough, exposition of the importance of this kind of work has been done by Kulka in relation to non-computational theories in psychology, using the terms 'theory amplification' (discovering necessary predictions, inconsistencies, complementarities and postdictions between theories and data) and 'simplification' (the application of different kinds of parsimony).[21,22]

5. A proposal

There are other benefits of modelling beyond this framework suggested by the consideration of models as tautologies. Modelling allows us to work with quantitative and multicausitive theories beyond the vague intimations of descriptive theories. Models can help us define a problem [23] or allow us to integrate different, even conflicting, theories at different levels of description within the same framework. Finally, models have considerable value for cultivating the intuitions of individual researchers. As Paul Krugman said, "We just don't see what we can't formalize".[24] For many modellers a primary value of modelling is the challenge to and cultivation of their intuitions that they make possible.

Notwithstanding these other benefits, I propose that modelling as an activity is only really justified by its relation to explanation. Because of this, the value of a model is tied to its structure as a tautology that corresponds to the known facts about the world, as outlined above.

Although there are diverse benefits of modelling, unless the driving purpose of a model is one of seeking to discover the implications of a theory (prediction) or to promote an explanation of some features of the world (sufficiency, insufficiency and existence proofs) then the modelling risks becoming a sterile exercise. Although models have a role in cultivating our intuitions, this must be taken beyond the level of the individual researcher and tested in the dissemination and contestation of the model by the scientific community.

Precisely because models are tautologies, the equations that comprise them don't have intrinsic meaning. It is not unambiguous which features of a set of equations that comprises a model are relevant to the theoretical issue at hand. Instead, the meaning of the model is created by the researchers who construct the model in their attempt to persuade others of their findings. When communicating their model and the implications which they derive from it, the obligation is upon the modeller to define which features of the model are supposed to correspond to which features of the world, and what the purposes of constructing a model like this are. Only when a proposal about the theoretical content of the model is offered can the value of the model be evaluated.

A good model is defined by the purposes you have; by whether you set out to deduce the consequences of the existence of certain entities to generate predictions, to test a proposal, prove necessity, sufficiency or insufficiency, or 'merely' to develop a formal framework for a problem. If the purposes of a model are not explicitly stated then its success and utility cannot easily be evaluated. Without a means by which the success of a model can be evaluated it will be difficult to integrate model findings in to a progressive programme of model development, something which is necessary for modelling to mature into a mature technique.[25]

6. Conclusions

Starting with the accusation that models are merely tautologies, I have attempted to turn this accusation around and argue that models can be informative about the world, but only when the correspondences between their parts is carefully articulated. I have used the analogy of a tautology to suggest a framework for some of the benefits of modelling with relation to explanation. There remains a strict sense in which modelling does not provide 'new facts' about the world, but for this to remain a criticism relies on both an unrealistic view of the reliability of the facts of psychology and neuroscience as provided by other tools of the scientific method[26] and on an overly conservative definition of what a 'new fact' is. If I use an equation to calculate the size of the earth from the length of a shadow at a particular spot at a particular time then I would say that I have discovered a new fact, even though this fact — the size of the earth — was inherent in the old facts of shadow length, time and position and nothing was added but the tautology of an equation.

This framework I have tried to outline of the benefits of modelling is not supposed to be comprehensive, but it does, I suggest, capture the core benefits of modelling, which are those relating to explanation. It is in these ways that modelling can help confirm, create, enhance or refute theories.

Models aid explanation in the same way as mathematics: by enhancing our perception beyond the horizon of individual reason and intuition.

Acknowledgements

Thanks to Hubert Petre for the loan of his flat in Brussels while I considered these issues, to Stuart Wilson for helpful comments on a draft of this article and to the students of the Computational and Cognitive Neuroscience Masters, University of Sheffield, for several useful discussions.

References

1. R. Ellis and G. Humphreys, *Connectionist Psychology : a text with readings* (Psychology Press Ltd, Hove, UK, 1999).
2. J. L. Elman, *Rethinking Innateness: A Connectionist Perspective on Development* (MIT Press, 1996).
3. R. C. O'Reilly and Y. Munakata, *Computational Explorations in Cognitive Neuroscience: Understanding the Mind by Simulating the Brain* (MIT Press, 2000).
4. S. Lewandowsky, *Psychological Science* **4**, 236 (1993).
5. S. Roberts and H. Pashler, *Psychological Review* **107**, 358 (2000).
6. P. Smolensky, *Behavioral and Brain Sciences* **11**, 1 (1988).
7. S. Segalowitz and D. Bernstein, Neural networks and neuroscience: What are connectionist simulations good for, in *The future of the cognitive revolution.*, (Oxford University Press, 1997)
8. M. McCloskey, *Psychological Science* **2**, 387 (1991).
9. D. Rumelhart, J. McClelland and the PDP Research Group, *Parallel Distributed Processing: Explorations in the microstructure of cognition* (The MIT Press, Cambridge, MA, 1986).
10. F. Crick, *Nature* **337**, 129 (1989).
11. K. J. W. Craik, *The Nature of Explanation* (Cambridge University Press, Cambridge, 1943).
12. R. Linsker, *Computer* **21**, 105 (1988).
13. J. L. McClelland and D. E. Rumelhart, *Psychological Review* **88**, 375 (1981).
14. D. E. Rumelhart and J. L. McClelland, *Psychological Review* **89**, 60 (1982).
15. K. Popper, *The Logic of Scientific Discovery* (Hutchinson, London, 1968).
16. D. C. Plaut and T. Shallice, *Cognitive Neuropsychology* **10**, 377 (1993).
17. A. Hurlbert and T. Poggio, *Daedalus* **117** (1988).
18. D. J. C. MacKay, *Information Theory, Inference and Learning Algorithms* (Cambridge University Press, Cambridge, UK, 2003).
19. I. E. Dror and D. P. Gallogly, *Psychonomic Bulletin & Review* **6**, 173 (1999).
20. G. Mayes, Theories of explanation, in *The Internet Encyclopedia of Philosophy*, (www.iep.utm.edu accessed 1/7/08, 2008)
21. A. Kulka, *Methods of Theoretical Psychology* (MIT Press, Cambridge, MA., 2001).

22. A. Kukla, *New Ideas in Psychology* **13**, 201 (1995).
23. D. Marr, *Vision: A Computational Investigation into the Human Representation and Processing of Visual Information* (Henry Holt and Co., Inc. New York, NY, USA, 1982).
24. P. Krugman, How I work, in *the Unofficial Paul Krugman archive*, (www.pkarchive.org accessed 1/7/08, 1993)
25. A. Roelofs, From Popper to Lakatos: A case for cumulative computational modeling, in *Twenty-first century psycholinguistics: Four cornerstones*, ed. A.Cutler (Lawrence Erlbaum, Mahwah, NJ, 2005)
26. P. Feyerabend, *Against Method (revised edition)* (Verso, New York, 1988).

Language, Learning and Development

A LOCALIST NEURAL NETWORK MODEL FOR EARLY CHILD LANGUAGE ACQUISITION FROM MOTHERESE

ABEL NYAMAPFENE

School of Engineering, Computing, and Mathematics, University of Exeter
North Park Rd, Exeter EX4 4QF, UK

This paper presents a localist multimodal neural network that uses Hebbian learning to acquire one-word child language from child directed speech (CDS) comprising multi-word utterances and queries in addition to one-word utterances. The model implements cross-situational learning between linguistic words used in child directed speech, the accompanying perceptual entities, conceptual relations and inferred communicative intentions. In 90 cases out of 117, the network successfully generates one-word utterances that may be viewed as being semantically equivalent to the CDS input used to train the network. The model also successfully emulates the one-word speech of a child in 12 out of 28 cases, despite its localist nature, thereby suggesting that Hebbian learning, as used in most models of cognitive development, is capable of cross-situational learning, a key component of multimodal temporal cognitive acquisition tasks, of which child language acquisition is one.

1. Introduction

Child language acquisition is a highly complex cognitive process that, despite holding the fascination of many researchers over the years, still remains unresolved. Recently neural network models have been used as a computational means for understanding the child language acquisition process. Examples include the autoassociation model by Plunkett, Sinha, Moller and Strandsby [1], models based on Miikkulainen's [2] Hebbian-linked self-organising maps architecture [3, 4], and, more recently, the counterpropagation network model by Nyamapfene and Ahmad [5].

In this class of models of child language acquisition a neural network model of child language acquisition is trained by submitting to it, on a cycle by cycle basis, single word forms and their associated extralinguistic information. For instance, the Plunkett et al model [1] is trained by submitting to it, on a cycle by cycle basis, an image representation and its associated word label. Similarly, in the Abidi and Ahmad neural multi-net model [3] and the Nyamapfene and Ahmad counterpropagation network model [5], training proceeds by submitting to the network, on a cycle by cycle basis, the phonetic representation of a single word taken from a child's speech corpus alongside its corresponding perceptual entity, conceptual relation and perceived communicative intention. Consequently, the training and simulation of current neural network models is akin to a child acquiring its first language through exposure to the linguistic output of another child undergoing the same process, and then emulating that child.

However, in real life the child is most likely to acquire her speech from her caregivers who in a family setting may be the child's parents and older siblings. In general, caregivers communicate with infants using a specially articulated version of normal speech known as "child directed speech" (CDS) or "motherese" [6, 7]. Unlike the training methodology adopted by current neural network models, the CDS that infants hear consists of multi-word statements and queries in addition to single word utterances. Firstly, infants have to segment the individual words in the CDS, and this they can do by the time they are seven and a half months old [8]. Then they have to associate the individual words in the CDS stream their corresponding referents in the linguistic environment. It is this second aspect of child language acquisition which is the focus of this paper.

It has been suggested that infants may learn word-meaning associations by pairing individual spoken words with several co-occurring possible referents over a period of time and then statistically deciding on the most appropriate word-referent pair. This form of learning is termed cross-situational learning [9]. In this paper a localist multimodal neural network uses Hebbian learning [10] to acquire one-word child language from child directed speech (CDS) through cross-situational learning.

The rest of this paper is organised as follows: In the next section a discussion of the role of child directed speech to the acquisition of child language is given. This is followed by a review of two computational models that, when given multi-word input, use cross-situational learning to map individual spoken words to their respective meanings. Following this, the localist neural network model for early child language acquisition from CDS is introduced, and the data used in simulating and analysing this model is presented. A discussion of the simulation results of the model is then presented. The paper then concludes by summing up the contributions of the model to early child language research, and reveals ongoing work to further improve the model.

2. Role of Child-Directed Speech in Child Language Acquisition

Language acquisition normally takes place in the context of a rich interaction between the child and its parents [11]. Early conversations are restricted to familiar settings and to objects that are present thereby greatly simplifying the child's problem of learning the words for things [6]. For instance, mothers' speech to one- and two- year olds consists of simple, grammatically correct, short sentences that deal with the child's interests: actions, objects, people and events that are present in the 'here' and now' [11, 14].

CDS possesses features that may help the child to segment speech into words, phrases and sentences [11]. For instance, single-word utterances are quite frequent, and words are articulated clearly and slowly with distinct pauses between sentences. In addition, mothers tend to repeat isolated phrases and words following the complete utterance. Consequently, CDS can be viewed as a highly specialized language with the necessary affective qualities to engage the child in language, and one which allows the child to remain focused on the provider of the input thereby maximizing language learning [7].

3. Related Computational Work

Siskind [12] developed a mathematical model based on cross-situational learning whose input is a series of multi-word utterances, each paired with a set of possible meanings for the utterance as a whole. Each utterance is viewed as an unordered collection of word symbols, and the model maps each word symbol in an utterance to a set of conceptual expressions that represent the meanings of different senses of that word. A set of inference rules embodying several constraints on the word-learning problem, including the constraint that the meanings of individual words in an utterance contribute non-overlapping portions to the meaning of the whole utterance, are then used over several trials to model the child's progression to mapping individual words to their meanings. Throughout the series of trials, as the model learns the meanings of some of the words, it uses that knowledge to further constrain the possible meanings of other words in an utterance, resulting in faster learning.

When presented with an artificial corpus, Siskind's model is able to learn a homonymous lexicon despite noisy multi-word input in the presence of referential uncertainty. However, the model's algorithm is very complex and unpractical for empirical mother-child corpora since it can not infer, through generalisation, or otherwise, the meanings of new multi-word utterances.

Yu and Ballard [13] have recently used a machine translation model to learn word-object association probabilities in a natural corpus comprising interactions between a mother and a pre-verbal infant. In their model, they assume that word-object pairs are latent variables underlying the spoken words and extra linguistic information that constitute the corpus. By formalising the task of child language acquisition as an expectation maximisation problem, they develop a learning algorithm that associates words and their referent objects in a manner that maximises the likelihood of the audio-visual observations in the corpus. Using word-object co-occurrence statistics, they assign initial values for word-object association probabilities, and on the E-step of the Expectation Maximisation algorithm, they compute counts for all word-object pairs. These values are then used on the M-step of the Expectation Maximisation algorithm to refine the word-object association probabilities. The E and M steps are repeated until the association probabilities converge. By weighting the word-object associations using prosodic information and joint attention information, the model demonstrated that recall improves in the presence of social cues. However, the model fails to take into account the speaker's communicative intention as well as the conceptual relations between the referent objects and events as suggested by the literature on child language acquisition [14, 15].

4. Experimental Method

Child language acquisition may be viewed as a form of 'social convergence' in which the child with a certain socio-cognitive capacity attempts to make sense of the contextualised language of the adults in her environment [16]. In this regard, the child learns to determine the entities the caregiver is speaking about, as well as the conceptual relations between the objects in the environment as well as the caregiver's communicative intentions and associates these with the linguistic words uttered by the caregiver. This task is simulated by a neural network that comprises five sets of nodes, namely spoken word nodes, actor nodes, object nodes, conceptual relation nodes and communicative intention nodes which are connected through learning. Each node encodes a single entity.

The word nodes encode the caregiver's utterances as multiword sequences. Each node encodes a word, and in our model, the nodes in a sequence are associated in accordance with temporal Hebbian links.

For each CDS utterance, the associated actor and object nodes are simultaneously activated, along with the corresponding conceptual relation and communicative intention nodes and Hebbian learning used to update the weights between activated modal nodes. Hence the extent to which individual words in each CDS utterance co-occur with agents, objects, conceptual relations and inferred communicative intentions is established in an automatic, self-organising manner in accordance with the Hebbian weight update equation [17, 18]:

$$\Delta w_{ij} = \varepsilon a_j (a_i - w_{ij}) \tag{1}$$

where Δw_{ij} denotes the change in weight from unit i to unit j, a_i and a_j denote the activation levels of units i and j respectively, and ε denotes the learning rate. The term $(a_i - w_{ij})$ ensures that weights do not grow without bound, thereby minimising the possibility of weight saturation. Eq. 1 captures the conditional probability that a sending end node was active given that the receiving node was active [17, 18], i.e.

$$w_{ij} = P(a_i / a_j) \tag{2}$$

Consequently, whenever a given receiving node *j* is active, if a sending unit *i* also tends to be active, the interconnecting weight will tend to be high. In contrast, whenever a given receiving unit is active, if a sending node tends not to be active, the interconnecting weight between the two will tend to be low. In this way, the Hebbian learning yields weights that reflect conditional probabilities of activities, and in turn yield interconnecting weights that represent correlations in the environment.

5. Data

The simulation described in this paper uses the child language acquisition data in the Bloom 1973 corpus [15]. This corpus is found in the Child Language Data Exchange System (CHILDES) corpora [19].

5.1. *Child-Directed Speech (CDS) Training Data*

The data set for training the network model and assessing its ability to generate one-word child language utterances is taken from the earliest sample in the Bloom 1973 corpus, i.e. the sample taken at age 1year 4 months and 21 days. This dataset comprises 195 utterances directed at Alison by her mother, the perceptual entities underpinning each utterance (as identified form the utterances and their accompanying annotations), the conceptual relationships between the entities, and the mother's communicative intentions as inferred from the discourse. The perceptual entities associated with each utterance were categorised into Actors and Objects based on the roles they play in the conceptual relationship between them. In this paper the term *extralinguistic information* is used to collectively refer to the communicative intention, conceptual relation, actors, and objects associated with a CDS utterance.

During network training CDS utterances and their associated extralinguistic information are simultaneously applied to the network on a cycle-by-cycle basis. A learning rate small enough to guarantee the convergence of the network weights to stable values is selected and the CDS utterances are applied until there is no change in the value of the weights. In the work reported in this paper a learning rate $\varepsilon = 0.01$ is used to train the network over 500 cycles.

To assess the trained network's ability to make one-word utterances, 117 distinct extralinguistic terms identified from the CDS training dataset are used. When an extralinguistic term is applied to the network, each word node computes individual activations for conceptual relations, communicative intentions, actors and objects. The resultant word activation is the product of these four individual modal activations, and the word with the highest activation product is deemed the winner.

5.2. *One-Word Stage Child Language Test Data*

According to Bloom [15], children at the one-word stage use single word utterances to talk about the conceptual relations between perceptual entities. 28 utterances made by the child Alison in the Bloom 1973 corpus [15] were identified, and for each utterance, the extralinguistic information encoding the perceived conceptual relation is applied to the trained model. In each case, the word node with the highest activation is deemed to represent the model's linguistic response to the input.

6. Results and Discussion

This section presents and discusses the results of the network in simulating one-word child language on the basis of extra-linguistic information derived from motherese utterances as well as the network's ability to emulate the one-word utterances taken from Alison's utterances in the corpus.

6.1. *One-Word Utterances from CDS Extra-Linguistic Data*

Table 1 lists examples of the one-word responses made by the trained network when prompted by extralinguistic information from the CDS training dataset.

Of the 33 single word CDS utterances in the training data, the model successfully recalled 32 of the utterances when prompted with the corresponding extralinguistic information. For instance, for the single word CDS input "up", the model correctly responds with the output "up".

In the failed response, the model responded with "fell" instead of "down". The concept of "down" had been trained using the situation when the doll fell down from the chair. In this situation, the CDS sequence is as follows:

1. Hey, look!
2. Your baby
3. Fell down
4. Down

Table 1. Examples of the network's one- word responses to extralinguistic information from the CDS training dataset.

Conceptual Relation	Communicative Intention	Actors	Objects	Single Word Response	Original Multiword-Input
person gets on chair	request	Alison	chair	up	up
Is-a	naming	chair	-	little	It is a little chair
Person gets off chair	query	mum	chair	off	Mommy off that chair?
jar lid covers lid	query	Alison and mum	Jar and jar lid	cover	Should we cover it up?
Person sit on floor	request	Alison and mum	floor	sit	let's sit down over there.

When presented with the extralinguistic information for the word "down" in line 4, the model responds with the word "fell". This is possibly due to the fact that both "fell" and "down" occur in the same situation, and other different situations would be needed to enable the model to correctly distinguish between them. The fact that the model successfully learns from single word utterances would suggest their importance as learning aids in child language acquisition, where it has been noted that single word utterances are quite dominant in CDS [20].

The remaining 84 extra-linguistic inputs with multi-word CDS utterances, the network manages to generate 57 one-word utterances that may be regarded as equivalent, in a semantic sense, to the associated multi-word CDS expressions. For the remaining 27 extra-linguistic inputs the network generates single-word utterances that are difficult to classify as having the same meaning as the associated CDS multi-word utterances.

An example of when the network gives a linguistic response that can be regarded as appropriate is when the network simulates Alison's response to extra-linguistic response associated with CDS utterances made as Alison and her mother covered a jar with its lid. In this case, the extra-linguistic information presented to the network is as follows: communicative intention – *comment*, conceptual relation – *lid covers jar*, actors – *Alison and mom*, objects – *lid and jar*. The network model responds to this extra-linguistic information with the single word 'cover' - i.e. the word 'cover' gives the highest output activation to this extra-linguistic information. Although Alison never uses the word "cover" in her one-word utterances in the corpus, the word "cover" seems to be an appropriate one-word equivalent for the corresponding multi-word CDS expression: 'OK, let's cover it up and put it away.'

Figure 1 shows all the words in the model that responded with non-zero activation to the extralinguistic information comprising: communicative intention – *comment*, conceptual relation – *lid covers jar*, actors – *Alison and mom*, objects – *lid and jar*.

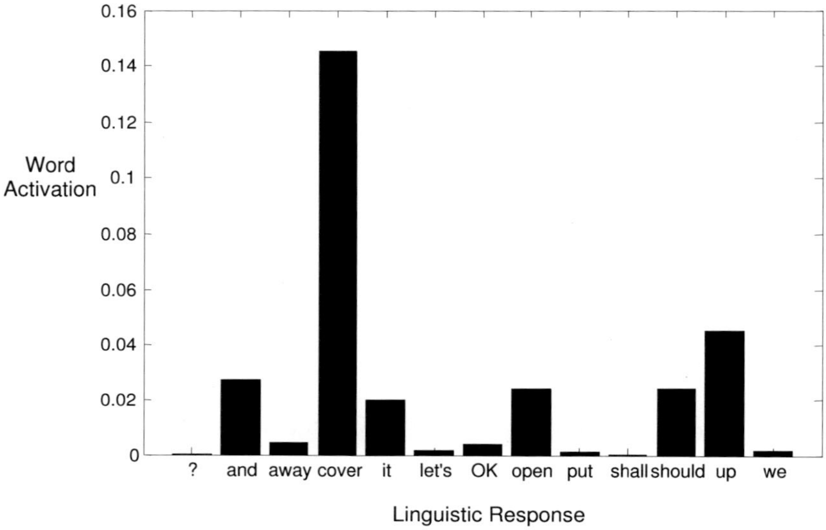

Figure 1. Activation plot for all the words that responded with non-zero activation to the extralinguistic information comprising: communicative intention – *comment*, conceptual relation – *lid covers jar*, actors – *Alison and mom*, objects – *lid and jar*.

An example of when the network gives a one-word utterance that may be regarded as inappropriate is when extralinguistic information associated with CDS utterance "there are no more cookies" is presented to the network. The extra-linguistic information for this CDS utterance is: communicative intention – *comment*, conceptual relation – *object disappearance*, actors – *cookies*, objects – *none*. The network model responds to this extralinguistic information with the single word 'are' - i.e. the word 'are' gives the highest word output activation to this extra-linguistic information.

Figure 2 shows all the words in the model that responded with non-zero activation to the extralinguistic information comprising: communicative intention – *comment*, conceptual relation – *object disappearance*, actors – *cookies*, objects – *none*. From Alison's one-word utterances, the correct response should have been 'gone', which is the second highest activation after 'are'. Also, the network responds with 'gone' when presented with extra-linguistic information for similar circumstances such as the disappearance of bubbles, and the disappearance of the microphone. This may be because the word 'gone' appears explicitly in the CDS expressions for the disappearance of bubbles and the disappearance of the microphone, which is not the case with the disappearance of the cookies where the expression uttered by Alison's mother is 'there are no more cookies'. This situation could possibly be remedied by incorporating inhibitory links between word nodes to ensure that inappropriate words are inhibited. Nevertheless, these results do suggest that the Hebbian weight update algorithm does try to associate applied extralinguistic information with the most appropriate one-word utterance, even in situations when such associations do not appear explicitly in the motherese used to train the model.

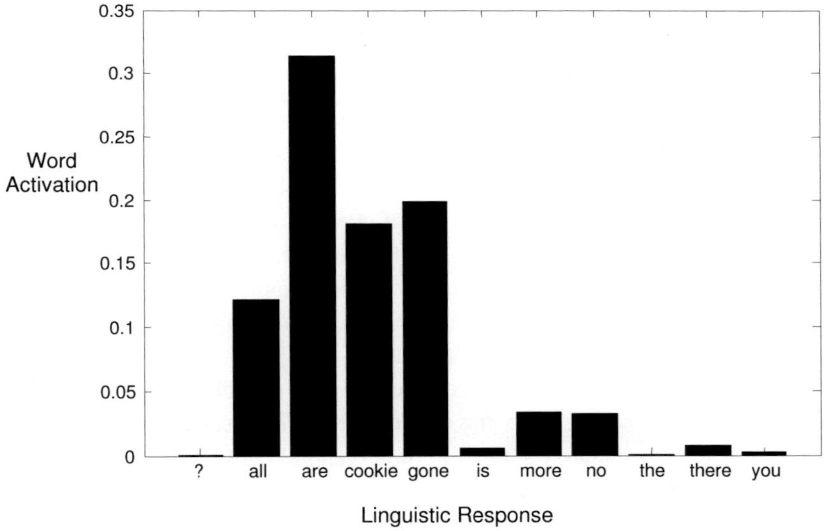

Figure 2. Activation plot for all the words that responded with non-zero activation to the extralinguistic information comprising: communicative intention – *comment*, conceptual relation – *object disappearance*, actors – *cookies*, objects – *none*.

6.2. *Emulating Alison's One-Word Child Language*

The output of the network, in response the extra-linguistic terms taken from Alison's utterances, falls into four categories when compared to Alison's utterances, as shown in Table 2:

Table 2. Categorisation of the network's One-word response to the extralinguistic information in Alison's one-word utterances.

Category	Exact Matches	Equivalent Matches	Unrelated Matches	No Output generated
Number of Utterances	6	6	8	8

There are six exact matches between the network's output and Alison's one-word utterances. In addition, the network output may also be considered to be equivalent to Alison's one-word utterances in another six of the data items. For example the network uses the word 'eat' instead of 'cookie' to request a cookie, and the word 'fell' instead of 'down' to refer to the event 'pig falls.' As we have discussed in section 6.1, this may be due to the word used by Alison being unavailable in the CDS used to train the network. However, the network is able to associate an appropriate word in the CDS utterance to the corresponding extralinguistic information.

In another eight of the data items, the network generated outputs which bear no discernible relationship to Alison's utterance in terms of semantic meaning. For instance, the network generated the word 'little' to name a chair and the word 'are' to refer to the disappearance of cookies. As discussed in section 6.1, this may be due to the word used by Alison being unavailable in the CDS used to train the network. In this instance, however, an inappropriate word in the CDS utterance is statistically matched by the Hebbian training algorithm to the corresponding extralinguistic information.

In the remaining eight utterances the network was unable to output a one-word utterance in response to the inputted extralinguistic information. In all these cases, the particular combination of perceptual entities, conceptual relation and inferred communicative intention in Alison's utterances had not been used at all in the CDS used to train the network. In these instances, the network failed to generalise to some appropriate linguistic output. This, in my opinion, is due to the localist scheme used in constructing the model whereby a single entity is represented by a single node. A distributed representation where data items are encoded as vectors of the features making them up would enable the network to generalise to data items used during training.

7. Conclusion and Future Work

As noted in [21], most cognitive processes, including language acquisition, "generally involve an interplay between a number of sources of information...each aspect of the information in the situation can act on other aspects, simultaneously influencing other aspects and being influenced by them." Incorporating multimodal processing in neural network models of cognitive processing, as has been done in this paper, may therefore help to make them more biologically plausible. In addition, the model presented in this paper is arguably one of the first Hebbian implementations of cross-situational learning. With cross-situational learning increasingly being viewed as an important cognitive learning mechanism, this model therefore presents some justification for the predominance of Hebbian learning in models of cognitive development [18].

As has been pointed out, however, the model presented in this paper exhibits some shortcomings as a consequence of its localist nature. An equivalent model based on distributed representation is currently being investigated. In addition, the progression of child language acquisition from one-word utterances to two-word utterances is also being investigated by incorporating multimodal temporal processing into the model as suggested in [22].

References

1. K. Plunkett, C. Sinha, M.F. Muller and O. Strandsby, *Connection Science* **4**, 293 (1992).
2. R. Miikkulainen, *Brain and Language* **59**, 334 (1997).
3. S. Abidi and K. Ahmad, *Journal of Information Science and Engineering* 13, 235 (1997).
4. P. Li, I. Farkas and B. MacWhinney, *Neural Networks* **17**, 1345 (2004).
5. A. Nyamapfene and K. Ahmad, *Proc. 20th IJCNN International Joint Conference on Neural Networks*, 783 (2007).
6. P.F. Dominey and C. Dodane, *Journal of Neurolinguistics* **17**, 121 (2004).
7. P. Matychuk, *Language Sciences* **27**, 301(2005).
8. P. W Jusczyk and R.N. Aslin, *Cognitive Psychology 29,* 1 (1995).
9. S. Pinker. *Learnability and cognition* (Cambridge, MA: MIT Press, 1989).
10. D.O. Hebb, *The Organisation of Behavior: A Neuropsychological Theory* (New York: Wiley, 1949).
11. P.A. de Villliers and J.G. de Villliers, *Early Language* (Havard University Press, Cambridge, 1979).
12. J. M. Siskind, *Cognition* **61**, 39 (1996).
13. C. Yu and D.H. Ballard, *Neurocomputing* **70**, 2149 (2007).
14. M. Small, *Cognitive Development* (San Diego: Harcourt Brace Jovanovich, 1990).
15. L. Bloom, *One word at a time: The use of single-word utterances before syntax* (The Hague: Mouton, 1973).
16. K. Nelson *Cognitive Development* **3**, 221 (1988).

17. D. E. Rumelhart and D. Zipser, Feature discovery by competitive learning. In *Parallel Distributed Processing: Explorations in the Microstructure of cognition, Volume 1: Foundations*, ed. D. E., Rumelhart and J. L. McClelland, and the PDP Research Group (Cambridge, MA: MIT Press, 1986).
18. Y. Munakata and J. Pfaffly, (2004). *Developmental Science* **7**, 141 (2004).
19. B. MacWhinney, *The CHILDES project: Tools for Analyzing Talk.* 3rd edition (Mahwah, NJ: Lawrence Erlbaum Associates, 2000).
20. A. Ninio, *Journal of Child Language*, **19**, 87 (1992).
21. J. McClelland, D.E. Rumelhart and G.E. Hinton, The appeal of parallel distributed processing. In *Parallel Distributed Processing: Explorations in the Microstructure of cognition, Volume 1: Foundations*, ed. D. E., Rumelhart and J. L. McClelland, and the PDP Research Group (Cambridge, MA: MIT Press, 1986).
22. A. Nyamapfene, *Unsupervised multimodal neural networks* (Unpublished PhD. Dissertation, University of Surrey, Guildford, England, 2006).

SYNCTACTIC GENERALIZATION IN A CONNECTIONIST MODEL OF COMPLEX SENTENCE PRODUCTION

H. FITZ*

Institute for Logic, Language and Computation, University of Amsterdam, Nieuwe Doelenstraat 15, 1012 CP Amsterdam, the Netherlands
**E-mail: fitz@science.uva.nl*
www.illc.uva.nl

F. CHANG

NTT Communication Science Laboratories, 2-4 Hikari-dai, Seika-cho, Souraku-gun, Kyoto 6190237, Japan
E-mail: chang.franklin@gmail.com

We present a neural-symbolic learning model of sentence production which displays strong semantic systematicity and recursive productivity. Using this model, we provide evidence for the data-driven learnability of complex yes/no-questions.

Keywords: Statistical learning; semantic processing; systematicity; recursion; polar interrogatives.

1. Introduction

Usage-based theories of language acquisition have emphasized the role of experience in the bottom-up construction of language knowledge (Tomasello,[1] Goldberg[2]). But since languages are lexically open and combinatorial in structure, no amount of experience covers their expressivity. These theories must therefore explain how children can generalize properties of their linguistic input to an adult grammar and, ideally, provide evidence that this explanation can be implemented explicitly. Connectionist models of language processing generally align well with fundamental tenets of usage-based theories, but they have frequently been criticized for not generalizing like humans (Marcus[3]). In this paper we present a neural network model of sentence production and syntactic development which generalizes in interesting ways, both lexically and structurally. In the second part of the paper, we will argue that our model might help to explain how complex yes/no-questions can be learned in the absence of direct experience.

2. The Dual-path model

Our modelling work built on the Dual-path model of Chang, Dell and Bock[4] which was adapted for the processing of multi-clause utterances. The model consisted of two pathways (Figure 1). One pathway, the sequencing system, was a standard simple-recurrent network.[5] This system learned distributional regularities over word sequences and developed syntactic categories at the compress-layer. The second pathway, called the message-lexical system, learned to use sentence meaning to activate words. The model learned from exposure to sentences paired with their meaning. Sentence meaning was represented by three components: concepts, thematic roles and event-structure. Concepts represented the meaning of individual words in the what-layer. Units in the where-layer represented thematic roles, such as the agent, patient or recipient of an action. These roles in the where-layer could be bound temporarily to sentence-specific content in the what-layer through dynamic weights. Hence thematic-role units could act like semantic variables. The event-semantics encoded the number and relative prominence of participants in an event. To represent a transitive event, for instance, an agent and patient feature were activated in the event-semantics-layer. Their relative level of activation biased the model towards selecting an active or passive construction. In multi-clause utterances, the event-semantics also encoded the relative prominence of basic events to signal the relation of clauses in the target utterance. Before production began, sentence meaning was activated in the message-lexical system. The model then mapped this message incrementally onto a sentence form. It learned in a standard error-based word-to-word prediction paradigm. The present model had the same architecture as in Chang et al.,[4] but it used extra units in the event-semantics- and where-layers to represent participant roles in relative clauses.

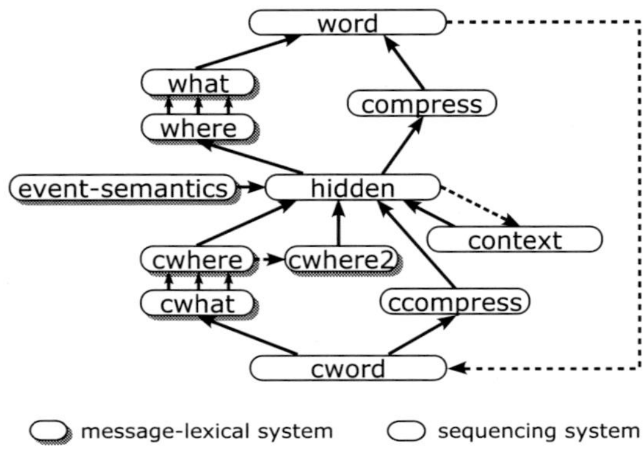

Fig. 1. Dual-path model architecture.

3. Strong systematicity

Children learn words in one semantic/syntactic context and reuse them in another. Strong lexical generalization requires that familiar words can be used correctly in novel sentences, at novel levels of embedding, in novel thematic roles. For example, children might learn the meaning of the word cat from simple sentences in which a cat is the agent of a transitive action and generalize its use to the recipient role of a dative embedding (Figure 2). This property of the human language faculty has been called strong semantic systematicity.[6] We trained the Dual-path model on an artificial English-like language with up to three nested relative clauses. This language contained intransitives, active and passive transitives, prepositional datives and obliques as basic constructions from which sentences with relative clauses were assembled. Over a lexicon of 48 words, particles and inflectional morphemes, it allowed the creation of 2.49×10^{18} distinct sentence tokens. 10.000 tokens were randomly selected for training out of which 40% were single-clause sentences and this proportion was decremented by 10% for each additional level of embedding. In training, the word cat only occurred in the agent slot of single-clause, active transitive sentences. The model was then tested on novel sentences with various numbers of relative clauses in which the word cat always occurred as a dative recipient in the deepest embedding. Model behavior on these items was compared with performance for the exact same sentences in which cat did not occur (Figure 3). The x-axis shows the amount of training, the y-axis measures performance in terms of 'perfect match' with the target utterance. The model learned to produce sentences with one and two relative clauses to perfection, sentences with three nested relative clauses were more difficult as the model reached only around 70% accuracy. For each level of embedding, however, the model reached comparable levels of accuracy whether the word cat filled the recipient slot of the deepest dative embedding or not. Since in training the word cat was not experienced in recipient slots, dative constructions, or relative clauses, this suggests that the Dual-path model displayed strong semantic systematicity in Hadley's sense.

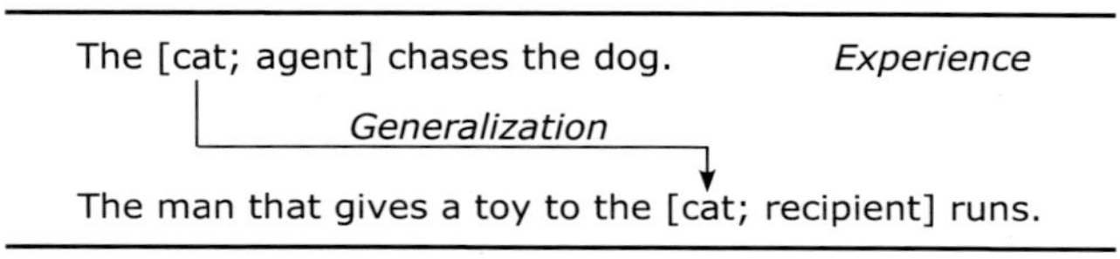

Fig. 2. Lexical generalization.

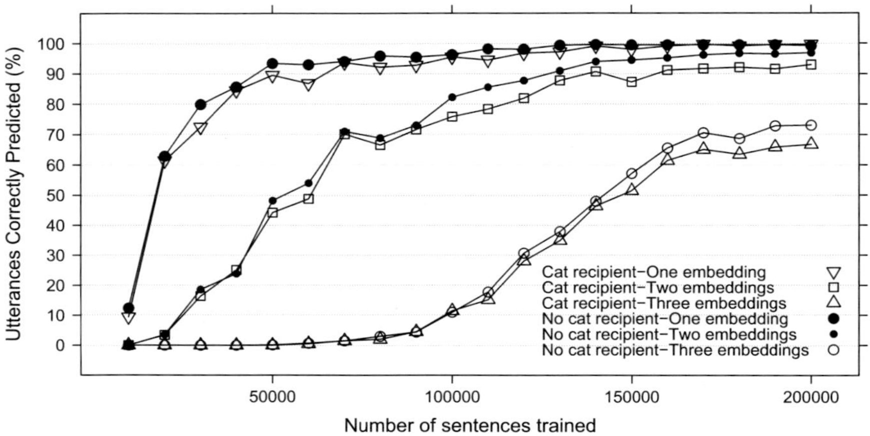

Fig. 3. Strong semantic systematicity in the Dual-path model.

How is systematicity achieved? The key component in the model is its weight-based message. To understand how this works, let's examine how the model would deal with the generalization in Figure 2. In the Dual-path model, this generalization has two parts. One part is learning the concept-word association, which in this case involves learning that the concept CAT (what-layer) maps to the English word cat (word-layer). This association can be learned from any input sentence about cats. The second part involves learning how to activate the appropriate recipient role Z (where-layer) at the embedded clause position where the word cat is supposed to be produced (i.e., gives the toy to the...). The model learned to activate this role from exposure to other sentences which contained embedded clause recipients (e.g., The woman that gave a stick to the dog jumped). This experience was sufficient because the message for the novel generalization in Figure 2 had a message link between the recipient role and the concept CAT (Figure 4). If

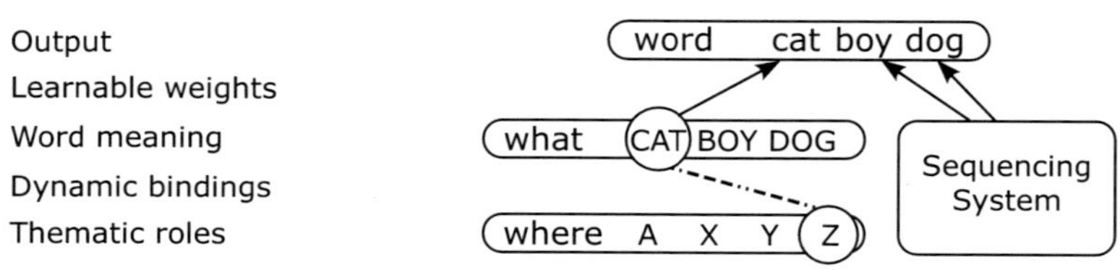

Fig. 4. Dynamic bindings (dashed line) enforce systematicity.

the recipient was activated, then the concept CAT was activated, and hence the word cat was produced. Thus, the Dual-path model could generalize systematically, because it could combine knowledge learned from different input utterances by means of its dynamic message.[7]

4. Recursive productivity

In structural generalization, familiar constructions are recombined into sentences with a novel hierarchical organization. By means of relativization, for example, the sentences

(1) The dog gave a toy to the cat.

(2) The girl that is chasing a dog was hit by the boy.

can form a novel structure with an additional embedding:

(3) The girl that is chasing a dog that gave a toy to the cat was hit by the boy.

To see whether the Dual-path model could generalize structurally, it was trained on a language with at most two relative clauses. Then it was tested on novel structures with three and four nested relative clauses (Figure 5). The model learned the training language with at most two embeddings

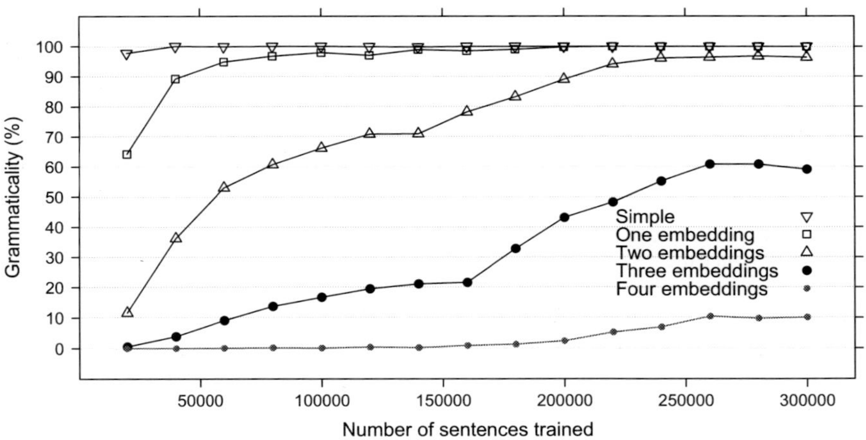

Fig. 5. Recursive productivity in the Dual-path model.

to perfection. In addition it produced 60% grammatical utterances with three embeddings and reached 10% grammaticality on sentences with four embeddings. For example, the model correctly produced sentences such as

(4) A dog that a boy that a teacher that gave the orange to a cat is carrying was attacked by is running with the toy.

without exposure to the syntax of three nested relative clauses in learning. The degradation of performance with depth of embedding is in line with human data.

Unlike systematicity, which depended on the role-concept weights, recursive productivity depended on another part of the message, the event-semantics. In training, the model learned to associate subparts of a sentence with the event-semantics of the proposition that controlled it (Figure 6). The model learned from simple messages how to sequence participants in single-clause transfer events (dog give toy to cat). Other features of the event-semantics controlled the position of relative clauses (X that) and the thematic role of the head noun in the relative clause (that *gap* VERB). When

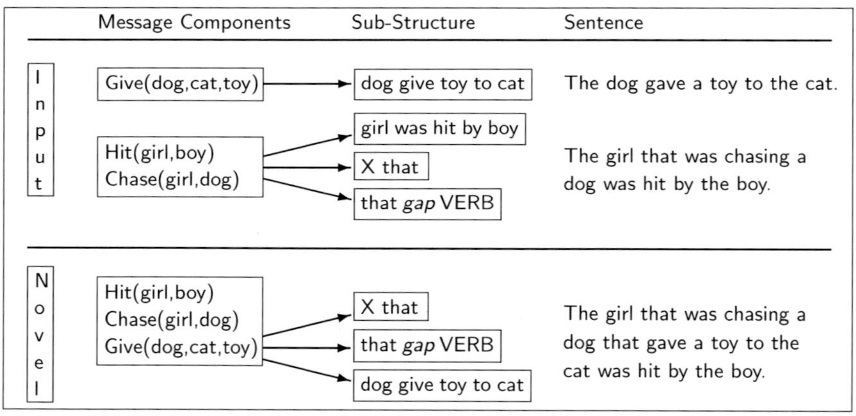

Fig. 6. Different components of the message control different subsequences of words in the target structure.

presented with a message for a novel construction, the model could use semantic regularities in the conceptual structure of the event-semantics and combine these regularities to generate additional embeddings.

From message-sentence pairs in training, the model learned which features of the event-semantics controlled which aspects of the hierarchical organization of complex sentences. Since novel messages shared features in the event-semantics with input messages, the model could generalize its learned subpart mappings and built novel structures from relevant message components. In this way, productivity was enabled by similarity-based meaning-to-form transduction.

5. The problem of auxiliary fronting in polar interrogatives

A major controversy in language acquisition revolves around the question which aspects of language, and syntax in particular, can be learned from experience and which aspects require some kind of language-specific biological endowment. Arguably, one of the most prominent issues in this debate concerns the learnability of yes/no-questions with relative clauses ('complex polar interrogatives'). A single-clause declarative such as

(5) The dog is barking.

can be turned into a yes/no-question by inverting the auxiliary is and the subject NP the dog:

(6) Is the dog barking?

Now consider the relative-clause sentence

(7) The dog that is chasing the cat is barking.

An ungrammatical question is obtained if the sequentially first auxiliary is moved to the front:

(8) *Is the dog that chasing the cat is barking?

This rule of forming complex questions disregards the hierarchical organization of the declarative (7) into main and subordinate clause. It is therefore a *structure-independent* rule. The correct rule requires that the main clause auxiliary be fronted across the relative clause; it is *structure-dependent*:

(9) Is the dog that is chasing the cat barking?

Simple questions such as (6) are quite frequent in child-directed speech. Chomsky argued that these questions support the structure-independent rule (8) because in both cases the auxiliary which is closest to the subject NP is placed in front. Complex yes/no-questions such as (9), on the other hand, seem to be virtually absent from child-directed speech. Consequently, a child has no inductive basis to infer the correct rule for question formation from the linguistic input. To explain why children acquire the syntax of yes/no-questions nonetheless, Chomsky proposed that children have an innate bias to induce hierarchical structures which allow for appropriate fronting constraints to be learned.[8]

Others have pointed out that structure-dependent auxiliary displacement also occurs in many other sentence types with subordinate or complement clauses[9,10] such as

(10) a. Could I have your French fries, if you're done with eating?
b. Why couldn't anyone who was at home close the window?

If these structures are sufficiently frequent in child-directed speech they might support learning the correct rule for yes/no-questions. A third approach comes from statistical learning with neural networks.[11,12] Reali & Christiansen, for instance, trained a simple-recurrent network on the Bernstein-Ratner corpus of mother-child interaction. In a grammaticality judgement task their trained model displayed a strong bias towards grammatical over ungrammatical yes/no-questions. Since these questions did not occur in the input to the model, this suggests that the linguistic environment of children might be rich enough for them to induce the correct syntax. The results of Reali & Christiansen were obtained by tagging the training corpus with parts of speech and they did not distinguish between verbs and auxiliaries or between different kinds of pronouns. Their account of question learning might only work under these assumptions and it remains to be seen whether children induce statistical constraints over similar types of categories.[a]

6. Question learning in the Dual-path model

In contrast to earlier approaches which emphasized the structural nature of the learning problem, our account of this generalization is based on meaning. We assume that children and adults who produce polar interrogatives represent a message that is made up of two propositions. We will show that a model which is given input messages with one and two propositions can learn proposition-specific syntactic constraints that allow it to generalize appropriately for polar interrogatives.

To describe our approach, we will first characterize the language that the Dual-path model was exposed to. This language contained basic single-clause constructions (intransitives, active/passive transitives, prepositional/double-object datives, and obliques), the combinatorially complete set of sentences with one relative clause composed from these constructions, simple yes/no-questions, and complex wh-questions:

[a]Similar results obtained with a more general n-gram model proposed in their paper, however, do not depend on these assumptions.

(11) Who is the cat that was chasing the dog playing with?

As many have argued, we suggest that the syntax of complex yes/no-questions can be assembled piecemeal from simpler and similar constructions which are warranted in a child's linguistic environment. Subject-auxiliary inversion might be learned from simple yes/no-questions in the input, and auxiliary displacement across a relative clause might be learned from complex wh-questions such as (11). In contrast to other approaches, our approach assumes that children use language-independent message information to help them produce polar interrogatives.

The Dual-path model was trained on message-sentence pairs from the language described above, and tested on novel sentences from this language and complex yes/no-questions (which were not in the training language). We obtained the learning curves of Figure 7. The x-axis represents the

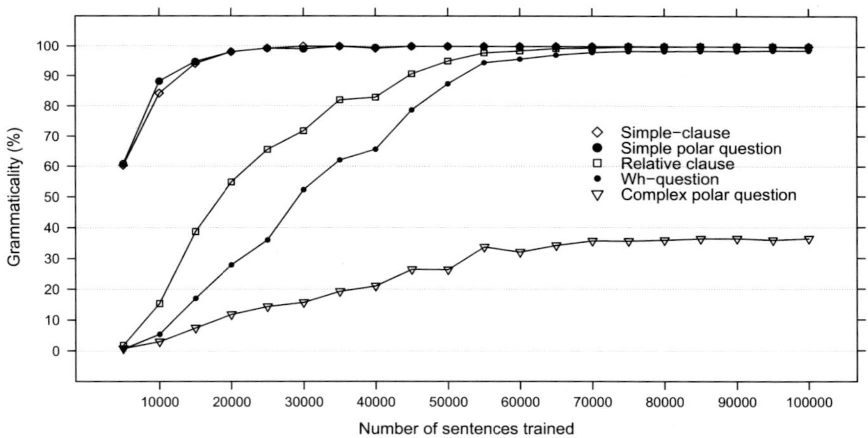

Fig. 7. Learning complex yes/no-questions.

number of sentences the model was trained on, the y-axis measures the grammaticality of the model's productions. Structures which were attested in the input were learned very well. The model correctly produced single-clause utterances and simple yes/no-questions quickly, followed by declaratives with relative clauses and wh-questions. When tested on the novel complex yes/no-questions, the model reached nearly 40% grammaticality. This shows that the model was able to use the two proposition message to help it learn the right generalization. Moreover, the model generalized in desirable ways in that it showed a clear preference for right-branching over center-embedded yes/no-questions and a preference for subject-relativized over object-relativized yes/no-questions (Figure 8).

Sentence meaning helped the model to segment utterances into the parts that correspond to the main clause, e.g., is the dog barking?, and the parts related to the embedded clause (that is chasing the cat, see Figure 6). Thus, the auxiliary in the main clause was controlled by a different part of the message than the auxiliary in the embedded clause. Questions were signaled in the event-semantics by question features which were neutral between clauses. Hence, the message for complex yes/no-questions did not bias the model towards selecting the main clause auxiliary. But the model learned to associate the question feature with the main clause auxiliary because it experienced simple yes/no-questions in training and because sentence-initial auxiliaries in complex wh-questions were never extracted from the embedded clause. These two types of information lead the model to shift the auxiliary that was controlled by the main clause message to the front when tested on complex yes/no-questions. In this way the system learned that picking the auxiliary closest to the subject NP was not appropriate.

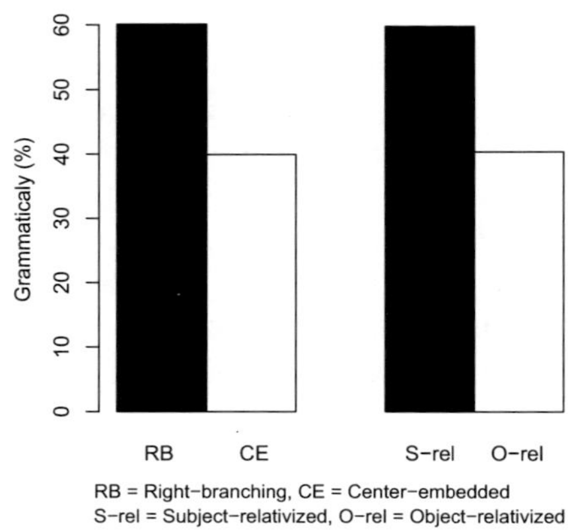

Fig. 8. Differential generalization for yes/no-questions.

Previous modelling work in this domain did not explain how question production could be achieved, and this is the first explicit model that can generate correct complex yes/no-questions from semantic representations, in the absence of these structures in the training corpus. The model did not reach an adult level of performance in which questions are produced flawlessly. However, the model's behavior is consistent with error levels found in English-speaking children age [4;7–5:7] in a study by Ambridge et al.[13] (mean correct production of center-embedded questions: children 27%, model 29%). Furthermore, errors that the model made did not result from structure-dependent auxiliary fronting. This can be verified by examining the initial segments of complex yes/no-questions the model produced in testing. Figure 9

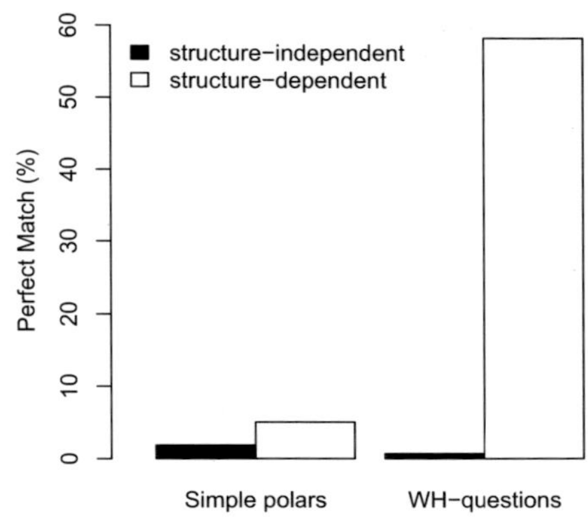

Fig. 9. Initial segments of yes/no-questions.

compares the results for two training conditions, one in which the only questions the model received in training were simple yes/no-questions (left bars), the other in which the model was also exposed to complex wh-questions (right bars). The y-axis shows the percentage of productions that perfectly matched either a structure-dependent initial segment (Is the cat that was chasing) or a structure-independent initial segment (*Was the cat that chasing) for 1000 test questions. In both conditions the model never extracted auxiliaries from the embedded clause. This indicates that errors in the Dual-path model's productions did not reflect a structure-independent hypothesis about auxiliary fronting in the absence of complex yes/no-questions in the input.

To compare our results with those of Reali & Christiansen, we tested the trained model on pairs of grammatical and ungrammatical center-embedded yes/no-questions. The model received a message input which was neutral between the two forms. The output was then compared to both targets, and classified as either grammatical or ungrammatical based on a graded performance measure (Figure 10). In 88% of the tested pairs the model's output was closer to the grammatical question. Quantitatively, these results are similar to those of Reali & Christiansen. Our test set, however, contained a considerable amount of structural variation[b] and our results did not depend on tagging the input in a specific way. These results demonstrate that structure-dependent auxiliary fronting can be learned

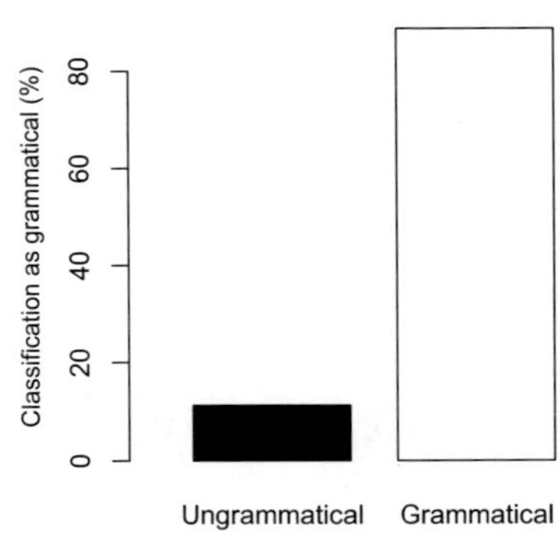

Fig. 10. Grammaticality judgement.

[b]Subject-relativized intransitive, transitive (active/passive), dative (prepositional/ditransitive) and oblique embeddings, and object-relativized embeddings when permitted.

from the structures that occur in child-directed speech as long as one assumes that children link syntax to meaning representations that distinguish different propositions in complex messages.

7. Conclusions

Adult speakers use language to convey meaning, and it has been argued that children must also use meaning in syntactic development if they are to acquire adult-like linguistic representations (MacNamara,[14] Pinker,[15] Tomasello[1]). We presented one of the few explicit models that uses meaning for syntax development. The model learned associations between parts of the message and subsequences of words, and it could combine these regularities in novel ways. This mechanism could explain generalization of words to novel slots and generalization of subsequences to novel embeddings. The Dual-path model could even generate polar questions without having experienced the target structure in training. Therefore, the structure of meaning may obviate the need for innate syntax-specific knowledge in the acquisition of adult-like language abilities.

References

1. M. Tomasello, *Constructing a Language: A Usage-Based Theory of Language Acquisition* (Harvard University Press, 2003).
2. A. Goldberg, *Constructions at Work: The Nature of Generalization in Language* (Oxford University Press, 2006).
3. G. F. Marcus, *Cognitive Psychology* **37**, 243 (1998).
4. F. Chang, G. S. Dell and K. Bock, *Psychological Review* **113**, 234 (2006).
5. J. L. Elman, *Cognitive Science* **14**, 179 (1990).
6. R. F. Hadley, *Mind and Language* **9**, 247 (1994).
7. F. Chang, *Cognitive Science* **26**, 609 (2002).
8. N. Chomsky, The linguistic approach, in *Language and Learning: The Debate between Jean Piaget and Noam Chomsky*, ed. M. Piatelli-Palmarini (Harvard University Press, 1980)
9. G. K. Pullum and B. C. Scholz, *The Linguistic Review* **19**, 9 (2002).
10. B. MacWhinney, *Journal of Child Language* **31**, 883 (2004).
11. J. Lewis and J. L. Elman, Learnability and the statistical structure of language: Poverty of stimulus arguments revisited, in *Proceedings of the 26th Boston University Conference on Language Development*, (Cascadilla, 2001).
12. F. Reali and M. H. Christiansen, *Cognitive Science* **29**, 1007 (2005).
13. B. Ambridge, C. E. Rowland and J. M. Pine, *Cognitive Science* **32**, 222 (2008).
14. J. MacNamara, *Psychological Review* **79**, 1 (1972).
15. S. Pinker, *Language Learnability and Language Development: The Acquisition of Argument Structure* (Harvard University Press, 1984).

A CONNECTIONIST MODEL OF READING FOR ITALIAN

GIOVANNI PAGLIUCA*
Department of Psychology, University of York, YO10 5DD
York, UK

PADRAIC MONAGHAN
Department of Psychology, University of York, YO10 5DD
York, UK

Classic connectionist models of reading have traditionally focused on English, a language with a quasi-regular (deep) relationship between orthography and phonology, and very little work has been carried out on more transparent (shallow) orthographies. This paper introduces a parallel distributed processing (PDP) model of reading for Italian. The model is successful in simulating a variety of behavioral effects such as the neighborhood effect and the morphological effect in nonword reading, previously accounted for by dual route architectures, and provides clear evidence that different grain sizes in the orthography to phonology mapping can be discovered even in a model trained with almost perfectly shallow stimuli.

1. Shallow orthographies and models of reading

Connectionist models of reading have been originally developed to explore the general cognitive architecture of the reading system but also the specific psycholinguistic effects that have been documented over the years for the English language. Very little work has been conducted to extend the parallel distributed approach or other modeling approaches to reading beyond the English language, despite the implicit claim that the principles that govern the reading system are universal and should therefore apply to all orthographies, both alphabetic and logographic, deep and shallow. PDP models of reading for English have been trained on small sets of monosyllabic words and have simulated a vast collection of behavioral effects related to monosyllabic single word reading [10, 11, 15]. One of the main practical difficulties in exporting a PDP architecture developed for English to other orthographies is due to potential distinctions in terms of the syllabic properties of the language. For example, some languages have very few monosyllabic words, and therefore a

*Corresponding author: g.pagliuca@psych.york.ac.uk

monosyllabic model would not be representative of the language as a whole. Or alternatively, the modeler must account for the constraints that a polysyllabic structure would impose on the model, such as those posed by stress assignment. A few attempts have nonetheless been made to model psycholinguistic effects in languages such as German and French within a general PDP framework.

Hutzler, Ziegler, Perry, Wimmer, and Zorzi [12] adapted Plaut and collaborators' [15] feedforward network to German monosyllabic words, and found a general advantage of this model compared to the English version in speed of learning, despite the striking similarities that the two languages share in both orthography and phonology (but not in the mapping between the two, German being more regular than English). Ans et al. [1] trained a polysyllabic connectionist network to read French. The model was trained on a large corpus of mono and polysyllabic French words, and could read successfully 96.32% of them, and account for accurate nonword reading, frequency and consistency effects, and simulate phonological dyslexia as well.

The reading process has generally been defined in the modeling literature in terms of forming a mapping between visual symbols and phonemes or syllables [15]. Learning to read can therefore be described as a process of learning to find shared "grain sizes" (or "what maps into what" pairs) between orthography and phonology [18] and models which implement distributed forms of representations can successfully discover these different functional units, as shown by Pagliuca and Monaghan [13]. Given the potential that PDP networks have to discover appropriate grain sizes in the orthography to phonology mapping, a core question is whether such a class of models can discover grain sizes larger than a single unit in an almost completely regular and shallow orthography, one for which the grapheme to phoneme mapping alone allows for an almost perfect recoding of orthography, and therefore almost perfect pronunciation. A possibility to test this ability is offered by the Italian language, whose spelling to sound mapping is almost perfectly regular, with a one to one correspondence between letters and phonemes. Nonetheless, several effects at the lexical and morpholexical level have been documented for Italian, suggesting that Italian readers show sensitivity to reading units larger than the single letter or pairs of letters in word naming and word recognition. This paper will describe and discuss a fully distributed model of reading for Italian, conceived in order to expand the PDP framework to transparent orthographies and further investigate the relation between orthography and phonology in the light of a grain size perspective on reading.

2. Properties of Italian orthography and phonology

Italian is an alphabetic orthography with an almost entirely compositional one-to-one mapping between spelling and sound. In Italian each letter regularly translates in a single phoneme, with few exceptions fully predictable by the orthographic context. For example, the letter B is always pronounced /b/, irrespective of the surrounding letters, but the letters C and G can obtain two different pronunciations according to the following vowel: /ʧ/ and /ʤ/ when followed by the vowels I and E, /k/ and /g/ when followed by the vowels O, U, A or by the letter H, which in Italian is unvoiced. The letter G can also be pronounced as a liquid if followed by the letter L in combination with I, as /ʎ/.

There are very few monosyllabic words in Italian, and most are function words. Given the polysyllabic structure of most words, Italian readers are confronted with the problem of stress assignment. Stress assignment in Italian is considered quasi-regular: for the vast majority of words (about 80%), stress is placed on the penultimate syllable, as in *al'bergo* (hotel) but there are many exceptions to this rule, with stress placed on the antepenultimate syllable in 18% of cases, as in *'albero* (tree) (see [17], for the estimated count). A small proportion of words, about 2%, have final stress, but in these cases the words are marked with diacritics in the written form, as in *papà* (dad), therefore stress assignment is fully predictable from these orthographic cues.

The Italian spelling to sound mapping has been studied extensively in the last few decades and a few benchmarks have been established for this transparent orthography. Despite the strong regularity in the spelling to sound mapping, which might alone promote the use of a nonlexical reading strategy with word naming primarily mediated by a sublexical code, and reliance on the use of grapheme-to-phoneme correspondence rules, as suggested in the past [9], a marked lexicality effect and frequency effect have been documented for Italian, even when using completely transparent stimuli [14], effects that cannot be explained solely by the use of sublexical conversion mechanisms or strategies.

Lexical contributions have nonetheless been found in nonword reading as well, challenging the claim that nonwords are solely read via a nonlexical serial mechanism [9], suggesting again that Italian readers do not simply rely on a set of rules to convert single letters onto phonological representations when reading nonwords. Arduino and Burani [2] found that nonwords which had a large cohort of lexical neighbors (nonwords that vary from other words by one letter only) were named faster than nonwords which had very few neighbors. This effect was found irrespective of the frequency of the neighboring words. The effect was ascribed to the contribution of a lexical lookup mechanism alongside a grapheme to phoneme set of rules within a dual route framework [7] with both mechanisms being active when reading nonwords as words.

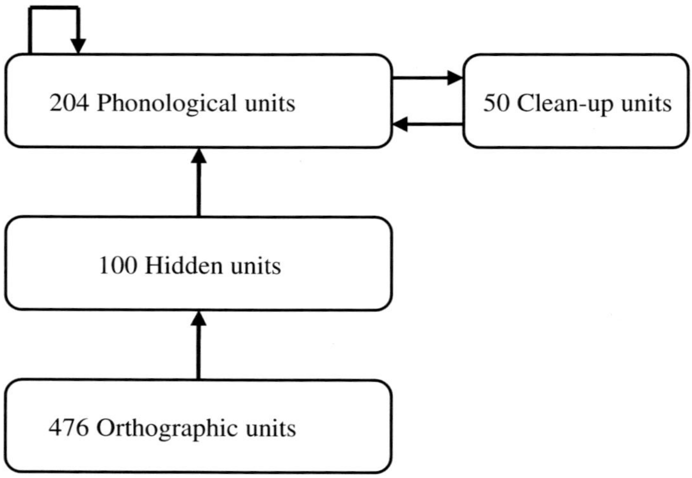

Figure 1: Architecture of the model.

What these results primarily show is that Italian readers can discover and make use of large grain sizes, shared by many words that provide information that goes beyond the reach of a strictly rule-base mechanism.

Morphological effects have also been documented for Italian. Italian readers seem to benefit from the presence of a morpheme in reading nonwords [5]. Nonwords containing real morphemic units (*donnista*, made up of a real root *donn-* and a real suffix *–ista*) were named faster than control nonwords (*dennosto*, which has no real root and no real suffix) matched for bigram frequency and length [5]. The authors suggest that the morpheme is an effective reading unit for Italian, complementary to whole-word lexical information, but again represents a unit larger than single letters or pairs of letters.

It seems evident from these reported studies that Italian readers can exploit the spelling to sound mapping beyond the smallest possible grain size (single letter), even when the mapping itself allows for an apparently sufficient and efficient one-to-one letter to phoneme recoding strategy. Italian readers show sensitivity to different grain sizes (graphemic, morphological, lexical), according to the stimuli they are asked to name aloud. However, this sensitivity does not necessarily imply that graphemic, morphemic and lexical information is stored and accessed independently, nor does it entail that there are intermediate units of representation between orthography and phonology that code explicitly for this kind of information. Nor does it require separate mechanisms that interact to generate the observed effects. A single-route PDP model that maps orthography onto phonology can in principle be used to explore some of the effects described so far, and account for them avoiding any recourse to a dual route mechanism. More importantly, a PDP architecture could discover the appropriate grain sizes that emerge in mapping Italian orthography onto phonology. This result would be even more striking given the extreme regularity of the mapping.

Next, a PDP model of reading is described, which, in line with other fully distributed architectures, does not implement localist units to represent lexical information nor does it instantiate distinct lexical and sublexical mechanisms to generate the appropriate phonology for each word. The model is then tested on a series of behavioral benchmark effects.

3. Modeling Italian reading

3.1. *Architecture and representation*

The architecture of the model is closely based on the Harm and Seidenberg's model of reading [10], and is shown in Figure 1. The orthographic layer comprised 476 units, the hidden layer had 100 units and the phonological layer contained 204 units. A set of 50 cleanup units was added to the network and connected bidirectionally to the phonological layer in order to create a phonological attractor. The phonological layer was self-connected to itself. Orthography in the model was represented in a slot based manner, with 3 slots for the onset, 2 for the vowels, and one for the coda for each syllable. The last syllable had no slot for the coda as typically Italian words do not end with a consonant. Up to three syllables could be represented in the orthographic layer, for a total of 17 slots (6 slots each for the first 2 syllables, 5 slots for the third syllable. Within each letter position slot, a total of 28 distinct letters were represented in the model's input. Stressed vowels that were marked in the orthography were represented as distinct letters.

Phonology in the model was rendered in terms of phonological features, in line with recent PDP models of reading [10, 15]. Each phoneme was described by a set of 11 standard binary phonological features [6]. An extra feature was added to the phonological matrix in order to distinguish stressed vowels from unstressed ones, bringing the total number of features to 12 for each phoneme.

3.2. *Training corpus*

In order to create a sizeable corpus of words to train the model with, two different databases were combined. Orthographic forms were initially extracted from the "Corpus e Lessico di Frequenza dell'Italiano Scritto" (CoLFIS) database [4]. This database contains frequency information from a corpus of 3million words, which was extracted as well. Plurals and inflected forms were included, not reduced to lemmas. The database contains mono and polysyllabic words. Words beginning with the letters H, J, Y, W, X were excluded from the corpus, as in Italian they appear almost only in loan words. Words containing the letters J, Y, W, X in any other position in the word were excluded as well for the same reason. Two more types of information about the lexicon were needed: syllabic boundaries for each word and stress position. This information was extracted from the De Mauro Italian Dictionary [8]. This database contains stress placement information and syllabic boundaries: each word is split into its constituent syllables (typographically separated by a hyphen) and the stressed syllable is marked by the use of a diacritic above the stressed vowel. Only primary stress is represented. The two databases were then matched and only those words that were present in both dictionaries were selected and extracted. A total of 29336 words resulted from this combination. Only monosyllabic, bisyllabic and trisyllabic words were further selected, resulting in a total of 9911 words. Words with more than 3 vowels in the nucleus were excluded from the corpus.

A phonological representation for each word was created using an algorithm to translate orthography onto phonology. Double consonants are true geminates in Italian and were coded as two separate phonemes. Diphthongs were not coded as different phonemes but were broken down into their constituent vowels. Frequency for each word was capped at 1000 and then compressed (square root compression).

3.3. *Training and testing*

The model was trained with continuous recurrent backpropagation algorithm [10]. The phonological attractor was pretrained until it reached a mean square error for the output of each pattern below 0.01. For 4 time ticks all phonological units were clamped with the appropriate values for the target word. For ticks 5-11 the output of each phonological unit was compared with the actual value of the word, and the difference was propagated backwards thought the network, generating error gradients for each word, and then updating the weights. The trained weights were then fixed in the reading model. A learning rate of 0.005

and momentum of 0.9 were used. The model was then trained for 1.2 million word presentations learning to map the orthographic input onto the phonological output, after which training was stopped and the model's performance was assessed.

4. Results

Naming accuracy and sum squared error (SSE) were computed to test the model's general performance. Euclidian distances were computed for each phoneme and the closest phoneme to the target was selected and reported as the models' final solution. A word was judged to be generated correctly if all of its phonemes were reproduced in each slot. SSE was computed from the model's output, as well as determining the nearest phonological output target.

After 1.2 million word presentations the model could read correctly 93.7% of all words. Of the errors 10% were classified as true phonological errors (*debacle* reads as *debaple*, with a phoneme substitution), while 26% were classified as "stress placement" errors (*im'pala* read as *'impala*). 64% of errors affected the reproduction of the vowels "o" and "e" along the open/closed dimension (an open "o" generated instead of a closed "o"). However this last type of response is usually not classified as error in the behavioral literature, due to large regional variation in the use of these 2 vowels. With the exclusion of this type of error, the model was 98% correct at reading the words in the corpus.

The model's performance on reading nonwords was assessed to evaluate its ability to generalize to novel stimuli. Three sets of nonwords were selected from the literature: 48 bisyllabic nonwords from the Pagliuca and collaborators' study [14]; 60 bisyllabic nonwords from the Arduino and collaborator's study [2] and 32 threesyllabic nonwords taken from Burani and collaborator's study [5]. The model was successful in reading correctly 98% of the nonwords, which is a level comparable to human performance. The model therefore shows a good level of generalization to novel stimuli.

In addition to the performance on words and nonwords, one of the benchmark effects that every computational model of reading should simulate successfully is the frequency effect. The frequency effect has been documented for all orthographies studied so far, from deep to shallow, including Italian, and has proven to be the most robust finding, with frequency being the psycholinguistic variable that accounts for the largest portion of variance in naming reaction times [3]. The model was trained 4 times with random initial weights and then each of the four simulations was tested on the 48 words (24 high frequency words and 24 low frequency words) from the Pagliuca and collaborators' study [14]. These stimuli do not contain any context-dependent rule and each letter in each word entails a perfect one to one mapping with phonology. The model showed sensitivity to frequency for completely shallow Italian words, as in the behavioral study.

4.1. *Morphological effect*

The study conducted by Burani and collaborators [5] sheds light on the sensitivity to large sublexical clusters that Italian readers develop in the course of learning to map orthography onto phonology. A PDP model of reading with no separate mechanisms for reading words and nonwords should still show sensitivity to large grain sizes that are shared by many words in the corpus. That should equally apply to a model that is trained with an extremely shallow orthography such as Italian.

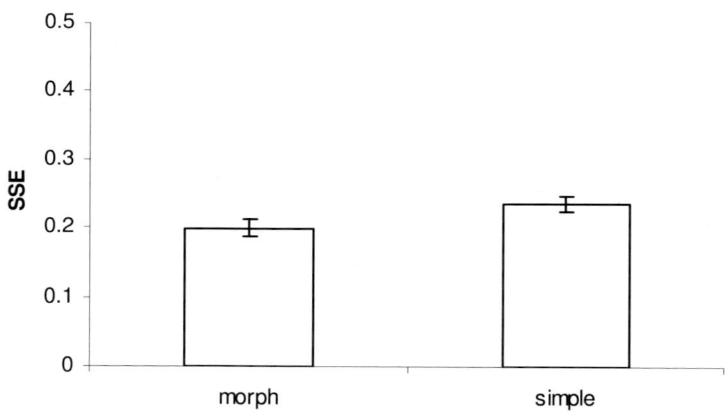

Figure 2: Mean SSE for morphologically complex (morph) and simple nonwords.

The two sets of 16 three-syllable pseudowords, morphologically complex (*donnista*) and simple (*dennosto*) from Burani et al. [5] were selected. Errors accounted for 3.9% of all responses. The model was tested as before, with four runs to simulate 4 "participants". As Figure 2 shows, the model developed sensitivity to large morphemic units, and performs better when tested with morphologically complex words than with control words.

4.2. *Neighborhood effect*

The study conducted by Arduino and Burani [2] provides helpful insights on the ability that readers of a shallow orthography as Italian have to discover and make efficient use of multiple grain sizes, larger than the single letter or bigram. In their study, the authors show that nonwords which share a large cohort of lexical neighbors are named faster than nonwords with a small cohort of neighbors, irrespective of the frequency of these words [2]. The effect has been ascribed to the supposed interaction between a lexical mechanism and a nonlexical one in reading these nonwords, with the lexical route boosting reaction times for nonwords that share many lexical neighbors, but not for nonwords with few neighbors. A different view on this effect is adopted by distributed approaches to reading, which assumes the reading system to be inherently fully interactive, with no partitions or separate modules for words and nonwords.

In order to explore the sensitivity of the model to this subtle effect, the 60 bisyllabic nonwords from Arduino and Burani [2] were selected. Half of these nonwords (30) have a large neighborhood size (Nsize) (as the nonword *bento*, which has many lexical neighbors that vary only by the first letter, i.e. *vento*, *sento*, *cento*, *lento*, *pento* etc.), while half (30) had a small Nsize (the nonword *biore*, which only has the word *fiore* as neighbor). The model was tested as before, with 4 runs to simulate 4 "participants", but failed to show any sensitivity to neighborhood size.

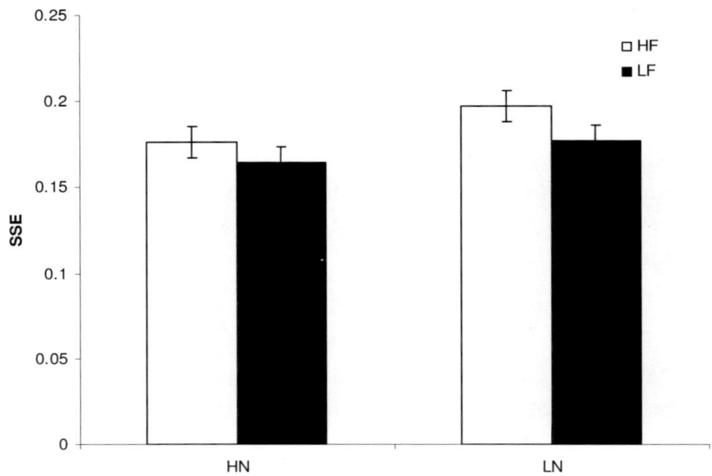

Figure 3: Mean SSE for high (HN) and low (LN) density neighbors nonwords as a function of frequency of the original words (HF: high frequency and LF: low frequency).

The lack of an Nsize effect could be ascribed to the necessity that the model has to be exposed to the corpus of words for a reasonable amount of repetitions in order to capture subtle effects such as the Nsize effect for a specific dataset of nonwords. The model was further retrained for 2 Million word presentation with random initial weights, and the test was rerun with the same testing words. The retrained model showed a marginally significant effect of neighborhood size, with nonwords sharing a large cohort of neighbors having lower SSE than nonwords sharing a small cohort of neighbors, as Figure 3 shows.

5. Discussion

This paper presented a connectionist PDP model of reading for Italian. The model inherits all the properties of standard distributed models of reading and extends the reach of this class of architectures to a transparent orthography and to a large corpus of polysyllabic words. Despite the extreme regularity of the mapping between Italian orthography and phonology, the model managed to show sensitivity to grain sizes larger than the single unigram or bigram and to capture subtle effects involving the use of these orthographic and phonological clusters, effects that have been documented in several behavioral studies, at the lexical (lexical neighborhood) and sublexical (morphological) level. The model, in line with classic PDP architectures, does so with no explicit localist representation of these large grain sizes (lexical and/or morphological units) and with no recourse to a lookup mechanism, as employed in dual route models of reading [7]. More importantly the model does not implement a set of grapheme to phoneme conversion rules [7], but it learns the relationships in the mapping during training, relationships that go beyond the single letter-phoneme mapping and encompass a wide range of grain sizes. Parallel distributed approaches to reading have proven a powerful tool to explore the reading system not just for deep orthographies, but for transparent orthographies as well.

Acknowledgments

This work was supported by an EU Sixth Framework Marie Curie Research Training Network Program in Language and Brain: http://www.ynic.york.ac.uk/rtn-lab. We are indebted to Jangfeng Yang for invaluable help provided during the development of the model.

References

1. Ans, B., Carbonnel, S., & Valdois, S., *Psychological Review*, **105** (1998).
2. Arduino, L.S., & Burani, C., *Journal of Psycholinguistic Research, 33* (2004).
3. Balota, D.A, Cortese, M.J., Sergent-Marshall, S.D., Spieler, D.H., & Yap, M., *Journal of Experimental Psychology: General*, **133**, 2 (2004).
4. Bertinetto, P.M., Burani, C., Laudanna, A., Marconi, L., Ratti, D., Rolando, C., & Thornton, A.M., *Corpus e Lessico di frequenza dell'italiano scritto (CoLFIS)* [lexical database] (2005).
5. Burani, C., Marcolini, S., De Luca, & Zoccolotti, P. Cognition, **108**, 1 (2008).
6. Canepari, L. *Italiano standard e pronounce regionali*, Padova, Cleup, (1980).
7. Coltheart, M., Rastle, K., Perry, C., Langdon, R., & Ziegler, J., *Psychological Review*, **108** (2001).
8. De Mauro, *Il Dizionario della Lingua Italiana*, Paravia (2000).
9. Frost, R., Katz, L., & Bentin, S., *Journal of Experimental Psychology: Human Perception and Performance*, **13** (1987).
10. Harm, M.W., & Seidenberg, M.S., *Psychological Review*, **106** (1999).
11. Harm, M.W., & Seidenberg, M.S., *Psychological Review*, **111** (2004).
12. Hutzler, F., Ziegler, J.C., Perry, C., Wimmer, H., & Zorzi, M., *Cognition*, **91**, 3 (2004).
13. Pagliuca, G., & Monaghan, P., *Proceedings of the Thirtieth Annual Conference of the Cognitive Science Society*. Mahwah, NJ: Lawrence Erlbaum (2008).
14. Pagliuca, G., Arduino, L.S., Barca, L., & Burani, C., *Language and Cognitive Processes*, **23**, (2008).
15. Plaut, D.C., McClelland, J.L., Seidenberg, M.S., & Patterson, K.E., *Psychological Review*, **103** (1996).
16. Seidenberg, M.S., & McClelland, J.L., *Psychological Review*, **96** (1989).
17. Thornton, A.M., Iacobini, C., & Burani, C., *BDVDB. Una base di dati per il vocabolario di base della lingua italiana* (*Seconda Edizione riveduta e ampliata*). Roma: Bulzoni (1997).
18. Ziegler, J., & Goswami, U., *Psychological Bulletin*, **131**, 1 (2005).

SIMULATING GERMAN VERB INFLECTION WITH A CONSTRUCTIVIST NEURAL NETWORK*

NICOLAS RUH
GERT WESTERMANN

Oxford Brookes University, Department of Psychology
Gipsy Lane, Oxford OX3 0BP

Taking seriously neurobiological and psychological evidence on the constructivist, experience dependent nature of brain development, we present a constructivist neural network model which builds its architecture in response to the task of learning German (past participle) inflection. Our model captures developmental profiles, as well as healthy and impaired adult performance, because two complementary processing pathways develop from the interaction of the constructivist learning mechanism and the distributional properties of the inflectional paradigm. Instead of a regular/irregular dichotomy it suggests an emergent dissociation between verbs that are easy or hard to learn, thus obviating the need for in-built assumptions such as verb type specific processing mechanisms or knowledge of grammatical class. We focus on the German participle in order to demonstrate that the performance of the model, though based on associative learning mechanisms, does not depend on the existence of a dominant 'default' class, as has been claimed by proponents of the dual-mechanism camp within the continuing past tense debate.

1. Introduction

The long standing, yet unresolved past tense debate bears a significance far outstretching its domain because it is exemplary of different theories of language acquisition and cognition in general.

Symbolic approaches postulate the psychological reality of transformation rules and stored exceptions from these rules, thus resulting in a dual-route account (e.g., [1]) of past tense formation where individual verbs are either inflected through application of the 'default' rule or retrieved through lexical look-up in an associative memory. U-shaped learning profiles, i.e., the observation that children often go through a period of temporarily producing incorrect, usually overgeneralized past tense forms of verbs that were previously inflected correctly (e.g., [2]), are seen as the result of the child's discovery of the default rule which, initially, is applied too widely. Correct performance is then

*This research was supported by ESRC grant Res-061-23-0129 to Gert Westermann

reached through a process of consolidation of the lexical entries for the exceptional (irregular) cases. This approach, however, struggles to explain why the onset of the overregularization phase is often gradual and why both correct and incorrect forms of individual verbs are often used intermittently for some period of time. Cases of irregularization, though infrequent, are also problematic for this theory. From a more general point of view it can be argued that the lack of a computational implementation of the symbolic, dual-mechanism theory hinders a rigorous evaluation of this approach.

Conversely, connectionist approaches (see [3]) have maintained that a single associative processing mechanism is responsible for the production of all exemplars. In this view, U-shaped learning profiles emerge because rote learning can lead to an initial correct performance while the vocabulary is small and processing resources are ample [4]. The rapidly expanding vocabulary then leads to increased competition for the limited resources until, eventually, a weight configuration is found that captures the underlying regularities and thus suits all verbs. These models have been criticized because their exhibiting a U-shaped learning profile crucially depends on the progressive expansion of the training set during the learning process. This is problematic because, arguably, a growing vocabulary should be an attribute of the child rather than the child's linguistic environment.

Another area of controversy is concerned with evidence from brain imaging studies that appear to reveal differences in the localization of processes relating to regular and irregular inflections (e.g., [5]). Similarly, verb type specific impairments have been observed in acquired (e.g., [6]) and developmental (e.g., [7]) neurological disorders. These studies imply that the various brain structures may be more or less involved in the processing of different verbs. Note, however, that the causal attribution of such dissociations to a verb's grammatical class is controversial ([8]).

These findings seem to support the notion of distinct processing pathways and are difficult to reconcile with homogeneous connectionist models. However, previous work on English past tense formation [9, 10] demonstrated the potential of constructivist neural network (CNN) models as an integral account of the above mentioned phenomena. CNN models adopt a decidedly developmental perspective by progressively allocating processing resources in response to experience with a task. This leads to progressive modularization in a single mechanism system where partial functional and structural dissociations emerge from distributional factors in the input-output mapping.

Previous connectionist models have also been criticized because, allegedly, their success crucially depends on a confound within the English inflection paradigm, namely the fact that the regular or 'default' case is also by far the most frequent one [11, 12]. German past participle formation has been suggested as a testing case because regular and irregular verbs are roughly equally frequent. In parallel to English, verb type specific dissociations have also been found in a broad range of studies for German [13].

In response to this challenge, we apply our CNN model to German verb inflection. It is demonstrated that the model captures a range of empirical phenomena (overgeneralization, U-shaped learning, generalization to pseudo-verbs) during the process of acquiring an adult level of performance. Moreover, we show that the constructivist growth process results in an emerging (partial) modularity where lesioning of different pathways within the network can lead to selective impairment of regular or irregular verbs.

1.1. *Past participle formation in German*

German past participles are formed with a phonologically conditioned prefix ge-, a verb stem and a suffix (-t or –n). In regular participles, an unchanged stem is suffixed with -t (1a-b), while irregular participles often show a modification of the stem vowel and usually take the ending -en (1c). Whether a verb is regular or irregular cannot be predicted from its phonological form (see Table 1).

Table 1: Past participle formation in German.

	Infinitive	Participle	Gloss
(1a)	tanz-en	ge-tanz-t	'dance'
(1b)	blink-en	ge-blink-t	'flash'
(1c)	trink-en	ge-trunk-en	'drink'

1.2. *Constructivist cognitive development*

The constructivist approach is based on recent empirical evidence which has demonstrated that brain development is dependent, to some extent, on the specific tasks that are processed [14-16]. From a functional point of view this suggests that activity dependent architectural modifications (constructive and regressive events) can alleviate the problem of finding a system whose structural properties are optimally geared towards the processing of the types of stimuli that are frequently encountered in a specific task. Learning theoretical work [17] has shown that incorporating activity dependent structural modification can enhance learning because it has the effect of optimizing the hypotheses space considered by the learning system. Extending the notion of learning and development in neural network models to include architectural properties can thus overcome many problems that are associated with standard, fixed-architecture systems.

In the light of these arguments we hold that plausible cognitive models should likewise be constructivist in the sense that they adapt their architecture in task dependent manner, essentially by allocating additional processing resources when and where they are needed.

1.3. *The Constructivist neural network model*

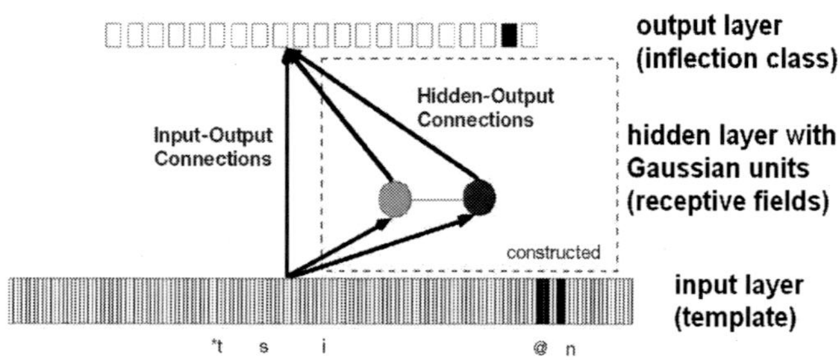

Figure 1: Initial architecture of the CNN. Arrows indicate full forward connectivity.

The CNN model starts out with a minimal architecture (see Figure 1) with predominantly direct connections between input and output. Hidden layer units have a Gaussian activation function, thus forming receptive fields (rf) for regions of the space spanned by the input vectors. A hidden unit will become maximally activated if its position (= the center of its rf) coincides closely with the feature values of the current input. For each input pattern, only the most active hidden unit contributes to the model's output. Additionally, this unit's connections from the input layer are adjusted slightly (learning rate = 0.001) so that the rf moves a fraction towards the position of the current input. All other connections in the model are adjusted via gradient descent (quickprop with a learning rate of 0.02 after each epoch).

The model attempts to learn the task with the given architecture until performance ceases to improve. When the global error has stagnated for at least five consecutive epochs, a new hidden unit is inserted. To comply with the idea of allocating additional processing resources where they are most needed, the novel unit is placed next to the rf whose activation previously caused the highest global error. Problematic areas in the input space thus become more densely populated with receptive fields. Hidden units that never (within one epoch) contribute to processing are pruned.

Using this constructivist training regime, the CNN starts out with just two units in the hidden layer, each being responsible for roughly half of the input space. As training progresses, more structural resources are inserted until the coverage of crucial areas of the input space is sufficient to solve the task. Because the network always attempts to find the optimal solution with a given architecture, it will be forced to constantly reorganize itself as it develops over the course of acquiring the task.

2. Simulations

The training data for the model was extracted from the German part of the CELEX database [18]. Prefixed forms of the same verb were combined into one simplex type with an accumulated frequency count. Entries with ambiguous past participle forms (including homophones) and verbs whose stem had more than three syllables or an accumulated frequency below 3 in 6 million were excluded. This resulted in a basic corpus of 967 verb types and 47523 tokens.

In order to keep computation times within limits and to simulate individual differences with regard to the linguistic environment, the training corpus of an individual simulation run was constructed by randomly extracting 20000 tokens from this basic corpus. Table 2 shows the statistics of a typical training set.

Table 2: Distribution of regular and irregular verbs.

	types	tokens
regular verbs	686 (81.5%)	11113 (55.6%)
Irregular verbs	155 (18.5%)	8887 (44.4%)
total	841	20000

For the input to the model, each phoneme was translated into a binary phonetic feature vector, representing features such as *high*, *low*, *rounded*, and *frontal* for vowels (6 bits) and *coronal*, *nasal*, *voiced* for consonants (7 bits). This representation was entered into a three-syllabic template of the form XCCCVCCC for each syllable (X = stress (one bit); V = vowel; C = consonant), resulting in a 147 bit binary input vector. Distributed representations for phonemes enable the model to represent degrees of phonological similarity between words; this property is relevant to the model's ability to generalize.

For the model's output (localist coding), verbs were classified according to how their past participle is formed, resulting in 21 inflectional classes. The first class represented the regular case (suffix –t, no stem change), the remaining 20 irregular classes accommodated all possible stem changes and suffixations (-t or –n). The main objective of this classification was to guarantee an unambiguous mapping of a stem to its past participle, given the inflectional class.

Training was non-incremental: the whole training set of 20,000 stem/past-participle-class pairs was presented in random order at each epoch. Hidden units were inserted depending on the learning progress (see previous section), and the network's performance on all verb types was tested at intervals of 10 epochs. Training was terminated when classification performance was 100% correct over five consecutive tests. Classification was deemed to be correct when the activation of the output unit standing for the correct class, but no other output, was higher than 0.7.

3. Results

Results are based on ten simulation runs with randomly initialized weights (in the range of +/- 0.1).

3.1. *Learning*

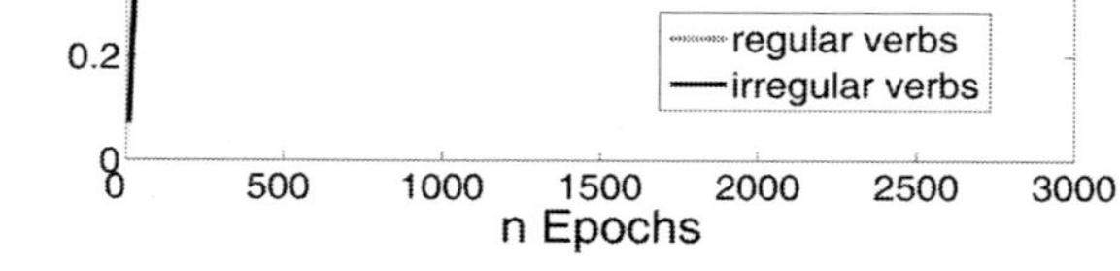

Figure 2: Mean performance during training (10 runs, dotted lines indicate standard deviations).

All ten networks reached the given performance criterion within 3000 epochs (mean = 2776.7, std = 103.9). By this time, the growing hidden layer contained on average 394.1 (std = 14.9) units. As shown in Figure 2, learning was stable and regular verbs tended to be classified correctly earlier than irregular verbs.

3.2. *Overgeneralization and U-shaped learning*

Figure 3 displays the proportion of verb types that were overgeneralized although they had been classified correctly at an earlier point in training. The model's performance shows a good fit with respect to the empirical data: reported overgeneralization rates during the acquisition of German verb inflection [19, 20] are in the range of 5-10%, 5-15% of which are incorrectly inflected regular verbs (irregularizations).

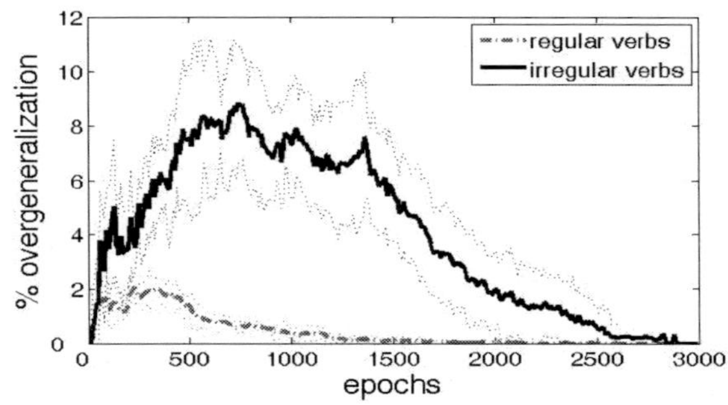

Figure 3: Mean overgeneralization error (and std) for the 10 networks during training.

In order to quantify this effect at a more detailed level we analyzed the network's performance on a subset of verbs that have been used in a recent empirical study with 5-7 and 11-12 year old children [21]. The 60 verbs used in this study were divided into 4 conditions by the factors 'verb type' (regular/irregular) and 'frequency' (high/low). The children were presented with a verb stem in a sentential context and had to produce the corresponding participle form.

Table 3: Mean percentage of suffixation errors (standard deviations in parentheses) of two age groups in German verb inflection, adapted from Clahsen et al. [21].

verb type	5-7 year olds	11-12 year olds
irregular high	6.3% (9.0)	0.3% (1.5)
irregular low	27.4% (15.8)	8.6% (9.4)
regular high	1.8% (3.8)	1.1% (2.6)
regular low	1.4% (2.8)	0.7% (2.1)

Comparison of children's performance (see Table 3) with the behavior of the model on the same 60 words (see Figure 4) yields a good qualitative and quantitative match with. Similar to the younger children, networks in the early stages of training have most problems with low frequency irregular verbs and, to a lesser extent, high frequency irregulars. Intermediate stages then see a drastic reduction in the error rates for irregular verbs, down to negligible with respect to high frequency items.

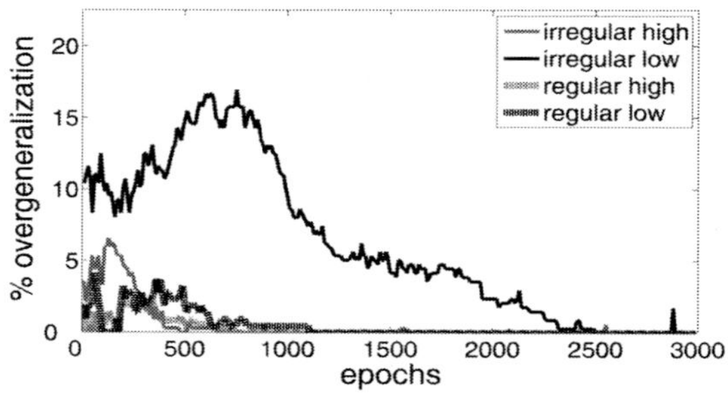

Figure 4: Mean overgeneralization rate of 10 networks for the four conditions in the Clahsen et al. [21] corpus.

A further result corresponding to child language data is concerned with the protection from overregularization by similar sounding irregulars: the four irregular verbs *rennen*, *brennen*, *nennen*, and *kennen*, for example, were hardly ever overregularized (0.7%) whereas equally frequent irregulars like *dürfen* (11.7%) or *mögen* (16.4%) were more likely to be transiently misclassified.

The CNN model was successful in capturing several phenomena related to U-shaped learning in verb inflection at a considerable level of detail. Note that this realistic developmental profile emerged in the absence of an external manipulation of vocabulary size [4, 22] or an essentially arbitrary parameter to control how often an exception verb has to be seen in order to be memorized [23, 24].

3.3. *Generalization to novel verbs*

The models were tested on a set of 13 pseudo-verbs (adapted from [11]) that were either constructed as rhyming with existing regular (3 items) or irregular verbs (3 items), or not phonologically related to any existing verb (7 items). While the overall ratio of regularizations (see Figure 5) is close to the rate observed in children (69-95%), the study by Clahsen & Weyerts [11] did not find a reduced tendency to regularize for the irregulars. Such an effect, however, was reported in a more extensive study with English pseudo-verbs [25] where the regularization rate for pseudo-irregulars was close to 50%, as opposed to

~90% for pseudo-regular verbs. This study also yielded a frequency effect for pseudo-irregular, but not for pseudo-regular verbs. Although the CNN model exhibits a similar tendency, the empirical basis (three verbs per group) with regard to German pseudo-verbs is insufficient to reliably address this issue.

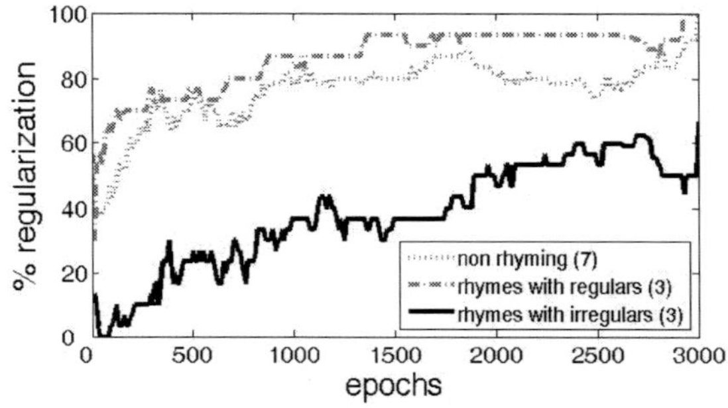

Figure 5: Mean regularization ratio of the 10 networks.

3.4. *Emergent modularity*

According to the dual-mechanism view, irregular forms are retrieved from associative memory whereas regular forms rely on the application of a mental rule. Observation of functional dissociations between verb classes in psycholinguistic experiments and in neurological disorders has been taken to support the notion of two distinct and generic pathways (e.g., [1]). In the CNN model, however, a partial functional dissociation between regular and irregular verbs emerges as a direct result of the constructivist learning process. This can be demonstrated by selectively lesioning the two pathways within the trained network (see Figure 6).

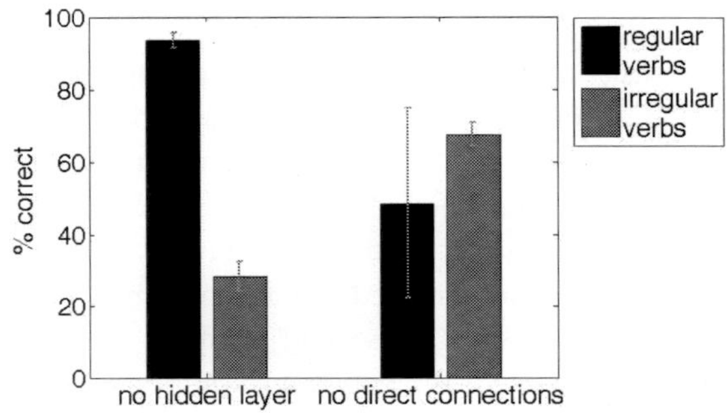

Figure 6: Performance of the lesioned networks.

Apart from demonstrating that the irregular verbs have come to rely more on the processing resources provided by the hidden layer, these findings are also reminiscent of similar double dissociations that have been observed in English patients (e.g., [26]). The model's account of German neurological data is reported elsewhere [27] in more detail.

4. Discussion

The simulations described in this paper demonstrate that constructivist neural networks can capture a host of phenomena related to the acquisition, processing and breakdown of German verb inflection. The ability of the CNN to develop its structure in response to the specifics of the learning task not only allowed it to allocate more structure to the difficult-to-learn irregular verbs, but also led to U-shaped learning curves and to emergent functional dissociations between regular and irregular verbs. Importantly, this (partial) functional modularity was not pre-specified but developed from the interaction of the constructivist approach and the distributional properties of the inflection paradigm.

The model's limited processing capacities at the start of training were insufficient to produce those verbs that are disadvantaged with regard to distributional factors (such as, e.g., neighborhood composition or frequency). With ongoing training, however, additional resources are inserted in close to stimuli that produced poor performance, thus shifting the responsibility for the production of those stimuli towards the hidden layer. This ongoing process of internal reorganization that chiefly affects distributionally disfavored verbs (many of which are irregular) is also responsible for those items' increased vulnerability to transient overgeneralization. It is this entanglement of processing and task structure which causes the model to closely follow the developmental profile observed in children and to reflect, in its final architecture, properties that can be found in normal and impaired adults. Together with the theoretical arguments for constructivist learning, these results offer compelling evidence for the usefulness of constructivist models in the study of cognitive development.

In view of the ongoing past tense debate, our model advocates two main theoretical contributions. The first is to emphasize that the number of routes and the number of mechanisms must not necessarily coincide. Constructivist models are capable of developing distinct processing pathways on the basis of a single underlying mechanism, without the need of built-in domain specific knowledge, e.g., about grammatical class. The second point is to emphasize that the emergent functional and structural dissociations are only superficially aligned with the regular/irregular distinction. What really matters to the network – and possibly to the brain – is how easy or hard it is to process a specific stimulus. (see [8] for a similar perspective). Therefore, what we should be doing is to identify the distributional factors or combinations of factors that determine easiness.

References

1. Pinker, S. and M.T. Ullman, *Trends in Cognitive Sciences* **6**, 11 (2002).
2. Marcus, G.F., S. Pinker, M. Ullman, M. Hollander, T.J. Rosen, and F. Xu, *Monographs of the Society for Research in Child Development* **57**, 4 (1992).
3. McClelland, J.L. and K. Patterson, *Trends in Cognitive Sciences* **6**, 11 (2002).
4. Plunkett, K. and P. Juola, *Cognitive Science* **23**, 4 (1999).
5. Beretta, A., C. Campbell, T.H. Carr, J. Huang, L.M. Schmitt, K. Christianson, and Y. Cao, *Brain and Language* **85** (2003).
6. Patterson, K., M.A. Lambon Ralph, J.R. Hodgesa, and J.L. McClelland, *Neuropsychologia* **39** (2001).
7. van der Lely, H.K.J. and M.T. Ullman, *Language and Cognitive Processes* **16**, 2-3 (2001).
8. Seidenberg, M.S. and A. Arnoldussen, *Brain and Language* **85**, 3 (2003).
9. Westermann, G., *Emergent modularity and U-shaped learning in a constructivist neural network learning the English past tense*, in *Proceedings of the Twentieth Annual Conference of the Cognitive Science Society*, ed. M.A. Gernsbacher and S.J. Derry (1998).
10. Westermann, G., *Constructivist Neural Network Models of Cognitive Development. PhD Thesis*. Division of Informatics, University of Edinburgh (2000).
11. Clahsen, H. and H. Weyerts, *Linguistische Berichte* **154** (1994).
12. Marcus, G.F., *Cognition* **56** (1995).
13. Clahsen, H., *Behavioral and Brain Sciences* **22** (1999).
14. Mareschal, D., M.H. Johnson, S. Sirois, M.W. Spratling, M. Thomas, and G. Westermann, *Neuroconstructivism: How the Brain Constructs Cognition* (Oxford University Press, 2007).
15. Quartz, S.R. and T.J. Sejnowski, *Behavioral and Brain Sciences* **20**, 4 (1997).
16. Westermann, G., D. Mareschal, M.H. Johnson, S. Sirois, M. Spratling, and M. Thomas, *Developmental Science* **10**, 1 (submitted).
17. Quartz, S.R., *Cognition* **48** (1993).
18. Baayen, H., R. Piepenbrock, and H. van Rijn, *The CELEX Lexical Database* (1993).
19. Clahsen, H. and M. Rothweiler, *Yearbook of Morphology* (1993).

20. Weyerts, H., *Reguläre und irreguläre Flexion: Psycholinguistische und neurophysiologische Ergebnisse zu Erwerb, Verarbeitung und mentaler Repräsentation. PhD Thesis*. University of Düsseldorf (1997).
21. Clahsen, H., M. Hadler, and H. Weyerts, *Journal of Child Language* **31**, 3 (2004).
22. Rumelhart, D.E. and J.L. McClelland, *On learning the past tense of English verbs: implicit rules or parallel distributed processing?*, in *Parallel Distributed Processing: Explorations in the Microstructure of Cognition*, ed. J.L. McClelland, D. Rumelhart, and the PDP Research Group (MIT Press, 1986).
23. Ling, C.X. and M. Marinov, *Cognition* **49** (1993).
24. Ling, C.X., *Journal of Artificial Intelligence Research* **1** (1994).
25. Prasada, S. and S. Pinker, *Language and Cognitive Processes* **8** (1993).
26. Tyler, L.K., P. deMornay-Davies, R. Anokhina, C. Longworth, B. Randall, and W.D. Marslen-Wilson, *Journal of Cognitive Neuroscience* **14**, 1 (2002).
27. Penke, M. and G. Westermann, *Cortex* **42** (2006).

HOW MANY WORDS DO INFANTS KNOW, REALLY?

JULIEN MAYOR* and KIM PLUNKETT

Department of Experimental Psychology, University of Oxford,
South Parks Road, Oxford, OX1 3UD, United Kingdom
**E-mail: julien.mayor@psy.ox.ac.uk*

For the last twenty years, many researchers interested in language acquisition have quantified the receptive and productive vocabulary of infants using CDIs – checklists of words filled in by the caregiver. While it is generally accepted that the caregiver can reliably say whether the infant knows and/or produces a given word, we lack an estimate for words that are not listed on CDI. In this study, we provide a mathematical model providing a link between CDI reports and a more plausible estimate of vocabulary size. The model is constrained by statistical data collected from a population of infants and is validated on a longitudinal study comparing diary report with CDI measures.

1. Introduction

How many words does an infant know? Traditionally, this question has been answered by counting the number of different words an infant produces within a representative period of time. Diary methods and home-based recordings provide an estimate of what the infant knows and offer a rich account of vocabulary knowledge in infants. They are, however, time-consuming and expensive strategies for assessing individual vocabulary sizes. Moreover, infants learn new words every day, while they do not use all their lexicon every day. Such direct measures face a dilemma; short recordings lead to a sub-sampling of the real lexicon whereas longer recordings, over a period of many days mask new acquisitions within that period. A further limitation of these approaches is that they only provide a measure of productive vocabulary which may inadequately reflect an infant's total vocabulary knowledge. Infants may understand many words they do not say and they man say words they do not understand.

As an alternative to diary methods and home-based recordings, one can interrogate parents about their infant's vocabulary knowledge. Parents are useful judges of whether their infant comprehends and/or produces a given word and can be asked to fill in checklists of words likely to be known by their infant. This method provides a snapshot of the infant lexicon on the day the form is completed. In addition, it takes just several minutes for the caregiver to complete the list and so is an efficient and inexpensive mean of assessment.

Many researchers assessing the vocabulary size of infants now prefer this method and rely on Communicative Development Inventories (CDIs). A CDI consists of a list of the most frequent words encountered by infants. The caregiver is asked to indicate whether every word on the list is understood (comprehension) and/or produced (production) by the infant. A straightforward method of estimating the typical vocabulary size at a given age is to average the total number of words known by all infants. This simple process leads to an accurate estimate, provided that the caregiver filled in the CDI reliably[1,2] and that CDI includes a suitable range of words likely to be understood or produced by infants. Experimental validation of an infant's knowledge of items reported by the caregiver has provided further support for the accuracy of the instrument[1–3] though see[4] for an alternative perspective. In constructing CDIs, researchers have strived to include a representative sample of words that infants know at different ages. However, the CDI is not intended to be an exhaustive listing of all the words that any infant might know.

When vocabulary size reaches a significant proportion of the CDI listing, the likelihood that infants would know words that are not listed on the CDI increases dramatically: "Although the present index might approach the status of an atlas for the younger children, it becomes an increasingly smaller subset of vocabulary for older children" [5, p.40]. A simple vocabulary count based on a CDI is therefore unlikely to be an accurate estimate for older infants In order to test the validity of the MacArthur-Bates CDI,[5] Robinson et al. (1999) compared the CDI-based productive vocabulary estimate with an exhaustive diary report based on data from a single child. The discrepancy increased dramatically with age, thereby confirming Fenson et al. (2003)'s concerns. Such findings would appear to undermine the utility of the CDI in providing accurate estimates of the number of words an individual infant knows. In particular, the CDI leads to provide a systematic underestimate of infant vocabulary knowledge. The goal of this paper is to demonstrate that this underestimate can be quantified even when the reported vocabulary size is a substantial proportion of the CDI listing. We will show that it is possible to offer a more accurate estimate of vocabulary size given a particular level of performance on the CDI. This new estimate takes into account both the idiosyncracies of an infant's individual vocabulary as well as general omissions of common words from the CDI and aims at providing an estimate of the real vocabulary size of an infant, when her reported vocabulary reaches a substantial fraction of the CDI size.

2. Method

We present a simple procedure for estimating more accurately the vocabulary of infants from direct measures on the CDI. The straightforward method is to count the number of word on the CDI that each infant knows and compute the average vocabulary size over all infants of the same age. However, this method has the problem each infant is likely to know words that are not present on the CDI. Consequently, the estimated vocabulary size is the average of inaccurate individual word counts.

CDI forms are compiled so that it is possible to determine the probability that a given word w_i is known by infants at a given age; $p(w_i)$. A basic rearrangement of these calculations shows that the straightforward method for measuring vocabulary – the average of individual vocabulary sizes over all infants – is equivalent to computing the sum, over all words on the CDI, of the probabilities that they are known by an infant.

$$\mathrm{Voc}_{est} = \sum_{i=1}^{W} p(w_i) = \frac{1}{N}\sum_{j=1}^{N} \mathrm{voc(j)} \tag{1}$$

where W is the number of words on the CDI and voc(j) measures the vocabulary size of infant j. The advantage of this formulation is that individual terms in the summation – $p(w_i)$ – approach the "exact" value as the number of infants increases, assuming that the caregivers respond accurately. Any inaccuracy is now the outcome of having a calculation that runs over words on the CDI and not over all words in the language, i.e, for a word not included in the CDI we lack information regarding the probability that it is known by an infant. We can estimate the real vocabulary size in terms of the direct CDI measure, plus a term that corresponds to the underestimate. The underestimate is simply the sum of the probabilities for words that are not listed on the CDI:

$$\mathrm{Voc}_{real} = \mathrm{Voc}_{est} + \sum_{i=W+1}^{W_\infty} p(w_i) \tag{2}$$

with W_∞ being the total number of words in the given language. This calculation is correct provided we can have an accurate estimation of all words that have not been included in the CDI.

We distinguish two sources of underestimation of an infant's vocabulary size. First, individual infant's lexicons are only partly overlapping. For example, an infant whose parent is a mechanic is likely to possess an early knowledge about car related words, otherwise rare among other infants. Idiosyncratic words cannot be listed in a CDI, despite their contribution to overall lexicon size, because they would greatly inflate the size of CDIs and the time taken to complete the form. The second source of underestimation derives from frequent words in the language that are not listed in the CDI. CDIs have been built by listing popular words in the infant's vocabulary. However, it is unlikely that the list is a perfect tabulation of *the W* most frequent words. For example, even highly frequent words have been omitted from the MacArthur-Bates CDI [a]. On the assumption that infants learn highly frequent words before lower frequency words, the CDI would necessarily underestimate vocabulary size in proportion to the number of highly frequent words not included in the CDI. We describe in the next section how to evaluate both effects in order to provide an accurate description of the lexicon size based on MacArthur-Bates CDI reports.

2.1. *The First Correction and Second Correction: An overview*

One can sort words according to the proportion of infants that know the word, in descending order and then plot the probability that infants know a given word as a function of its rank. For example, a word that is know by a vast majority of infants ("daddy") will be ranked high on the list, and a word known by only a small fraction of infants will have a low rank. This probability distribution that a word is know to a given infant is a decreasing function where words of low probability occur in the tail of the distribution. Idiosyncratic words – the first correction – correspond to words that are only known to a small minority of infants. These are words that occur in the tail of the distribution. The size of this underestimate thereby corresponds to estimating the length of the tail. Commonly occurring words absent from the CDI – the second source of underestimation – change the shape of the probability distribution. Quantification of the length of the tail and estimation of the parameters for the correct shape of the probability distribution permits a more accurate estimate of an infant's vocabulary size.

[a]Bag, back, come, computer, digger, down, floor, gate, hole, lift, pigeon, ring, sea, tower, warm, wheel

2.2. *First Correction; Adding idiosyncratic words to the lexicon*

We choose to model the distribution of knowledge using a standard sigmoid function that describes the probability $p(w_i)$ that a word is known given its rank i among other words:

$$f(w_i) = 100(1 - \frac{1}{1 + e^{\frac{-(i-a)}{b}}}) \approx p(w_i) \quad (3)$$

This equation has only two free parameters, a and b. Therefore, finding an optimal value for the parameters is likely to be unique, and the algorithm for finding the solution fast and stable. It also reduces the risk of over-fitting the data, since the number of free parameters is much lower than the number of data points used to constrain the optimisation. Moreover, it provides an intuitive fit of the distribution of knowledge of the words: One expects to have values close to 100% for highly ranked words (very common words, known by everybody) to values closer to 0% for low ranked words, known to only a very small subset of the population. The first free parameter – a – determines overall vocabulary size. More precisely, a determines the location of the rank order of words that are known to 50% of the infants. The second free parameter – b – determines the overlap of word knowledge across the population of infants. A very low value for b corresponds to a steep probability distribution whereas a high value yields a shallow distribution. Shallow distributions correspond to low overlap of individual vocabularies whereas low values correspond to high overlap. This sigmoidal function possesses another useful property: When the number of words in the language is large and far beyond the sample words included in the CDI, the sum over all words of the function becomes a simple expression of parameters a and b:

$$\text{Voc}_{Corr1} = b \cdot ln(1 + e^{a/b}) \quad (4)$$

where ln is the natural logarithm. Quantification of a and b allows us to determine the value of the first correction.

2.3. *Second Correction: The role of frequent words missing from the CDI*

We assume that the CDI contains the most frequent words known to infants. However, the probability that the CDI lacks a particular word increases with decreasing rank. This is because experienced researchers can reliably list the most common words in the infant's lexicon but will be more prone to error as the word list expands to include less common words. In other words, the more items an infant is reported to understand on the CDI, the greater is the number of potential missing items from the vocabulary estimate. The second underestimate is therefore directly related to the number of words that an infant is reported to know. The fraction of omitted words can be written as:

$$f_{omission} = \alpha \mathrm{Voc}_{Corr1} \tag{5}$$

The only way to quantify this underestimate is by direct comparison with exhaustive word lists that individual infants know such as that reported by.[6]

3. Results

The validity of the procedure for the first correction is tested by applying it to the Lex2005 database,[7] based on the American MacArthur-Bates CDI,[5] for both production (Words and Sentences) and comprehension (Words and Gestures). Overall, results suggest that the underestimation due to the absence of idiosyncratic words on the CDI increases with age, while the degree of overlap between individual vocabularies remains relatively constant. A simple analytical prediction of the underestimation when vocabulary size reaches a significant proportion of the CDI size is presented. A strong, non-linear, increase of estimated vocabulary size is predicted as the measured vocabulary size becomes large with respect to the CDI.

We investigate the impact of the absence of frequent words in the CDI on the estimated vocabulary size. This second correction is applied to production data on the McArthur-Bates CDI and the number of missing words is estimated, based on a comparison of a diary count and CDI count for a single case study.[6] The addition of these two corrections enables us to predict a more accurate estimate of vocabulary size for individual infants as well as typical mean vocabulary sizes from 8 to 18 months of age in comprehension and from 18 to 30 months of age in production.

3.1. *First Correction: Underestimation due to the absence of idiosyncratic words*

The method is applied for both production (16 months to 30 months old) and comprehension (8 months to 18 month olds), based on the MacArthur-Bates CDI.[7] For each age group, words are sorted in descending order from those that are known by most infants to the least known words. A regression is applied to identify the parameters a and b that minimise the squared error between the data and the model. All fits of the CDI data explain at least 80% of the variance, indicating that a regression using Equation 3 is applicable. The vocabulary size as predicted by the model is obtained by computing Equation 4 with the measured parameters a and b. Figure 1(a) depicts a comparison of the vocabulary in comprehension from the CDI data and from the model (top panel). The model (solid line) predicts a

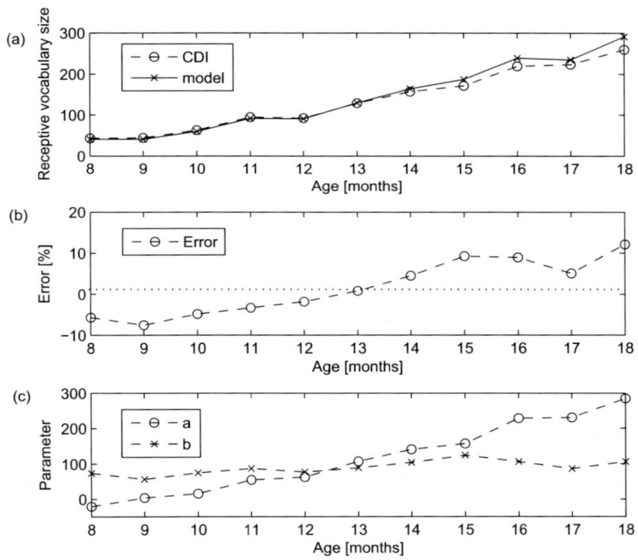

Fig. 1. Comprehension. (a) comparison of vocabulary estimates from the CDI and from the model, (b) discrepancy between the two estimate, (c) evolution of the two free parameters with age.

higher vocabulary size for older age groups (14 months and older) than direct CDI measures (dashed line). The model also indicates a smaller vocabulary size than the direct estimate for younger age groups (up to about 11 months). The discrepancy is plotted in Figure 1(b). The negative error at 8-11 months may be due to over-reporting from the caregiver, or to an unsuitable equation to describe these early words or proto-words (in ranked order; mommy, daddy, bye, peekaboo, bottle, no, hi). Note that this source of error is not itself a measure of idiosyncratic words in the infant vocabulary, but an indirect effect of estimating the parameters a and b which quantify the idiosyncratic contribution. As expected, the direct CDI measure underestimates the vocabulary size as age increases. At 15–18 months of age, the model suggests that the CDI underestimates vocabulary size by the order of 8–10%. However, for the ages ranging from 11–13 months, the estimate based on a direct count is reliable.

Both parameters a and b are plotted for the different age groups in Figure 1(c). The decomposition of the vocabulary curve into two parameters allows us to disentangle the contribution to overall vocabulary growth, a, and of overlap of vocabulary knowledge across infants, b. Figure 1(c) shows that parameter a mirrors the overall vocabulary growth, approximating the typical vocabulary size of the infants. Parameter b shows that the amount of overlap across infants in the vocabulary space stays relatively constant and that the number of "unique" idiosyncratic words stays approximately constant over the age range under consideration.

The same procedure has applied to the productive vocabulary of toddlers, from 16 months to 30 months of age, using the MacArthur-Bates CDI in English (not shown, due to the limited space). The model predicts a higher vocabulary size than a direct count from the age of 19 months of age, with a discrepancy that increases with age. From about 19 months of age, the underestimate of vocabulary size increases steadily to reach about 18% at 30 months of age. The gradual increase with age suggests that the underestimate of productive vocabulary based on a direct count will be even greater for older toddlers. Parameters a and b can also be computed for productive vocabulary and parameter b remains essentially constant after 19 months of age, indicating that shared productive vocabulary does not change over time.

Having estimated the parameters a and b from the CDI population data, we can estimate the size of a individual infant's vocabulary given a CDI score. We have established that for both receptive and productive vocabulary, there is an increase in the magnitude of underestimation as the total vocabulary increases. The absolute underestimate is determined by the overall size of the CDI and the parameters a and b that we have used to fit group scores to the direct measure of the CDI.

$$\text{Absolute underestimate} = \sum_{W+1}^{W_\infty} f(w_i) = b \cdot ln(1 + e^{\frac{a-W}{b}}) \qquad (6)$$

where W is the overall size of the CDI and $f(w_i)$ is the model's estimate that an infant knows the words w_i given the word ranking i.

We have seen that the overlap of knowledge is essentially constant for older age groups. Therefore, we assume that the magnitude of the underestimation can be calculated using the same value of parameter b for the oldest age groups. Equation 6 predicts the magnitude of the error as the overall vocabulary becomes a substantial proportion of the CDI size W.

3.2. *Second Correction: Evaluation of the role of omission of frequent words on CDIs*

We have assumed so far that the CDI is "perfect", in the sense that *all* the W most frequent words are present on the CDI. Another source of underestimation is the omission of words that should be listed on the CDI that have been left out of the selection of the words known by most infants. The omission of such words may also have an impact on the estimate of parameters a and b, because it changes the shape of the probability distribution, thereby leading to a biased estimate of the contribution of the tail of the distribution of word knowledge to the overall vocabulary. In order to disentangle the impact of the absence of frequent words from the contribution of idiosyncratic words, we randomly deleted a percentage of words on the CDI and compared the direct vocabulary count with the model estimate. If the omission of a fraction of words on the CDI has the same impact on the direct count and the model estimate, this would indicate that missing frequent words do not induce complex biases when estimating the tail of the distribution of word knowledge. In a separate simulation (not shown for space constraints), we showed that both effects do not interfere with each other.

The linearity of the impact of omitting frequent words on the CDI is important. It implies that the two effects – absence of idiosyncratic words and omission of frequent words on the CDI – don't interfere with each other, at least to a first approximation. Consequently, the overall procedure for estimating the correct vocabulary size for infants can be decomposed into two parts. First, based on the CDI, one can estimate the parameters a and b, defining respectively the overall vocabulary size and the overlap of vocabulary knowledge across the population of infants with Equation 3. We can then use Equation 4 to provide the estimated vocabulary size of the infants – Voc_{Corr1} – including the contribution of idiosyncratic words, not listed on the CDI. Finally, an estimate of the fraction of words that should be on the CDI (i.e., among the W most known words) is used to increment the total vocabulary by the same *fraction* rather than the absolute number of words missing from the CDI: $\text{Voc} = \text{Voc}_{Corr1}(1 + f_{omission})$

As mentioned earlier, the fraction of words missing on the CDI is likely to be smaller amongst the most frequent words, where an exhaustive list of well-known words can be established relatively easily, compared to less frequent items, where listing all the better-known words is a difficult task. Therefore, we assume that the fraction of missing words increases linearly with the lexicon size, according to Equation 5. An exhaustive comparison of productive vocabulary based on a detailed diary report with a CDI-based estimation is presented in Robinson & Mervis (1999). They reported the vocabulary production of one male child from about 10 months of age to 2 years of age and identified, on a monthly basis, the total number of different words produced and counted how many of these words were listed on the MacArthur-Bates CDI. As predicted, the underestimation (the words produced that are not on the CDI) increased with vocabulary size. This comparison allows us to constrain the free parameter α of Equation 5 of the second correction by fitting the fully corrected curve to the data provided by Robinson & Mervis.

Note that the first correction for the absence of idiosyncratic words is a mathematical property of computing a definite integral of a sigmoidal curve, and is defined by the measured overlap of vocabulary knowledge and by the size of the CDI form. With this first correction, the shape of the corrected vocabulary size based on direct measurement is defined. The fit to Robinson & Mervis' data is a linear transformation of the first correction. The strong non-linearity predicted by the model derives from the first correction introduced by idiosyncratic words. The omission of frequent words on the CDI serves only to modulate this non-linearity.

Figure 2 depicts corrected vocabulary sizes based on measured productive vocabulary scores, from several different data sources. The triangles correspond to the individual corrections based on the MacArthur-Bates CDI (each triangle corresponds to a different age group with a slightly different overlap parameter b) whereas the dashed line corresponds to the first analytical correction for the role of idiosyncratic words in individual lexicons (only one parameter b for all age groups). The non-linearity of estimated vocabulary size (first correction) based on the number of words reported on the CDI is already apparent. The empty circles are based on the data reported by Robinson & Mervis (1999), where they compared the lexicon size of an infant based on dairy report to the lexicon size as measured by the CDI. The solid line corresponds to the prediction of vocabulary size based on the fully-corrected model. The fit to the Robinson & Mervis (1999) data confirms the strong non-linearity of underestimation as the number of words in the lexicon increases. This clear agreement between experimental data and the model suggests that the two corrections account for the increasing underestimation of the lexicon as the number of words reported on the CDI increases.

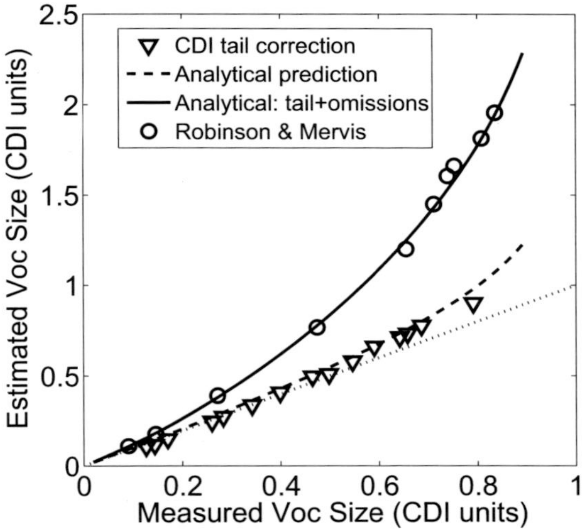

Fig. 2. Estimated productive vocabulary size as a function of measured vocabulary, according to the first correction (triangles pointing downwards and dashed line for the analytical prediction) and both corrections (solid line). For comparison, the comparison of diary data with CDI data from Robinson & Mervis (1999) is shown (○). See text for further details.

4. Discussion

We have proposed a mathematical model for estimating the vocabulary size of infants given their CDI scores. Two corrections are applied to the raw CDI measurements: First, the number of idiosyncratic words is estimated via a measure of the overlap of individual vocabularies in the infant population. Second, an estimation of the number of omitted words on the CDI is constrained by a comparison of dairy reports and direct CDI counts.

The model is applied to the MacArthur-Bates CDI database. The model suggests that, as predicted by its creators, the underestimation of vocabulary size increases with the number of words known on the CDI. Moreover, the magnitude of the underestimation is highly non-linear; for small vocabularies the straight CDI count is relatively accurate whereas when infants know 90% of the words on the CDI, they are likely to know about three times as many words.

This non-linearity has important implications. For example, CDIs are a widely used tool for diagnosing language delays. Whereas criteria for identifying delays are not absolute, we advocate against their use based on the raw CDI scores. For example, imagine that a whole data-set consists of just three infants; infant A is reported to know one word on the CDI, infant B six words and infant C nine words. A diagnostic based on the raw data would suggest infant B knows about 10% more words (6.0) than an average infant (5.3). However, after a non-linear transformation, this result does not hold. If, as an example, actual vocabulary sizes are the square of direct CDI scores, infant B would then know about 10% *less* words than an average infant (36 vs. 39.3).

The results can also offer additional information for those interested in characterising the vocabulary spurt often observed at the end of the second year of life. Many researchers attempt to identify an inflection point in the increasing vocabulary size. Often, direct measure from the CDI indicates a slowing-down in the speed of acquisition of new words after the spurt. Again, the non-linearity of the correction suggests more caution in the analysis of vocabulary sizes as the deceleration is likely to disappear after the vocabulary size correction.

Finally, the analysis of the amount of overlap between individual vocabularies suggests that the absolute number of idiosyncratic words does not change with age, over the considered age range. This observation may offer some important boundary conditions in the attempt to apply statistical models of lexicon growth such as preferential attachment[8] or preferential avoidance.[9]

References

1. P. Dale, E. Bates, S. Reznick and C. Morisset, *Journal of Child Language* **16**, 239 (1989).
2. P. Dale, *Journal of Speech, Language and Hearing Research* **34**, 565 (1991).
3. S. Styles and K. Plunkett, to appear in *Journal of Child Language.* (2009).
4. C. Houston-Price, E. Mather and E. Sakkalou, *Journal of Child Language* **34**, 701 (2007).
5. L. Fenson, P. Dale, S. Reznick, D. Thal, E. Bates, J. Hartung, S. Pethick and J. Reilly, *MacArthur communicative development inventories: User's guide and technical manual* (Singular Press, San Diego, 1993).
6. B. Robinson and C. Mervis, *Journal of Child Language* **26**, 177 (1999).
7. P. Dale and L. Fenson, *Behavior research methods, instruments & computers* **28**, 125 (1996).
8. M. Steyvers and J. Tenenbaum, *Cognitive Science* **29**, 41 (2005).
9. T. Hills, M. Maouene, J. Maouene, A. Sheya and L. Smith, Categorical Structure in Early Semantic Networks of Nouns, in *Proceedings of the 30th Annual Conference of the Cognitive Science Society*, eds. K. M. B. C. Love and V. M. Sloutsky (Cognitive Science Society, Austin, TX, 2008).

MODELLING SENSORY INTEGRATION AND EMBODIED COGNITION IN A MODEL OF WORD RECOGNITION*

PADRAIC MONAGHAN

Department of Psychology, Lancaster University, Lancaster, LA1 4YF, UK

TATJANA A. NAZIR

Institut des Sciences Cognitives, Centre National de Recherches Scientifiques, Lyon, France

Performing conceptual tasks that do not involve overt sensory and motor processes, can nonetheless implicate sensory and motor regions of the brain. In models of "embodied" cognition, the sensory and motor brain regions are seen as integral to the representation of the concept. Alternatively, "disembodied" theories of concept representation assume that these activations are peripheral and epiphenomenal to the representation itself. We review three sources of data for embodied cognition – the activation of sensory and motor regions for conceptual tasks, the effect on conceptual task performance when motor areas are otherwise engaged, and behavioral influences on reading in patients with impaired sensory and motor areas. We show that such data is consistent with a connectionist model of embodied cognition, and discuss the sources of data that can distinguish between embodied and disembodied accounts.

1. Theories of "embodied" and "disembodied" cognition

When performing conceptual tasks that do not directly implicate overt sensory or motor processes, sensory and motor regions of the brain still appear to be engaged, see [5, 20] for reviews. One view of this phenomenon is that these sensory and motor areas are integral to the conceptual representation, we term this the "embodied" model. Alternatively, the sensory and motor regions, though apparently activated, may be epiphenomenal to the representation – a mere byproduct of interconnected brain regions [14]. In this paper we consider sources of evidence for and against each of these accounts, and present a computational model that aims to provide explanatory adequacy to account for the observable behavior taken as support for models of embodied cognition.

*This work was supported by an EU Sixth Framework Marie Curie Research Training Network Program on Language and Brain: http://www.hull.ac.uk/RTN-LAB/.

2. Evidence for embodied cognition

There are three sources of evidence taken as supporting views of the direct involvement of motor and sensory regions in concept representation. First, there is brain activity in these regions for tasks that do not directly require sensory input or motor output. Second, manipulating cortical motor activity with transcranial magnetic stimulation or through overt motor behavior alters responses to verbal descriptions of body movements. Third, impairment to motor or sensory input regions of the brain has an observable impact on performance on language tasks.

2.1. *Sensory/motor activity for conceptual tasks*

Goldberg, Perfetti, and Schneider [8] asked participants to read a set of concrete words. The words were repeated in blocks and in each block, the participants had to decide whether the words described an object with a particular property. The properties varied in terms of the sensory modality to which they referred. For the visual modality, participants had to decide whether the object was green, for the auditory modality, whether the object was associated with loud noise, for touch, whether the object was soft, and for taste, whether the object was sweet. Participants were placed in a fMRI scanner, and signal responses in several regions of interest were recorded for each block.

Despite the stimulus being identical in each of the blocks, the judgment task resulted in very different patterns of activation. For the visual task, greater signal increase was observed in the ventral temporal cortex, a region associated with visual processing, whereas no signal change was found for the other modalities. For the auditory task, there was a significant signal increase in the superior temporal sulcus, but not for the other blocks. For the tactile block, there was significant signal change in motor and premotor areas (premotor cortex, pre-central and post-central gyrus), and for the taste task, signal change in the gustatory cortex – orbitofrontal cortex – but not for the other task blocks.

However, the Goldberg et al. study may be seen to directly implicate the sensory and motor areas due to the nature of the task. Hauk, Johnsrude, and Pulvermüller [9] (see also [24]) found that specific activity within the motor region could be observed for different types of action words even when the task was abstract and not directly related to action or tactile perception. In a fMRI study, participants passively read action words that were associated with leg-, arm-, or face-movements. In another block of the experiment, participants were required to make movements to the leg, arm, or face. For the silent reading and the movements, a similar topographic arrangement in motor and premotor cortex was observed, with leg words/movements eliciting activity in the ventral regions, arm words/movements resulting in dorsolateral activity, and face words/movements both producing activity in perisylvian cortex (see [20] for a review).

2.2. *Sensory/motor interference for conceptual tasks*

An additional source of evidence for the involvement of the sensory and motor areas as integral to conceptual representation is derived from evidence showing occupying these regions in other tasks, or affecting their processing, has an impact on conceptual task performance. Pulvermüller, Hauk, Nikulin, and Ilmoniemi [21] were given a lexical decision task to action words related to arm or leg movements. Simultaneously, transcranial magnetic stimulation, which temporarily disrupts cortical activity, was applied to regions of the motor cortex corresponding to the arm or the leg in the left or right hemisphere. They found that only when transcranial magnetic stimulation was applied to the language dominant left hemisphere were response times to the words affected, indicating particular involvement of the left motor cortex as a facet of word representation.

Glenberg and Kaschak [7] required participants to judge the grammaticality of sentences by responding with a push or a pull movement. They found that participants' responses were affected by the meaning of the sentence. So, for the sentence "close the drawer", when the grammatical response was a push movement responses were quicker than when the grammatical response was a pull movement (see also [6]). Similarly, Boulenger et al. [3] showed that perceiving words that describe motor actions can modify a reaching movement within the 200ms after onset.

2.3. *Sensory/motor impairment and conceptual tasks*

Other sources of support for embodied cognition views of conceptual representation are derived from behavioural impairments for abstract conceptual tasks following brain injury to motor, pre-motor, or sensory regions. Neininger and Pulvermüller [18], for instance, tested patients with lesions in right frontal or right inferior temporo-occipital lobes. The first lesion site was more likely to impair motor and premotor processing, wheras the more posterior lesion site was hypothesized to affect more visual processing regions. Patients were given a speeded lexical decision task, reading action words, or concrete object words. As predicted, the patients with frontal lesions were less accurate for action words than object words, whereas the patients with posterior lesions were less accurate in lexical decision for object words than action words.

Relatedly, Boulenger et al. [3] examined effects of priming in lexical decision in 10 patients with Parkinson's disease. Parkinson's disease is caused by a dopinamergic deficiency of the nigrostriatal region, which manifests behaviourally in terms of akinesia, bradykinesia, rigidity, or tremors. The symptoms of Parkinson's disease can be ameliorated by dopinamergic treatment.

All the participants in the study were undergoing dopinamergic treatment with Levadopa. They were asked to refrain from their medication for 12 hours prior to testing, and were subsequently tested within 60 minutes of receiving a high dose of Levadopa. The participants were given a masked priming lexical decision task with 70 action verbs and 70 concrete nouns. The target word appeared after either a consonant string or an identity prime (the prime word was the same as the target word: WALK-walk). Typically, identity primes increase accuracy and response time for lexical decision, and this pattern of results was found in the patients that were on Levadopa treatment. For both the nouns and the verbs there was a significant advantage of identity over consonant string primes. When the patients were tested off Levadopa treatment, by contrast, the advantage of identity over consonant primes was still observed for nouns but no longer for verbs. Impairment of motor functions can thus accompany selective deficits in processing verbs (see Figure 2).

The summative evidence from these studies suggests that motor and sensory brain regions are engaged in abstract conceptual representation. However, Mahon and Caramazza [14] argue that these data are also consistent with models of disembodied cognition. Motor/sensory area activity is observed because the motor and sensory areas are connected to the abstract conceptual representation. The abstract conceptual representation therefore passes activation to the motor and sensory areas, though these are secondary and inessential to the representation itself. The effects of sensory/motor interference and impairment on conceptual task performance can be explained similarly. The presence of these behavioural effects is entirely compatible with an account where activation is passed to and from the motor and sensory areas via an abstract conceptual representation. The effects of interference and impairment are therefore contained within the sensory and motor areas, and do not impact upon the conceptual representation itself.

Conceiving of alternative accounts in descriptive models is a useful first step in validating a theory, however, implemented computational models enable a precise testing of the adequacy of particular representations, and as the architecture must be specified, they enable a clearer statement about the divergence between possible models of imaging and behavioural data. In the next section we consider possible modeling foundations for an account of embodied cognition, in order to contrast it with views of disembodied cognition.

3. Computational models of embodied cognition

A starting point for models of embodied cognition is that the representation of a concept is entirely specified by activations within the sensory and motor systems and the connections between them. One branch of computational models that have taken this approach are models that have attempted to specify the cognitive impairments observed in semantic dementia patients [12, 23]. Such patients have difficulties in forming mappings between representations of different modalities, whereas tasks involving comparison of representations within the same modality appear to be relatively spared in these patients. Hodges et al. [11], for instance, found that patients had difficulty naming objects or pictures, and Luzzi et al. [13] found difficulties in this group in naming smells, or matching pictures to smells. Semantic dementia results from atrophy of the anterior inferior and lateral temporal cortex [16]. Rogers et al. [23] identified the superior temporal gyrus (STG) as a critical brain region that forms a "hub" for linking between representations of different modalities.

Dilkina, McClelland, and Plaut [4] constructed a model using an integrative layer to represent the STG in an action and object word naming task to simulate patients with semantic dementia. The integrative layer was connected to and received connections from an action layer, a vision layer, as well as an orthography and a phonology layer. The aim of their study was to implement the involvement of semantics in word naming tasks, in particular the greater involvement of semantic representations when reading irregularly pronounced words. Half the words related to actions and half to objects, and the model learned to associate activations of orthography, phonology, and either motor or visual layer activations. The motor and visual layers were selectively activated by a task-unit which indicated which of these layers were involved in the current task. The model effectively simulated a range of behavioral deficits, but the distinction between object and action words was not an aim of this model.

Lambon Ralph et al. [12] also produced an integrative layer model that contrasted semantic deficits in semantic dementia patients with herpes simplex virus encephalitis (HSVE) patients. The latter typically demonstrate category specific errors, whereas the impairment is more generic in semantic dementia patients. The model incorporated an integrative layer that mapped between phonological and visual representations. Impairment was simulated by adding general noise across the integrative layer, which simulated impairment for the

HSVE patients, and resulted in distortion of semantic representations. Semantic dementia was simulated by a "dimming" of the model's performance, by removing connections to and from the integrative layer, resulting in lowering of general activity passed between the other representational layers in the model.

Yoon, Heinke and Humphreys [25] produced another integrative layer model, called the naming and action model, which simulated selection of actions as a combined result of input from general semantic information and direct visual information. The model implemented an abstract semantic representation as the integrative layer, with input from an orthographic and a visual representation of an object, and passed output to a phonological and a motor output. There were also direct links between the orthography and the phonology, and between the visual and motor layers. Optic aphasia was simulated by lesioning the visual to integrative layer connections, anomia was simulated by lesioning the connections between the integrative and phonological layers, and visual apraxia was simulated by damaging the direct route between visual and motor representations. In all cases, the model was able to simulate patient data.

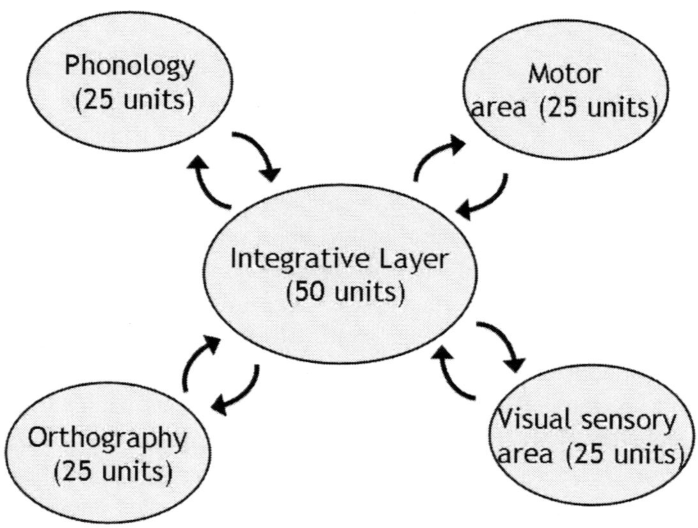

Figure 1. The integrative layer model of embodied cognition.

4. Modeling motor impairment in visual word recognition

We constructed a computational model based on the integrative layer modeling framework, to simulate masked priming effects for lexical decision in Parkinson's patients [3].

4.1. *Architecture*

The model is shown in Figure 1. A central, integrative layer was connected to and received connections from a motor layer, a visual layer, and a phonological layer, each of which operated both as input and output layers. An orthographic input layer was also connected to the integrative layer. The integrative layer was self-connected.

4.2. *Training and testing*

The model was trained on 100 words, 50 of which were actions and were associated with a representation in the motor layer of the model, the remaining 50 were objects and were paired with a representation in the visual layer. The phonological representations were generated by randomly activating an average of 5 of the 25 units in the phonological layer for each pattern. The orthographic representation was identical to the phonological representation, and so the model had to learn the compositional nature of this mapping in order to read. The motor and visual representations were produced by again randomly activating an average of 5 from 25 units, and these patterns were arbitrarily paired with the phonological representation. Active units in the patterns had an activation of 1, all other units had initial activation of 0.

Activity in the model circulated for 25 time steps in each pattern presentation, with activity passing between each layers in a continuous, graded manner, such that the activation of a unit was 0.8 times its current activation plus 0.2 times the sigmoid of the sum of the inputs to the unit. During training, the input pattern was presented for five time steps, at which point its activation started to reduce due to the continuous, graded activation update for units. At time steps 6 to 25 the model was required to produce the target pattern. The model learned five separate mappings, which were randomly selected during training. The model learned to map between phonological representations and motor representations for the action words, and between phonological and visual representations for the object words, in both directions. In addition, the model learned to map between orthographic and phonological representations, to simulate the word recognition task. Note that the motor and visual layers were not directly implicated for this reading task. The model was trained using backpropagation over time with cross-entropy as the error measure, and learning rate of 0.05. Error was computed for time intervals 11-25, the earliest point at which complete activation could pass from the input to the output layer. Weights were adjusted at time interval 25. Training was halted after 10,000 patterns had been presented to the model.

To simulate the priming task, we generated additional random patterns with mean of 5 from 25 units active to represent the consonant strings. At time steps 1-5 the consonant string was presented, which then decayed between time steps 6-10, then at time step 11-15 the orthography of the word was presented. The model had up to 35 time steps to settle to a response. For the identity prime condition, the orthography was presented at times steps 1-5 and 11-15. We assessed the model's performance by measuring the point at which the model produced a phonological representation closer to the target than to any other pattern in the training set.

In fMRI studies, Parkinson's disease is associated with reduced activity in regions associated with motor-planning, including the striato-frontal loop [1, 22], and so we simulated impairment to the motor system by reducing the activity of units in the motor layer in the model to zero. The simulations were repeated twenty times each, with different randomly-generated patterns, and different randomized starting weights.

4.3. *Results and discussion*

The model learned all the mappings to a high degree of accuracy (>98% correct). There were two aspects of the model's performance that we wanted to determine. First, whether activation was observed within the visual and motor areas of the model for the lexical decision task which did not directly implicate these regions. Second, we wanted to test for the impairment to priming effects for action words in the model with impairment to the motor layer.

For each of the words input in the orthography layer to the model, we measured the change in activation in the visual and motor layers of the model. Large changes in activation are taken to indicate greater involvement of these regions in the task (see [15] for further justification of this measure). For the motor layer, verbs resulted in a mean activity change of 4.44 and nouns resulted in a smaller activity change of 4.17. For the visual layer, the opposition pattern was found, with verbs resulting in a mean activity change of 4.16 and nouns 4.23, which was a significant interaction. There was substantial activity in these regions, even though not directly implicated in the reading task, however the interaction was only marginally significant, indicating large variation in the activity changes in the model.

Simulations where there was a difference in accuracy greater than 4% between the noun and verb priming effect for the intact model were omitted. There were some small fluctuations between different runs of the simulation due to the different randomisations, and consequently 10 simulations were included in the analyzed data. Figure 2 shows the priming effect for the model with the impairment to the motor layer in terms of delayed response time for the consonant prime compared to the identity prime. For response times, there was a significant main effect of prime type, $F(1, 9) = 36.95$, $p < .001$, there was also a significant main effect of word type, $F(1, 9) = 11.59$, $p < .01$, and, importantly, a significant interaction between prime and word type, $F(1, 9) = 5.17$, $p < .05$. There was a larger priming effect for the nouns compared to the verbs for the impaired model, and difference from zero was only significant for the nouns ($p < .001$, $p = .09$ for the verbs). The results indicate that the priming effect for nouns was larger than that for verbs in the impaired model, providing a qualitative reflection of the Parkinson's patients' performance.

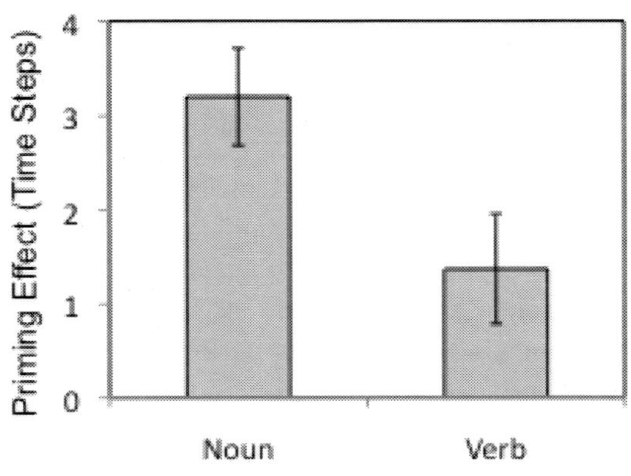

Figure 2. The priming effect (consonant prime time steps minus identity prime time steps) for nouns and verbs in the impaired model, error bars show ±1 standard error of the mean.

5. Discussion: Deciding between models

The set of computational models using an integrative layer to map between different modalities of representation have indicated that such an approach is a plausible framework for how semantic representations are implemented in the neural architecture of the brain. The current version of this framework, to simulate the word recognition data from patients with impaired motor skills, highlights that even though the visual and motor areas were not required for the task, due to previous experience on tasks mapping between motor/visual and phonological representations, these regions become activated for an abstract conceptual task – that of word recognition. The model performs the task by activating regions of the model that are associated with the spoken form of the word, even when these are not directly implicated in the model's performance. The temporal pattern of the activation for the reading task suggests that the motor and visual layers of the model produced an activation as a direct consequence of the orthographic input and not only as a consequence of indirect activation via the phonological layer. This indicates that the hidden layer produced a distributed representation for each word that combined motoric, visual, as well as phonological information. When the motor layer of the model was impaired, the stability of the activation to and from the hidden and motor layers was affected, resulting in a reduction of activation for the phonological representation of words early in processing. This had the largest effect for the priming of verbs. For the nouns, when the prime was a consonant string then the model's visual representation was not coherent and therefore had little effect on the subsequent activation of the word, but for primed nouns, the model could utilise the preactivation in the visual layer to assist in producing the phonological representation of the word.

Furthermore, the model demonstrates that the motor/visual areas are likely an integral part of the model's representation. Changing the activation of the motor layer in the model resulted in changes in the activation in the integrative layer, which influenced the model's orthography to phonology mapping.

However, proponents of a view of abstract conceptual representations could adapt the current model by introducing an abstract semantic representation in place of the current integrative layer, and performance would be similar: the effects of motoric impairment on word recognition would be due to impairment to the clarity of the abstract semantic features activated.

This raises the question of whether the issue between these models can ever be settled. If the abstract conceptual representation connects to and from all the sensory and motor areas, and impairment to these peripheral regions results in alterations to the abstract conceptual representation, then there seems to be convergence in terms of the general architecture of the cognitive system of representation, but differences in terms of the nature of representations in the integrative layer.

Mahon and Caramazza (2008) suggest that the issue can be resolved by finding evidence of patients with impaired motor systems but intact abstract conceptual representations. Negri et al. [17] present data from a set of apraxia patients who dissociate in terms of impairment to object recognition compared to their ability to use an object. Hence, if activity in the motor cortex is critical to the semantic representation then object naming should be affected. However, though there is a dissociation for individual patients, as a group the apraxia patients show a high correlation between impairment to object use and object recognition, precisely as would be expected from a range of impairments in a distributed integrative layer account (see, e.g. [19]), where the motor representation *is* a part of the entire conceptual representation. Implemented models of each of these accounts require a specification of the mechanisms involved, and are likely to illuminate the convergence of apparently theoretically-opposed theories. Computational models of such alternative accounts will provide a useful means for not only providing theoretical tests of behavioral data, but also for informing more general debates about the nature of representation in abstract conceptual tasks.

Acknowledgments

This research was supported by the EU Sixth Framework Marie Curie Research Training Network in Language and Brain.

References

1. G.E. Alexander, M.R. DeLong, and P.L. Strick, *Ann. Rev. Neurosci.* **9**, 357-381 (1986).
2. L.W. Barsalou, W.K. Simmons, A.K. Barbey, and C.D. Wilson, *Trends Cog. Sci.* **7**, 84-91 (2003).
3. V. Boulenger, L. Mechtouff, S. Thobois, E. Broussolle, M. Jeannerod, and T.A. Nazir, *Neuropsychologia* **46**, 743-756 (2008).
4. K. Dilkina, J.L. McClelland, and D.C. Plaut, *Cog. Neuropsych,* **25**, 136-164 (2008).
5. M.H. Fischer and R.A. Zwaan *Q. J. Exp. Psychol.* **61**, 825-850 (2008).
6. S.P. Gennari, S. Sloman, B. Malt, and T. Fitch, *Cognition* **83**, 49-79 (2005).
7. A.M. Glenberg and M.P. Kaschak, *Psychon. Bull. Rev.* **9**, 558-565 (2002).
8. R.F. Goldberg, C.A. Perfetti, and W.Schneider, *J. Neurosci.* **26**, 4917-4921 (2006).
9. O. Hauk, I. Johnsrude, and F. Pulvermüller, *Neuron* **41**, 301-307.
10. O. Hauk and F. Pulvermüller, *Hum. Brain Mapp.* **21**, 191-201 (2004).
11. J.R. Hodges, N. Graham, and K. Patterson, *Memory* **3**, 463-495 (1995).
12. M.A. Lambon Ralph, C. Lowe, and T.T. Rogers, *Brain* **130**, 1127-1137 (2007).

13. S. Luzzi, J.S. Snowden, D. Neary, M. Coccia, M. Provinciali, and M.A. Lambon Ralph, *Neuropsychologia* **45**, 1923-1931 (2007).
14. B.Z. Mahon and A. Caramazza, *J. Physiol.* **102**, 59-70.
15. P. Monaghan and S. Pollmann, *J. Exp. Psych. Gen.* **132**, 379-399 (2003).
16. C.J. Mummery, K. Patterson, C.J. Price, J. Ashburner, R.S.J. Frackowiak and J.R. Hodges, *Ann. Neurol.* **47**, 36-45 (2001).
17. G.A.L. Negri, R.I. Rumiati, A. Zadini, M. Ukmar, B.Z. Mahon and A. Caramazza. *Cog. Neuropsych.* **24**, 795-816.
18. B. Neininger and F. Pulvermüller, *Neuropsychologia* **41**, 53-70 (2003).
19. D.C. Plaut, *J. Clin. Exp. Neuropsych.* **17**, 291-321 (1995).
20. F. Pulvermüller, *Nat. Rev. Neurosci.* **6**, 576-582 (2005).
21. F. Pulvermüller, O, Hauk, V.V. Nikulin, and R.J. Ilmoniemi. *Eur. J. Neurosci.* **21**, 793-797 (2005).
22. O. Rascol, U. Sabatini, F. Chollet, N. Fabre, J.M. Senard, J.L. Montastruc et al., *J. Neur. Neurosurg. Psych.* **57**, 567-571 (1994).
23. T.T. Rogers, M.A. Lambon Ralph, P. Garrard, S. Bozeat, J.L. McClelland, J.R. Hodges et al., *Psychol. Rev.* **111**, 205-235 (2004).
24. M. Tettamanti, G. Buccino, M.C. Saccuman, V. Gallese, M. Danna et al., *J. Cog. Neuro.* **17**, 273-281.
25. E.Y. Yoon, D. Heinke, and G.W. Humphreys, *Vis. Cog.* **9**, 615-661 (2002).

COMPETITION AS A MECHANISM FOR PRODUCING SENSITIVE PERIODS IN CONNECTIONIST MODELS OF DEVELOPMENT

MICHAEL S. C. THOMAS

Developmental Neurocognition Lab, School of Psychology
Birkbeck College, University of London, Malet St., London, UK

Marchman's [1] framework for simulating sensitive periods in development was extended to investigate whether *competition* is a mechanism that might contribute to reductions in functional plasticity with age. Under this view, the ability to learn new behaviors is reduced when old established behaviors are unwilling to give up shared representational resources. The simulations supported this hypothesis, but indicated that a range of factors modulated competition effects: the similarity between old learning and new learning, the level of representational resources, the prevailing plasticity conditions within the system, the timing of introduction of new learning, and the complexity of the problem domain.

1. Introduction

1.1. *Age-related changes in plasticity*

Cognitive development frequently exhibits non-linear profiles of change. One of the most studied is the phenomenon of the critical period in development, in which functional plasticity appears to reduce with age. Research on plasticity is typically informed by three sources of empirical evidence: (i) the rate and upper limit of behavioral change at a given age; (ii) the effects of early deprivation on subsequent development; and (iii) recovery from damage at different ages. Research in this area has drawn several conclusions [2]. First, because plasticity is rarely ever eliminated in older individuals, the term *sensitive period* is viewed as more appropriate for age-related changes. Second, there are multiple varieties of sensitive period ranging from sensory processing to high-level cognitive abilities, often exhibiting different profiles. Third, multiple neurocomputational mechanisms may underlie changes in plasticity, including processes of entrenchment, pruning and assimilation [3]. Fourth, many sensitive periods may be a consequence of the basic processes underlying postnatal brain development, including the emergence of functionally specialized structures. In this paper, we employ connectionist modeling to explore another potential source of reductions in plasticity with age: *competition for resources*.

1.2. *Evidence for competition as a mechanism that mediates plasticity*

Competition effects on plasticity are proposed to occur under circumstances of sequential learning, where one behavior is learned after another (and the first behavior is continued). It is the later age at which the second behavior is acquired that would give the appearance of a sensitive period in development, all other things being equal. Strabismus (squint) in young children provides evidence for the importance of competition effects. Where the input to one eye is disrupted by a squint, infants often develop dominant fixation in the other eye. In this case, the squinting eye can lose vision, termed *amblyopia*. The loss of function is viewed as a consequence of competition for synaptic sites, where the dominant eye invades the areas of representation of the squinting eye, thereby disrupting the development of the normal geniculo-cortical connections [4]. Amblyopia can be reversed by patching the dominant eye and forcing the child to use the squinting eye. That all other things are not equal is illustrated by the fact that such reversal is only possible up until 6-7 years of age [5], implying that other conditions of plasticity are altering within the visual system.

Modulation of competition has been argued to affect recovery from acquired brain damage. For example, in adult humans suffering hand paralysis following stroke, recovery of function in the paralyzed hand is aided by restraining the other functionally intact hand [6]. This is consistent with the view that recovery of the motor behavior in the paralyzed hand exploits the representational resources of the intact hand, but cannot do so while the intact hand is utilizing these resources. Similarly, it has been argued that following insult to the left cerebral hemisphere, language can be developed in the right hemisphere only before the age at which the right hemisphere has developed its normal functional circuits [7]. That is, once the right hemisphere resources are being used for their typical function, they are less plastic to accommodate other functions.

Competition for resources implies that the resources are themselves limited. Evidence regarding exact levels of resource allocation in cognitive development is hard to come by. However, *crowding effects* following focal brain damage in children are suggestive that resources are not effectively infinite in cognitive development. Following focal damage, the long-term consequences are a general lowering of abilities across the child's cognitive profile, rather than specific behavioral deficits [4]. The implication is that the residual resources are no longer sufficient to develop cognition to the expected level.

If competition reduces plasticity, then when the conditions of the competition alter, new functional plasticity should be revealed. However, such plasticity may not always be adaptive. It has been argued that phantom limb pain in amputees may in part be due to reorganization of primary somatosensory cortex, following an attenuation of the normal input from the amputated limb and invasion of adjacent areas into the limb's representational zone. For example, following the loss of an arm, the representation of the cheek was observed to take over the arm and hand representations in somatosensory cortex [8].

Second language acquisition provides a strong test of the sequential learning paradigm. Here, it has been observed that when the second language *replaces* the first language before the age of 6, the second language can overwrite the first language, removing evidence of it both at behavioral and brain level [9]. Again, the fact that this is a phenomenon of early childhood suggests that there are other plasticity conditions changing across development. By contrast, when the second language is *added to the first*, brain-imaging evidence suggests that the higher the proficiency of the second language, the more its use is associated with activation of areas used by the first language, as if the second language must compete for the optimal functional circuits established by the first language [10]. Moreover, bilingualism is not a static condition but subject to continuous slow shifts in dominance depending on relative usage of the two languages.

1.3. *Computational modeling of changes in functional plasticity*

Connectionist models have been used to explore how different mechanisms may produce a reduction in functional plasticity, providing a necessary level of analysis intermediate between behavior and brain [11]. The following four models have generated influential findings. O'Reilly and Johnson [12] constructed a model of filial imprinting in the chick brain using a self-organizing network. After a certain level of exposure to an input stimulus, no amount of training on a subsequent stimulus could cause the network to shift its preference to the second stimulus. McClelland *et al.* [13] also used a self-organizing network to simulate the ending of a sensitive period in non-native language phoneme discrimination. After a certain amount of training on a given phonemic class, the system could no longer learn a subtle distinction between two new similar-sounding phonemes. Marchman [1] used an associative connectionist network acquiring the English past tense to explore sensitive period effects in recovery from brain damage, arguing that connectionist networks exhibit slower recovery from damage the later the damage occurs in development. Lambon Ralph and Ehsan [14] used similar associative networks to explore age-of-acquisition effects – the idea that patterns appearing earlier in training show stronger learning and are subsequently less vulnerable to damage.

Connectionist networks typically contain a learning rate parameter in their learning algorithms. This parameter modulates the size of connection weight changes induced by each learning experience. A reduction of plasticity with age could be achieved simply by reducing the value of this parameter across training. It is of note that none of the four preceding models used this method, holding the learning rate constant. Effective reductions in functional plasticity thereby revealed alternative mechanisms for generating sensitive periods, characterized respectively as self-terminating sensitive periods, assimilation and entrenchment.

The simulations presented here extend the framework employed by Marchman [1] to consider the role of *competition* in reducing functional plasticity. The following **key questions** were addressed:

1. In a sequential learning paradigm, does the functional plasticity of the learning system reduce when a later training set must compete for representational resources with an earlier (and continuously refreshed) training set?
2. Are competition effects modulated by the level of resources, in this case the number of hidden units in a three-layer backpropagation network?
3. Are competition effects modulated by the similarity between later and earlier training sets?
4. Are competition effects modulated by on-going changes in the intrinsic plasticity conditions within the system, for instance if resource levels are reducing (equivalent to pruning) or the learning rate is reducing (equivalent to a reduction in the availability of functionally unspecified synapses [4])?
5. If intrinsic plasticity conditions do change across development, does the timing of the introduction of the later training set matter? In other words, are competition effects worse at older 'ages' of the network?
6. Are competition effects modulated by the encoding of the problem domain, which alters the complexity of the mappings that the network must learn?
7. How do all of the above factors interact?

2. Simulation Methods

2.1. *Basic model*

For the base learning system, Marchman's [1] model of acquisition, loss, and recovery in connectionist networks was extended to consider competition. The simulations employed the well-understood domain of English past tense formation, which has often served as a test bed to illustrate the importance of the frequency and consistency of associative mappings in shaping performance.

These features are argued to influence many aspects of cognitive development (e.g., [15] for wider arguments in language development). The English past tense is of note because it is characterized by a predominant rule (e.g., *talk-talked*, *drop-dropped*, etc.) that extends to novel stems (e.g., *wug-wugged*), but also contains irregular verbs of different types (*go-went*, *hit-hit*, *sing-sang*). The past tense serves as a useful test domain because it allows us to examine the effects of problem type on competition, and in particular the modulating effects of consistency, type frequency, and token frequency on functional plasticity.

The regular past tense has the highest type frequency and forms a consistent set of mappings (reproduce the stem, add an inflection). The different classes of exception verb fall on a continuum of inconsistency, with no-change past tenses (*hit-hit*) least inconsistent (reproduce the stem but don't add an inflection), vowel change past tenses (*sing-sang*) at an intermediate level (partly reproduce the stem, no inflection), and arbitrary past tenses (*go-went*) most inconsistent (no relation between stem and past tense). Arbitrary past tenses have the lowest type frequency but require the highest token frequency in order to be acquired.

The following simulations had a modest objective. Marchman's model was relatively simple, both in its topology (a 3-layered feed forward network) and in its learning (the backpropagation rule). It was a cognitive model rather than a model of a language-related brain area, and some of its assumptions have restricted biological plausibility. Nevertheless, it provides a transparent framework in which to consider the direct consequences of five potentially interacting factors on competition effects: resource level, pattern consistency, intrinsic plasticity conditions, timing, and mapping complexity.

2.2. *Simulation details*

Architecture: The architecture comprised a three-layer feedforward network with 90 input units and 100 output units. Resources levels were manipulated by varying the number of hidden units, from 30 (low resources: just sufficient for successful learning) to 50 (medium resources) to 100 units (high resources).

Intrinsic plasticity: Models were trained with the backpropagation algorithm using the cross-entropy error measure. Three conditions of intrinsic plasticity were considered, shown in Figure 1. Under the *constant* condition, the learning rate was fixed at 0.1 (momentum = 0). Under the reducing learning rate or *redux* condition, the learning rate started higher and stepped downwards across training. The network's 'lifetime' was 400 epochs. The learning rate changed as follows: epoch 1=0.3; 2=0.2; 12=0.1; 200=0.05; 300=0.01. Under the *pruning* condition, after a certain point in training, unused connections were probabilistically lesioned. Beginning at 100 epochs, connections were permanently lesioned with a probability of 0.1 if their magnitude was less than 0.5. Figure 2 demonstrates the result of pruning on the number of connections in an equivalent weight layer in a medium or a high resource level network. Solid lines indicate the number of weights when the network underwent training, while dashed lines indicate the number of weights when the network was untrained across the same period. This plot shows that many fewer connections are pruned when the network undergoes training (because the weights become larger than the pruning threshold), and proportionately fewer connections are lost in networks that start with lower resource levels.

Simulation parameter values – hidden units, learning rate (constant or reducing), pruning onset, threshold, and rate – were calibrated to ensure successful learning of the full training set within the 400 epochs allotted to each network's 'lifetime', under conditions of minimal resources.

Overall training and testing sets: The training set was an artificial language comprising tri-phonemic verbs stems represented using an articulatory feature-based phonological code (30 bits per phoneme). There were 410 regular verbs (adding *–ed* to form past tense); irregular verbs were of three types: 68 vowel change verbs, 20 no-change verbs, and 10 arbitrary verbs. The generalization set comprised 410 novel verbs that rhymed (shared two phonemes) with the regular verbs in the training set. The output layer included 10 units to encode the inflectional morpheme. To explore the role of increased mapping complexity, an alternative coding of the training set was employed. Phonemes were represented over a much more compact code, using 6 bits per phoneme [16]. This latter architecture employed 18 input units and 20 output units.

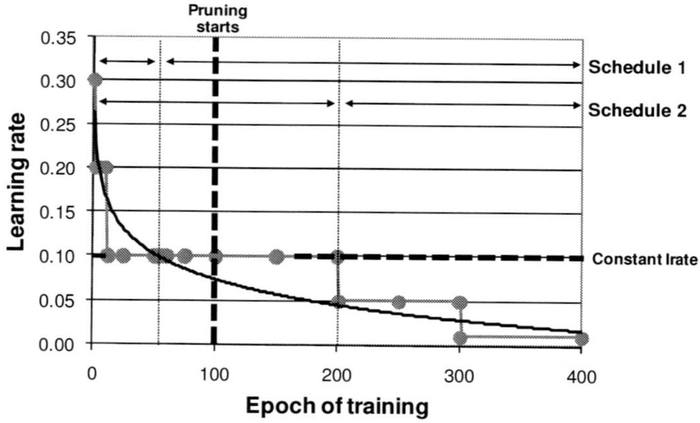

Figure 1. The three *Intrinsic plasticity* conditions.

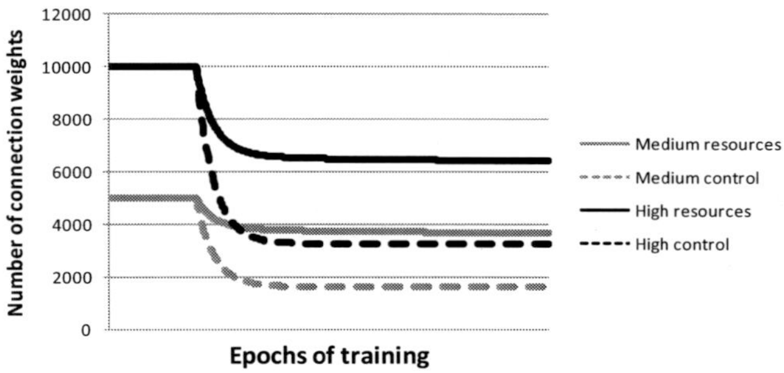

Figure 2. The effects of pruning on the number of connection weights in equivalent layers of a medium resource and a high resource network. Solid lines indicate networks undergoing training. Dashed lines indicated networks that do not undergo training.

Early and late training sets: To capture the sequential learning paradigm, the overall training set was split in two ways, either to *maximize* the inconsistency between early and late training sets, or to *minimize* the inconsistency. To maximize the inconsistency, the overall set was split into regular vs. irregular past tenses. To minimize the inconsistency, the training set was split into two equal halves, A and B.

Training schedules: For simplicity, we refer to the early training set as L1 and the later training set as L2. In the maximum inconsistency condition, we considered both the situations where L1 comprised regular verbs and L2 irregular verbs, and the situation where L1 comprised irregular verbs and L2 comprised regular verbs. In the minimum inconsistency condition, L1 and L2 comprised the two equal halves of the training set, which were counterbalanced.

To explore *timing effects*, competition either occurred when the network was relatively 'young' or when it was somewhat 'older'. *Young:* L1 was trained for 50 epochs; L2 was then either added to or replaced L1 and training continued to 400 epochs. *Older:* L1 was trained for 200 epochs; L2 was then either added to or replaced L1 and training continued to 400 epochs.

2.3. *Design*

The simulations were run in two parts. In the first part, a combinatorial design was used with four factors: Resources (low, medium, high), Intrinsic plasticity (constant, redux, pruning), Similarity (maximum inconsistency, minimum inconsistency), and Timing (Young, Older). There were six replications of each condition with different random seeds. This yielded 3x3x2x2x6=216 individual simulations. In the second part, this design was repeated but omitting the Resource factor (medium resources were used throughout) and adding a Domain

Complexity factor (normal encoding, atypical encoding), yielding a further 2x3x2x2x6=144 individual simulations.

3. Results

Our central question was whether competition reduced functional plasticity. The key contrast was the rate and final level of acquisition of the later training set when it was added to, and therefore had to compete with, the earlier training set (L1+L2) compared to when it replaced the earlier training set (L2). The *rate* was assessed by deriving the mean disparity between the developmental trajectories of L2 in the two conditions; the *final level* reflected performance on L2 at the end of training (400 epochs).

Network performance was assessed via percent correct on each verb class in the training set (**Regular**s and the three exception types), as well as the network's ability to extend the past tense rule (add *–ed*) to novel verb stems, referred to here as **Rule** patterns. Network responses were derived by using a nearest neighbor method to convert output activations to phoneme strings, which were then compared to the target output. In the following, performance on exception patterns is referred to via the abbreviations **EP1** (*hit-hit*), **EP2** (*sing-sang*), and **EP3f** (*go-went*). The **EP** number emphasizes the degree of inconsistency of the verb class with the regular past tense, while the **f** indexes the greater token frequency of the arbitrary verb class. Mean results are reported averaged over the six replications, along with the standard error of the mean.

Figures 3 and 4 depict the delay and final performance levels for the Similarity condition. These two figures illustrate several points. First, competition indeed reduced functional plasticity, both in the rate of learning and final level of proficiency: there are positive differences in Figure 3 for all pattern types in the training set. Second, competition effects were much smaller in the *minimum inconsistency* condition. In the *maximum inconsistency* condition, reductions in plasticity were more marked for generalization; they increased with greater inconsistency (from EP1 to EP2) but were attenuated by high token frequency (EP3f). Lastly, delays in learning were sometimes (irregular verbs) but not always (regular verbs) associated with reductions in the final level of proficiency. High type frequency was therefore a protective factor for final levels of performance in the face of competition.

Figure 5 demonstrates that the competition effects were significantly worse when there were fewer representational resources available. With high resource levels, competition effects still reduced plasticity in terms of rate of learning (albeit to a lesser extent) but final performance levels were now unaffected. Figure 6 indicates that reductions in plasticity due to competition interacted with the intrinsic plasticity conditions prevailing within the learning system, and were particularly exaggerated when processes of pruning reduced the level of resources available. By contrast, Figure 7 indicates that as a main effect, the timing of the introduction of the second training set did not modulate reductions in plasticity due to competition.

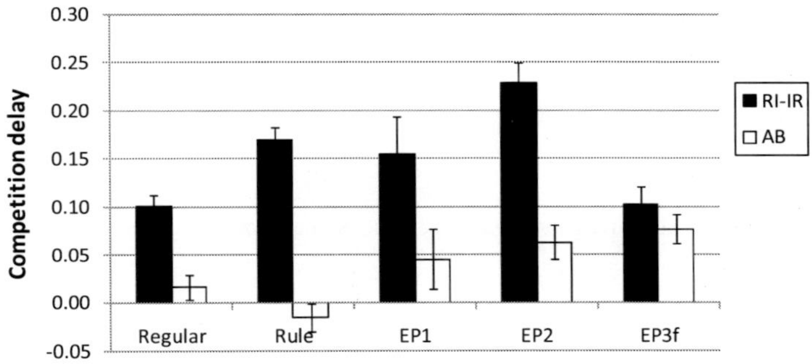

Figure 3. The delay in acquiring each pattern in its role as L2. RI-IR shows the *maximum inconsistency* condition: For Regular and Rule, irregular verbs were the corresponding L1. For EP1, EP2, and EP3f, regular verbs were the corresponding L1. AB shows the *minimum inconsistency* condition where for all pattern types, the corresponding L1 was the other half of the training set.

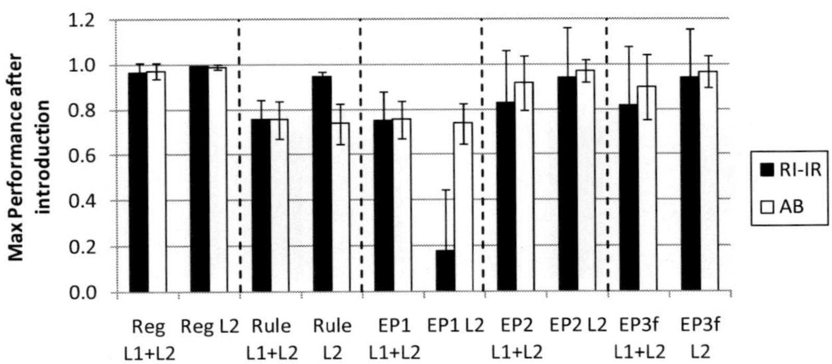

Figure 4. Final performance level for each pattern type in its role as L2, either when competing with the earlier training set (L1+L2) or replacing the earlier training set (L2). Results are shown separately for maximum (RI-IR) and minimum (AB) inconsistency conditions.

However, Figure 8 suggests that timing did interact with other factors. This figure depicts a 4-way interaction between timing, similarity, resource level, and intrinsic plasticity, and reveals complex interactions between these factors. Most notably, competition effects were exaggerated late in training when there was high inconsistency and intrinsic plasticity had itself reduced. Lastly, Figure 9 depicts the situation of an increase in the complexity of the mappings that the system was required to learn, implemented via a change in the encoding of the problem domain. This factor was also found to increase competition effects.

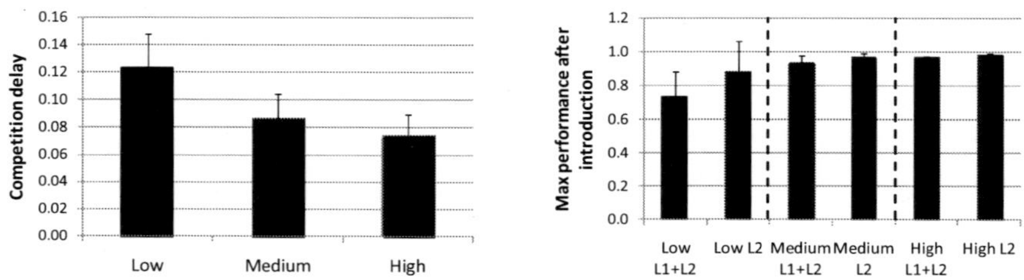

Figure 5. Delay and final performance level depending on the amount of representational resources.

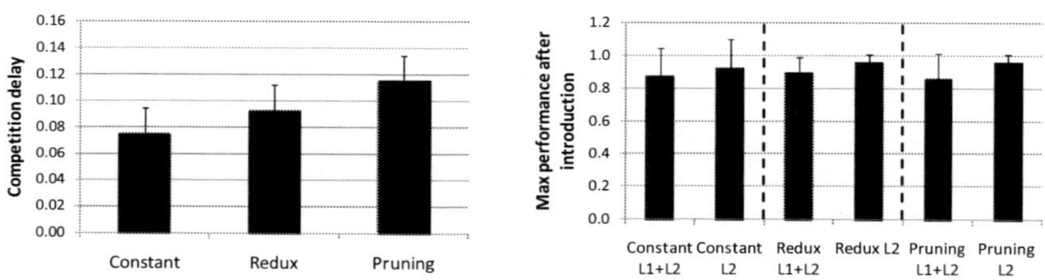

Figure 6. Delay and final performance level depending on intrinsic plasticity conditions.

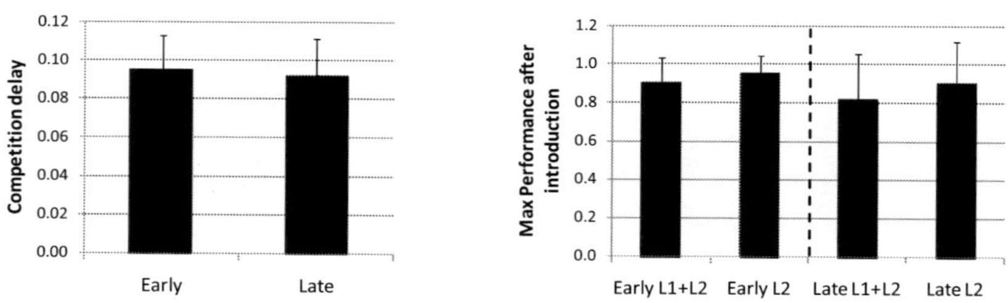

Figure 7. Delay and final performance level depending on the timing of introduction of L2.

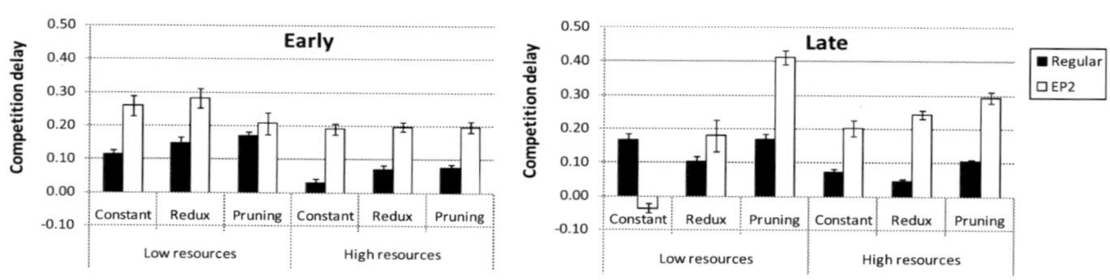

Figure 8. 4-way interaction: Timing x Pattern similarity x Intrinsic plasticity conditions x Resources.

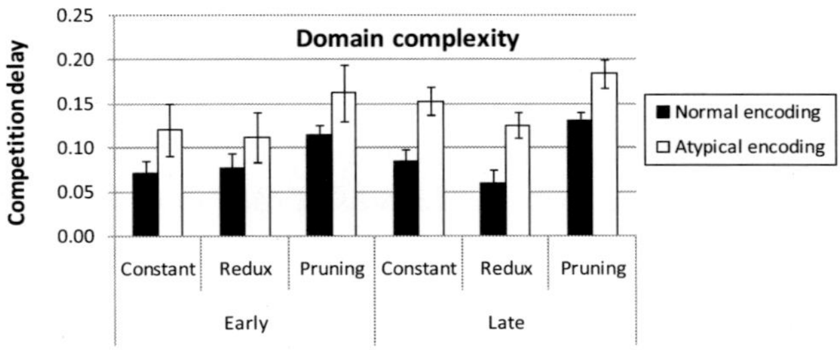

Figure 9. An increase in the complexity of the problem domain also exaggerated reductions in functional plasticity via competition for resources.

4. Discussion

The Marchman [1] simulation framework was extended to explore whether competition for representational resources may be a contributory mechanism to reducing functional plasticity across development. Under this view, the ability to learn new behaviors is reduced when old established behaviors are unwilling to give up shared representational resources. The simulation results offered support for the hypothesis.

Mechanistically, the reduction in functional plasticity due to competition can be viewed as related to effects of entrenchment. Both competition and entrenchment are consequences of previous learning. Entrenchment puts the system in a state where it can less readily respond to new learning. Competition additionally interferes with the attempts of the new learning to reconfigure the representational resources. Competition effects may have contributed to changes in plasticity reported in previous computational models of development [3].

The simulation results were notable for the number of interactions observed. Competition effects depended on consistency between old and new learning. They were mitigated by high type and token frequency in the later training set; but they were exaggerated by inconsistency, since this increased the extent to which the later training set had to fight to reconfigure the representational resources. Competition effects were made worse by other intrinsic reductions in plasticity conditions and when this occurred, the timing of introduction of the later training set became important. Competition operates over a restricted amount of resources: competition effects were attenuated when those resources were greater. They were exaggerated when the complexity of the mappings was increased, because greater complexity requires greater resources. Lastly, reductions in rate and final performance level did not always co-occur. There was therefore a dissociation between the two behavioral markers of functional plasticity.

These are, of course, preliminary findings, which need to be extended to other training sets and other learning architectures to evaluate their generality. The motivation for modeling work of this type is ultimately to establish an inventory of the mechanisms that may serve to reduce functional plasticity with age, and to identify the behavioral hallmarks of each mechanism. The aim is to prescribe appropriate interventions where people are struggling to achieve a desired behavioral change. What are the hallmarks of reductions in plasticity due to competition? Timing effects, consistency effects, and similarity effects were observed but are unlikely to be unique to competition. Competition is implicated if there are any indications of low resource levels (e.g., low IQ, developmental disorders, previous damage to the system). However, the most salient evidence that competition is responsible for reducing functional plasticity is that greater plasticity is revealed when the competing behavior is removed.

Acknowledgments

This work was supported by MRC grant G0300188.

References

1. V. Marchman, *J. Cog. Neurosci.*, **5**, 215-234 (1993).
2. M. Thomas & M. Johnson, *Curr. Dir. Psych. Sci.*, **17**, 1-5 (2008).
3. M. Thomas & M. Johnson, *Dev. Psychobiol.*, **48**, 337-344 (2006).
4. P. Huttenlocher, *Neural plasticity*, Harvard Uni. Press: Cam. Mass. (2001).
5. A. Assaf, *Br. J. Opthalmol.*, **66**, 64-70 (1982).
6. E. Taub *et al.*, *Arch. Phys. Med. Rehab.*, **74**, 347-354 (1993).
7. S. Knecht, *Brain*. **127**, 1217 (2004).
8. H. Flor, L. Nikolajsen and T. Jensen, *Nat. Neuro. Rev.*, **7**, 873-881 (2006).
9. C. Pallier *et al.*, *Cerebral Cortex*, **13**, 155-161 (2003).
10. J. Abutalebi, S. Cappa and D. Perani, in J. Kroll and A. de Groot (eds.) *Handbook of Bilingualism*, 497-515, OUP: Oxford (2005).
11. M. Seidenberg and J. Zevin, in Y. Munakata and M. Johnson (eds.) *Processes of Change in Brain and Cognitive Development*, OUP: Oxford (2006).
12. R. O'Reilly and M. Johnson, *Neural Computation*, **6**, 357-390 (1994).
13. J. McClelland *et al.*, in J. Reggia, E. Ruppin and D. Glanzman (eds.) *Disorders of Brain, Behavior and Cognition*, 75-80, Elsevier: Oxford (1999).
14. M. Lambon Ralph and S. Ehsan, *Visual Cognition*, **13**, 928-948 (2006).
15. E. Bates & B. MacWhinney, in B. MacWhinney (ed.) *Mechanisms of Language Acquisition*, 157-193, LEA: Hillsdale, NJ (1987).
16. K. Plunkett and V. Marchman, *Cognition*, **38**, 1-60 (1991).

NEUROEVOLUTION OF AUTO-TEACHING ARCHITECTURES

EDWARD ROBINSON and JOHN A. BULLINARIA
School of Computer Science, University of Birmingham
Edgbaston, Birmingham, B15 2TT, UK
e.robinson@cs.bham.ac.uk

This paper explores the idea that auto-teaching neural networks with evolved self-supervision signals can lead to improved performance in dynamic environments where there is insufficient training data available within an individual's lifetime. Results are presented from a series of artificial life experiments which investigate whether, when, and how this approach can lead to performance enhancements, in a simple problem domain that captures season dependent foraging behaviour.

1. Introduction

Neural networks with reinforcement or supervised learning algorithms are known to be excellent at acquiring complex behaviours if they are given a large enough amount of training data. However, humans and other animals often need to operate in environments in which there is insufficient information available to enable an individual to configure their behaviour mechanisms appropriately. This can render such lifetime learning techniques inadequate, despite their generally good potential.

Learning, however, can take place over two rather different time-scales: lifetime adaptation during the life of an individual, and evolutionary adaptation over much longer periods. If the learning task remains constant across many generations of evolution, then it is possible that the necessary behaviours could become specified innately, making the need for lifetime learning unnecessary. If lifetime learning has a cost, such as periods of relatively poor performance, then it is best avoided if possible. It is certainly known that the Baldwin Effect can lead to the genetic assimilation of appropriate learned behaviours (Baldwin, 1896; Bullinaria, 2001). However, if the behaviour to be learned changes within the individual lifetimes, or varies between individual environments, or changes too quickly for evolution to track it, or is too complex for easy genetic encoding, then evolution will not be able to help in this way.

Another approach that has been suggested for resolving the problem of insufficient training data during a lifetime involves employing *auto-teaching*

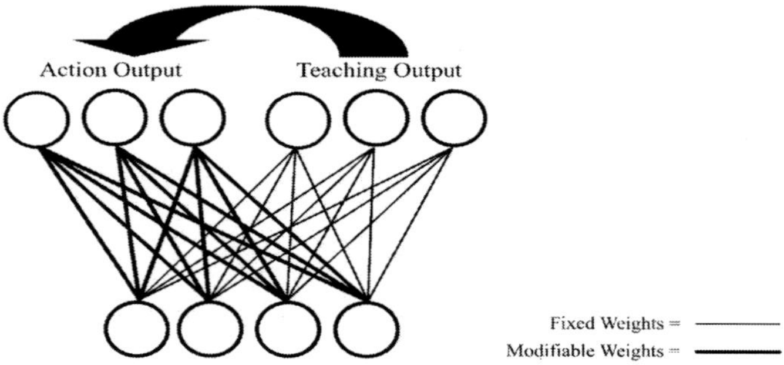

Figure 1: Simple auto-teaching neural network architecture.

networks. These are neural networks that can generate their own "supervision signal", based on evolved innate connection weight parameters (Nolfi & Parisi, 1993, 1996). The idea is that evolution can lead to neural structures that do not completely encode particular behaviours themselves, but instead they facilitate the lifetime learning of appropriate behaviours. Previous research in this area has shown, using a number of different learning tasks, how simulated individuals using these teaching architectures can out-perform similar individuals that do not have an "auto-teaching" mechanism.

The previous experiments involved simple artificial life agents evolved to perform a foraging task. Their neurocontrollers had a feed-forward architecture, in which the inputs were environmental stimuli and the outputs specified behaviour in the environment. This paper presents further simulations following a similar approach, but explores the evolution of auto-teaching networks more systematically, and assesses the performance of this approach on new and more difficult tasks in a novel dynamic environment.

The remainder of this paper will begin with a review of past work on auto-teaching networks, and then describe in detail how the new simulations were set up. This is followed by a presentation of the key simulation results, and some discussion and conclusions.

2. Auto-Teaching Neural Networks

Auto-teaching networks have traditional connection weights w_{ij} that are updated during the individual's lifetime, but instead of the usual external training signal, which will not be available in many realistic scenarios, they have an internal training signal coming from an additional set of neurons driven by the same sensory inputs via evolved fixed teaching weights W_{ij} (Nolfi & Parisi, 1993). A simple feed-forward auto-teaching network architecture is shown in Figure 1.

For each input pattern, the outputs are computed as in a standard feed-forward network, but rather than updating the weights w_{ij} to minimize the output errors relative to externally provided target outputs, they are updated using targets provided by the internal teaching outputs. The idea is that evolution provides an appropriate teaching signal depending on the current sensory inputs, as a substitute for the feedback information lacking in the environment.

The aim of this paper is to explore whether, when and how this architecture performs better than traditional networks. Nolfi & Parisi (1993) devised a simple foraging task within a 'grid-world' artificial life environment to do this, and used a genetic algorithm to evolve agents that were good at finding food items to consume. They used a multi-layer perceptron with sensory inputs that provided the direction and distance to the nearest food item, and action outputs that specified the agent's next movement. After each movement, the teaching outputs were used to update the modifiable weights using a standard gradient descent algorithm. Nolfi & Parisi (1993) presented results indicating that their auto-teaching networks performed better than networks in which the main network weights were evolved but fixed during an individual's lifetime. However, Williams & Bounds (1993) analysed a similar task and found that simple perceptrons performed better than the more complex multi-layer networks with auto-teaching architectures.

The environment used by Nolfi & Parisi (1993) had randomly distributed food items, but was of the same form for each new agent, and static during an agent's lifetime. It seems likely that, for any predictable static environment, any useful search policy that evolves to be encoded in fixed network weights would remain suitable throughout each agent's life, and there will consequently be no advantage to having an auto-teaching mechanism too. Whether auto-teaching might usefully interact with evolution to facilitate the acquisition of better evolved behaviour in such circumstances is less clear (Nolfi & Parisi, 1993; Williams & Bounds, 1993).

Nolfi & Parisi (1997) designed a more challenging changing environment, and used simple perceptrons with auto-teaching to control simulated Kherpera robots. These robots had to move to a randomly pre-defined target in a finite environment, and to do well (i.e. complete the task quickly) the robots had to explore the environment as efficiently as possible. However, there were two distinct environments, and each new agent was placed randomly into one of them, which meant that two distinct search policies were needed. Evolved robot controllers that could auto-teach during their lifetime were found to outperform those with fixed weights, because they could adapt to the right policy rather than rely on some inferior compromise policy. In general, it is easy to see how

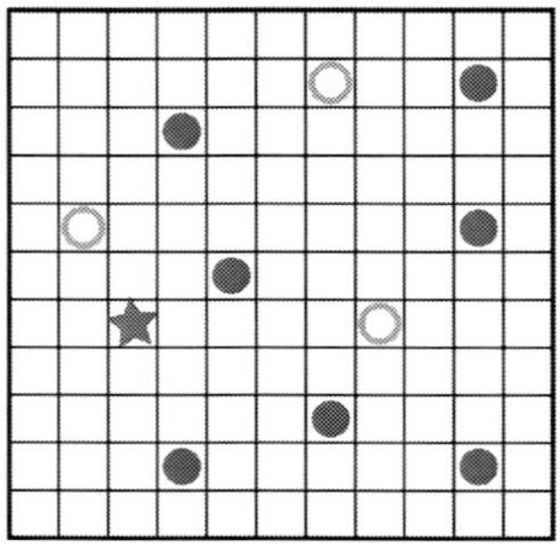

Figure 2: Grid-world environment, with agent ★, food ● and buried food ○.

limited sensory information could be used with auto-teaching to switch at birth to the appropriate one of many evolved behaviours that have been acquired though exposure to many potential environments over evolutionary history.

What remains to be explored is the dynamic case in which the form of the environment is the same for all agents, but its nature changes during the agent's lifetime, possibly many times.

3. Simulations with Dynamic Environments

To explore auto-teaching in dynamic environments, agents were simulated that had to forage for randomly placed food items in a grid-world environment of the form shown in Figure 2, as in the Nolfi and Parisi (1993) study. Adaptation is required because the availability of food varies throughout the agents' lifetimes. Each time-step is one agent *day*, and 600 days is one agent *year* made up of two *seasons*: first summer with plenty of food items, and then *winter* with none (Figure 3). Agents must bury some food during the summer to consume later to survive through the winter. Simulation results will be presented for a 20×20 cell world, with agents that start with 100 energy units and expend energy at the rate of one unit per time-step. Each food-item consumed is worth another 35 energy units, but agents can only store 100 units of energy at any time. Given appropriate sensory information, this task is linearly separable (Williams & Bounds, 1993), so a simple perceptron controller was adequate.

At each time-step, the agents' simple perceptron networks (as in Figure 1) have their weights and activations updated and then have their output actions implemented. The agents had different sensory input information available depending upon the experimental condition. They always had the normalized coordinate distances to the nearest food item. In the first set of simulations, they also had a sinusoidal representation of the time of year (i.e. the season), and

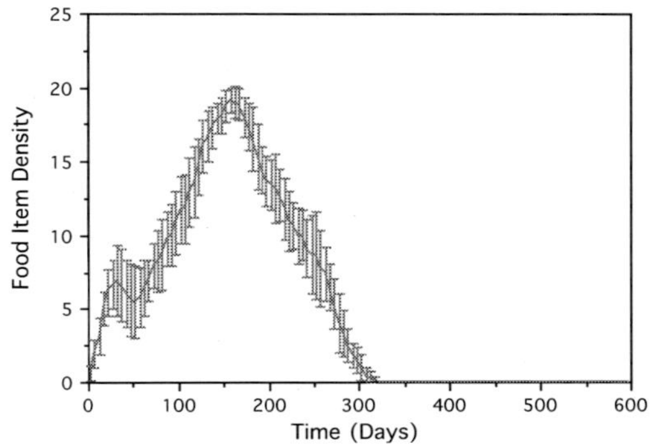

Figure 3: Density of food items in the environment at different times of year.

their current normalized energy level, but these were absent in the second set of simulations. Each of the agents' three output unit activations specified one of their three potential actions: namely move left/right, move up/down, and consume/bury food. These outputs were all thresholded, so that activations in the range [–0.2, +0.2] meant no action, while higher or lower values meant unit action in the appropriate direction. The consume/bury action always takes precedence over the movements. If an agent is situated in the same cell as a food-item, and the consume/bury output neuron has output +1/–1, the agent will consume/bury the food-item, and not move. Only if the consume/bury output is 0, or the agent is not situated on a food-item, will the agent perform the action corresponding to its movement outputs.

In line with the previous studies described in Section 2, an evolutionary algorithm was used to evolve populations of fit agents. The genotype to be evolved consisted of the network connection weights and biases, and, when lifetime auto-teaching was allowed, the learning rate. For tasks with n input units and m output units, that means $(n+1)m$ evolvable parameters for the fixed networks and $2(n+1)m + 1$ for the auto-teaching networks – consisting of the $(n+1)m$ main initial weights w_{ij}, $(n+1)m$ auto-teaching weights W_{ij}, and one learning rate. At the beginning of each simulation, a population of 100 random individuals were generated, with network weight values taken from a uniform distribution with the range [–1, +1]. Fitness was taken to be the length of time survived, which provided a measure of the agent's foraging skills. To smooth the statistical variations inherent in the simplified task, each agent's fitness was averaged over three independent runs. A steady state genetic algorithm with tournament selection was used, replacing the least fit fraction of the population at each stage by children of the fitter individuals (Eiben & Smith, 2003). A

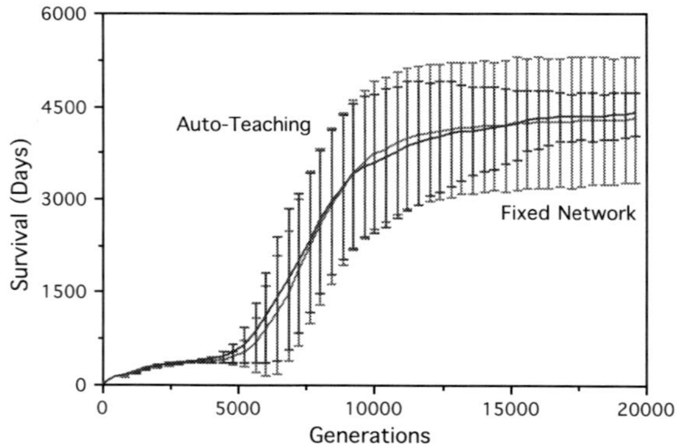

Figure 4: Evolution of performance when all the sensory information is available.

recombination process produced the children by crossover and mutation. Crossover randomly took parameters from both parents, but with an increased probability (of 66%) that sets of weights corresponding to a single output were kept together. That minimized the disruption to existing correctly functioning output units. Then, with 1% probability, an individual would have one of its parameters randomly mutated with a Gaussian distribution. This process was repeated over many generations until the performance level stabilized.

4. Simulation Results and Analysis

Three distinct sets of experiments were run to elucidate the advantages, if any, of auto-teaching networks in the artificial life environments described above.

4.1. *Simulations With Full Set of Sensory Information*

First the performance was evaluated for auto-teaching architectures that had all the sensory-information available to them: coordinate distances to nearest food-item, time of season, and internal energy levels. Although this environment is different to that used by Nolfi & Parisi (1993), it is qualitatively similar in that the agents have all the information necessary to perform well on the task. Thus it can again be asked whether auto-teaching networks provide an advantage over standard fixed neurocontrollers.

Figure 4 presents the survival times, with means and variances over twenty evolutionary runs, with foraging episodes of up to 5000 days. This shows that there is no statistically significant increase in foraging performance when auto-teaching networks are employed on this task. Contrary to the Nolfi & Parisi (1993) study, it is found here that, in this case where the task is linearly separable, a good behavioural policy can be specified via evolution alone, with simple fixed perceptrons performing just as well as those that adapt during their lifetimes, and there is no difference in the rate of evolution. The overall lifetime performance will always be better when the agents can behave correctly from birth, rather than at some later point in life after learning, so it follows that auto-teaching networks are of no benefit here.

Observing the behaviour of individual agents confirmed that those with fixed networks possess the correct behavioural policy from birth. It was useful to determine, at this point, exactly how evolution had specified the ability to solve the task. The agents could easily evolve the capacity to quickly approach food via the most optimum path, because the available distance information inputs trivially indicate the direction to move at each stage. How the agents evolved to deal with the issue of when to bury or consume food-items, or indeed when to neither bury nor consume them, was not so straightforward. It was found that the best evolved agents used a combination of time-of-year and internal-energy sensory inputs to decide on the appropriate action at each time-step. The main criterion for what an agent should do with a food-item was the time of season. During the winter months, because of the lack of new food-items available for burying, agents only consumed food-items. During the summer months, agents only buried items, unless the winter period was imminent or their internal energy became low. This meant that they generally maximised the number of food-items buried during the summer months, and only consumed food-items when necessary. Another use for the internal-energy sensory input was to maximise the length of time during the winter months when the agent was not consuming its previously buried food-items. Agents did this by remaining still until their energy became low, in which case they headed to a previously buried food-item and consumed it.

4.2. *Simulations With Limited Sensory Information*

The first objective of this work has been achieved by establishing, in this scenario, that auto-teaching networks do not always perform better than fixed networks in artificial-life environments. Next the simulations were varied to determine under what conditions auto-teaching networks can outperform fixed evolved networks. Analysis of the experimental results so far indicated that the evolved agents relied heavily on the internal-energy and seasonal-time sensory inputs. With these two sensory stimuli, a fixed-network can display a wide enough range of actions to survive indefinitely in the environment. However, if these stimuli were removed, the agents would need another mechanism to change their behaviour during their lifetime in order to survive longer than the initial

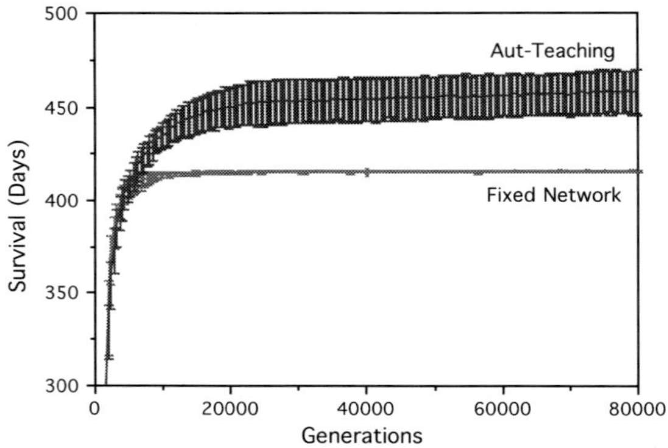

Figure 5: Evolution of performance when only food location input is available.

summer months. This is because, with only the position information available, an agent's network input will always be the same whenever it is positioned on a given food-item. Therefore, for the network outputs to be different, e.g. –1 for bury or +1 for consume, the network connection weights must be different, which means the agent needs to adapt during its lifetime.

However, given the nature of the neural learning mechanism being used, it is not obvious whether the necessary adaptation is possible, given that the external teaching signals are limited, and the way an agent teaches itself is fixed during its life (because the teaching weights are fixed). In particular, the agents must use the environment to generate appropriate auto-teaching stimuli, and if the environmental stimuli are limited to the position information of the nearest food-item, it is not clear whether that can lead to appropriate consume/bury signals. To explore this issue, the simulations were re-run with only the food location information as sensory inputs. The results, presented in Figure 5, show that all the performance levels are considerably lower than the previous experiment, due to the increased difficultly of the task resulting from the lack of sensory stimuli. However, there is now a clear and significant improvement in the performance of the auto-teaching networks over fixed networks.

The fixed networks evolve to simply consume food-items whenever they find them, and that allows them to survive until shortly after the end of summer-time, i.e. ~410 simulated days. It is clear from the improved mean performance of ~450 days that agents with an auto-teaching architecture are changing their behaviour (with regard to what action to perform when on a food-item) during the task. They are now, at birth, burying food-items whenever they encounter them. However, at some point during their life, the agents change their behavioural policy to one that involves consuming the food-items whenever they

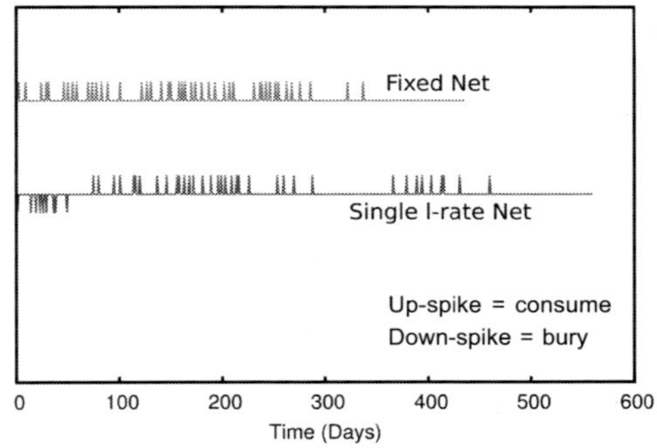

Figure 6: Actions taken by typical evolved agents during the foraging task.

are encountered. This allows them to bury some food-items to be consumed during the winter part of the task when there are no other food-items available. Since the agents no longer have any sensory information about the time of year, nor their internal energy levels, the evolutionary process is managing to select for teaching-weights that ensure this behaviour change happens at the most appropriate point in time, given the stochastic nature of the task. Figure 6 illustrates how these behaviours take place in typical evolved agents, with the up/down spikes representing successful consume/bury actions. This graph also illustrates the difference in resultant life-times.

From these results, it is clear that the auto-teaching networks do not evolve sophisticated continuous learning – the agents only change their consuming/ burying behaviour once during their lifetime. To do better at the task, they would need to be able to switch between the two behaviours multiple times during a lifetime spanning many years. In effect, the evolved auto-teaching mechanism needs to encode the fact that there are seasons of particular lengths, and adjust the agents' behaviours at appropriate times of each year. The current framework is such that evolution cannot find such a mechanism, probably because the sensory inputs provide insufficient information to allow it to take place with the learning mechanisms available.

4.3. *Simulations With Multiple Learning Rates*

To give the auto-teaching mechanism more flexibility, and to provide evolution with a better chance of finding improved behaviours, more sophisticated neural networks were considered. The auto-teaching signal provides target outputs, and the single evolved learning rate specifies the rate at which the adaptable weights change to achieve those targets. If numerous different rates of change were allowed in the network, it is likely that a wider range of dynamics would be

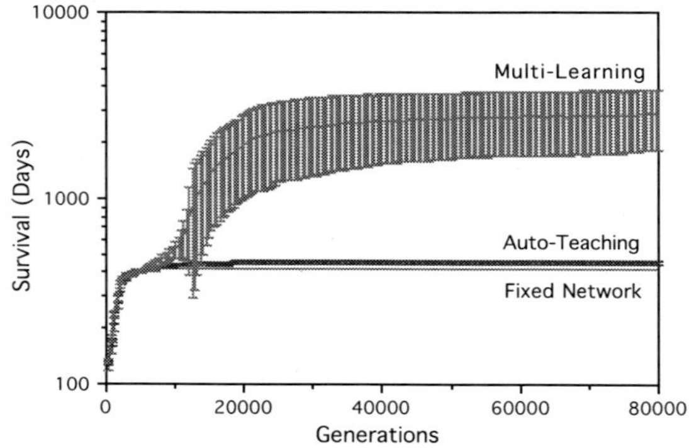

Figure 7: Evolution of performance for multiple learning rate agents.

evolvable. Consequently, the previous approach was extended to allow the possibility of a different learning rate to evolve for each adaptable network weight. This would allow (if it proved beneficial) independent weights to change at different speeds during the life of an agent, possibly with some being fixed, and this could allow more complex behaviours to emerge.

The previous simulations were thus repeated with multiple learning rates. For networks with n input units and m output units, that meant increasing the size of the agent genotypes to $3(n+1)m$ – consisting of $(n+1)m$ initial values for the adaptable weights w_{ij} and $(n+1)m$ auto-teaching weights W_{ij} as before, but now with $(n+1)m$ learning rates instead of only one. All the other simulation details remained exactly the same as before, with a similar pattern of crossover and mutation employed for the learning rates as for the network weights. Figure 7 shows how the new multiple learning rate auto-teaching networks significantly outperform both the previous single learning rate auto-teaching architectures and the non-learning fixed networks.

The new multiple learning rate architectures are able to modulate their behaviour during life, allowing them to change between consuming and burying policies multiple times. It is clear, from the average population fitness, that agents using this new architecture are surviving well beyond a single simulated year, which is encouraging because the previous auto-teaching networks were not capable of this. In fact, the maximum foraging time of 5000 days is once again being regularly achieved, and it is now actually possible for agents to survive indefinitely in the environment.

The season dependent behaviour is seen more clearly in Figure 8, which presents a plot of a typical agent's actions when encountering a food-item, for their first 2500 days. Analyzing the details of the evolved networks reveals that

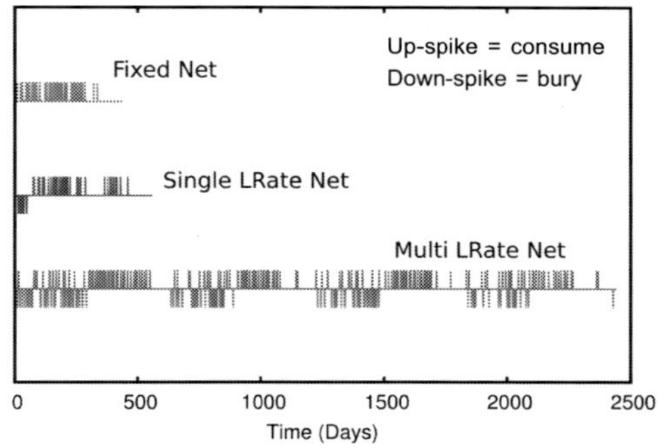

Figure 8: Actions taken by typical evolved multiple learning rate agents.

there are actually many different mechanisms that can emerge to enable this improved behaviour. The auto-teaching signals always vary rapidly during the agents' lifetimes, and these interact with complex patterns of learning rates to modulate the rates of consuming and burying at different times of each year. Exactly how this is achieved is found to vary considerably across individuals from independent evolutionary runs, with different sub-sets of the weights w_{ij} becoming fixed in different individuals. It is certainly clear from Figure 8 that the evolved behaviour is more complex than the simple switch between burying and consuming at appropriate times each year that one might think would be the easiest way to survive over many years. Burying only takes place during the summers, but apart from that, the choice between burying and consuming appears random. Determining the precise range of mechanisms that allow this improved behaviour will require considerable further study. The important issue here is that, within this relatively simple framework, it is possible for evolution to reliably find such mechanisms.

5. Discussion and Conclusions

The study presented in this paper has used artificial life simulations, in a simple foraging domain, to test the effectiveness of auto-teaching neural networks for agents operating in dynamic environments. It showed that, contrary to previous indications in the literature, simpler fixed weight networks can exhibit equally good performance on some tasks. However, if the sensory input information is sufficiently limited on the same tasks, then auto-teaching networks can show significant performance improvements over fixed networks. In general, if the task is predictable, but varies during an individual's lifetime, it will depend on the nature of the task and the available sensory inputs whether auto-teaching will be beneficial. Fortunately, the evolutionary approach adopted in this paper is easily applicable to determine the efficacy of auto-teaching neural networks for any novel problem domain.

For the simple foraging task studied, the performance enhancement provided by standard auto-teaching neural networks, with a single learning rate for all the modifiable weights, was relatively limited. However, by allowing a slightly more general auto-teaching mechanism, with a potentially different learning rate for each modifiable weight, it was demonstrated that auto-teaching architectures can, in certain scenarios, evolve to modulate behaviour successfully in line with the environmental dynamics, and thus out-perform the standard auto-teaching networks by a large margin.

While it is clear that evolved auto-teaching networks can perform better on the simple foraging task considered than evolved networks with fixed weights, it remains to be seen how useful auto-teaching is for more complex behaviours that require more complex neural networks. For example, for the dynamic task studied here, a neural network sophisticated enough to allow the implementation of a timer or oscillator would quite likely allow the evolution of a fixed network that could allow individuals to survive over many years just as easily as the auto-teaching network. It remains a topic for future work to establish the limits of the auto-teaching approach, and to determine if and when it has advantages over other approaches for other tasks. If auto-teaching allows simpler networks to solve a particular task, it is quite possible that evolution will favour it as a mechanism for implementing the appropriate behaviour.

References

Baldwin, J.M. (1896). A new factor in evolution. *American Naturalist*, **30**, 441-451.

Bullinaria, J.A. (2001). Exploring the Baldwin Effect in evolving adaptable control systems. In R.M. French & J.P. Sougne (Eds), *Connectionist Models of Learning, Development and Evolution,* 231-242. Springer.

Eiben, A.E. & Smith, J.E. (2003). *Introduction to Evolutionary Computing*. Berlin, Germany: Springer-Verlag.

Nolfi, S. & Parisi, D. (1993). Auto-teaching: networks that develop their own teaching input. In: J.L. Deneubourg, H. Bersini, S. Goss, G. Nicolis & R. Dagonnier (Eds), *Proceedings of the Second European Conference on Artificial Life*. Brussels.

Nolfi, S. & Parisi, D. (1996). Learning to adapt to changing environments in evolving neural networks. *Adaptive Behavior*, **5**, 75–98.

Williams, B. & Bounds, D. (1993). Learning and evolution in populations of backprop networks. In: J.L. Deneubourg, H. Bersini, S. Goss, G. Nicolis & R. Dagonnier (Eds), *Proceedings of the Second European Conference on Artificial Life*. Brussels.

Sensory Processing and Attention

MORE IS NOT NECESSARILY BETTER: GABOR DIMENSIONAL REDUCTION OF VISUAL INPUTS YIELD BETTER PERFORMANCE THAN DIRECT PIXEL CODING FOR NEURAL NETWORK CLASSIFIERS

M. MERMILLOD[1], D. ALLEYSSON[2], S. C. MUSCA[3], M. DUBOIS[4], J. BARRA[5], T. ATZENI[6], R. PALLUEL[2] and C. MARENDAZ[2]

[1]*Université Blaise Pascal, LAPSCO (UMR CNRS 6024), 63037 Clermont-Ferrand, France*

[2]*Grenoble Université, LPNC (UMR CNRS 5105), 38040 Grenoble, France*

[3]*Universidad de Málaga, Departamento de Psicología Básica, Causal Cognition Group, Campus de Teatinos s/n, 29071 Málaga, Spain*

[4]*Université Catholique de Louvain, Cognition and Development Lab, B-1348 Louvain-la-Neuve, Belgium*

[5]*Université Paris-Descartes, LPNC (UMR CNRS 8189), 92774 Boulogne-Billancourt, France*

[6]*Université Victor Segalen, LPSQV (EA 4139), 33076 Bordeaux, France*

V1 receptive fields show different sensitivities to different scales suggesting spatial frequency coding of visual information. The purpose of the present paper is to determine whether such a spectral decomposition at a perceptual level would be efficient for non-linear categorization purposes. Specifically, we compare the advantage of providing an artificial neural network with this biologically plausible visual information vs. direct pixel information in a natural scene classification task. In order to keep information qualitatively constant in the two conditions, original images were downsampled in a way that preserved the same amount of data in the spatial frequency domain. Results show that a standard back-propagation neural network aimed at classifying visual images yields better performances when provided with data from Gabor receptive fields (simulating V1 biological neurons) than with direct pixel coding data. This result suggests that artificial and possibly biological neural systems would be better off using reduced Gabor filtered information in the spatial frequency (or spectral) domain rather than direct spatial information in the visual classification of natural scene images.

1. Introduction

Using an image's pixels as an input to a connectionist neural network is often undesirable due to the excessively large amount of data involved. Indeed, with such a coding, a n *x* n-pixel image would require n^2 neurons in the input layer. Many different methods are used in connectionist modeling to compress visual information. For example, the use of Principal Component Analysis (PCA) allows one to describe a pattern of data in an orthogonal space. Therefore, each stimulus in the original space can be indexed in this new reduced space by the value of its projection along the axis describing the larger variability of the inputs. Applying this method to a gender categorization task of human faces, Abdi, Valentin, Edelman, O'Toole [1] showed that reliable gender categorization can be obtained using a posteriori features automatically derived from the statistical structure. They reported a correct classification rate of 91.8% when associated with a multi-layer perceptron (MLP) and 90.6% when associated with a Radial Basis Function network. Similarly, Cottrell [2] proposed compressing visual information by using the hidden layer of a back-propagation auto-associator. This process, generally considered as a non-linear version of PCA, results in compressing the input patterns presented to the input layer into "holons".

Another method consists of using local receptive fields that handle different parts of the input layer (the image), and associating their centers with category nodes. These types of neural networks, such as Radial Basis Function (RBF) networks [13] seem to be reliable for identification and classification purposes [5, 6,]. Nonetheless, Jones & Palmer [11] have shown that Gabor functions are better at simulating receptive fields of biological visual neurons than Gaussian functions. Therefore, Wiskott [15]; Wiskott, Fellous, Krüger & Von der Malsburg [16]; Dailey, Cottrell, Padgett & Ralph [4] used the convolution of Gabor wavelets at specific locations of the original image in the spatial domain in order to compress visual images. However, this last technique requires an additional (and not biologically motivated) step, generally PCA, to compress visual information for MLP.

Gabor [8] has shown that his function efficiently describes the informative content of a signal in the frequency domain while losing a minimum of information in the spatial domain. Thus, recent articles have proposed applying Gabor filtering in the frequency domain for visual categorization purposes [9, 10, 12]. This method is a common tool for simulating spatial invariance properties observed at the level of the striate cortex (which is not the case for visual pathways from the retina to the lateral geniculate nucleus). Unfortunately, the spectral analysis of visual information in these previous papers was not compared to a direct spatial analysis of visual images in identification and categorization tasks. Accordingly, the aim of the present paper is to test the reliability of neural computation of the Gabor technique compared to the raw code provided by natural images *per se*. More recent spiking neuron networks use the raw pixel code to perform fast and reliable categorization (Thorpe, Delorme & VanRullen, 2001 [17]; VanRullen & Thorpe, 2002 [18]). The aim of the present paper is not to ompare these different families of neural networks but, instead, to test different perceptual information pre-processing methods widely used in connectionist modeling for the *same* PDP classifier. In other words, our current goal is to show that for a given non-linear classifier, a biologically inspired spectral integration of visual data could outperform spatial coding. In order to conduct a qualitatively fair comparison of these inputs one must keep the same amount of data in both simulation conditions. Therefore, visual compression was performed in the spatial domain by means of a regular downsampling of the low-pass filtered original image that was identical to the low-pass filtering applied before computing the spectral domain. At a quantitative level, Gabor wavelet filtering will result in a drastic dimensional reduction of information (56 length-input vector compared to 1024 length-input vector for direct pixel coding).

2. Gabor filters and stimuli pre-processing

In order to avoid a boundary effect in the subsequent Fourier transformation, a Hann window was first applied. Boundary effects could result in a bias toward an over-representation of cardinal orientations, and the Hann window is a common tool to eliminate this bias. The following formula describes the Hann window applied to each image:

$$w(i) = 0.5 + 0.5 \times \cos\left(\frac{2\pi i}{N}\right)$$

Then the following spectral or spatial processing was applied to the images.

2.1. *Spectral analysis*

The purpose of this section is to use of Gabor wavelet filtering to describe a visual stimulus in terms of orientation and spatial frequency information that is similar to V1 cortical neurons. Computationally, this spectral analysis is widely used because it relies on well-known mathematical signal decomposition tools, such as the discrete Fourier transform (DFT). A low-pass filter was then used to remove high spatial frequency information. This step was performed in order to retain the same amount of information in the Fourier domain as in the spatial domain, for the downsampled images. Downsampling of visual images is possible because high spatial frequency information is removed. Therefore, we used the same low-pass filter to reproduce the removal of high spatial frequency information in the spectral domain.

Images were 256x256 pixels in size. This defines spatial frequencies up to 128 cycles/image. The low-pass filtering suppressed all the frequencies up to 16 cycles/image in order to be able to represent images in an array of size 32x32. The filter was applied in the Fourier domain; it is a step function which sets all frequency values greater than 16 cycles/image to zero as shown in Figure 1.

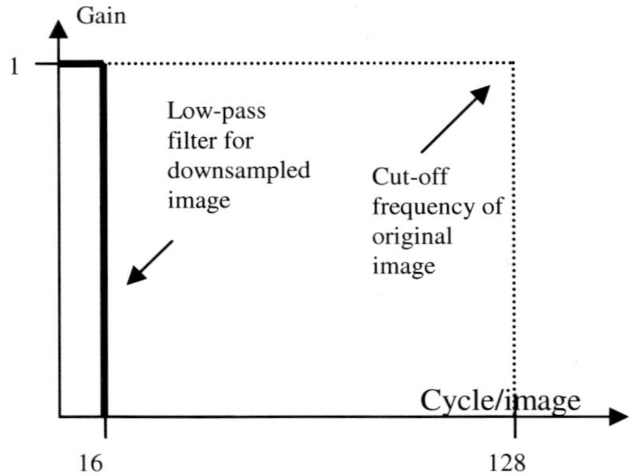

Figure 1. Spectral cut-off and spatial downsampling.

Then, we applied Gabor receptive fields in the spectral domain. A Gabor function has the shape of a sine wave modulated by a Gaussian filter. However, it is also possible to perform the filtering in the frequency domain by multiplying the spatial frequency information by the kernel of the Gabor function:

$$G(x, y, f_c, \theta) = \frac{1}{2\pi\sigma_r\sigma_t} e^{-\frac{(x.u)^2}{2\sigma_r^2}} e^{-\frac{(x.u_\perp)^2}{2\sigma_t^2}} e^{j2\pi \underline{x} f_c}$$

With: $\left| \begin{array}{l} \underline{x} = [x, y]^t, f_c = [f_0 \cos\theta, -f_0 \sin\theta]^t \\ u = [\cos\theta, \sin\theta]^t, u_\perp = [\sin\theta, \cos\theta]^t \end{array} \right.$

A Gabor filter is constructed with a Gaussian modulated by a complex exponential: parameters σ_r and σ_t of the Gaussian determine the spatial extent of the filter (figure 1). The vector f_c with module f_0 and direction θ describes this sine wave.

Each individual image was transferred into the Fourier domain and filtered by a set of Gabor filters. The filtered outputs were used to determine energy coefficients by coding the local energy spectra. We applied a bank of 56 Gabor wavelets corresponding to seven different spatial frequency bands and eight different orientations (0, π/8, 2π/8, 3π/8, 4π/8, 5π/8, 6π/8, 7π/8). The distance between two consecutive centers was one octave and spatial extent increased by one octave per spatial frequency channel [7].

2.2. *Spatial analysis*

Spatial analysis consisted of a downsampling in the spatial domain that keeps the same amount of information as the low-pass cut-off applied in the Fourier domain (figure 2). In other words, it is possible to convert the downsampled image in sine wave decomposition in the Fourier domain and then return to the spatial domain without any loss of information. This makes it possible to retain the same amount of information in the spectral and spatial domains for further neural computation processes. The downsampling was applied in the following way.

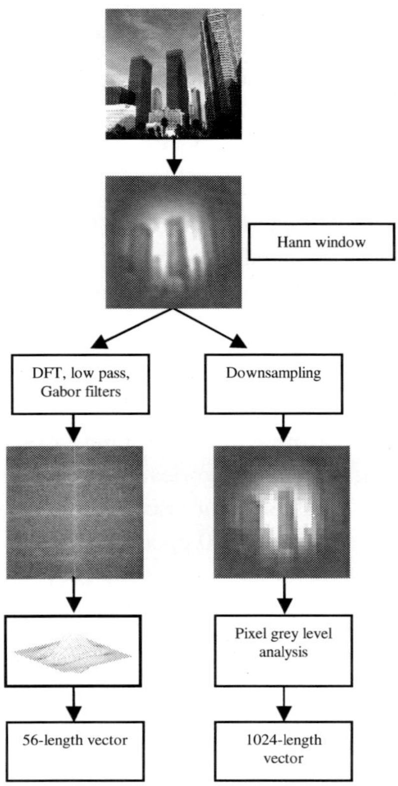

Figure 2. Spectral and spatial image processing.

3. Neural network processing

The connectionist network is a 3-layer back-propagation neural network, initialized with random connection weights in the range [0;1]. In order to associate each of the different category exemplars with a specific output vector coding for the corresponding category, the standard hetero-association training algorithm that minimizes the sum squared error [14] was used.

An important point of this paper is that neural network modeling was not proposed as a simulation of cortical processes proper, but rather as a tool allowing us to explore the statistical properties of the two input signals for a non-linear classifier.

4. Simulation 1: Testing spatial information in a connectionist network

4.1. *Network*

The connectionist architecture was the standard 1024-512-6 backpropagation hetero-associator described above.

4.2. *Stimuli*

Stimuli were composed of 72 exemplars from 6 categories of natural scenes that were downsampled. The detailed description of the stimuli is presented in section 2.2. Data were normalized between 0 and 1 across all category exemplars for neural network computation.

4.3. *Procedure*

The training phase was performed on 36 training exemplars randomly chosen from each of the 6 natural scene categories (6 training exemplars per category). The training consisted of associating each exemplar with a specific vector category during a fixed number of 200 epochs. Output vectors were 000001 for the beach category, 000010 for the village category, 000100 for the mountain category, 001000 for the indoor category, 010000 for the city category and 100000 for the forest category. The learning rate was fixed to 0.1, momentum to 0.9 and the Fahlman offset to 0.1. The only difference between the two simulations was the nature of the input vectors: Downsampling of grey level pixels vs. spectral information provided by Gabor filters.

The test phase consisted of exposing the 6 remaining exemplars per category to the neural network. The observed output was gathered through the whole set of test vectors and a winner-take-all algorithm was then applied to the output nodes in order to determine which node provided the strongest activation associated with each input vector.

Fifty runs of this training/test procedure were conducted and a ratio of correct responses was computed for each run.

4.4. *Results*

Results show weak classification performance on the Forest category (35.3% of correct categorization) and average performance for the City (57.7%), Indoor (65.3%), Mountain (69%), Village (52.3%) and Beach (64.7%) categories. Surprisingly, the neural network often confused Mountain exemplars (31.3%) with other category exemplars, especially the Forest and Village exemplars. An exhaustive confusion matrix is reported in Table 1.

Table 1: Confusion matrix produced by the neural network after training on spatial information provided by downsampled data.

	NEURAL NETWORK CLASSIFICATION					
INPUT VECTOR	Forest	City	Indoor	Mount	Village	Beach
Forest	35.3	5.0	7.3	31.3	13.7	7.3
City	7.3	57.7	9.0	15.7	6.7	3.7
Indoor	3.7	1.3	65.3	14.7	6.3	8.7
Mountain	8.3	2.7	2.0	69.0	7.3	10.7
Village	7.0	6.7	5.7	20.0	52.3	8.3
Beach	4.7	3.3	0.3	12.7	14.3	64.7

4.5. *Discussion*

Neural network performance was fair or average in almost all categories (except for the Forest category, where a significantly lower performance was observed). For most categories, the neural network seems to be able to use the spatial information provided by direct grey level pixels to generalize categorization to new exemplars after training on a random set of exemplars.

5. Simulation 2: Testing spectral information in a connectionist network

5.1. *Network*

The connectionist architecture was a 56-28-6 backpropagation neural network corresponding, in terms of hidden unit compression, to the neural network used in simulation 1. All parameters were kept identical to simulation 1.

5.2. *Stimuli*

Stimuli were the same 72 exemplars from the 6 nature scenes categories used in simulation 1. However, the stimuli were filtered by means of a low-pass cut-off applied in the Fourier domain, in order to keep the same amount of information as for the downsampled stimuli. Subsequently, a bank of Gabor filters was applied in the frequency domain. Each filter provided an average energy value relating to one spatial frequency and one orientation channel resulting in a 56-component vector for neural network processing.

5.3. *Procedure*

The training/test procedure was identical to that used in simulation 1.

5.4. *Results*

Reliable categorization performances were obtained for each test condition. The Forest category produced 89.9% correct categorization, the city category 88.3%, the Indoor category 88.3%, the Mountain category 91%, the Village category 68%, and the Beach category 79%. The confusion matrix is reported in Table 2. For each category, spectral information provided by Gabor wavelet filtering provided a slightly better categorization performance than the spatial information provided by pixel grey levels. The effect is significant for the Forest category, $F(1, 98) = 136.2$, $p<0.001$, the City category, $F(1, 98) = 77.6$, $p<0.001$, the Indoor category, $F(1, 98) = 41.6$, $p<0.001$, the Mountain category, $F(1, 98) = 19.7$, $p<0.001$, the Village category, $F(1, 98) = 12.2$, $p<0.001$ and the Beach category, $F(1, 98) = 14.5$, $p<0.001$.

Table 2: Confusion matrix for the neural network after training on spectral information provided by Gabor wavelet filtering.

	NEURAL NETWORK CLASSIFICATION					
INPUT VECTOR	Forest	City	Indoor	Mount	Village	Beach
Forest	89.0	0.0	3.0	1.0	4.3	2.7
City	1.7	88.3	3.7	1.0	4.0	1.3
Indoor	0.0	4.7	88.3	4.0	1.7	1.3
Mountain	1.3	0.7	1.7	91.0	4.0	1.3
Village	20.7	3.0	3.7	1.7	68.0	3.0
Beach	1.0	0.0	3.0	11.7	5.3	79.0

5.5. *Discussion*

Globally, these results imply that the spectral information coded by Gabor filters in the Fourier domain seems to permit better categorization performance of new category exemplars. This effect was obtained on a standard non-linear classifier based on parallel and distributed processing.

6. Conclusion

Among the different techniques used to compress visual information for subsequent connectionist processing, spectral decomposition of visual images seems to be a promising tool. Gabor filtering of spectral information combines a biologically inspired method for signal analysis with an efficient coding of visual inputs for categorization tasks. The striking result is that, despite the drastic dimensional reduction produced by Gabor wavelet filtering (input layer was a 56-dimensional space for Gabor filters Vs. a 1024-dimensional space for pixel analysis), Gabor filters produced better categorization rates than pixel analysis. Spectral analysis is less sensitive to translation within the same image or among different or similar details relating to different exemplars of the same category. For example, if the horizontal lines characterizing a beach appear at different places in the beach images, spectral analysis will be less sensitive than spatial analysis to these changes.

Compared to RBF networks, combining Gabor filtering with MLP has the advantage of optimizing receptive fields within both Fourier and spatial domains. In addition, this combination also permits parallel and distributed processing, allowing non-linear dynamic classification to occur.

To summarize, this work shows the advantage of using the spectral domain compared to the use of a raw coding of the images in a categorization by a connectionist network. We propose that the perceptual system may have many advantages in processing spatial frequency information, which is actually the case for biological neurons [11]. In this paper, we used Gabor filters as a computational shortcut to perform this scale processing but [18] have shown that spiking neuron networks would be able to transform spatial pixel coding into scale decomposition for cognitive processes.

Finally, there are new types of connectionist networks that use Gabor patches directly in the spatial domain by means of a sliding window across the entire image. This technique requires an additional PCA at the output of these filters, thus allowing compression of visual information for MLP (Dailey & Cottrell [3]; Dailey, Cottrell, Padgett & Ralph [4]). An interesting step now would be to compare spectral Gabor filtering with spatial Gabor filtering (in addition with PCA) for connectionist networks.

Acknowledgments

This work has been supported by a grant from the French Research National Agency (ANR Grant BLAN06-2_145908) to MM and the CNRS to MM, CM, DA, JB, & RP.

References

1. Abdi, H., Valentin, D., Edelman, B.E., O'Toole, A.J. (1995). More about the difference between men and women: Evidence from linear neural networks and the principal component approach. Perception, 24, 539-562.
2. Cottrell, G.W. (1990). Extracting features from faces using compression networks: Face, identity, emotion, and gender recognition using holons. In Proceedings of the 1990 Connectionist Models Summer School, (eds. D. Touretsky, J. Elman, T. Sejnowski & G. Hinton) Kaufman, 328-337.
3. Dailey, M. N. & Cottrell, G. W. (1999). Organization of Face and Object Recognition in Modular Neural Networks. Neural Networks, 12(7-8), 1053-1074.
4. Dailey, M. N., Cottrell, G. W., Padgett, C., & Ralph A. (2002). EMPATH: A neural network that categorizes facial expressions. Journal of Cognitive Neuroscience 14(8), 1158-1173.
5. Duvdevani-Bar, S., & Edelman S. (1999). Visual recognition and categorization on the basis of similarities to multiple class prototypes. International Journal of Computer Vision, 33(3), 201-228.
6. Edelman, S. & Duvdevani-Bar S. (1997). A model of visual recognition and categorization, Proceedings of Royal Society, London, 352, 1191-1202.
7. Field, D.J. & Brady N. (1997). Visual sensitivity, blur and the sources of variability in the amplitude spectra of natural scenes. Vision Research, 37, 3367-3383.
8. Gabor, D. (1946). Theory of communication. J. Inst. Electr. Eng, 93, 429-457.
9. Guyader, N., Chauvin, A., Peyrin, C., Hérault, J., & Marendaz, C. (2004). Image phase or amplitude? Rapid scene categorization is an amplitude based process. C. R. Biologies 327, 313-318.
10. Hérault, J., Oliva, A., & Guerin-Dugue, A. (1997). Scene Categorisation by Curvilinear Component Analysis of Low Frequency Spectra. Proceedings of the 5th European Symposium on Artificial Neural Network, Bruges, Belgium, pp. 91-96.

11. Jones, J.P. & Palmer L.A. (1987). The two-dimensional spatial structure of simple receptive fields in cat striate cortex. Journal of Neurophysiology, 58(6), 1187-1211.
12. Oliva, A., Torralba, A. B., Guérin-Dugué, A., & Hérault, J. (1999). Global semantic classification of scenes using power spectrum templates. Proceedings of the Challenge of Image Retrieval (CIR99), Newcastle.
13. Poggio, T. & Edelman, S. (1991). A network that learns to recognize three-dimensional objects. Nature, 343, 263-266.
14. Rumelhart, D. E., Hinton, G. E., & Williams, R. J. (1986). Learning internal representations by error propagation. In Parallel Distributed Processing: Explorations in the Microstructure of Cognition (eds. D. E. Rumelhart, J. L. McClelland & The PDP Research Group), MIT Press, 318-362.
15. Wiskott L. (1997). Phantom Faces for Face Analysis. Pattern Recognition 30(6), 837-846.
16. Wiskott, L., Fellous, J.M., Krüger, N. & Von der Malsburg C. (1999). Face Recognition by Elastic Bunch Graph Matching. In Intelligent Biometric Techniques in Fingerprint and Face Recognition, eds. L.C. Jain et al., CRC Press, 11, 355-396.
17. Thorpe S.J., Delorme A. & VanRullen R. (2001). Spike-based strategies for rapid processing. Neural Networks, 14(6-7), 715-726.
18. VanRullen R. & Thorpe S.J. (2002). Surfing a spike wave down the ventral stream. Vision Research, 42(23), 2593-2615.

NEURAL MODELS OF PREDICTION AND SUSTAINED INATTENTIONAL BLINDNESS

ANTHONY F. MORSE†

COIN Lab, School of Humanities & Informatics, University of Skövde, Sweden

Increasingly cognitive scientists view prediction as central to cognition, from philosophical and psychological theories such as the enactive approach and sensorimotor perception [1-3], to computational neuroscience and modelling e.g. [4-7]. Indeed, as our experiments show, prediction can significantly increase the recognition of task relevant input features in models of cortical micro-columns (Echo State Networks) [8-11]. Here, feedback into the cortical micro-column is simply the output activity of single layer perceptrons trained to identify input features from the activity of the cortical micro-column. The surprising result is that while this feedback or prediction enhances recognition of features relevant to making that prediction, it consistently reduces performance at recognising non-prediction-task-relevant-features and hence provides a model of sustained inattentional blindness. This is confirmed in our computational model of a sustained inattentional blindness task demonstrating the role of feedback in successfully tracking the attended object, and how this can result in blindness to the presence of an unexpected object. The model therefore suggests that tuning input filters with predictions of what the sensory system should expect, may be the cause of inattentional blindness. While Simons and Chabris [12] note that "we perceive and remember only those objects and details that receive focused attention." p. 1059, our model suggests that the relevant information simply was not there to be attended.

1. Introduction

The ability to predict or anticipate sensory changes is increasingly suggested to underpin our ability to perceive the world around us. According to Noe [1], perception is both dependent upon and grounded in our possession of sensorimotor knowledge, i.e. "practical knowledge of the ways movement gives rise to changes in stimulation" [p. 8]. Hence we predict the consequences of our actions in terms of anticipated sensory change. For example, we may perceive something as round, not because it projects 'roundness' or even a round image to our retina but because being round leads to a particular profile of change. Hence while a wheel or a plate may, from many angles, project an elliptical image it

†This work was supported by a European Commission grant to the project "*Integrating Cognition, Emotion and Autonomy*" (IST-027819, www.iceaproject.eu), as part of the European *Cognitive Systems* initiative.

nevertheless appears or is perceived as round because we anticipate or predict how our sensory contact with the object would change as we move. Where these expectations are contradicted by subsequent experience, as in forced perspective experiments, or when one's foot fails to contact the floor as expected while walking, the discrepancy is immediately brought to our attention. Such an account of perception is in line with Gibsonian affordances [13] in that predictions of the (sensory) consequences of actions map well onto object affordances interpreted as the actions that an object permits. Such profiling of sensorimotor predictions, as a consequence of affordance perception then enables the perception of objects.

The neuroscientific basis for anticipation and prediction, at least at the neural level, is well founded and pervasive. Downing [5] provides a review of computational neuroscience models of the cerebellum, basal ganglia, neocortex, hippocampus, and the thalamocortical loop, all of which involve anticipatory neural circuits of one kind or another suggesting that anticipation is central to the functioning of the brain. Such anticipatory mechanisms are present throughout the brain and should not be marginalised or considered as an subsidiary process. With respect to the idea of anticipating sensory change resulting from movement or action, Gallese and Lakoff [7] cite extensive neuroscientific evidence of anticipation specifically in the sensory-motor systems of the brain, and also propose a theory of conceptual knowledge rooted in sensory-motor prediction, and with some similarities to Noe and O'Regans theories [1, 2]. Neural links between sensory and motor streams, are however insufficient on their own to account for the prediction or anticipation of changes at the level of perception. This is largely due to the temporal and non-linear aspects of the relationship between sensory and motor streams which must be further explained before a perceptual account can be given [14]. The temporal problem results from the fact that the consequences of an action may not be immediate and may result from a sequence of actions. Temporal problems therefore often manifest a form of the credit assignment problem whenever experience is supposed to guide future expectations. The non-linear aspect of this relationship between sensory and motor streams provides a limit on the computational abilities of known forms of neural plasticity which approximate to some degree Hebbian plasticity [15]. Such plasticity at the neural level can only account for high level perceptual or psychological phenomena where the neural and conceptual levels coincide, i.e. under localist interpretations (e.g. [16, 17]) or more importantly where linear separation of localist interpretations from the neural substrate is in principle possible. Under such conditions psychological phenomena are not only prolific but readily modelled and explained with intuitive associative accounts (e.g. [14, 18-20]). The remainder of this paper details a simple neurocomputational model demonstrating how to bring about these conditions and further providing a demonstration and non-standard account of the psychological phenomenon of sustained inattentional blindness.

2. The Conditions for Conditioning

While many complex structures and circuits exist in the cortex, the basic unit repeated throughout is the cortical micro-column [6, 21]. Cortical micro-columns themselves involve a rich structure; however, here we are concerned with two specific properties, their capacity to act as a fading analogue memory and their intrinsic implementation of high dimensional kernels. The first property, formally defined as the separation property in [22], draws an analogy between the activity 'reverberating' around large recurrent networks and the ripples on water, in that information about the disturbance causing the ripples (or the input causing the activity) is preserved over time. The second property follows any warping expansion of dimensionality from relatively few inputs to relatively many neurons in a network. This transformation from input activity to network activity constitutes a continual warping rendering many highly complex and non-linear relationships in the original input data to be linearly separable in the networks' activity ([8-11, 22-24]). In recent years this approach has gained significant popularity in the pattern recognition community.

To those unfamiliar with these formalisations, such approaches to computational modelling may seem complex; however, their implementation is easily achieved. As a highly abstract model of a cortical micro-circuit, Echo State Networks (ESN) display the same properties. An *Echo State Network* (ESN) [8-11] is a large, sparsely connected recurrent neural network, randomly configured to implement a single null point attractor. Here we use a random sparse (30% connectivity) weights matrix, and then divide it by the maximum absolute Eigenvalue of that matrix plus 0.001. This effectively produces the weights for a random recurrent neural network with a single null attractor. The resulting network is then cycled asynchronously according to the following update rules.

$$\text{Input activity to neuron: } \boldsymbol{a}_i = \Sigma \boldsymbol{y}_j\, \boldsymbol{w}_{ij} + i_i$$
$$\text{Output activity of neuron: } \boldsymbol{y}_i = \tanh(\boldsymbol{a}_i)$$

In the experiments documented in this paper, the network is cycled 10 time steps for every single time step of the simulation, i.e. external input was only updated every 10 cycles of the network, thus approximating a continuous time recurrent neural network (CTRNN). Input fed by random connections into such networks perturbs their state differently for different input values, generating complex dynamics as the system's trajectory decays back toward the null state. The lack of any other attractor within the system ensures that all activity reverberating around the reservoir is related to its recent input history rather than resulting from cyclical generators or other non-null attractors. Such networks make principally possible the linear separation of complex non-linear and temporally extended features of the input stream and therefore bring about the conditions under which Hebbian learning can readily model, produce, and account for various psychological phenomena including conditioned learning [16, 20].

3. Sustained Inattentional Blindness

There is increasingly much psychological research highlighting that our perception of the world around us is not quite as it seems. Probably the most startling of these perceptual investigations involves the phenomenon of sustained inattentional blindness where humans can be shown to be experientially blind to highly salient and temporally extended events, even when they are looking directly at them. In a clear demonstration, Simons and Chabris [12] perform an experiment in which human subjects watch a video showing two intermingled groups of people, one dressed in white and the other in black, each passing a basketball between members of their own group. Subjects are asked to count how many times the ball is passed by one particular group (either those dressed in white or those dressed in black, depending on which condition the subject is in). Somewhat surprisingly, many "observers fail to notice an ongoing and highly salient but unexpected event…[a] gorilla walked from right to left into the live basketball passing event, stopped in the middle of the players as the action continued all around it, turned to face the camera, thumped its chest, and then resumed walking across the screen" (p. 1069). Observers in this study "were consistently surprised when they viewed the display a second time, some even exclaiming, 'I missed *that*!?' " (p. 1072). In accounting for this phenomenon Simons and Chabris [12] note that "we perceive and remember only those objects and details that receive focused attention" (p. 1059). Though it is not entirely clear in this context what attention is, similar claims have been made by many researchers, e.g. [1, 2, 12]. Many follow-up experiments have been devised and carried out to investigate the extent of sustained inattentional blindness and identify the relevant factors. For example, the effect of similarity between the attended (the team the subject is watching), distracter (the other team) and unexpected objects (the gorilla) has been systematically varied, showing that close similarity between the attended and unexpected objects reduces the occurrence of inattentional blindness [12, 25-28]. In a more easily modelled task, Koivisto and Revonsuo [25] asked human subjects to count how many times balls of one colour bounce off the edge of a computer screen, while balls of a different colour also bounce around the screen (see figure 1 below). In this experimental setup the unexpected object appears on the left of the screen and travels across it until it exits on the right. Subjects engaged in the counting task often miss the unexpected object and thereby display sustained inattentional blindness. Koivisto and Revonsuo [25] systematically varied the number of distracter objects and their similarity to the attended objects showing that (a) distracter objects have little or no effect and that (b) sustained inattentional blindness can occur even in the absence of any distracters. In a different scenario Most et al, [26, 27] varied the luminance of the attended and unexpected objects, showing that increasing similarity (in terms of luminance) decreases the likelihood of failing to detect the unexpected object, in the experiments detailed in this paper the same result is upheld for close similarity but not for dissimilar objects.

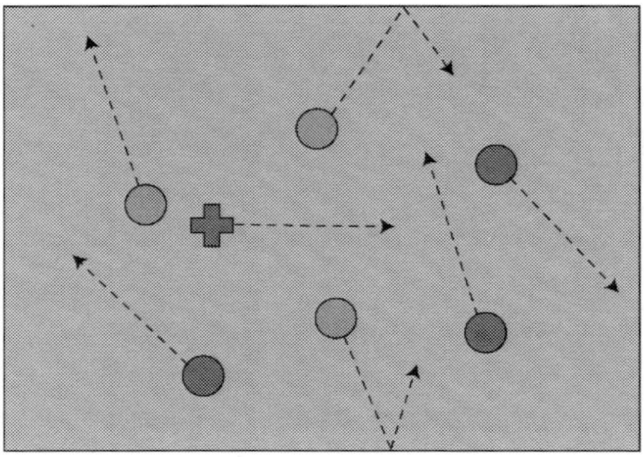

Figure 1. Illustration of Koivisto & Revonsuo's task. Human subjects count how many times the lighter balls bounce, while ignoring the darker balls. The unexpected object, here a cross, moves across the screen, often undetected. Experiments vary the number of distracter (darker) balls and the similarity of the unexpected object to the attended (lighter) balls. Dashed lines here only indicate the direction of movement for the reader, but are not visible during the experiment.

4. Building a Model

In the computational modelling experiments detailed herein we simplified Koivisto and Revonsuo's task (see figure 1) in the following ways. First we removed all distractor objects as the number or presence of distracter objects was found not to significantly alter the extent of sustained inattentional blindness in experiments carried out in [25]. Second we reduced the number of attended objects to 1 so as to simplify the modelling task. The visual area was then divided up into a 4 x 4 grid and the average green or blue pixel values of each cell provided two inputs respectively from each cell. This provided a total of 32 inputs to an ESN at every time step. The task here is to constantly track the vertical aspect of the direction of the attended simulated object, i.e. is the blue ball moving upward or downward (ignoring left and right movement).

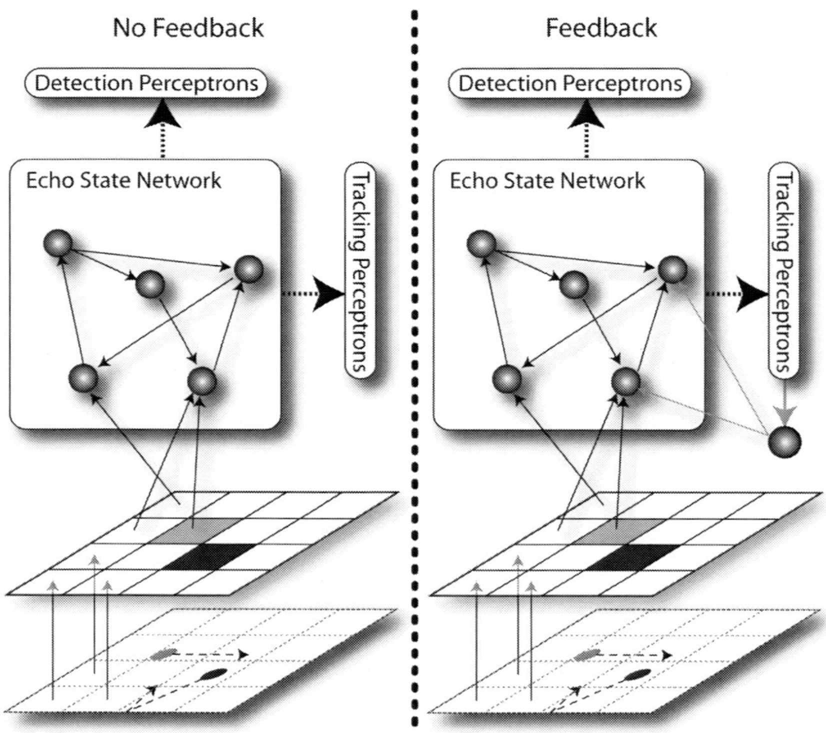

Figure 2. Visual input is averaged over a 4 by 4 grid and then passed as input to the ESN. Perceptrons are trained to read the ESN, and in the feedback condition (right) the average of their current activity also provides an input to the ESN.

In further experiments the horizontal aspect was also tracked with similar results to those presented here. This variation on the task requires continual attention rather than identifying discrete events and thereby simplifies training. While this task is slightly different from counting the ball bounces, it is reasonable to assume that humans do track objects as a pre-cursor to acts such as counting the bounces. Furthermore, as the network can see the whole image 'all at once' we wanted to avoid solving the counting problem using sensitivity to the edge of the image. An alternative would have been to restrict the area of the image the network can see at any one time thus forcing it to move around the image to do the counting task, however; this would clearly also involve tracking the vertical position of the ball.

4.1. *Training*

One hundred randomly configured ESNs were set up following the details provided earlier, corresponding to 100 computational 'subjects'. Each randomly configured ESN had two separate sets of single layer perceptrons trained, fully connected to the ESN, one set trained to identify the vertical direction of movement of the ball, and the other set trained to indicate the presence or absence of the unexpected object. Each network then took part in two different conditions, one in which no feedback was present, and the other where feedback was present from the ball tracking (see figure 2). Separate sets of perceptrons were trained in the feedback and no-feedback conditions. To provide more detail, for each randomly set up ESN, 100 perceptrons were trained in parallel, to identify whether the attended object was moving up or down. As we are concerned with linear separation we train many perceptrons (to avoid local minima) but then take only the results from the single best performing perceptron. Each perceptron was trained with no feedback to the ESN for 10,000 time steps (an average of 40 changes in direction of the attended object, and an average of 10 appearances of the unexpected object). A second set of 100 perceptrons were similarly (but separately) trained with feedback to the ESN. This feedback took the form of a single input to the ESN the value of which was the average value of this second set of 100 perceptrons trained to track the direction of movement of the ball. That means the feedback indicated what direction the network 'thought' the ball was moving in and is therefore seen as anticipatory.

An additional 200 perceptrons were also trained for 10,000 time steps to identify when the unexpected object was present, 100 of which where trained in the condition where feedback was present from the perceptrons tracking the attended object, and 100 of which were trained in the condition where feedback was not present. Note that feedback is only from the perceptrons trained to track the ball and is not from those trained to detect the unexpected object.

4.2. *Testing*

Each randomly configured model was tested by recording the performance of all trained perceptrons during a period of 1,000 time steps with no feedback to the ESN, and again for a period of 1,000 time steps with feedback to the ESN from the perceptrons trained to track the attended object (see figure 2). This gives us the second condition, whether feedback was present during testing or not. Each perceptron's performance was judged as correct during a time step if its output was within 0.5 of the target (e.g. 1 for up and 0 for down, or 1 for present and 0 for not present). The performance of each perceptron is then the percentage of time steps in which it gave correct answers. During all testing the unexpected objects were present for exactly 50% of the time, thereby removing any bias (e.g. the possibility of always responding that there is no unexpected object and being correct most of the time).

4.3. *Results and Analysis*

In all cases we take the results obtained by the best performing single perceptron (of 100) in each condition. This is intended to indicate the percentage of time in which the relevant features (i.e. for tracking or for detecting) are separable by a single linear boundary. As can be seen in figure 3 (left) the presence of this feedback clearly improved tracking performance, however from figure 3 (right) we can also clearly see a degraded performance at detection.

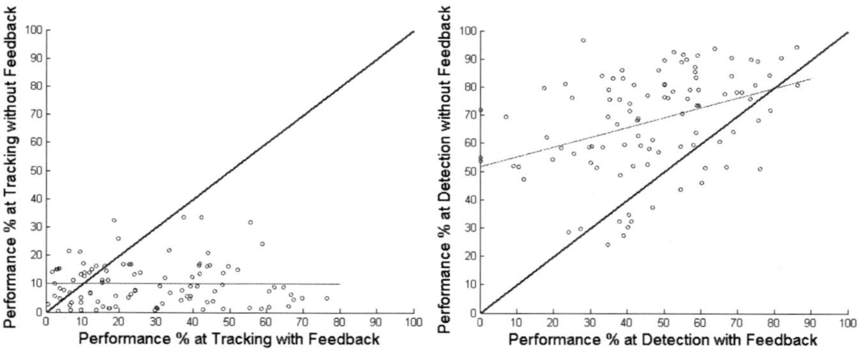

Figure 3. (Left) comparing performance at tracking with and without feedback, and (Right) comparing performance at detection with and without feedback.

The conditions in this experiment were;

- Whether the task data was for tracking or detecting
- Whether the perceptrons were **trained** with or without feedback from the tracking perceptrons
- Whether the perceptrons were **tested** with or without feedback from the tracking perceptrons

A 2 by 2 by 2 repeated measures ANOVA was performed on the complete data from 100 individuals, resulting in both significant main and interaction effects. All interaction effects had a probability of $p < 0.01$, however of theoretical importance here is the interaction between the task (i.e. tracking the ball or detecting the unexpected object) and the presence of feedback during testing. For this interaction to confirm inattentional blindness we would expect the presence of feedback to improve performance at tracking (task 1 in figure 4 below), and to degrade the performance at detection of the unexpected object (task 1 in figure 4 below). Further simple measures tests established that the upper and lower bounds of each condition combination do not overlap, and thereby confirmed the significance of this interaction effect and the hypothesis that such anticipatory feedback for tracking could be the cause of sustained inattentional blindness.

5. Experiment 2: Varying Similarity

We repeated the previous experiment ten times, varying the similarity between the unexpected object and the tracked object. This was achieved by varying the intensity of the two color input channels while keeping the total intensity constant, thus a similarity of 10% means that for the tracked object one colour channel has a value of 0.05, while the other has a value of 0.95, while for the unexpected object the first color channel has a value of 0.95, and the second 0.05. At 20% we use 0.1 and 0.9 and so on. A similarity of 100% therefore means both channels had a value of 0.5 for both the unexpected and tracked objects which were therefore identical in their colour. It should be noted that the shape and size of the attended object and unexpected object remained identical throughout, though their movement was consistently different. In the previous experiment the similarity was always 50%.

5.1. *Results*

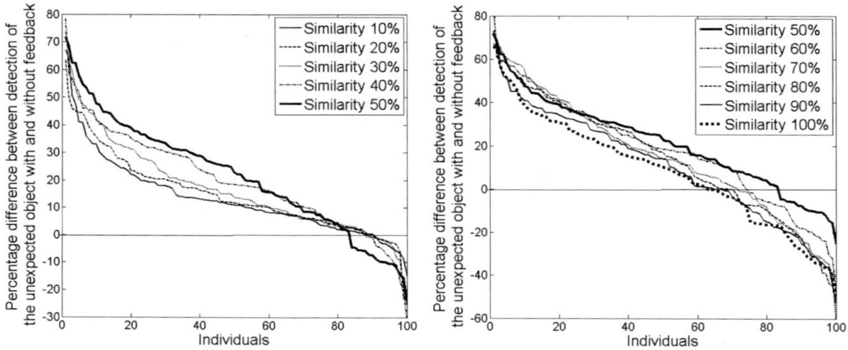

Figure 4. The effect of varying similarity between unexpected and attended objects on the deficit in detection of the unexpected object with feedback, by comparison to the same individual without feedback, **(Left)** from 10% to 50%, and **(Right)** from 50% to 100%.

The statistical tests performed in the first experiment were repeated for each variation in similarity with the same significant effects found for all variations, $p < 0.001$. Varying the similarity between the unexpected and tracked objects revealed an unexpected result, increasing the similarity from 10% to 50% dramatically increased the effect of feedback and the likelihood of displaying sustained inattentional blindness. In Figure 4 we can see the effect of each gain in similarity (the area under each line indicates the extent of the effect), so that for example, with a low (10%) similarity, 11% of the population displayed a difference greater than 30% in their likelihood of failing to detect the unexpected object. Thus we could propose that 11% of the population would fail to see the unexpected object while engaged in the tracking task. For a similarity of 50% the figure rises to 38% of the population. This result seems to contradict both 'common sense' expectations and the psychology literature on human sustained inattentional blindness, where dissimilarity between the attended and unexpected objects increases rather than decreases the likelihood of failing to see the unexpected object. However, as we continue to increase the similarity, this effect is reversed (see figure 4 right). While there is not a great deal of change in the higher end of figure 4 right, until the similarity reaches levels of 90% to 100%, there is a clear change in the mid and lower sections of the graph, showing a drop in the size of the effect, corresponding to a reduction in inattentional blindness.

6. Discussion

This paper suggests a potential non-standard explanation of the sustained inattentional blindness phenomenon. While standard explanations appeal to attention processes, the work presented in this paper suggests that sustained inattentional blindness results not from lack of attention, but rather from a comparatively well defined process of prediction or anticipation. While it is not surprising that this feedback alters performance at detection, it was unexpected that it would consistently degrade detection performance. The second experiment varies the similarity between the tracked and unexpected objects supporting the findings of others in similarity ranges from 50% to 100% similar (in terms of colour variation), in that as similarity increases the size of the effect of sustained inattentional blindness is reduced. This experiment, however, leads to a second unexpected result, that as similarity decreases, i.e. the tracked and unexpected objects become more dissimilar, past 40% similarity, that the effect would also be reduced. We are not currently aware of any psychological data confirming or refuting this finding. Further work is now underway extending this model to investigate the relationship between sustained inattentional blindness and priming.

References

1. Noë, A., *Action in Perception*. Cambridge, Mass: MIT Press (2004).
2. O'Regan, K. and A. Noë, A sensorimotor account of visual perception and consciousness. *Behavioral and Brain Sciences*. **24**: p. 939-1011 (2001).
3. Thompson, E., *Mind in Life: Biology, Phenomenology, and the Sciences of Mind*. Harvard University Press (2007).
4. Downing, K.L., Neuroscientific implications for situated and embodied artificial intelligence. *Connection Science*. **19**(1): p. 75-104 (2007).
5. Downing, K.L., Predictive models in the brain. *Connection Science* (In Press).
6. Hawkins, J. and S. Blakeslee, *On Intelligence*. Times Books (2004).
7. Gallese, V. and G. Lakoff, The brain's concepts: The role of the sensory-motor system in reason and language. *Cognitive Neuropsychology*. **22**: p. 455-479 (2005).
8. Jaeger, H., The echo state approach to analysing and training recurrent neural networks, German National Institute for Computer Science (2001).
9. Jaeger, H., Short term memory in echo state networks, German National Institute for Computer Science (2001).

10. Jaeger, H., Tutorial on Training Recurrent Neural Networks, Covering BPPT, RTRL, EKF and the "echo State Network" Approach, GMD-Forschungszentrum Informationstechnik. (2002).
11. Jaeger, H., Adaptive Nonlinear System Identification with Echo State Networks, in *Neural Information Processing Systems (NIPS)* (2002).
12. Simons, D.J. and C.F. Chabris, Gorillas in our midst: Sustained inattentional blindness for dynamic events. *Perception*. **28**(9): p. 1059-74 (1999).
13. Gibson, J.J., *The Ecological Approach to Visual Perception*. Boston: Houghton Mifflin (1979).
14. Morse, A.F. and T. Ziemke. Cognitive Robotics, Enactive Perception, and Learning in the Real World. in *CogSci 2007 - The 29th Annual Conference of the Cognitive Science Society*: Erlbaum: New York (2007).
15. Hebb, D.O., *The Organization of Behavior: A Neuropsychological Theory*. John Wiley & Sons (1949).
16. Morse, A.F., Autonomous Generation of Burton's IAC Cognitive Models, in *EuroCogSci03, The European Cognitive Science Conference*, Schmalhofer, Young, and Katz, Editors, LEA Press (2003).
17. Page, M., Connectionist modelling in psychology: A localist manifesto. *Behavioral and Brain Sciences*. **23**(04): p. 443-467 (2001).
18. Morse, A.F., Scale Invariant Associationism, Liquid State Machines, & Ontogenetic Learning In Robotics, in *AAAI Technical Report Developmental Robotics (DevRob05)* (2005).
19. Morse, A.F., Psychological ALife: Bridging The Gap Between Mind And Brain; Enactive Distributed Associationism & Transient Localism, in *Modeling Language, Cognition, and Action: Proceedings of the ninth conference on neural computation and psychology*, A. Cangelosi, G. Bugmann, and R. Borisyuk, Editors, World Scientific. p. 403-407 (2005).
20. Morse, A.F., *Cortical Cognition: Associative Learning in the Real World.*: DPhil Thesis, Department of Informatics, University of Sussex, UK (2006).
21. Mountcastle, V.B., An Organizing Principle for Cerebral Function: The Unit Model and the Distributed System., in *The Mindful Brain.*, Edelman and Mountcastle, Editors, MIT Press (1978).
22. Maass, W., T. Natschlager, and H. Markram, Real-Time Computing Without Stable States: A New Framework for Neural Computation Based on Perturbations. *Neural Computation*. **14**(11): p. 2531-2560 (2002).
23. Maass, W., T. Natschlager, and H. Markram, A Model for Real-Time Computation in Generic Neural Microcircuits, in *Advances in Neural Information Processing Systems 15* (2003).
24. Maass, W., T. Natschlager, and H. Markram, Computational models for generic cortical microcircuits. *Computational Neuroscience: A Comprehensive Approach* (2003).

25. Koivisto, M. and A. Revonsuo, The role of unattended distractors in sustained inattentional blindness. *Psychological Research*. **72**(1): p. 39-48 (2008).
26. Most, S.B., et al., What you see is what you set: Sustained inattentional blindness and the capture of awareness. *Psychological Review*. **112**(1): p. 217-242 (2005).
27. Most, S.B., et al., How Not to Be Seen: The Contribution of Similarity and Selective Ignoring to Sustained Inattentional Blindness. *Psychological Science*. **12**(1): p. 9-17 (2001).
28. Rensink, R.A., J.K. O'Regan, and J.J. Clark, The Need for Attention to Perceive Changes in Scenes. *Psychological Science*. **8**(5): p. 368-373 (1997).

DECOMPOSITION OF NEURAL CIRCUITS OF HUMAN ATTENTION USING A MODEL-BASED ANALYSIS: sSoTS MODEL APPLICATION TO fMRI DATA

EIRINI MAVRITSAKI
HARRIET ALLEN
GLYN HUMPHREYS

Behavioral Brain Sciences Centre, School of Psychology, University of Birmingham, UK, B15 2TT

The complex neural circuits found in fMRI studies of human attention were decomposed using a model of spiking neurons. The model for visual search over time and space (sSoTS) incorporates different synaptic components (NMDA, AMPA, GABA) and a frequency adaptation mechanism based on I_{AHP} current. This frequency adaptation current can act as a mechanism that suppresses the previously attended items. It has been shown [1] that when the passive process (frequency adaptation) is coupled with a process of active inhibition, new items can be successfully prioritized over time periods matching those found in psychological studies. In this study we use the model to decompose the neural regions mediating the processes of active attentional guidance, and the inhibition of distractors, in search. Activity related to excitatory guidance and inhibitory suppression was extracted from the model and related to different brain regions by using the synaptic activation from sSoTS's maps as regressors for brain activity derived from standard imaging analysis techniques (FSL). The results show that sSoTS pulls-apart discrete brain areas mediating excitatory attentional guidance and active distractor inhibition.

1. Introduction

In order to understand both the functional mechanisms and the underlying neural substrates of brain functions, investigators are increasingly combining behavioral studies with fMRI. However, given the limited spatial and temporal resolution of fMRI, it is often difficult to separate the different functional processes that may contribute to visual selection. More specifically, for visual selection different functional processes can combine to influence selection. One way to advance the functional analysis of fMRI data is to link the data to an explicit model of performance, which does distinguish between the different functional processes, and which can be used to predict the variation in fMRI signal as the different processes take place. Here we present an example of this using the Spiking Search over Time and Space (SSoTS) model of visual search [1]. We show how sSoTS can be used to distinguish fMRI signals associated with excitatory and inhibitory processes in search, providing a more detailed analysis of the relations between cognitive and neuronal function.

1.1. *Human visual search*

Traditionally, in visual search tasks participants are asked to find a known target item amongst irrelevant distracter items, and the time it takes participant to identify the target is measured (the reaction time (RT)). Watson and Humphreys [2] devised a new version of visual search where the temporal as well as the spatial features of targets and distracters were varied. They adapted a standard color-form conjunction task, but presented half of the distractors (the preview) prior to the other distracters and the target (when present). They showed that this preview search condition was facilitated relative to the standard conjunction search, with search efficiency approximating that found when the new items were presented alone (the 'single feature baseline'). Watson and Humphreys [2] proposed that temporal prioritization in search tasks depends, at least in part, on the active ignoring of old items – a process they termed visual marking. Humphreys et al. [3] showed that visual marking is disrupted when a secondary task must be conducted during the preview, consistent with the secondary task disrupting top-down ignoring of old items. In addition this, there is also evidence for top-down excitatory biases influencing search. For example a positive bias for expected target properties can offset the effects of an inhibitory bias against the features of old distracters [4] (induced by, for example, instructions or changes in display).

There is now considerable evidence that search is contingent on a network of neural circuits in frontal and parietal cortex that control both voluntary and reflexive orienting of attention to visual information [5]. The inter-play between the different parts of this fronto-parietal circuit however remains much less understood.

Brain imaging studies of preview search [6, 7] which converge in demonstrating that the preview period is associated with activation within the superior parietal cortex and the precuneus. Allen et al. [8] examined preview search both when a preview task was carried out alone and under conditions of secondary task load (a visual memory task was interleaved with preview search). In a single feature baseline, the participant had to locate a blue house target amongst red house distracters. In a conjunction condition, the same target had to be found amongst blue faces and red house distracters. In the preview condition, the preview items (blue faces) appeared 2 sec before the search display (red houses and blue house target). In the visual memory task participants had to memorize the positions of dots presented before the preview display. The, after the presentation of the preview, either the dots re-appeared or the search display was presented. When the dots re-appeared the task was to judge whether one had moved location. This study used faces and houses as search items rather that the typical lines or letters. This allowed Allen et al [8] to draw conclusions about the activity in stimulus-specific cortex (e.f. fusiform face area). Although there are differences in behavior with these more complex stimuli, crucially, Allen et al. [8] found a behavioral advantage for preview search which decreased when there was a memory load. Active ignoring of the preview display was associated with activation in a network of brain areas in posterior parietal cortex. These same regions were active during the visual memory task and decreased their activation for preview displays when the memory task was imposed.

1.2. *Modelling human search*

Over the past ten years, increasingly sophisticated computational models of visual search and selection have been proposed [9-12]. The importance of these models is that they generate a system-level account of performance, emerging from interactions between different local components. This provides a means of examining how interactions within a complex network generate coherent behavior.

The majority of models to-date have used relatively high-level connectionist architectures, where (e.g.) activity within any processing unit typically mimics the behavior of many hundreds rather than individual neurons [see [9] for an example]. Such models not only operate at a level of abstraction across individual neurons, but they also very often include network properties divorced from real neuronal structures (e.g., with units being both excitatory and inhibitory, depending on the sign of their connection to other units). One exception to this approach comes from the work of Deco and colleagues [10, 13] who have simulated aspects of human attention with models based on 'integrate and fire' neurons. These networks utilize biologically plausible activation functions and generate outputs in terms of neuronal spikes (rather than, e.g., a continuous value, as in many connectionist systems). Deco and colleagues have shown how classic 'attentional' (serial) aspects of human search can be simulated by such models even when the models have a purely parallel processing architecture. This provides an existence proof that a model incorporating details of neuronal activation functions can capture aspects of human visual attention.

One attempt to simulate human search over time as well as space has been made using the spiking Search over Time and Space model (SSoTS)[1, 14], which represents an extension of the original work of Deco and Zihl [10]. sSoTS uses a system of spiking neurons modulated by NMDA, AMPA, GABA transmitters along with an I_{AHP} current, as originally presented by Deco and Rolls [13] (see also Brunel & Wang [15]). sSoTS is separated into processing units that encode the presence of independently coded features (e.g. color and form) (see Figure 1). The feature maps can be thought as high-level representations for groups of low level of features. There is in addition a 'location map' in which units respond to the presence of any feature at a given position. At each location (in the feature maps and the location map), there is a pool of spiking neurons, providing some redundancy in the coding of visual information. The feature maps may correspond to collections of neurons in the posterior ventral cortex (e.g., V4), while the location map may correspond to collections of neurons in dorsal (posterior parietal) cortex (for more information for the model see [1]). Over time, the model converges upon a target, with reaction times (RTs) based on the real-time operation of the neurons.

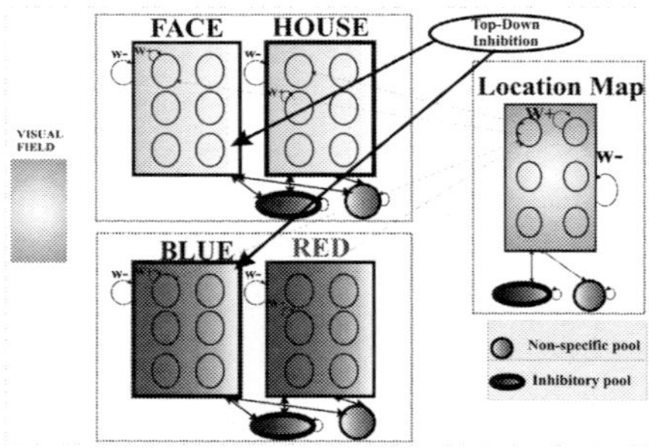

Figure 1: The architecture of the sSoTS model: The maps outlined in bold (Blue and House maps) receive top-down excitation (for the expected target) and the maps linked to the external inhibitory pool (the Blue and Face maps) receive the top-down inhibition (for the features of the preview).

Search efficiency in sSoTS is determined by the degree of overlap between the features of the target and those of distracters, with RTs lengthening as overlap increases and competition for selection increases. Consequently, search for a conjunction target (having no unique feature and sharing one feature with each of two distracters) is more difficult than search for a feature-defined target (differing from the distracters by a unique feature). Mavritsaki et al. [1, 14] showed that search in the conjunction condition also increased linearly as a function of the display size, mimicking 'serial' search.

In addition to modeling spatial aspects of search, SSoSTs also successfully simulated data on human search over time, in the preview search paradigm [2, 16]. Provided the interval between the initial items and the search display is over 450 ms or so, the first distractors in preview search have little impact on behavioral performance [2, 16]. The sSoTS model generated efficient preview search when there was an interval of over 500ms between the initial preview and the final search display. sSoTS mimics the behavioral time course due to the contribution of two processes: (i) a spike frequency-adaptation mechanism generated from a slow $[Ca^{2+}]$-activated K^+ current, which reduces the probability of spiking after an input has activated a neuron for a prolonged period [17], and (ii) a top-down inhibitory input that forms an active bias against known distracters. The slow action of frequency-adaptation simulates the time course of preview search. The top-down inhibitory bias matches data from human psychophysical studies where the detection of probes has been shown to be impaired when they fall at the locations of old, ignored distractors [18, 19]. In addition, in explorations of the parameter space for SSoTS, Mavritsaki et al. [1, 14] found that active inhibition was necessary to approximate the behavioral data on preview search. These results, using the sSoTS model, indicate that processes of co-operation and competition between processing units may not be sufficient to account for the full range of data on human selective attention and that factors such as frequency adaptation are required in order to simulate the temporal dynamics of visual attention.

1.3. *Linking the model to fMRI*

As we have noted, imaging studies have shown a network of regions in posterior parietal cortex (PPC) (including superior parietal cortex and precuneus, extending into occipital cortex) associated with successful prioritization of the new target and successful ignoring of the old distracters. However, the increased activation in these regions found in preview search is inherently ambiguous, because preview search is influenced by both positive expectancies for targets and inhibitory suppression of distracters [20]. This ambiguity is not apparent in the sSoTS model, though, where effects of top-down expectancies and inhibitory biases against distracters can be distinguished. For example, the map associated with the feature of the old distracters that does not re-occur in the search display (i.e., the map for face stimuli, in the experiment of Allen et al. [8]) uniquely receives top-down inhibition in SSoTS. The map corresponding to the feature of the target not present in the old distracters (i.e. houses in Allen et al [8]) uniquely receives top-down activation. The changes in activity over time in these maps may be used to predict changes in the fMRI signal linked, respectively, to top-down expectancies and inhibition in preview search. The distinct time courses of activation in the model may then be used to pull-apart activity from within the regions linked to preview search, allowing us to isolate the neural regions concerned with excitatory and inhibitory modulation of processing. We report an analysis of fMRI data on preview search taking this approach.

2. sSoTS architecture

sSoTSs consists of spiking neurons organized into pools containing a number of units with similar biophysical properties and inputs. The simulations were based on a highly simplified case where there were six positions in the visual field, allowing up to 6 items in the final search displays. SSoTS has three layers of retinotopically-organized units, each containing neurons that are activated on the basis of a stimulus falling at the appropriate spatial position. There is one layer for each feature dimension ("color" and "form") and one layer for the location map (Figure 2). The feature maps encode information related to the features of the items presented in an experiment – in this case, Allen et al. [8]. For Allen et al. [8], the two different features encoded are colour and object shape, which in this case is house or face. Here the feature dimension "color" encoded information on the basis of whether a blue or red color was presented in the visual field at a given position i, (i=1,...,6) (creating activity in the red and blue feature maps). The feature dimension "form" encoded information on the basis of whether there is a house or face present in the visual field at a given position i (i=1,..,6). The pools in the location map sum activity from the different feature maps to represent the overall activity for the corresponding positions in the visual field. Each of the layers contains one inhibitory pool (see also [13]) and one non-specific pool, along with the feature maps.

The system used and the connections are illustrated in Figure 2. More details about the architecture of sSoTs, the organisation of the units (neurons) in the network and the neuronal characteristics can be found in Mavritsaki et. al [1]. The parameters for the simulations were established in baseline conditions with 'single feature' and 'conjunction' search tasks as reported by Watson and Humphreys [2] and Allen et al. [8] (conjunction search: blue house target vs. red houses and blue faces distracters; feature search: blue face target vs. red houses distracters). The generation of efficient and less efficient (linear) search functions in these conditions replicates the results of Allen et al. [8]. These same parameters were then used to simulate preview search. RTs were based on the time taken for the firing rate of the pool in the location map to cross a relative threshold (*thr*), (for more details see [1]). Detailed simulations were run at the spiking level only, to match the experimental results [8]. Additionally, to simulate the working memory effect, we reduced slightly the top-down inhibition during the 'working memory' trials – assuming this is equivalent to the effects generated when human participants hold another stimulus in working memory during the preview period.

3. Applying the sSoTS model to fMRI data

3.1. *Extraction of activation maps for top down inhibition and excitation*

During the preview period activation in the model is affected by several factors: top-down excitation (for the target), top-down inhibition (for old distractors) and passive inhibition caused by frequency adaptation. In order to be able to compare the fMRI data with the activation patterns in the model we extracted activation maps from the model related to the above mechanisms. For example, consider preview search for a new blue house target amongst previewed blue faces and new red houses distracters (see [8]). In SSoTS there is a positive bias applied to maps representing the features of targets, for Allen et al. [8] the target is the blue house, therefore the map that encodes the shape "house" and the map that encodes the color "blue" receive top-down excitation. Furthermore, there is an inhibitory bias applied to maps representing the features of old distracters (distracters presented before the presentation of the search display), these distracters are blue faces, so the map that encodes the shape "face" and the map that encodes the color "blue" both receive top-down inhibition. By tracing activity in the house, face and blue maps, we can correlate brain activity with active excitatory and inhibitory biases in the model. Note that we are interested in activity relating to these biases and processes, not to the distracter features or colors.

To extract the brain activity relating to these processes, we first extracted a time course of the activity in each of the sSoTS maps (2 x shape, 2 x features and the location map) over the experiment of Allen et al [8]. These time courses were convolved with a standard estimate of the heamodynamic function and used as regressors for the fMRI activity (see below). To estimate the activations associated with positive biases for targets and inhibitory biases against distracters (see Table 1) we compared the activations found for each map (for both the conjunction and preview search conditions). Thus, for conjunction search, the positive top-down bias was given by:

(Target form – distractor form) + (Target colour – Distractor Colour)
i.e: *(House – Face+ Blue - Red)*

For preview search it was given by:

(Map with only Positive Bias –Map with no bias)+(Map with Positive and Negative Bias- Map with only Negative Bias)
i.e: *(House-Red+Blue-Face)*

For preview search the top-down inhibition was given by:

(Map with only Negative Bias – Map with no Bias)+(Map with Positive and Negative Bias – Map with only Positive Bias)
i.e: *(Face-Red+Blue-House)*

Table 1. Map extraction for Single Feature (SF), Conjunction (CJ) and Preview (PV) search.

	SF and CJ Top-Down Excitation	**SF and CJ Top-Down Inhibition**	**PV Top-Down Excitation**	**PV Top-Down Inhibition**
Face	NO	NO	NO	**YES**
House	**YES**	NO	**YES**	NO
Blue	**YES**	NO	**YES**	**YES**
Red	NO	NO	NO	NO

3.2. *Comparison of fMRI data with model bold responses*

Activation in sSoTS was linked to the human fMRI data by taking into account the delay that is present in the fMRI bold signal (about 5-9 sec) [21]. To do this, activity in the model was convolved with a haemodynamic response function (HDR) [22-24]. Previous work by Gorchs and Deco [22] simulated the bold response by taking the average pool activity in a given location in the model and convolved this with a Poisson distribution. The result from the convolution was then compared with bold responses taken from the fMRI data (from the corresponding simulated region). Furthermore, instead of using the average pool activity the synaptic activity can also be employed. Deco et al. [24] used the synaptic activity from his model and convolved it with the haemodynamic response function suggested by Glover [23]. In our effort to compare our theoretical data with the fMRI experimental data we used the average synaptic activity from the pools in the model's feature maps. The comparison took place in two steps; (i) first we compared qualitatively the bold response from the fMRI data with the activation function with top-down inhibition similarly with previous work [22-24], (ii) the average synaptic pool activity was then directly compared with the observed bold data from Allen et al. [8], using the synaptic activity as regressors for the fMRI analysis.

We note that there was no top-down inhibitory bias applied during conjunction search. However, activity in the same maps was examined in order to provide a baseline with the preview search task. After extracting the activity maps from the model, we averaged over 20 trials for each condition and we took the changing time course of activity reflecting top-down inhibition and top-down excitation activity for each condition. This activity was convolved using an assumed haemodynamic response function [24] to create a time series of predicted bold activity. This time series was then used as a regressor for the fMRI data in the contrasting search conditions.

fMRI analysis was done using FEAT, part of fsl (www.fmrib.ox.ac.uk/fsl). The data were pre-processed as in Allen et al. [8], including correction for head movement, within scan signal intensity normalisation, high pass temporal filtering (to remove slow wave artifacts). The time course for each map in the model was entered as a separate regressor. Positive and negative biases were estimated by combining the regressors for each map as desribed above. Z (Gaussianised T/F) statistic image were thresholded using clusters determined by Z>2.3 and a (corrected) cluster significance thresholded of P=0.05.

4. Results

The behavioural results generated by sSoTS matched the classical findings on single feature, conjunction and preview search [2]. In the single feature condition (the half set baseline), the search slope was 14 ms/item; for the preview condition it was 12 ms/item, and it was 46 ms/item for the conjunction condition (the full set baseline). When a working memory task was added (the loaded search condition), the slope of the preview condition increased to 19 ms/item (see Figure 3).

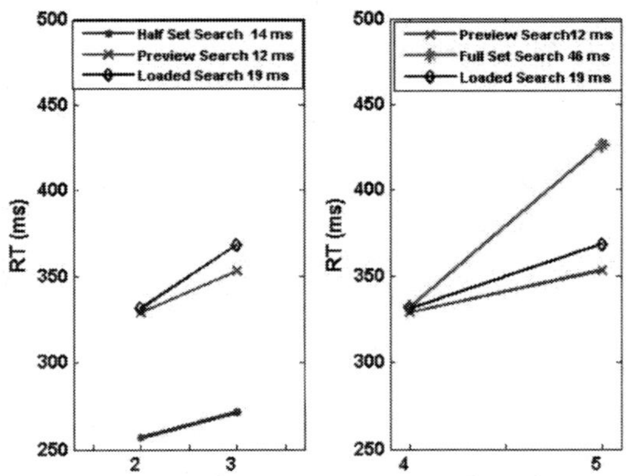

Figure 2: The slopes generated by sSoTS for single feature search (the half set baseline), conjunction search (the full set baseline), standard preview search and preview search with a working memory load (the loaded search condition).

Activity linked to top-down inhibition in the maps was compared with the fMRI data in precuneus by convolving the activation with the HDR. We found that the HDR for top-down inhibition in the preview condition was increased for preview search compared with conjunction search – a result that reflects the greater salience of the target in preview compared with conjunction search, and not the difficulty of the search tasks (conjunction search being the more difficult). This matches data reported by [8] for the precuneus (see Figure 3).

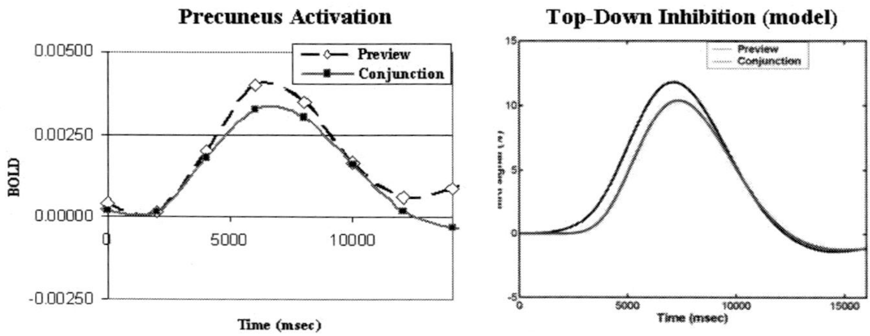

Figure 3: The haemodynamic response found in the precuneus in preview and conjunction search, in Allen et al. [8] and the simulated haemodynamic response in the location map in sSoTS.

We then took the time courses of activation reflecting the top-down excitatory and inhibitory activity in sSoTS's feature maps and applied these as regressors to the fMRI data associated with the preview condition reported by Allen et al. [8]. In this study we sought areas where BOLD activity was related to excitatory and inhibitory activity. Allen et al. [8] reported activation in posterior parietal cortex (superior parietal lobe and precuneus) linked to the dummy preview condition. We found a reliable correlation ($p<0.001$ for all correlations) in right lateral parietal cortex for top-down excitatory activity predicted by sSoTS. In contrast, top-down inhibitory activity in the model was correlated with fMRI activation in the medial precuneus (Z=50) (Figure 4A). Here the model-based analysis distinguishes two functionally different operations taking place when observers attempt to ignore the preview and to prioritise search to new items [20].

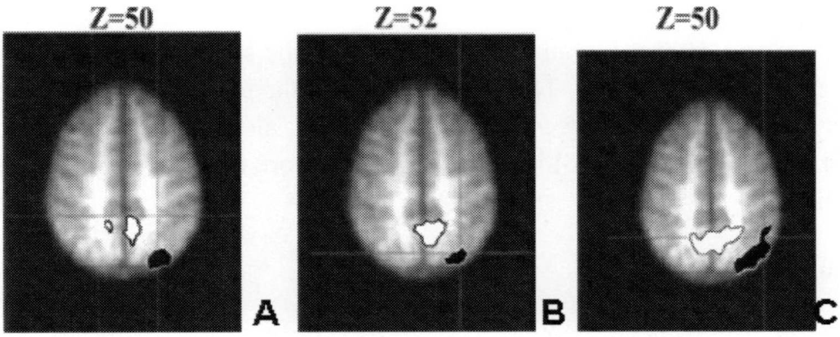

Figure 4: A. Top-down inhibition in the model (white area correspond to maps: (1-4)+(3-2)) was associated with activity the medial precuneus, while top-down excitation in the model (black area corresponds to maps: (2-4)+(3-1)) was associated with activity in the lateral parietal cortex (right hemisphere). B. Comparisons between preview and conjunction search (the full set baseline). The white regions reflect correlations between (i) top-down inhibitory activity in sSoTS and (ii) increased activation in preview compared with conjunction search. The black regions reflect correlations between (i) top-down excitatory activity in sSoTS and (ii) greater activation in conjunction search compared with preview search. C. Comparisons between the standard preview condition and the condition where preview search was conducted with a working memory load (the loaded search condition) [2]. The white regions reflect correlations between (i) top-down inhibitory activity in sSoTS and (ii) increased activation in standard preview search compared with the loaded search condition. The black regions reflect correlations between (i) top-down excitatory activity in sSoTS and (ii) increased activation in the loaded search condition compared with standard preview search.

We also examined the differences between bold activity in the preview and conjunction search conditions in relation to the activation differences between these conditions apparent in sSoTS (comparing activity in the critical maps in preview and conjunction search). In SSoTS these activation differences are driven by the application of top-down inhibition in preview search. The results showed a reliable correlation between the activation differences in sSoTS and increased activation in the precuneus in preview search compared with the conjunction condition. There was also a correlation between differences in activity in the conjunction and preview conditions in SSoTS and increased activity for the conjunction condition over the preview condition in lateral parietal cortex (see Figure 4B). This may reflect the increased role of excitatory guidance to the target in the conjunction condition.

Finally, we evaluated the differences in activity between the standard preview condition and preview search conducted with a memory load. The differences in activity between these two conditions in sSoTS was correlated with (i) an increase in bold activity in the standard preview compared with the working memory condition in the precuneus, and (ii) an increase in bold activity in the working memory condition compared with the standard preview in lateral parietal cortex (Figure 4C). These results fit with there being reduced inhibitory activity under conditions of working memory load, along with an increased role for top-down activation for the target under the more difficult working memory condition.

5. Conclusions

sSoTS replicated successfully the behavioral results from Allen et al. [8]. Activity in the model linked to top-down excitation and inhibition also correlated with the bold signal in posterior parietal cortex. Prior fMRI studies have demonstrated increased activity in posterior parietal cortex linked to preview search, but differences in excitatory and inhibitory influences have not been separated. In SSoTS the activation associated with top-down excitation and inhibition can be distinguished. We showed that bold activity in the precuneus was associated with top-down inhibition in the model, while activity in more lateral parietal areas (particularly in the right hemisphere) correlated with top-down excitation in the model. Activation in these two regions also changed across the search conditions in accord with changes in SSoTS. Higher activation in the precuneus in preview search compared with (i) conjunction search and (ii) the working memory condition was correlated with greater inhibitory activity in the model. In contrast, there was increased activity in lateral parietal cortex associated with increased activation in (i) conjunction search and (ii) the working memory condition, compared to standard preview search, linked to increased top-down excitation in SSoTS. These data suggest that top-down inhibition may play a driving role in generating efficient preview search compared with less efficient search conditions (conjunction search and preview search with a working memory load). Top-down activation, on the other hand, appears to play a greater role in inefficient search (conjunction search, preview search with a working memory load) than in efficient preview search. This may reflect the more prolonged search taking place, which enables a greater role for top-down excitation, for the target, to emerge. The analysis demonstrates that the model-based analysis can help to identify the functional role of different brain regions in search, providing a more accurate account of the neural substrates of visual selection.

Finally it should be noted that, relative to the neuronal structures controlling attention and search in the human brain, the sSoTS model is very simplistic. For example, in a more realistic model, the top-down modulation of excitation and inhibition would come from external neurons, whose own operation should vary according to the neurotransmitter functions involved. In addition input coming into the maps should more accurately reflect the properties of neurons in earlier visual areas, there would be topological organization within feature and location maps, and local grouping in addition to global inhibitory or excitatory modulation. It will be both important and interesting to explore the functional consequences of adding in these extra factors. For now, however, the results indicate the utility of even a simple model for pulling apart functionally distinct activations at a neural level.

Acknowledgments

This work was supported by grants from the BBSRC and MRC (UK).

References

1. Mavritsaki, E., et al., Journal of Physiology *Paris*, 2006. 100: p. 110-124.
2. Watson, D. and G. Humphreys, Psychological Review, 1997. 104: p. 90-122.
3. Humphreys, G.W., D.G. Watson, and P. Joliceour, Journal of Experimental Psychology: Human Perception and Performance., 2002. 28: p. 640-660.
4. Miller, E.K., ed. Attention space and Action: Studies in cognitive neuroscience, ed. G.W. Humphreys, J. Duncan, and A. Treisman. 1998, Oxford University Press: Oxford.
5. Corbetta, M., et al., Nature Neuroscience, 2002. 3(3): p. 292-297.
6. Pollmann, S., et al., NeuroImage, 2003. 18: p. 310-323.
7. Olivers, C.N.L., et al., Human Brain Mapping, 2005. 24: p. 69-78.
8. Allen, H., G.W. Humphreys, and P.M. Matthews, Journal of Experimental Psychology: Human Perceptionand Performance., 2008. 34(2): p. 286-297.
9. Heinke, D. and G.W. Humphreys, Computer vision and image understanding., 2005. 100(1/2): p. 172-197.
10. Deco, G. and J. Zihl, Visual Cognition, 2001. 8(1): p. 119-140.
11. Itti, L. and C. Koch, Vision Research, 2000. 40: p. 1489-1506.
12. Mozer, M.C. and M. Sitton, *Attention*, Pashler, Editor. 1998: East Sussex, UK. p. 341-388.
13. Deco, G. and E. Rolls, Journal of Neurophysiology, 2005. 94: p. 295-313.
14. Mavritsaki, E., et al., Neurocomputing, 2007. 70: p. 1925-1931.
15. Brunel, N. and X. Wang, Journal of Computational Neuroscience, 2001. 11: p. 63-85.
16. Watson, D., G. Humphreys, and C. Olivers, Trends in Cognitive Sciences., 2003. 7(4): p. 180-186.
17. Madison, D. and R. Nicoll, Journal of Physiology, 1984. 345: p. 319-331.

18. Agter, A. and M. Donk, Journal of Experimental Psychology-Human Perception and Performance., 2005. 31: p. 722-730.
19. Allen, H.A., G.W. Humphreys, and H. Bridge, Vision Research, 2007. 47(6): p. 766-775.
20. Braithwaite, J.J. and G.W. Humphreys, Perception and Psychophysics, 2003. 65: p. 21.
21. Friston, K.J., J. P., and R. Turner, Human Brain Mapping, 1994. 1: p. 153-171.
22. Gorchs, S. and G. Deco,. NeuroImage, 2004. 21: p. 36-45.
23. Glover, G.H., NeuroImage, 1999. 9: p. 419-429.
24. Deco, G., E. Rolls, and B. Horwitz, Neurocomputing, 2004. 58-60: p. 729-737.

AUTHOR INDEX